ANNUAL REPORTS

OF THE

COMMISSIONERS OF EMIGRATION

OF THE

STATE OF NEW YORK,

FROM THE

Organization of the Commission, May 5, 1847, to 1860, inclusive:

TOGETHER WITH

TABLES AND REPORTS, AND OTHER OFFICIAL DOCUMENTS, COMPILED AND PREPARED UNDER RESOLUTION ADOPTED BY THE BOARD, AUGUST 29, 1860.

NEW YORK:

1861.

JOHN F. TROW, Printer,
50 Greene Street.

PREFACE.

Previously to the year 1847, the subject of the care and support of alien emigrants was left either to the general quarantine and poor laws or to local laws and ordinances, varying sometimes as to the provisions, very often as to the practical administration. A general tax, under State authority, on all passengers arriving at the port of New York was applied to the support of the Marine Hospital at Quarantine; and aliens (as well as others) arriving in that port, suffering under contagious or infectious disease, as yellow fever, ship fever, &c., were there received, but no further provision was made from that fund for their relief under other circumstances, or after their arrival. Local laws authorized the requiring of bonds by the city authorities from the owners of vessels bringing such emigrants, to indemnify the city and county in case of the emigrant becoming chargeable under the poor-laws. With the great and rapidly increasing emigration from 1840 to 1847, these provisions were found very inconvenient to the ship-owner, and wholly inadequate to the important end of necessary aid and relief to the emigrant falling into disease and destitution. The bonds remaining uncancelled for a long time, were onerous to the better class of ship-owners; whilst they sometimes, as to others, were found of no value when enforced. But a much more serious objection to the system was, that it did not efficiently provide for the care and relief of the emigrants who might most require aid. No general aid or protection was provided for those who might need it from other causes than disease alone; whilst it led to the establishment, from motives of economy, of small private hospitals for the sick and infirm, who might otherwise be chargeable to the public institutions. The number of such diseased emigrants was increased beyond the proportion of the increase of emigration, from the overcrowding of the vessels and the wretched provision often made for the comfort, sustenance, and health of the passengers. In such crowded private hospitals, without any public supervision, with none of the provisions as to space, ventilation, and other comforts, now common in all good sanitary establishments, great suffering and much mortality were the necessary consequences.

This state of things was becoming more distressing as emigration grew larger, and it even threatened danger to the public health. A number of citizens, to whose notice these facts were specially and frequently brought—to some from their connection with commerce and navigation, to others from their personal sympathy with the children of the land of their own nativity,—met about the close of 1846, or the winter of 1847, and consulted on the means of remedying these evils. They prepared and agreed upon a plan of relief, which was presented to the Legislature of the State of New York, and was passed into a law in the session of 1847. The system then recommended and adopted was, that of a permanent Commission for the relief and protection of alien emigrants arriving at the port of New York, to whose aid such emigrants should be entitled for five years after their arrival, the expenses of their establishments and other relief being defrayed by a small commutation payment from each emigrant.

The whole government and property of the Quarantine Hospitals, created under this law, were also transferred to the Board. This original system has since been, at different periods, altered or modified in its details, as experience pointed out, or legal or practical difficulties occurred, but it continues substantially the same as created and organized in 1847; since which date its operations and beneficent results have swelled to a magnitude far beyond any thing contemplated when the system was first devised.

Its history will be found stated officially in the following reports, from year to year.

This volume contains a reprint (abridged merely as to some repetitions, which were necessary at the time) of all the annual and other reports of the Commissioners of Emigration, made to the Legislature of the State of New York, as provided by law, since the organization of the Commission in 1847. These are accompanied by the statistics, tables, reports of their medical and other officers, and other documents, which were appended to the several reports in their successive years.

The present Commissioners were induced to collect and reprint these reports and documents, from the conviction that they contained a great body of useful information of great value in many respects. They present, when taken consecutively, the annals of the most remarkable and important, as well as by far the most numerous, emigration to distant lands which is recorded in modern history. They show, in detail, how, from May, 1847, till the close of 1860, the remarkable aggregate of two millions six hundred and seventy-one thousand eight hundred and nineteen emigrants (see general tabular statement, page 288) landed at the port of New York, seeking on this side of the Atlantic,—what was certainly found by most of them,—relief from the wrongs or the misery which they experienced themselves, or dreaded for their children, in their native land. Here are shown the respective nationalities of these emigrants, fluctuating from year to year in numbers and proportion, from various causes connected with great events or circumstances which have now become of interest to every student of history or political economy.

The history of great changes in the character of our navigation and that of other commercial nations, may be here traced through every stage, especially that of the immense amelioration of the sanitary treatment and condition of passengers on shipboard, which has been effected within the last few years, and was caused by wise legislation here and in Europe, and, also, in no small degree by the honorable and humane efforts of the navigating interest itself. The prevention of the hardships, misery, disease, and deaths formerly so frequent among the humbler class of emigrants on their passage or immediately upon landing, is one of the most honorable and beneficent of the services to the cause of humanity which have distinguished our age.

The relative proportion of different native countries, and the manner in which this great element of our population has been diffused over our own land, are also shown in this volume, and will afford valuable matter to the historical or the political inquirer now and hereafter.

There are yet other subjects of still more immediate and more practical utility on which these reports throw much light, and the more so, because they were framed from the constant experience of each year without any view to theoretical opinions. They show the workings of a vast sanitary and charitable system for a number of years, which system has the rare and peculiar merit of being self-supporting, and that without any serious burden on these who contribute to its support. There are shown the formation and gradual expansion and improvement of that system, growing out of the experience of each year, and the economy combined with efficiency, which has resulted in no small degree from the fact of the fund administered by the Commission and their officers, being always limited in proportion to the number entitled to be aided by its expenditure.

The manner in which actual experience has taught the successive administrators of this great and beneficent trust to guard over the resources committed to them—the various and efficient aid given to many who had recourse to their assistance, without lessening their feeling of self-reliance, so essential to their future success, and even to their independent support, together with other fiscal and economical details appearing in these reports, and the tables, etc., appended, are full of instruction for all intrusted with the legislation, direction, or administration of establishments for the relief of the diseased or helpless. These objects cannot but receive much illustration from the details here contained of the expenditure of above five millions of dollars in the care, relief, or assistance of 893,736 persons (see tabular statement, page 379), of whom a large proportion were hospital patients, requiring and receiving the aid of high medical and surgical skill, and the best hospital care and attendance.

Moreover, these Reports present the details and results of the practice for above thirteen years of two public hospitals, among the largest in the civilized world. One of them, the former Marine Hospital at Quarantine, was always devoted chiefly, and of late years entirely, to the reception of infectious or contagious diseases, as to cases of yellow fever, cholera, ship-fever, small-pox, etc., of which the diseases, the deaths, and cures of 56,877 patients are here stated. During the same term and for nearly fourteen years, the Ward's Island Hospitals, together with the Refuge for the infirm and helpless, requiring frequent medical advice and aid, though not regular hospital care, and which has been aptly termed the Dispensary department of the Ward's Island Hospitals, show the records of 129,641 cases. The tables of medical and surgical diseases and operations with their results, the proportion of mortality to cases treated, and facts or circumstances connected with them, reported by the medical and surgical officers, and embodied in the official Reports, constitute an immense body of medical and surgical statistics too valuable for professional and sanitary purposes, to be suffered to remain almost inaccessible in scattered pamphlets, and annual legislative documents.

In addition to these more general classes of information, many facts and many suggestions and opinions of professional men, and other particulars of interest and utility, may be found scattered through this volume. Thus it is trusted that this volume cannot but be useful and instructive, as well for the purposes of medical science, as for the practical administration of sanitary or benevolent establishments.

NEW YORK, *April* 17, 1861.

ANNUAL REPORTS

OF THE

COMMISSIONERS OF EMIGRATION

OF THE

STATE OF NEW YORK.

First Annual Report

FROM MAY 5, TO DECEMBER 31, 1847.

TO THE LEGISLATURE OF THE STATE OF NEW YORK:

The Commissioners of Emigration, in conformity with Section 8 of the Act concerning passengers in vessels coming to the city of New York, passed May 5th, 1847, respectfully submit the following Report of the amount of moneys received under the provisions of said Act, and the manner in which the same has been appropriated during the period commencing on the 8th of May, 1847, when the Board was organized, and terminating December 31st, 1847.

The Commissioners have embodied the required information in the following form.

The statistics of Emigration to this port, and the number of passengers arrived from May 5 to December 31, 1847, for whom commutation and hospital money was paid, and of the relief afforded to sick and destitute aliens under the operation of this Commission, present the following results:

Total number of alien passengers landed from May 5 to December 31, 1847, was 129,062. Of these 53,180 were natives of Germany, 52,946 of Ireland, and 22,936 of other countries. (For particulars see Table A.)

Number sent to Emigrant Refuge and Hospital, Ward's Island, from May 5 to Dec. 31, 1847		1,629
(For particulars see Table C.)		
" in Marine Hospital, May 5, 1847	256	
" admitted to do. from May 5 to Dec. 31, 1847, from the city	2,802	
" admitted to do. from vessels	3,416	
Total treated at Marine Hospital	——	6,474
(For particulars see Table B.)		

Number sent to Dr. Wilson's Hospital	208
" " Dr. Williams' "	18
" " New York City Hospital	25
" " " " Alms House	720
" forwarded to various sections of the country	798
" temporarily relieved	503
" of lunatics supported by the Commission from May 5 to Dec. 31, 1847	22
" sent to Leake & Watts' Orphan House	7
" " Home for the Friendless	17
" " Deaf and Dumb Asylum	1
" of out-door poor in the city buried at the expense of the Commission	172
Grand total of persons relieved, provided for, &c., from May 5 to Dec. 31, 1847	10,594

On the first day of January, 1848, there remained in the institutions under the control of the Commissioners, 1,110 sick or destitute, of whom 762 were natives of Ireland, 162 of Germany, and 186 of other countries.

Table No. 1 is an account current of the Commutation and Marine Hospital Funds, closed on the 31st of December, 1847, with the receipts and disbursements, and showing a balance on hand at the end of the year of $64,155 89 for the former, and a deficit of $17,910 26 for the latter fund.

Table E shows the amounts paid for emigrants who became chargeable to the Commutation Fund in cities, towns, and counties of this State.

Deducting the deficit in the hospital fund from the excess of the commutation account, the available means in the hands of the Commissioners on the 1st day of January in this year, was $46,245 63. But to show the actual condition of the funds at the disposal of the Commissioners, they must add, that since the 1st of January the total expenditures have exceeded the total receipts by $19,780 29 ; and that the available means are now reduced to $26,465 34.

The great deficit in the hospital fund, which, but for the sums drawn from the treasury of the State, would amount to $40,950 68, arises principally from the fact that a large portion of the hospital money, amounting since the 5th of May last to $34,785, was paid under protest and retained separately on deposit, until the decision of the Supreme Court of the United States on the question of the constitutional right of the State to impose this tax. This sum did not, therefore, come into the hands of the Commissioners.

By Section 17 of the Act of May 5th, 1847, the Commissioners are authorized to supply any deficiency of expenditure, chargeable properly to the Commutation Fund, out of the surplus moneys of the Mariners' Fund. The pressing necessities of the last summer and autumn, requiring large immediate expenditures for additional buildings, and permanent furniture, &c., for the quarantine establishment, the Mariners' Fund, (diminished as it was by the large amounts paid under protest,) contrary to the expectation of the legislature, proved inadequate to meet the demands upon it, whilst the Commutation Fund has been thus far sufficient to meet all the present claims upon it, leaving a considerable surplus for the future charges upon it which may arise. Though such claims may perhaps hereafter prove very large, yet, acting under the urgent circumstances of the case, the Commissioners, whilst carefully distinguishing the accounts of expenditures and receipts of each fund, and keeping distinct bank accounts with the city chamberlain for the Marine Hospital Fund and Commutation Fund, still found themselves compelled to overdraw their account for the Marine Hospital Fund, while the commutation account always exhibited a favorable balance, thus virtually borrowing from the one fund to meet the pressing exigencies which should be defrayed from the other.

It is hoped that the necessity of extraordinary outlay at the Quarantine Hospital, having thus far been fully supplied, a similar state of the two funds will not hereafter often occur.

But it is respectfully submitted to the consideration of the Legislature, whether as the two funds are for the benefit of the same class of persons, it may not be proper to authorize the Commissioners, in case of necessity, to direct a transfer from the surplus of the Commutation Fund to the Marine Hospital Fund for such amount, and under such regulations for refunding the same, when practicable, as may be fixed by a vote of the Board.

The Commissioners, at this early period of their operations, do not find themselves able to express any decided opinion as to the sufficiency of the present commutation tax to meet all the demands which will arise under "the act of May 5." In view of the fact that the term for which emigrants are entitled to be supported out of the fund is *five years*, present experience admonishes us that not only will a rigid economy be always necessary, but it is possible that unforeseen contingencies may, in spite of every precaution, render the fund insufficient hereafter for the full indemnity of the cities, towns, and counties.

The Commissioners have to express their regret that a law "for the protection of immigrants arriving in the State of New-York," which passed the House of Assembly in 1847, is not now upon the statute book.

It is a matter of almost daily observation by persons in the employ of the commission, that the frauds exposed in the report of the select committee, appointed last year "to examine frauds upon emigrants," continue to be practised with as much boldness and frequency as ever. A regular and systematic course of deception and fraud is continually in operation, whereby the emigrant is deprived of a large portion of the means intended to aid him in procuring a home in the country of his adoption.

On the third of July last, the Board appointed Mr. David Neligan their agent in Albany, with instructions to see the emigrants on their arrival there, and by his advice and counsel render them all the benefit he could. We have reason to be well satisfied with the labors of Mr. Neligan ; and as he is in a position to discover many of the impositions practised upon the unsuspecting foreigners, his weekly reports continue to furnish strong evidence of the necessity of the law which has been alluded to. To him we would refer the Legislature for additional testimony, similar to that submitted by him to the committee appointed to "investigate frauds upon emigrants."

The bill which was then introduced, is again presented to the Legislature, and it is earnestly hoped that it will obtain your early consideration, and that its provisions, or others of equal efficacy, for the protection of the inexperienced stranger, will be adopted.

It is the constant effort of the Commissioners to assist the able-bodied portion of those who are thrown upon our hands in finding opportunities of self support. For this purpose, correspondence has been opened with the contractors of many of the public works, through which channels we have been enabled to dispose of a larger number of able-bodied men and their families, and who otherwise would have been a serious burden upon the funds of the commission.

Through the enterprise of a single individual, a resident of the State of New Jersey, comfortable homes and the means of self support have been found for several hundred of our dependants. He has established an agency in that State, whereby he not only renders much assistance, in the disposal of many able-bodied people, but is also of much assistance to his neighbors for thirty miles around him, who may be in want of farm labor of various kinds.

The Board have a melancholy duty to perform, in announcing the death of their friend and fellow-laborer, Robert Taylor, their late general agent. From the first organization of the Board, Mr. Taylor was indefatigable in aiding to commence and carry on the arduous duties of the commission, and was of invaluable assistance, in meeting with his sound judgment, great practical experience, and energetic spirit, the pressing emergencies which arose. Assiduously devoted to his duties, and untiring in his zeal for the benefit of the emigrant, he fell a martyr to his fearless benevolence.

On the 26th of January the Commissioners appointed John H. Griscom, M. D., to the office of general agent, made vacant by the death of Mr. Taylor. Dr. Griscom immediately entered upon the duties of his office. He is well known in this community as a physician of acquirements and ability, and his long connection with hospitals and other institutions of public benevolence, appeared, in the judgment of the Commissioners, to give him peculiar qualifications for many of the duties of their executive chief officer, especially in the inspection and care of the extensive sanitary establishments under their charge.

During the preparation of this report we have been called upon to mourn the loss of another and valuable officer. An occupancy of less than two months of the office of Physician and Superintendent of the institution at Ward's Island, had begun to justify our hopes that in Dr. John Snowden we had found one fully competent to the arduous duties of the post, when he also fell a victim to his untiring devotion to the sick under his care.

Dr. Snowden had become early marked for his studious habits, his practical character, and his steady application to his immediate duties, when, at the premature age of 32 years, as he was beginning to reap additional honors, he was removed from the scene of his usefulness. Thus have the Commissioners been deprived of two of their most efficient agents.

These afflicting events, occurring as they did, one at the close of the last, the other at the commencement of the present year, together with the sickness of several others in the employ of the commission, much interrupted its business; on which account the Board are compelled to ask the indulgence of your honorable body for the delay which occurs in the rendition of the present report.

These losses and interruptions have been incidental to the peculiar exposure to which all connected with the commission have been and must continue to be, more or less subject. But the additional measures which have been recently adopted for more effectually ventilating and purifying the offices and institutions under our care, afford us great reason to hope that the danger will in future be much diminished.

All of which is respectfully submitted.

G. C. VERPLANCK,
J. BOORMAN,
JACOB HARVEY,
ROBERT B. MINTURN,
DAVID C. COLDEN,
ANDREW CARRIGAN,
WM. V. BRADY,
FRANCIS B. STRYKER,
LEOPOLD BIERWIRTH,
GREGORY DILLON.

NEW YORK, *February* 15, 1848.

Second Annual Report

FOR THE YEAR 1848.

TO THE LEGISLATURE OF THE STATE OF NEW YORK:

By Section 8 of the Act of May 5, 1847, the Commissioners of Emigration are required to furnish, during the legislative Session of every year, a report of the moneys received under the provisions of said act, during the preceding year, and of the manner in which they have been applied, and a further annual statement is required of them by Section 5 of the Act of December 15th, 1847.

Looking at the great interests placed under their care, the magnitude of which could hardly have been foreseen at the time when this Commission was first established, and with the view of throwing as much light as possible on so important a subject, as the enormous emigration at this port now proves to be, the Commissioners deem it their duty, not to confine themselves to a mere statement of their money transactions, as required by law, but to report at large upon the more important matters connected with the trust confided to them.

Emigration—its Extent, Condition, &c.

The number of passengers arrived at the port of New York during the year 1848, and for whom commutation and Hospital money was paid, was 189,176; of whom 98,061 were natives of Ireland, 51,973 of Germany, and 39,142 of other countries. (See Table A.)

The total number of passengers who arrived by sea, including citizens not subject to the payment of commutation money, was 195,509. (See Table A.)

All these passengers, with the exception of about 2,000, arrived in 1,041 vessels. Of which 531 were American, 341 British, 125 German, and 44 others.

The ratio of the sick, out of every *one thousand*, was 30 on board British, $9\frac{2}{5}$ on American, $8\frac{3}{5}$ on German vessels.

The statistics of relief, &c., afforded to sick and destitute emigrants, under the operation of this Commission, during the year 1848, present the following results :

Number remaining in Marine Hospital, Staten Island, January 1, 1848	550	
" sent to Marine Hospital during the year from the city	4,167	
" " " from vessels	3,944	
(For particulars see Table B.)		
	——	8,661
Number remaining in Emigrant Refuge, and Hospital, Ward's Island, Jan. 1, 1848	389	
" admitted to do. during the year 1848	3,491	
" born at do	177	
(For particulars see Table C.)	——	4,057
Number chargeable in various counties of this State to this Commission		5,369
" remaining at Dr. Wilson's Hospital on Jan. 1, 1848, chargeable to this Commission	49	
" sent to do. during the year	233	
	——	282
Number sent to Bedlows Island		46
" " Blackwell's Island Hospital		35
" " City Hospital during the year		49
" " City Alms House		6
" " Deaf and Dumb Asylum		1
" " Institution for the Blind		2
" " Lunatic Asylum		51
" forwarded to various sections of the country		2,102
" of persons temporarily relieved		6,640
" of out-door poor in the city buried at the expense of the Commission		222
Grand total of persons relieved, provided for, &c., by the Commission during the year 1848		27,523

The place of nativity of many of the persons admitted at the Marine Hospital, from shipboard, and of those who have become chargeable in other counties than New York, cannot be ascertained. Of those applying and relieved at the office of the Commissioners, being in all 16,820, there were 12,264 Irish, 4,157 Germans, and 399 others.

The temporary relief granted to 6,640 persons, consisted principally of a supper, a night's lodging, and a breakfast; and, in some instances, temporary relief was allowed to parties in their dwellings, when too sick to be removed to the hospital. As far as possible, the Commissioners have strictly adhered to a resolution adopted January 12, 1848, which is as follows:

"*Resolved*, That relief shall be given only in the institutions of the Commissioners, except in cases where persons entitled to relief, are too sick to be removed, in which cases assistance may be given by the general agent; he reporting the same to the Board at its first meeting thereafter; such relief to be discontinued so soon as said persons may be in a condition to be removed."

Further details of these subjects will be found in the annexed statements.

It appears evident that the emigration from Europe to this port is still on the increase, and will probably continue for years to come, so long as the rewards of labor are far greater, and life and property find more security here than in most parts of the old world.

By far the greater number of last year's emigrants were natives of Ireland. The Germans were less numerous than in the preceding year, on account of political troubles which detained many, who, if they could have disposed of their property, would have emigrated. Others again were prevented from leaving, by the war with Denmark leading to the blockade of the German ports in the North Sea, during several of the best months of the year, which caused a great want of shipping.

The personal condition in which the passengers arrived was, on the whole, decidedly better than during the preceding year. The frightful loss of life among emigrants on their passage across the Atlantic, and immediately after their arrival in the

American ports,* arising from the misery in which they lived before embarkation, and from an insufficient supply of food and want of ventilation on shipboard, has at last attracted the attention of the governments in both hemispheres, and led to the enactment of laws which have eminently lessened the evil.

The British act of Parliament of March 28, 1848, and that of our Congress of May 17, 1848, (in the preparation of which last-named act the members of this Board had the pleasure of co-operating with the Chamber of Commerce of New York,) which had been preceded by similar legislation on the part of governments of continental Europe, have had the beneficial results contemplated. For many months past, no instance has come to the knowledge of the Board, of an actual want of provisions on the passage ; and of ship fever, so prevalent in 1847, only 1,002 deaths at sea have been reported, and 3,079 cases on arrival of vessels, bringing in all 195,509 passengers.

The American packet ships, and the majority of transient vessels under the American flag, still maintain a superiority in their arrangements and management over the generality of British emigrant vessels ; but there is a marked improvement in the latter, and if the laws of the respective governments concerning the ventilation and provisioning of passenger vessels be faithfully executed, there cannot be any essential difference between the two flags, so far as regards the safety and comfort of the passengers.

The foreign vessels from ports in the north of Europe, more particularly those from Hamburg and Bremen, have landed their passengers generally in as good condition as the best of the American ships. Ship fever and want of food are almost unheard of on board of vessels from Northern Europe, but instances of small-pox have been of very frequent occurrence.

* It has been estimated by medical statisticians that not less than 20,000 emigrants perished by ship fever at sea, and in the various emigrant hospitals in American ports, during the year 1847; a large proportion of which mortality occurred in Canadian ports.

Marine Hospital.

The sick wards in the different buildings of the Marine Hospital, independent of the public stores, are calculated to hold conveniently about six hundred beds. It was from the beginning, the wish of the Board to receive regular and correct reports of the number of inmates in the Hospital, but in this they have experienced great difficulty.

To remedy this, the Board appointed a clerk, to whom the physicians were requested to make daily reports of all the patients received and discharged by them, to be by him entered in proper books, and daily returned to the office of the Commissioners.

By thus relieving the physicians of that unprofessional part of their former duty, the Commissioners have been enabled to keep, as they believe, a nearly accurate record of the persons admitted to, and discharged from the Marine Hospital. In addition to the daily reports of the admissions and discharges, a weekly return taken from the clerk's books, has been customary by the health officer, of the whole number of patients. The Board have also lately required of the steward a report of the number of patients ascertained by actual count at a certain hour every week.

The steward's reports, the first of which was received on the 21st June, and since which time they have come regularly, show that the number of the sick up to the first week in December never exceeded 675, the average being 500, or 100 less than the wards can hold beds; consequently there was nearly at all times ample room for the patients, while the public stores at no time contained more than 280 convalescents, and were never crowded.

By the Act of Dec. 15, 1847, the Marine Hospital is placed under the sole and exclusive control of the Commissioners of Emigration; but at the same time, the Act leaves with the health officer the power to appoint his own medical assistants, and the sanitary treatment of the inmates is left entirely to his discretion, or that of the Commissioners of health. These powers granted to the health officer seem to imply a certain control over the institution, and to conflict with the reading of Section 1 of said Act, according to which, the sole and exclusive control is vested in the Commissioners of Emigration. The health officer naturally exercises to their full extent the powers given him by law, and as the Commissioners of Emigration deem it equally their duty to perform all the duties enjoined upon them as trustees for the State, by the series of laws under which they act, difficulties have arisen between the health officer and the Commissioners of Emigration, which could not but be detrimental to the interest of the emigrant, and interfere with the harmonious and successful action of the establishment. The propriety of so amending the law as to avoid in future all similar difficulties, is respectfully submitted to the wisdom of the Legislature.

Convalescent Hospital.

The use of the public stores on Staten Island was granted by the United States Government, and intended by the Commissioners solely for occupation by convalescing patients. It was desirable to use the wards in the hospital buildings for the treatment of the sick only, and to have them as speedily as it could be done with safety, disencumbered of the convalescents, while at the same time it was equally desirable to place the latter in comfortable quarters until a relapse need no longer be apprehended. The Commissioners had had frequent occasion to complain of a too early discharge of patients. Emaciated and feeble, incapable of any bodily exertion, such discharged patients would ask for support at the office of the Commissioners, and the consequence was, that they had to be sent back to the hospital or to Ward's Island, and in either case their entire recovery was greatly protracted by the premature dismissal from the hospital.

The Board have reason to believe this addition of a house expressly devoted to convalescent patients, where they may be detained in a pure atmosphere until health is completely restored, to be the first instance of the kind in any similar institution, and its value has been satisfactorily proved by the small number of cases returned to the hospital in consequence of renewal of disease.

On the 2d day of December the ship New York arrived from Havre, with 324 steerage and 21 cabin passengers. The latter were permitted to leave Quarantine immediately, and proceed to the city ; but the 324 steerage passengers, among whom a disorder which was pronounced to be Asiatic cholera, had broken out during the voyage, and of which seven persons had died at sea and ten were sick on arrival, were all taken on shore and lodged in the public stores.

In consequence of these difficulties arising from the crowded state of the Quarantine establishment, it was determined to accept a tender of the use of Bedlows Island, one of the islands in the harbor of New York, used for the defence of the port. A temporary grant of its use for hospital purposes to the city authorities had been obtained some weeks before, from the Secretary of War, by a committee of the inhabitants of Staten Island, but had been then declined by the Commissioners, on the ground that nothing but unavoidable necessity could authorize them to remove any part of the Marine Hospital from Staten Island without legislative sanction. That necessity was now thought to have arrived, and after some delay arising from unforeseen circumstances, the island was occupied for the purposes, and under the authority detailed in the following resolution of the Board of Health.

At a meeting of the Board of Health, held Dec. 8, 1848, the following preamble and resolutions were adopted :

"Whereas, The Secretary of War has consented to yield the possession of Bedlows Island temporarily to the city of New York, and whereas, the Commissioners of Emigration have made application for permission to occupy said Island for the purpose of affording accommodation to persons arriving at this port, who are not affected with contagious or infectious diseases, the same to be furnished and provided with all other necessary and suitable accommodations at their expense ; said Commissioners to indemnify, and save harmless the said city, against any and all loss or damage which may occur to the buildings or other works upon said Island during their occupation thereof; therefore

"*Resolved*, That the application of the said Commissioners for the use of said Island, for the accommodation of persons arriving at this port, who may not be afflicted with contagious or infectious diseases be, and the same is hereby granted, upon condition that none but immigrants not affected as aforesaid, shall be removed to said Island, and that the necessary arrangements for their transportation and accommodation be made at the proper cost and expense of the said Commissioners, and that they indemnify and save harmless the said city against any and all loss or damage which they may sustain or be put to by reason of any damage to the works or buildings on said Island, by reason of such occupation; and provided also, that all such immigrants as may be removed to said Island, shall not be permitted to leave there, without permission of the mayor and Health Commissioners.

"*Resolved*, That the mayor be requested to notify the officer in command of said Island, that the city will accept the temporary possession thereof, for the time and upon the conditions mentioned in the letter of the Hon. the Secretary of War, to Jno. Anthon, Esq., under date of 7th November last."

(Signed) D. T. VALENTINE, *Clerk*.

There is one point in relation to this extensive charity, to which the Board would earnestly solicit the early attention of the Legislature, as it involves a serious question of humanity. The law provides for the admission into the Marine Hospital of "any passenger who shall have paid hospital moneys, during any temporary sickness within one year after such payment." Now, it is well known that into a quarantine hospital there must necessarily be received all those who on arrival are ill with "small-pox, yellow, bilious, malignant, or other pestiferous or infectious fever," and the records, as furnished by the health officer's weekly reports, show, that during the past year, there have actually been received from ship board, and from the city into, and have occurred at, the Marine Hospital, not less than 666 cases of small pox, 25 of yellow fever, over 3,000 cases of typhus (ship) fever, and from 60 to 70 cases of cholera, all of which are of the most malignant and pestiferous character, and that in the case of neither of these diseases, has their destructive influence been confined to the individuals who originally introduced them, but they have pervaded the institution more or less extensively, attacking many, and destroying the lives of some who, with only some mild and temporary sickness, had sought the benefits of the institution, to which they were entitled, but whose tickets of admission have proved, as it were, their death warrants.

No subject has given the Commissioners more anxiety and concern, than the necessity they were under, without any alternative, of sending within such precincts, persons applying for medical aid for ills not of an infectious character (such as fractured limbs, diseases of lungs, rheumatism, &c.). They trust to the humanity of the Legislature of the State to relieve them and the unfortunate subjects under their charge, of this cruel necessity, by authorizing them, without delay, to employ as much as may be necessary of the Marine Fund, to erect hospitals elsewhere than at Quarantine (say on Ward's Island), for the reception of all mild and non-infectious diseases, occurring either on board ship, or after arrival, within the period now prescribed by law.

Temporary accommodation for the sick, in Institutions not under the control of the Commissioners.

In our first Annual Report, mention was made of arrangements then existing, by which a large number of those entitled to relief from the Commission, were, from want of room in our own establishment, boarded in certain private institutions near the city. This arose from the necessary relinquishment of the U. S. Public Stores at Quarantine, which had been granted for a limited period, but when on the 1st of March last, the use of those stores was again granted to the Commissioners by the U. S. Government, in a manner, and on terms justifying arrangements for permanent occupation, the Board felt a reasonable assurance of ample hospital accommodations for the Quarantine establishment for a long time to come.

When thus assured of ample room in the Marine Hospital for all those who by law have a claim to medical treatment therein, the Commissioners withdrew their people from these private institutions, the last of the inmates placed there by the Commissioners having been transferred to Ward's Island, and the Marine Hospital, on the 21st of April. Since then the Commissioners have been able to provide for all applicants entitled to assistance in institutions entirely or measurably under their own control, with the exception of lunatics, and 35 small-pox patients, for whose treatment in the institutions on Blackwell's Island they have made arrangements with the city authorities.

The Commissioners are not at present prepared for the complicated arrangements required for the treatment of lunatics, of whom there have been since 5th May, 1847, sixty-one under their care. For several months most of our lunatics were received at the Bloomingdale Asylum, but on the appearance of the ship fever in that institution, introduced doubtless by a recent emigrant, the Governors declined keeping or receiving our insane patients.

Application was subsequently made for their reception in the State Asylum at Utica, which was also declined, the superintendent replying as follows:

"We have now all that we ought to have in this institution (usually 500), and the vacancies that are made by patients leaving are usually engaged before they occur. We need more public accommodations for the insane in this State."

The small-pox patients sent to the hospital on Blackwell's Island, were such as were taken with the disease in the city, and could not be sent to the Marine Hospital for want of a conveyance, arising from the impossibility of finding persons willing to risk themselves or their vehicles in the transportation of patients with this disease.

Law of December 15, 1847. *Property of patients in Marine Hospital, and of orphan children.*

By Section 5 of the Act of December 15, 1847, the personal property of emigrants dying on the passage, or in the Marine Hospital on Staten Island, and leaving minor children, shall be taken in charge by the Commissioners of Emigration, to be by them appropriated for the sole benefit of said minor orphan children. The Commissioners, in accordance with this law, on the 23d August adopted the following resolution:

"*Resolved,* That in conformity with Section 5 of an act entitled an act to amend an act entitled 'An act concerning passengers in vessels coming to the city of New York, passed December 15, 1847,' the health officer be requested to furnish daily reports to the Commissioners of Emigration, of all the persons dying in the Marine Hospital on Staten Island, and that he mention in said reports, whether or not such persons have had any personal property with them, and if they have left any such property, to furnish a correct inventory of the same."

This regulation not having been complied with by the health officer, the Commissioners, on the 25th Oct. adopted the following By-Law:

"It shall be the duty of the Steward to examine every patient as soon as possible after entering the hospital, and ascertain from them whether they have about their persons, or in their baggage, any money, papers, or other property of particular value which they wish taken care of, and to offer to take charge thereof, and give a receipt therefor; a duplicate of which receipt shall also be given by the Steward to the health officer. All property thus received shall be immediately entered in a book, to be kept for that purpose, with the name, age, vessel, date of arrival, and date of admission of the owner; and all property thus received shall be handed over to the Commissioners of Emigration properly endorsed.

"*No other person than the Steward* shall receive any property or effects from patients; and any person violating this order, shall be immediately discharged. Any information obtained by any person employed in the Marine Hospital, respecting the property of patients, must be immediately communicated to the Board."

Since the adoption of the plan prescribed in this By-Law, and up to Dec. 31, 1848, 186 parcels, containing money or jewelry, have been deposited with the general agent of the Commissioners by the Steward, as belonging to patients in the Marine Hospital, of which 54 parcels have been reclaimed by the owners after the recovery of their health, and 132 parcels remain in the hands of the general agent; and $349 84, belonging to orphans, have been deposited in the Seaman's Savings Bank.* (For particulars of this latter, see Table No. II.)

The Board would respectfully call the attention of the Legislature to what appears to be an omission in the first part of the fifth Section of the Law of Dec. 15, 1847.

It has happened, and doubtless will again, that minor children will be left orphans, by their last surviving parent dying in the institution at Ward's Island, or at some other place in the city or State soon after their arrival; when, whatever effects are left by them, unless taken in charge by some authority, may be either lost, or fall into the hands of dishonest persons who make no representation of it.

The law makes no provision for our guardianship over such, and we respectfully suggest an amendment thereto, as follows: to strike out "in Marine Hospital on Staten Island," and insert in lieu thereof, "or in any institution under the care of the Commissioners of Emigration; or in any other part of the State, within five years after their arrival at said port."

Extension and Improvement of the Emigrant Refuge on Ward's Island.

The Board saw, at an early period of the year, that far more extensive establishments than were then at their disposal, would be required for the accommodation of feeble and destitute emigrants, who could not find employment, or had not the strength to work. They also began soon to feel the want of a

* Transferred to the Emigrant Industrial Savings Bank, July 8, 1852.

proper place for those requiring medical treatment, and not entitled by law to the benefits of the Marine Hospital. The Commissioners therefore determined to have a hospital of their own, on Ward's Island, within a short distance of the building used as a Refuge. They were desirous of erecting a substantial stone building, but considering the funds at their disposal, and that it was necessary to have the building fit for occupation within as short a time as possible, they resolved upon a wooden structure. The contracts for the erection of this building were concluded on the 28th day of June with E. F. Rogers, carpenter, for the wood work, and with J. A. Hopper, for the mason work, and it was finished and occupied on the first of November.

The building is of wood, filled in with brick. It has a west front of 119 feet, and two wings, running east and west, of 40 feet long by 25 feet wide. It contains, besides apartments for physicians, apothecary and nurses, and the apothecary's shop, eleven large rooms, each 40 feet by 25, for patients, affording accommodations for 250 beds. It is heated by furnaces on an improved plan, and the ventilation is excellent. The entire cost of the building, as it now stands, including fixtures, was $13,839.

The Commissioners are satisfied that, considering its extent and accommodations, it is thus far the cheapest of all the buildings erected for hospital purposes in this city or at the Quarantine, and that for every purpose of utility, it will compare favorably with any similar edifice in the State.

While this hospital was in the course of construction, the Board became satisfied that still more ample accommodations would soon be needed, that more particularly a proper establishment for children (the number of whom had then increased to over 300, and is now upwards of 400) was imperatively demanded ; and further, that suitable arrangements for the instruction of the young, and for the performance of religious services, had become in the highest degree desirable. They therefore concluded to erect a *nursery-building*, to contain, besides dormitories, and play-room, a school-room and chapel.

In the month of January, before the buildings were crowded

to their present excess, a school was established, and one of the inmates of the Refuge appointed teacher, when his daily report exhibited an average attendance of 70 to 80 pupils of both sexes. But the pressure of numbers, which rapidly increased as winter approached, rendered it necessary to occupy the school-room for other purposes, and the school was, therefore, much to our regret, discontinued ; to be resumed, however, in the new nursery building, now nearly completed, in the plan of which ample accommodations have been included.

It became essential to have more ground than was then in the possession of the Commissioners, and acting on the conviction obtained from experience, and a careful examination of the vacant spots in and near the city, that no site or locality could be found more suitable in every respect than Ward's Island for a permanent establishment, such as is required to carry out the objects and provisions of the law, and several lots or parcels of land on Ward's Island happening at this time to be for sale, it was resolved to take advantage of the opportunity, and in the month of July the following purchases were made, viz. : Lot No. 1, from A. R. Lawrence, containing 2 acres, 3 roods and 15 perches, including a dwelling-house and barn ; lots Nos. 46 and 47, from Lambert Suydam, 6 acres, and 37 perches ; lot No. 48, from Mrs. Lawrence, 3 acres, and 10 perches ; making in all 12 acres and 22 perches, the aggregate cost of which was $12,289 38.

The contract for the erection of the nursery building was concluded on the 29th of September, with William Twine, for the carpenter's work, at a cost of $10,500 ; and with J. A. Hopper, for the mason work, at a cost of $3,989 13. This building is now sufficiently advanced to be ready for occupation within a short time. But it is quite clear to the Commissioners, that even these additional accommodations will soon be filled to overflowing, that they will have great difficulty in making them suffice for the present winter, and that to meet the probable wants of the next, more structures will be required.

In view of this contingency, and in order to have ample room for their buildings, and to prevent their being placed too near each other, the Commissioners purchased from F. Price, the lot containing two acres, at $500 per acre, adjoining their former purchase from Abm. R. Lawrence, making the aggregate of their possessions 25 acres, two roods and 14 perches, including 11 acres, 1 rood, and 32 perches, which they hold on a lease.

The following extract from the Report of the Executive Committee, recommending the erection of the Hospital, will show the reasons which actuated the Board in placing this Hospital on ground not yet owned by them in fee simple. After demonstrating that further and more extensive accommodations are needed, the Report says: "It only remains to consider where they should be erected."

In determining the question, the Committee have been much embarrassed by the consideration that the ground now occupied by the Commissioners, on Ward's Island, does not belong to them, that they hold it on a short lease; and hence the propriety may be doubted of spending a large sum of money on buildings which, by the terms of the lease of the ground, may have to be abandoned within about two years without the certainty of receiving a fair remuneration for the outlay.

But the Committee, nevertheless, have finally and unanimously decided to have the Hospital on Ward's Island, on the land leased from Mr. Minturn, for the following reasons:

"It would be extremely difficult, if not impossible, to find a locality answering the purpose as well as Ward's Island, and it would be highly injudicious to scatter our establishments still more than they are already. We must have the Hospital near the Poor House, and so long as the latter is at Ward's Island, the former must be there also. We must hope, that by the time the lease of the ground expires, the parties from whom we hold it, may be induced either to extend the same for a long term of years, or sell the land to us at a fair price. It may reasonably be supposed that another suitable locality will easily be found for the accomplishment of the object for which the premises on Ward's Island were originally intended by the present owners, and the Commissioners will, no doubt, be prepared to pay a fair price for the spot, than which none can be found better, or equally well adapted to their purpose."

There are now on Ward's Island the following buildings occupied by the Commissioners:

The large stone (or old factory) building, five stories high, 130 ft. long by 40 wide, with a brick addition 40 by 40 ft., the latter containing the offices, dining and bed-rooms, cutting and sewing rooms, and kitchen and store-house.

A wooden building two stories high, 204 feet long by 23 wide, in the rear of the former, and connected with it by a covered walk, containing a dining room for the inmates, and dormitory for children.

A barn and stable in the rear thereof.

A small frame house, used for store-room and summer kitchen.

A small wooden dwelling-house with a barn belonging to it, occupied by the superintendent of the institution.

A frame building temporarily used as a wash-house.

The New Hospital and

The New Nursery building already described, erected within the last six months.

The buildings with their contents are insured for $49,600 in seven different offices.

Besides the buildings enumerated, there was a small old wooden house, of little value, which in the month of November, before the Hospital was finished—the other buildings being then filled to overflowing—was used as a Hospital for about 20 children affected with ophthalmia. In the night of Sunday the 26th November, this building took fire, and was entirely destroyed. Thanks to the presence of mind, and the intrepidity and energy of Dr. Greene, not one of the children, of whom many were fast asleep, received the least injury, but were all taken from the burning building in safety.

The Emigrant Refuge on Ward's Island (as the establishment has been named,) is under the immediate superintendence of Enoch Greene, M. D., who, on the 19th of April, after having attended in the Institution nine weeks to the entire satisfaction of the Board, was appointed superintendent and physician, at a salary of $1,000 per annum.

Law of April 11, 1848.

The Act of April 11, 1848, was intended to guard against the frauds on emigrants practised by forwarders, boarding-house keepers, agents, runners, &c. ; but it is feared that the benevolent intention of said act has, thus far, not been fully realized, owing to the inability on the part of the Commissioners to comply with all its provisions. Experience has satisfied the Commissioners that the essential prerequisite of any control over those enemies of the emigrant (the runners), is the possession of a large dock or pier, where all the emigrants should be landed, and where none would be allowed to enter without permission of the Commissioners, and where the emigrant could be cautioned and put on his guard against the wiles of those who await him on arrival. Such a pier or dock the Law of April 11th of last year authorizes the Commissioners to purchase or lease, and on the strength of this authority they leased on the 8th May from the Common Council, for a term of five years, at the annual rent of $3,000, the large and commodious pier at the foot of Hubert street. This pier lies rather farther up town than is desirable for the purpose intended, but considering its peculiar shape and size, the Commissioners preferred it to any other they could get at the time, and they congratulated themselves upon its possession.

It was anticipated that it would be in proper order for use by the middle of July, but to the surprise of the Commissioners they were, immediately after the lease was executed, served with an injunction, obtained by some of the residents in the neighborhood of the pier.

The case was successively argued before Judge Hurlbut and Judge Morse, of the Supreme Court, and the injunction sustained.

The Commissioners conceived it to be their duty to appeal from this decision, in order to have the question finally settled, whether indeed the landing of emigrants on a pier specially appropriated for the purpose, and placed under strict superintendence, with preservation of order and decorum, can be judicially inhibited as a nuisance.

It was understood that the principal reasons which influenced the granting and the sustaining of the injunction were, that the landing of emigrants at the foot of Hubert street, in the vicinity of St. John's Park, would bring into a quiet part of the city, a noisy population, without cleanliness or sobriety, would endanger the health and good morals of the ward, and seriously affect the value of its real estate.

If there be any force in these arguments, they cannot apply to that part of the city, where the nuisance, if such it can be called, already exists where the emigrants are now, and have been for a number of years landing, in the lower part of the city; and the Commissioners, therefore, while they took all proper means to have the injunction, as stated, removed, endeavored at the same time, to get some other landing-place within the region just mentioned. They were in constant intercourse on the subject with the Common Council, whom they considered in a measure bound to furnish a pier, and whom they repeatedly memorialized on the subject. But though the Common Council seemed favorably disposed, yet no other pier could be procured, and rendered suitable for the purpose for which it was intended, without a considerable expenditure. The apprehension of similar resistance to its occupation, as prevented the obtaining possession of the Hubert street pier, has thus far defeated this plan.

Being without a pier or landing-place under their control, the Commissioners could not enforce Section 1 of the Act of April 11, 1848, as to licensing steamboats or lighters, and hence the owners of vessels used for the conveyance of passengers from shipboard to the city, have been as little affected by that act as the emigrant runners.

The use of a pier or dock for the exclusive landing of emigrants, is the principal feature of the Law of April 11, 1848, by which it was hoped and intended that the enormous frauds which had before been practised upon the emigrants, would be effectually prevented. It was upon that pier that the Commissioners or their officers were authorized and intended to be the first to meet the emigrants, and to give them such counsel and instruction as, "strangers in a strange land," and particularly liable to imposition, they would need, and put them upon the best and most economical route to their ultimate destination.

As already stated, we have been unable to obtain the use of a pier for this purpose, and consequently, being unable to reach the emigrant before he falls amongst those who stand ready to deceive him, frauds which formerly excited so much indignation and sympathy, are continued with as much boldness and frequency as ever.

Sections 3 and 4 of said Act, relating to emigrant boarding-house keepers, have no doubt, on the whole, acted beneficially, inasmuch as they have checked exorbitant charges, and saved the luggage of many a poor emigrant who had been enticed into these taverns, to spend his little cash, instead of using it for travelling expenses to some part of the country where he might find work, and lay the foundation of a permanent home. In several cases, where the boarding-house keepers refused the delivery of the luggage, the property withheld has been reclaimed, and the penalty inflicted according to law. It may also be remarked, that of late, robberies of luggage from emigrant boarding-houses have become a frequent occurrence, so as to have excited the suspicion that in some instances the keepers of the houses are not altogether free from participation in the robbery. If the tavern keeper has reason to apprehend that the lodger will not be able to pay his bill, and knowing that the law prohibits his retaining the luggage, he may think it proper to secure his claim without law.

The Commissioners would respectfully suggest, that the act be so amended as to require the mayor to withdraw the license from those who have been more than once legally fined for a violation of the act, and in whose houses robberies have been more than once committed on the property of boarders.

As there is a doubt how soon, if ever, we shall have a pier, it is desirable that the whole system of emigrant runners should be materially altered, if, indeed, it would not be an improvement to abolish it altogether, and make it an illegal business.

It is decidedly believed, that the emigrant would be essentially benefited, if there were no runners at all, neither for boarding-houses nor for forwarding offices ; if the emigrant were left at liberty to take lodgings, or engage his passage, wherever he thought best, after listening to the advice of the agents of the Commissioners, who would always be sure to meet him on board the ship which brings him. Certain it is, that the license system has not resulted in any essential improvement of the character of the runners ; that the license is no proof of their honesty ; that their calling is, what it always has been, *to force* their services upon the emigrant, and make him pay for them, and that the system has aggravated, rather than lessened, the old evil, inasmuch as the "badge" gives the runner a certain degree of authority and credit, which formerly, without his badge, he had not. Even should the emigrant, duly cautioned against those who await his appearance, arrive with the determination to avoid them, the first person he meets is a bold and decided-looking man, who obligingly offers his services, while at the same time he warns the new comer against the rascals in the rear of him. He points to his badge, "licensed emigrant runner," and soon satisfies the perplexed emigrant that he, the licensed runner, is the person especially appointed to look after the stranger, and protect him from the danger of being imposed upon ; he often even succeeds in making the emigrant believe that he (the emigrant) *must* do as the *licensed* runner tells him.

If there are constitutional obstacles in the way of suppressing the runners' business altogether, it might be nevertheless expedient to abolish the license system. The object thereby contemplated, of having a better class of men than heretofore, engaged in the business, cannot be obtained ; its advantages (if there are any) are neutralized by its drawbacks, and the small revenue derived from the licenses cannot be taken into account, the less so, as it is sure eventually to come out of the pockets of the emigrant.

Should it not be deemed expedient to repeal the whole of section five of the Act of April 11, 1848, a revision and correction of its phraseology seems necessary. The last sentence of the section reads as follows :

"Every person who shall solicit alien emigrant passengers, * * * *without such license*, shall be deemed guilty of a misdemeanor, and shall be punished by imprisonment * * * and shall also *forfeit his license.*"

An amendment of Section 3 of the same law is necessary. As will be seen on examination, it requires all persons keeping houses for boarding emigrant passengers, to have a license; *but it imposes no penalty for not taking out a license.*

The Commissioners of Emigration have abundant evidence that many of the emigrant boarding-house keepers are as unscrupulous as the runners, in the advice they give to emigrants regarding the routes to the interior of the country, and on other matters connected with their sojourn in this city, and that, more particularly, they make it their business to prevent the emigrant from asking and obtaining advice and counsel of those who would honestly give it.

The Commissioners, therefore, would respectfully suggest, that the Act of April 11, 1848, be so amended as to require the keepers of emigrant boarding-houses to cause to be kept conspicuously posted in the public rooms of such houses, any and every publication or handbill which the Commissioners may deem proper to issue, for the purpose of putting the emigrant on his guard against overcharges in the price of passage to the interior, and other frauds.

To the long list of frauds on emigrants, noticed in the former reports of the Commissioners, they have to add another which is practised on the emigrant, before he leaves Europe, and which is to induce him there to engage and pay for his passage hence to the place of his destination, in the interior of the country. Among others, the American Consul at Havre kindly directed to the subject, the attention of the Commissioners, who adopted the only means at their command to arrest the evil, which was to issue a circular exposing the fraud, a copy of which is hereto appended (see Appendix No. 1), and to have the same published in Europe, in several languages. They asked the assistance of the General Government for the purpose of insuring greater publicity to the subject, and they are happy to acknowledge that assistance was readily granted. (The correspondence between the President of the Board and the Secretary of State, will be found in Appendix No. 2.)

The Commissioners fulfil an agreeable duty in here noticing, with sincere thanks, the proofs of kind consideration they have received in the performance of their duties, from several of the officers high in place, and in the esteem of the country. The Secretary of State, the Secretary of the Treasury, the Secretary of War, the Collector of the port, Major-General Gaines, Major Delafield, and other officers in command at the various military stations in the harbor, have on various occasions testified by their acts a lively interest in the cause of the commission. Their thanks are due also to the consuls of foreign powers residing in this city, and to several of our own consuls abroad.

Financial matters.

The Marine Fund is formed by the payment of $2 for every cabin passenger (citizen or alien), arriving from a foreign port; and for each steerage passenger, 50 cents, and for each passenger in a coasting vessel (with certain exceptions), 25 cents. (See Act of May 7, 1844, 2 R. S. Pt. 1, Chap. XIV., Title IV., Section 7.)

The Commutation Fund is formed by the payment of $1 per head for each passenger not a citizen of the United States, arriving in this port, and is applied to the support and relief of those of them who would otherwise become chargeable as paupers on the city and county where they may be.

The receipts and expenditures of the Commutation and Hospital Funds, for the year 1848, will be found in Table No. III.

Economical Measures.

It has been the earnest endeavor of the Commissioners to introduce and adhere to, the strictest economy, in all their money transactions, and to reduce the expenses to the lowest possible standard. For this object the following changes among others of less consequence, have been made during the year 1848.

A separate hired office, formerly kept by the Commissioners of Health, for receiving applications for admission from the city into the Marine Hospital, with two clerks, has been discontinued, and the business done at the office of the Commissioners of Emigration. This effects a yearly saving of $1,300. The wages of the boatmen at the Quarantine had been for some years, at a rate much above that ever allowed by private persons for similar services, so that these places had become regarded as rewards for partisan, political services. The wages have been reduced to what is still a liberal compensation, commanding an eager competition for the places, whenever they happen to be vacant. A practice had grown up of furnishing the health officer and others with passage tickets for the ferry boats between Staten Island and the city, which were distributed and used without restriction, so that about twelve hundred dollars were paid in the course of the year for these tickets.

Since the 8th of May, 1848, this expenditure has been wholly retrenched, with the exception of a small commutation fee for a messenger, and occasional tickets purchased for visits of business, making a saving of about $1,100 annually.

On the 10th of May the Commissioners had a conference with the health officer, informing him that they found no legal authority for the payment to the deputy or assistant health officer of the salary of $1,500 per annum, from the hospital moneys, and which he had hitherto received, he being strictly in the personal employment of the health officer. That payment has therefore been discontinued. The medical and other officers of the hospital had long been boarded at the public table, the expense of which it was impossible to supervise or restrain, and was necessarily left to accidental discretion. By an arrangement satisfactory to those immediately interested, and made with their consent, an annual allowance, in addition to their several salaries, has been substituted in lieu of board. The pecuniary amount of this retrenchment cannot be precisely stated, but it is confidently believed that the result is in all respects most beneficial.

On the 5th of May, 1848, the Board passed the following resolution :

"*Resolved*, That the wine, brandy, beer, porter, &c., furnished to the Marine Hospital, are intended for the use of the patients solely, and that the Steward be instructed to deliver them upon the requisition of the physicians for that purpose only."

One of the most important savings effected, is in the mode of conveying from the city, persons entitled to the benefits of the Marine Hospital, and the Institution on Ward's Island. The Commissioners originally employed the Staten Island ferry boats for the conveyance of patients to the Marine Hospital ; but when the proprietor of these boats refused to carry such patients any longer, the Board was obliged to arrange for their transportation with the owner of some other steamboat. This involved an average expense of $1,111 per month. For the conveyance of people to Ward's Island, the Board employed a coach of their own.

The enormous expense of these modes of transportation had been a constant source of trouble to the Commissioners. And some other more economical mode of communication with the various institutions, was very desirable. In the month of August, the general agent of the Commissioners suggested a proposition, which was submitted to the Alms House Commissioners of New York, for our joint use of a steamboat to do the transportation of both institutions—the cost to be divided equally between them. The proposition was immediately accepted, and was carried into effect on the 1st of October, by chartering the steamboat "Stranger" for $35 per day. The saving to the Commissioners of Emigration by this arrangement may be safely estimated at $9,500 per annum, and thus far, the arrangement has met our expectations.

The Board has, during the past year, also made fresh contracts, for supplying the Marine Hospital, and the Emigrant Refuge and institutions at Ward's Island with bread, milk, and meat, by which an essential saving on the former contracts has been effected. The bread is now furnished at $2\frac{5}{8}$ cents per pound, milk at $3\frac{1}{2}$ cents per quart, and meat on the following terms:

Shoulders (shin off), sockets (whole), necks (button off), legs (first cut-round off), each 4 cents per pound. Corned beef (plates, navels, and briskets), roast beef (chucks, six ribs on), beef steaks (sirloin, chuck, and round), pork, lamb, mutton, and veal (in quarters), each 7 cents per pound. Shins 10 cents each.

The enfeebled and broken-down condition of a large majority of the people under our care, is such as to require the articles of consumption to be of the best and most nutritious quality, such being deemed the most economical. The meat and bread will compare favorably with those articles used at most public tables.

Finally, the arrangement with Messrs. Craig & Lane (stated in the first report of the Commissioners), was modified, by reducing their compensation from 5 to 3 per cent. commissions on the amount of their purchases for our account. This is considered a reasonable compensation for the services rendered, and the great trouble and risk connected therewith. The Board is satisfied that by no other arrangement could they obtain their supplies better or cheaper. The articles which Craig & Lane have to furnish, may be called innumerable, requiring great judgment in the selection, and much time and labor to collect; and the delivery at the respective establishments is at their risk. They are paid only on producing the original bills of the parties from whom the goods are purchased, and a certificate that they have been duly received at Ward's Island or the Marine Hospital, as the case may be.

In the mode of procuring supplies, the Commissioners have learned by experience, that permanent contracts could be satisfactorily made for certain articles of consumption only, such as bread, meat, milk, and fuel, while others, such as medicine, clothing, &c., are so varied in character, and required in smaller and more uncertain quantities, and at longer intervals, as to be most economically obtained, through responsible purchasers, in such quantities, as from time to time are needed.

3

The total amount of savings effected by the above-mentioned and other minor changes, cannot fall short of $19,000 per annum.

In the year 1838, the average expense per patient, as appears from the report of Dr. Stevens (who was appointed by the Legislature to examine into the affairs of the Marine Hospital, and report all matters connected with it), was $5 12 per diem, or $35 87½ per week. In 1842 and 1843, as appears from reports of commissioners appointed to examine into expenditures of hospitals in the first Senate district, the expense per patient per week was about $15.

The Commissioners are unable to find the data necessary to form an estimate of the average expenses of the Marine Hospital for the succeeding years, but they cannot state any fact showing more conclusively the economy now practised at the institutions under their charge, than that during the past year, the expense per patient was as follows :

IN MARINE HOSPITAL.

	PER DIEM.	PER WEEK.
For food	$0 13·25	$0 92·75
" medicines, liquors, &c.	5·66	39·62
" salaries, wages, &c.	16·18	1 13·26
" clothing, dry goods, &c.	1·64	11·48
	$0 36·73	$2 57·11

IN EMIGRANT REFUGE.

	PER DIEM.	PER WEEK.
For food	$0 09·20	$0 64·40
" medicines, liquors, &c.	·78	5·46
" salaries, wages, &c.	3·20	22·40
" clothing, dry goods, &c.	5·25	36·75
	$0 18·43	$1 29·01

The cost of land, buildings, permanent fixtures, &c., are not included in the above estimates.

Moneys paid under protest.

Notwithstanding the introduction of rigid economy and the strict adherence thereto, it will be seen by the statement of the Marine Hospital account, that the money authorized by law to be collected from emigrants for the use of that institution, is altogether insufficient for the support of the establishment. The deficiency arising during the year 1847, was, in a considerable degree, caused by the erection of sundry buildings, and other improvements ; but the expenses under this head for the year 1848 were only $5,963 78, and, nevertheless, there arose a deficiency of means required for the support of the hospital, calling for appropriations from other sources to the amount of above $20,000.

But it does not follow, that the hospital money of fifty cents on every steerage passenger is altogether inadequate to meet the expenses of the Marine Hospital. This deficiency arises in great part from the fact that a large portion of these moneys continues to be paid under protest, and thereby becomes unavailable. The Commissioners are still inclined to think that the money collected under existing laws would furnish sufficient means for the support of the hospital, if the whole amount thereof were placed at their disposal. But, considering the uncertain result of the suit now before the Supreme Court of the United States, regarding the constitutionality of the law, and that until a decision shall have been given, a large part of the fund will be continued to be paid under protest, the Commissioners would respectfully suggest that the hospital money for aliens be abolished, and in lieu thereof, the commutation money be raised to one dollar and fifty cents. There would then be no more payments under protest on their account, the whole amount of moneys collected would be available as soon as deposited with the Chamberlain, and there would be no necessity for keeping two separate accounts. There would be but one fund created by the moneys collected in the manner stated, out of which fund provision could be made for the maintenance and support and medical treatment of such persons, in the manner prescribed by Sections 4 and 5 of the Act of May 5th, 1847, and by Section 18 of the Act of May, 1846.

The Commissioners received information, that the case before the Supreme Court of the United States regarding the constitutionality of the hospital tax, would be reargued before that court, immediately after its opening in December. They were confident that the interest of the fund would be safe in the hands of the present able Attorney-General, but believing that the intimate knowledge of the case possessed by his immediate predecessor, who argued the same last year, might prove of essential benefit, if brought into requisition on the present occasion, and anxious not to omit or neglect any steps calculated to insure a favorable result, the Commissioners thought it important to engage him to assist Mr. Jordan.

Payments.

The manner in which payments are made by the Board, is as follows :

The auditing committee reports at the weekly meetings of the Board, the bills examined and passed by them, stating the several items, for the aggregate amount of which, if approved by the Board, a warrant is issued on the Chamberlain to transfer said amount to the credit of the general agent. The latter then attends to the payment of the various bills by drawing a separate check for each, to the order of the party who is to receive it, which check is countersigned by one of the Commissioners.

It will thus be seen that the expenses of the Commission are settled weekly as fast as they are incurred ; and no accounts are allowed to remain unsettled beyond the time necessary to be satisfied of their correctness.

Prospective Considerations.

It is extremely difficult to give a prospective statement of the funds of the Commission, with any degree of accuracy, but the matter is deemed too important to be omitted entirely in this report, and the Commissioners respectfully invite attention to the following *exposé :*

Amount of available means on hand, Jan. 1, 1848............	$46,245 63
" " " Jan. 1, 1849............	82,293 07
Number of persons chargeable in the Institutions of the Commission, Jan. 1, 1848..................................	1,110
Do. Jan. 1, 1849..................................	1,855
Number of alien passengers arrived since May 5, 1847, Jan. 1, 1848	129,062
Do. do. do. Jan. 1, 1849	318,238

Thus it is shown, that the available means of the Commissioners now are about $36,000 more than a year ago ; but the number of persons actually supported at its expense exceeds that of last year by 745, and the number of those having claims on the funds of the Commission is about 150 per cent. larger than at this time last year.

Last year the funds were exhausted before the end of April, and in order to prevent a suspension of the operations of the Commission, the Legislature had to make provision for the then existing, and prospective deficit, to the amount of $60,000.

After the beginning of April, the receipts overran the expenditures, and continued to do so until November, since when, the reverse has been the case. Our means are now again rapidly decreasing, and there is reason to apprehend that they will not suffice to carry us through the winter. The subject will have the constant attention of the Board, and unless the money, now held under protest, is released by a favorable decision of the United States Supreme Court, the Commissioners will be obliged to call upon the Legislature for aid from some other source.

Changes.

The changes in the organization of the Board during the past year, were as follows :

Wm. F. Havemeyer resigned, and, in his stead, Andrew Carrigan was appointed a Commissioner by the Governor and Senate, and took his seat on the 9th of February, 1848. The seat of our esteemed associate, Jacob Harvey, was made vacant by death on the 10th of May, and, on the 19th of July, Wm.

M. McArdle, having been appointed Commissioner by the Governor in place of the deceased, appeared and took his seat, having previously taken the oath of office.

Gulian C. Verplanck was, on the 1st of March, unanimously elected President of the Board, for the remainder of the year 1848.

All of which is respectfully submitted.

G. C. VERPLANCK,
J. BOORMAN,
DAVID C. COLDEN,
ANDREW CARRIGAN,
WM. M. McARDLE,
WM. F. HAVEMEYER,
FRANCIS B. STRYKER,
LEOPOLD BIERWIRTH,
GREGORY DILLON.

NEW YORK, *January* 13, 1849.

Third Annual Report

FOR THE YEAR 1849.

To the Legislature of the State of New York:

The Commissioners of Emigration respectfully present to the Legislature their report for the past year.

In this report, following the example of former years, they have not confined themselves to the financial and other returns specially required by law, but have added such other facts, statements and suggestions, as seemed most important to be presented to the consideration of the Legislature, for the due supervision of the great interests confided to the Commissioners, and the improvement of the system which they administer.

For the better understanding of the subsequent statements and details of this report, it will be proper, first, to present a brief recapitulation of the judicial and legislative action upon the subject of the Marine Hospital and alien-passenger laws of this State during the past year.

In their last annual report, and in their subsequent communications to the Legislature and the State officers, the Commissioners stated the embarrassments with which they were threatened by the legal opposition to the provision of the Revised Statutes, imposing a tax upon all passengers arriving in the port of New York, for hospital money, and to the later act of 1847, requiring an additional payment of one dollar for each alien emigrant so arriving. A large proportion of the payments thus required and appropriated to the objects of this Commission, were made under protest, and paid directly over into the State treasury, to be held subject to the decision of the Supreme Court of the United States, before which tribunal the decisions of our own State courts, sustaining the constitutionality of our State legislation, had been carried by appeal. The proportion of the moneys thus paid, to the whole amount, continued to increase with great rapidity, from the conclusion of the year 1848 until the decision of the cause, which was delayed by various circumstances. In the mean time, the regular receipts of the Commissioners were exhausted, and the establishments under their charge must have been closed, had it not been for an unexhausted balance of the commutation fund, arising from the receipts of former years, and the authority given by law to transfer a portion of it to meet the deficiencies of the Marine Hospital fund. But even with this resource, they were barely able to meet the great and pressing demands of the winter, after the payment of commutation money ceased entirely.

The Supreme Court of the United States having finally adjudged the invalidity of the several laws of New York on this subject, the Legislature of 1849 proceeded to a revision of the system, which was finally passed the 11th April, 1849.

By the act of that date, the former laws establishing a provision for alien emigrants who might require public relief, were so modified as to obviate the constitutional objections on the subject sustained by the Supreme Court; and by the requisition of bonds with ample security, or a commutation in lieu thereof, with other provisions for special cases, to provide the means of preventing emigrants, in case of sickness or destitution, from becoming a charge upon the counties.

The separation of the Quarantine Hospital from the charge and control of the health officer, made in the same law, and the restrictions as to the persons received there, whilst they improved the efficiency and good order of the establishment, served also to remove certain constitutional difficulties founded on the diversion of money collected from emigrants, to other purposes.

Since the date of the act, no legal objection has been raised, and the several requirements of the law, as to bonds, commutation, &c., have been promptly complied with.

It must, however, be remarked, that although the Commissioners were thus relieved from the serious embarrassments arising from the contested payments under the old law, yet they were obliged to recommence under the new system with many outstanding debts and claims, with a large number of emigrants who were entitled to relief under the law of May 7th, 1847, and without any surplus at their command from former receipts, such as they might have calculated upon, had the legislation of the State been sustained in the court of last resort.

The emigration of 1849 from Europe to this port, has fully realized the expectations expressed by the Commissioners in their last report, being one-sixth greater than the aggregate of 1848.

The emigration from Ireland still continues to increase, to exceed largely that from any other country, and to bear nearly the same proportion to the whole, being last year 2,290 more than half, and having been in the year preceding, 3,473 more.

Our latest accounts from England give information of a temporary check to the large emigration from Great Britain and Ireland; yet there is probably no good reason to expect any great diminution of emigration from those quarters during the present year. The information from Germany leads the Commissioners to believe, that the emigration thence will be somewhat lessened, though doubtless still large. The emigration from Holland, Norway and Sweden, shows a considerable increase over the small numbers of former years, and there is good ground to expect a regular and considerable augmentation, from year to year of emigrants (chiefly agricultural), from those countries.

The personal condition and health of the passengers in 1849, was as in 1848, far better than during the first year of this Commission.

Although the number claiming and receiving aid or relief in various ways from the commutation fund during 1849, was nearly one-third more than in the year preceding; still, as the whole number entitled to claim such relief, includes all within this State who have come under the operation of the emigrant laws, since May 1847, and is probably more than double the number entitled to such relief in the year 1848, a cheering indication is given, that the proportion of destitution in the whole mass, is decidedly diminishing.

The beneficial operation of the recent legislation in America and Europe for the protection of the health and comfort of passengers on shipboard is constantly felt ; notwithstanding that occasionally the requirements of these laws are evaded to some extent, and thus their important objects, though not entirely frustrated, are less perfectly obtained.

Evidence of such evasions, and of their consequent evils, having from time to time come to the knowledge of the Commissioners, they thought that it was their duty to tender to the Collector of the port such aid and information as they might thus be able to afford in enforcing the laws of the United States.

The Collector's attention had already been actively devoted to the subject, and one of the officers of the customs put specially in charge of it. This officer was instructed to confer with the officers of this Board, and to receive such information and suggestions as might assist in giving efficacy to the act of Congress of the 18th May, 1848.

It is due to the character of the navigation of this port to add, that the cases alluded to are comparatively few, and merely exceptions, in part, to the great and general amelioration in the mode of carrying passengers, which has taken place during the last two years.

But the remembrance of the dreadful amount of suffering and death, which occurred in former years, from the neglect of proper sanitary precautions on board vessels bound to our ports, and still more in those conveying emigrants to the British colonies, powerfully impresses the duty of unremitted vigilance in providing, as far as possible, against the recurrence of similar calamities.

The statistics of emigration to this port, and of the relief or assistance afforded to destitute aliens under the operation of this Commission, presents the following results :

Total number of passengers who landed at the port of New York in 1849, 234,271.

Of these 13,668 were citizens, and 220,603 aliens ; of whom 112,591 were natives of Ireland, 55,705 of Germany, and 52,307 of other countries. (For particulars, see Table A.)

All these passengers (with the exception of about 4,000) arrived in 1,651 vessels; of which 594 were American, 371 British, 85 German, and others 601. (For statement showing the relative ratio of mortality, &c., during the voyage, see statement accompanying Table A.)

The statistics of relief, &c., afforded to sick and destitute emigrants under the operation of this Commission, during the year 1849, present the following results:

Number remaining in Marine Hospital, Staten Island, Jan. 1st, 1849	605	
" sent to Marine Hospital during the year	5,554	
(For particulars see Table B.)		6,159
Number remaining in Emigrant Refuge and Hospital, Ward's Island, Jan. 1st, 1849	1,147	
" admitted to do. during the year 1849	6,827	
" born at do.	346	
(For particulars see Table C.)		8,320
Number chargeable in various counties of this State to this Commission		5,566
" of lunatics chargeable to this Commission		171
" sent to Bedlows Island during the year		645
" forwarded to various sections of the country		2,999
" of persons temporarily relieved		16,854
" of out-door poor in the city buried at the expense of the Commission		544
Grand total of persons relieved, provided for, &c., by the Commission during the year 1849,		41,258

Estimated number of days of inmates on Ward's Island	468,000	
Whole number of days of inmates in Marine Hospital	174,258	
Total number of days of persons chargeable to Commission in both Institutions		642,258

Number of licenses granted for boarding-houses	97
Do. do. to forwarders	26
Do. do. to runners	92

Of the whole number received and supported at Ward's Island, about one-third (or a weekly average of about 600) are children under twelve years of age.

Of the remainder, a large but varying proportion (often half) are under medical treatment.

Marine Hospital.

Under the acts which were in force for the first three months of the year 1849, the Marine Hospital was under the joint government of the Commissioners of Emigration and of the health officer of the port; the former having the financial responsibility and the power over the property and supplies, whilst the health officer was the chief physician of the establishment, with authority to appoint his medical assistants.

By the laws establishing the Marine Hospital, all passengers, whether citizens or aliens, arriving at the port of New York, were subject to a tax, the payment of which entitled them absolutely, for a year, if requiring gratuitous medical care, to be received into that establishment at Quarantine.

All infectious and contagious cases from shipboard were of course detained there. Thus this hospital has of late years been filled to excess, whilst crowds of patients suffering under milder or non-contagious diseases, or requiring only surgical aid, were exposed to ship fever, small-pox, yellow fever, or cholera, in spite of every precaution. These difficulties, with others incident to the former organization, continued to exist in various degrees during the winter of 1848–'49.

Bedlows Island and the United States public stores, the temporary occupation of which had been granted by the Secretary of the Treasury (as stated in last year's report), were filled with the overflow of patients from the Marine Hospital.

The cost of fitting up Bedlows Island, and the keeping up a distinct organization there, contributed to augment the expenses beyond the previous proportion of hospital support.

By the Act of April 11, 1849, the Marine Hospital was specially restricted to the reception of contagious and infectious cases, and placed under the separate charge of a physician in chief, and four medical assistants, leaving the Commissioners the control over its financial and other concerns.

The patients not coming within the regulations of this law, were removed to Ward's Island, as soon after as practicable, and the extra accommodations at Bedlows Island being now required for military purposes, were delivered up to the proper authorities.

Since this change, the number of patients at the Marine Hospital have varied from 699 to 228, being a weekly average of 498.

The Commissioners have every reason to be satisfied with the general operation of the new system.

During the wide-spread pestilence and mortality of the last summer, when, under the former system, no human precaution could have prevented their extension over crowds of other patients, the new classification and superintendence were found powerfully efficacious.

The mode of supplying the hospital by contract with meat, bread, milk, fuel, and whatever else it could be beneficially applied to, has been continued as heretofore. Other articles are supplied in the manner detailed in last year's report, by purchases made on requisitions, for which the officers of the hospital are made responsible as to amount and nature. In addition to the office of steward as heretofore, the Commissioners thought it expedient that a resident superintendent should be vested with the general inspection and control of the whole establishment, to carry into effect their by-laws, and to act under their authority in matters of discipline, which often require prompt and decided action.

This office is not incompatible with the duties of physician-in-chief, neither, on the other hand, are its duties necessarily connected with his. Various circumstances induced the union of the whole authority in one person for the contemplated purposes, which has thus far been found convenient and salutary.

By the fifth section of the Act of 10th April, 1849, the Commissioners of Emigration were bound, as soon as practicable after the passage of the said law, to procure a new burial-ground for the Marine Hospital, and cease burials in the old ground. After many fruitless attempts to secure a favorable and unobjectionable ground, the Commissioners succeeded in buying four acres of land in the township of Castleton, Staten Island, so situated as to be at the greatest possible distance from an inhabited neighborhood, and over forty rods from the nearest public road, yet not more than about a mile distant from the Marine Hospital.

About one-half of this ground has been enclosed by a high close fence, with well-secured gates, inside of which all burials have taken place since the 15th of August last.

In front of this enclosure, a small house has been erected for the permanent residence of the person in charge of the burial-ground.

The Commissioners believe, by this arrangement, to have satisfied on this point, all reasonable wishes of the inhabitants in the neighborhood of the Marine Hospital.

By the 19th section of the Act of 11th May, 1849, the selection and appointment of the nurses and orderlies at the Marine Hospital, are given to the several assistant physicians, each for his own department, the number being determined by the chief physician, whilst the compensation of each of them is to be fixed and determined by the Commissioners of Emigration.

In fixing the general rate of compensation, the Commissioners have always cheerfully complied with the recommendation of the chief physician. But it may sometimes occur that the good order, economy, or morals of the establishment may, in the view of the Commissioners, be promoted by the dismissal of some one or more of these subordinates. The language of the act in giving the Commissioners authority over the wages, would seem to imply that the authority was not confined to general regulation, but may be exercised in any individual instance.

It is, however, respectfully submitted, whether the Commissioners may not with propriety be invested with the power to discharge any such nurse or orderly, leaving the right of selection and appointment in the hands of the physicians.

This is an authority which runs no risk of being exercised capriciously or frequently, but may occasionally contribute to the general efficiency and character of the hospital services.

In connection with the same subject, it may also be observed, that it would seem reasonable that the chief of the department, who is responsible for its general good order and moral character, should have some authority to guard against ill-judged appointments, and to remove those disobedient to the regulations of police and order.

For this end the physician of the Marine Hospital might with great propriety, and with probable beneficial effect, be also invested with the power of discharging all nurses and orderlies, and all appointments by the assistants might be made subject to his approval.

Another subject connected with the Quarantine establishment is so important in relation to the health and commerce of the State, that although it does not come within the immediate authority of the Commissioners, they feel it to be their duty to present it to the consideration of the Legislature.

Under the laws in relation to "the public health," the whole care and responsibility of maintaining a Quarantine were confided to the health officer, who was also the chief physician of the Marine Hospital. By the late law dividing the duties of that officer, it is expressly declared "that the health officer shall have no other authority over the hospital, than as provided in the act." This authority is there limited to the privilege of visiting and inspecting the hospital, and the granting discharges of patients. Thus, no provision is any longer made to secure the objects of a Quarantine *on land*, so far as intercourse with patients sick of contagious or infectious diseases is concerned. *On water*, the health officer is still vested with ample and efficacious powers to enforce his regulations and orders for the protection of the public health. The exclusive control of the Marine Hospital is, indeed, given to the Commissioners of Emigration, but unaccompanied with the other powers necessary to enforce a strict Quarantine ; nor, indeed, would they be the the proper depositories of a discretionary authority which could only be executed by deputy. But it would seem to be on all accounts proper, as well as expedient, that the chief medical officer of the Marine Hospital, appointed by the State, should be intrusted with such powers, and made responsible for the maintenance of the quarantine on shore, and the regulation of intercourse with the sick and other inmates of the institution. This could be effectually done only by extending to the physician of the Marine Hospital, the same powers in relation to enforcing quarantine at and near the hospital, as formerly belonged to the health officer in relation to the hospital and its inmates.

From the increase of the commerce of this port, and the consequently increased claims upon the attention and time of the health officer, the Legislature judged it advisable to divide his duties with a new officer. This officer is now the only person fitted, from his office, to take charge of the enforcement of quarantine on shore. During the season when this is most essential, the health officer is frequently detained upon the water for hours at a time, and if his control on shore were restored, his other duties would rarely permit him to pay proper attention to the subject of intercourse between the sick in the hospital, and others who might be the means of diffusing infection far and wide.

The Commissioners therefore respectfully recommend, that the physician of the Marine Hospital should be authorized to exercise all the power and authority in respect to the enforcement of quarantine on or about the Marine Hospital, heretofore possessed by the health officer, as physician of the same.

Emigrant Refuge and Hospitals, Ward's Island.

The experience of almost three years has fully justified the propriety of the selection of Ward's Island for the location of our establishments for the reception of destitute emigrants, coming under the operation of the passenger laws.

Its vicinity to the city, and its easiness of access at all seasons, combined with its isolation from the inconveniences and annoyances of a thickly-settled neighborhood, and the means it afforded of procuring lands of sufficient extent to meet the increasing demands for its use, at a much more reasonable rate than could be obtained elsewhere within the same distance, and with the same facilities of conveyance thither, all originally recommended that selection. The Commissioners have not been disappointed in the result, now that the demands for its use and occupation have swelled to a magnitude much beyond what they could have at first anticipated.

At the beginning of the year 1849, the establishment there consisted of the following buildings : The large old stone building (originally built for a factory), five stories high, 170 feet by 40, as fitted up and enlarged for the purposes of the commission in 1847. A wooden building, two stories, 204 feet by 23, parallel to and connected with the former. Several smaller houses and out-buildings, as stable and barn, house for superintendent, &c. The new nursery building and the hospital building, as described in our former reports ; the former contains accommodations for children, with school room and chapel, and other apartments. The hospital affords accommodation for about 250 patients.

But the Commissioners soon realized the expectation, confidently expressed in their last Annual Report, "that these accommodations will soon be filled to overflowing, that there would be great difficulty in making them suffice for that winter, and that to meet the probable wants of the next, more buildings would be required." The numbers of destitute emigrants, either incapable of finding immediate employment, or wholly incapacitated from profitable occupation by age, infirmity, or infancy, who had become entitled to relief under two years operation of the commutation law, so much exceeded those of the past, that enlarged accommodation was immediately required. The alteration of the Quarantine hospital system, excluding from that institution numerous cases (other than those afflicted with infectious or contagious diseases), formerly received there, added to the number required to be received at Ward's Island and provided with hospital accommodation.

Their funds at that time being inadequate for the erection of a hospital building of a permanent and durable character, and the rapidly increasing pressure of numbers demanding the speediest possible accommodations, the Board determined upon the construction of buildings of the simplest kind compatible with health and comfort. They accordingly, during the past spring and summer, erected twelve temporary buildings of wood, each of a single story, 125 feet long by 20 wide, and 13 feet high to the ceiling, filled in with brick, lathed and plastered. Each of these buildings will accommodate fifty patients, and they are partitioned off into two, and some into three separate apartments, thus admitting of abundant classification of patients.

They are placed at distances from each other, and from the more valuable buildings, sufficient for all the purposes of convenience and security against the spreading of fire.

The prudence of the precaution of securing a considerable extent of land by the purchases and agreements of 1848, was now manifest. But the high probability of a still further increase of inmates for some time to come, the necessity of considerable extent of ground for exercise, health, and various employments, urged the propriety of additional purchases of adjoining lands, which were now offered. To these considerations were added others in reference to the morals and good order of the establishment, which, it was evident, would be materially promoted by a large extent around the buildings, bringing within the bounds of our authority all the lots in the immediate vicinity, by squaring the whole property, and also of having the control of the adjoining water rights which were held under a grant from the Commissioners of the Land Office, distinct from the title of the shore and upland.

All these objects have been satisfactorily attained by the purchase of 95 acres 3 roods 6 perches, exclusive of 11 acres 1 rood 13 perches, held on a lease, with some leases of water rights, to cost, on the whole, $63,818 83. Of this sum, $43,818 83 has been paid for part of the land, the rest being conveyed, and the payment of the consideration money to be made during the present year.

The demand for a more ample supply of good water for baths, washing, and all other purposes of health and cleanliness requ red by an average of 1,600 inmates, the greatest part of whom are either children, infirm or diseased persons, was such as was imperfectly supplied by wells and cisterns. The example of the adjoining City Alms House, on Randall's Island, showed that this deficiency could best be supplied from the Croton aqueduct, and carrying the water across or under the channel which separates Ward's Island from the Island of New

York. An arrangement to this effect was made with the Croton aqueduct department, the conveyance of the water to be under the charge of the Commissioners of Emigration, and at their expense. This work was commenced in December last, and is now nearly completed, and will cost about $10,000, a portion of which has been paid.

In connection with this supply of water, it was deemed advisable, and indeed necessary, to erect a spacious and substantial wash-house, with drying rooms, disinfecting apartments, baths, and other conveniences.

In settling the plan, it was found that both convenience and economy would be consulted, by so enlarging the wings of the proposed building, as to provide apartments or wards, which might be used for various classes of patients or others. The building is now in progress, and will soon be completed.

The largely increased hospital service soon demanded the exclusive attention of a physician-in-chief, devoted solely to that duty. The former office of superintendent and physician was therefore divided. Dr. Theodore Tellkampf was appointed to the chief medical office, and the former superintendent continued until the commencement of the present year, to discharge the proper duties of that station.

Since our last report, the Board have prepared and adopted a new set of rules for the government of the officers of the Institution, more minutely specifying their duties, and embodying such regulations as experience had suggested. It is hoped that they will materially contribute to the good order and usefulness of the establishment.

The supplies for Ward's Island have been furnished in the manner heretofore reported, by contract by public competition for the articles of larger and regular consumption, and having the other innumerable articles required for such an establishment in smaller quantities purchased at the lowest possible cost.

The Commissioners have always kept in view, that this establishment should, as far as practicable, be used only as a refuge for the infirm, diseased, or helpless, such as would otherwise fall under the charge of the local administrators of our poor laws. Yet in spite of every precaution, some not coming within this class, must be received ; some others entitled to aid by disease, may, when restored to health, continue for a time in the refuge. But the Commissioners and their officers have taken pains to find employment for all capable of it, on our public works, and in private employment in the interior or in the city. Where such demand for labor was at a distance, many destitute emigrants (either from Ward's Island or the city) were often aided by advances of the costs of transportation.

Thus during the last year, large numbers were sent to various parts of the country at the expense of the fund, and many others were provided with occupation at the charge (if any) of their employers.

Many of those remaining on the Island are employed in work for the establishment. But the Commissioners regret that they have not been able to give full and useful occupation to all who are capable of it. The subject, always a difficult one, is more than usually so, in relation to the peculiar circumstances of those under the charge of the commission. The subject will continue to receive the serious attention of the Commissioners.

Salaries of Resident Physician and others.

The Act of 11th April, 1849 (Section 8), expressly enacts that "the moneys received as commutation money or upon bonds given for, or on account of, any persons or passengers landing from vessels at the port of New York, or elsewhere, shall not be applied or appropriated to any other purpose or use than to defray the expenses incurred for the care, support, or maintenance of such persons or passengers."

This enactment was evidently intended to guard the act from the constitutional objections which had been successfully raised against the former legislation on this subject, under which a part of the hospital moneys were applied to other collateral purposes and uses of the State.

The Commissioners, therefore, doubted whether they were any longer at libeıty to pay from the moneys thus collected, now composing nearly the whole of their revenue, the salary of the resident physician of New York, made payable out of the hospital moneys by former laws, or the salary of the health commissioner, except that part expressly allowed by the present law as a compensation for duties performed in relation to alien passengers.

The payment of the wages of the boatmen of the health officer, hitherto paid by the Commissioners, also seemed clearly to fall under the same restrictions.

The opinion entertained by the Commissioners was confirmed by the Attorney-General, as will be seen more fully by the correspondence between the President of the Board and the late Attorney-General. (See Appendix No. 3.)

None of these payments have, therefore, been made.

The Commissioners are far from considering the curtailment cf the compensation of the medical officers of the Board of Health as a proper measure of economy. Their action was founded only on the requirements of the act, which seemed to leave them no discretion, especially as the express words of the statute were in conformity with the spirit of the decision of the Supreme Court of the United States, to meet which the anterior legislation of the State had been so recently amended.

Amendments of the Acts respecting Alien Passengers.

In addition to these important points suggested in the foregoing report, as requiring legislative action, the experience of the past year has pointed out several omissions and incongruities in the laws of the last session in relation to alien passengers, and the care and protection of emigrants. These relate mainly to details not at all affecting the general principle of the laws, but of much importance to their practical operation, being such omissions and questions of doubtful interpretation, as not unfrequently arise in acts only partially amendatory of former legislation. The correction of these, will give additional efficacy to the law, and doubtless prevent future litigation and delay. There are, also, two or three other provisions (as one in relation to the property of minor orphans, for account of which see Table IV.), where a due regard to private rights requires some alteration of the existing law.

The Commissioners, considering these legal details as not coming within the sphere of the present report, have prepared, and will soon communicate to the Legislature, a statement of the several defects in the legislation of the last session to which they refer, together with the corrections which appear to them proper to be made, as well for the public interest as for the welfare and protection of those aliens within our State jurisdiction.

Receipts, Expenditures, and other Financial Matters.

Since the Act of the 11th of April, 1849, the distinction between the Marine or Hospital Fund, and the Commutation Fund, as found previously throughout the Reports and accounts of the Commission, no longer exists.

The funds of the Commission are now derived from the payment of $1 50 for each alien passenger, in commutation for bonds and other securities demanded by law, together with such sums as may be collected from bonds given by owners or consignees, or received from penalties or compromises, for violation of the requirements of the act.

For the accounts of receipts and expenditures for the Emigrant Refuge at Ward's Island, and those for the Quarantine Hospital, which are kept separately, these two establishments being entirely distinct in their medical and economical government and superintendence, see Table No. V.

In addition to the special disbursements for buildings and the purchase of land, rendered necessary by the increased number to be accommodated at Ward's Island, under the new law, the ordinary expenditures were increased by the following causes, as well as by the augmented numbers.

The Marine Hospital at Quarantine, which formerly received patients of all classes, is now specially devoted to contagious and infectious diseases, most of which require in their treatment, a much larger attendance of physicians and nurses, and often a far greater expenditure in other respects, than the average of hospital cases.

Thus, in the New York Hospital (one of our best managed institutions), it has been found that whilst an average charge of three dollars per week is sufficient to pay necessary expenses for patients of all kinds, those suffering under ship fever cost more than double that amount.

Considering, therefore, the character of the diseases, the increased salary assigned by the act to the head of the medical staff, and the large proportion of nurses, the Commissioners find no reason to be dissatisfied with the average amount of cost for each patient for the year, which is found to be $3 29½ per week. This includes all expenses of support and attendance, and the general expense of the establishment as salaries, &c., and excludes only payments for land, buildings, and permanent fixtures. The total expenditure for the Marine Hospital during 1849, is $32,617 96 less than that of 1848.

At Ward's Island, the hospital department was formerly a small part only of the establishment. The increased proportion of sick persons to the whole number there, has caused an addition to the current expenses, as well as rendered necessary an immediate outlay for additional buildings and more land.

Although the island was happily exempted from any extensive ravages of cholera in its worst form, yet the prevalence of that disease, both in itself and in its known influence upon general health, contributed to swell the number requiring medical care during the last summer. Thus the average cost of the inmates at Ward's Island, has been found to exceed that of the last year, being about $1 60 for each per week, and requiring a weekly expenditure of about $2,300.

The prevalence of this disease also contributed largely to increase the amount reimbursed to many counties.

The interruption of receipts under the former law for the first hundred days of the year 1849, and the great diminution during the latter half of 1848, with the accompanying circumstances of unexpected and necessary expense during the winter, left the Commissioners with an empty treasury at the commencement of the operation of the new law, whilst they had to meet all the claims of those who were entitled to relief under the former acts. The pressing necessity of increased accommodation, requiring payment for lands and buildings, some already made, others to be met during the first six months of this year, with the cost of introducing the Croton water to Ward's Island, exhausts their funds as fast as they are received; and thus, should the ordinary claims of the next summer for support or relief, exceed, or even equal those of the past, there is much reason to anticipate the most serious embarrassments.

But as the apprehended deficiency will be caused by permanent improvements, and a large addition to the real estate of the commission, it will mainly arise from throwing upon the income of the present year, the expenditures which ought, in part, to be borne by succeeding years; and any serious difficulty can be avoided by enabling the Commissioners to divide these charges amongst some two, three, or at most, four years.

The lands held by them are of great value, and those lately purchased will, in the prospective growth of the city, probably much more than repay the present advances.

It is, therefore, believed, that if authority be given to the Commissioners by law to borrow, if necessary, on mortage on the lands held by them, such sum or sums as may be approved by the Governor or the State officers, under such restrictions as may seem proper, this provision will be sufficient to meet any probable contingency for the present year.

Without this precaution, or unless other means be placed at their disposal, the Commissioners have no confidence in being able to meet the imperious necessities which may arise during the recess of the Legislature.

All of which is respectfully submitted.

G. C. VERPLANCK,
DAVID C. COLDEN,
ROBT. B. MINTURN,
CYRUS CURTISS,
GEO. E. KUNHARDT,
C. S. WOODHULL,
EDWARD COPELAND,
ANDREW CARRIGAN.

NEW YORK, *January* 23, 1850.

Fourth Annual Report

FOR THE YEAR 1850.

TO THE LEGISLATURE OF THE STATE OF NEW YORK:

The Commissioners of Emigration respectfully present their report for the year ending December 31st, 1850:

The whole number of aliens, subject to bonds or commutation, who arrived at the port of New York during 1850, was 7,902 less than during the preceding year.

This decrease arose entirely from the diminished emigration from Germany, conforming with the expectation expressed by the Commissioners in their last Annual Report. The falling off of this class of emigration amounts to about one-fifth, the number of Germans arriving at this port being 45,535, against the 55,705 of the year 1849.

The emigration from Ireland has continued, as heretofore, to exceed largely that from any other country, and to increase both numerically, and in proportion to the whole, having exceeded by 21,280 the whole number arriving from other countries.

The statistics of emigration to this port, and of the relief afforded to destitute diseased aliens, under the operation of this Commission, present the following results:

Total number of passengers landed in 1850, 232,768. Of these 19,972 were citizens, and 212,796 aliens. Of the aliens 117,038 were natives of Ireland, 45,535 of Germany, and other countries, 50,223. (For particulars see Table A.) These passengers arrived in 1,912 vessels.

Number in Emigrant Refuge and Hospital Ward's Island, Jan. 1, 1850	1,674	
" born during the year	384	
" admitted during the year	8,098	
Total number cared for	——	10,156
" sent to Small-Pox Hospital, Blackwell's Island		106
" in Marine Hospital, Jan. 1, 1850	343	
" admitted from the city during the year	2,241	
" " vessels " "	827	
Total number treated	——	3,411
" relieved in several counties of this State and chargeable to this Commission		5,937
" forwarded to inland places at the expense of this Commission, from the city of New York		2,248
" returned to Europe, at the expense of this Commission		53
" provided with situations through the office of this Commission (partly estimated), females		3,000
" provided with situations through the office of this Commission (partly estimated), males		5,000
" supplied with lodging, supper, and breakfast		12,946
" received in lodging-house in Chambers street		14,368
Being an average per night of	43	
Of the above the males were	8,672	
" " females were	5,696	
Number of lunatics in city Asylum supported by this Commission during the year		161
Grand total of persons relieved, provided for, &c., by the Commission during the year		57,386
Total number of days of inmates in Refuge and Hospital, W. I.		646,409
Number of days spent in Marine Hospital by inmates		103,066
" of licenses issued to emigrant boarding-houses		80
" " " " runners		83
" " " " bookers		33

The great amelioration of the mode of carrying passengers since 1848, has continued generally to exercise its beneficial influence during the last year. Some few exceptions, chiefly in foreign vessels, have, by the disease and mortality produced from defective ventilation, crowded ships, and bad food, strongly attested the importance of the general improvement, and the necessity of rigidly enforcing all laws for the prevention of such evils.

From the general character of the shipping transporting them, and also to a large extent from their own character and means, a great part of the year exhibited a better personal condition of the passengers than the average ; but during the latter months a considerable proportion of the emigration from Ireland has been of a necessitous and suffering class.

The whole number of persons who have, in various ways, been chargeable to the Commissioners for occasional temporary aid, to long-continued support and medical care, was over 50,000, or above 10,000 more than during 1849. This increase naturally results from the annual increase of the whole number entitled to claim assistance until the expiration of five years from the time of commutation. In the last year, the necessitous portion of the emigration for above three years and a half, in all parts of the State, claimed assistance. The whole number of commuted persons still living is probably not much less than one-third more than those of the preceding year. Thus it will be seen that the increase of persons actually demanding aid is in a less proportion, indicating how large a number have found the means of independence or self support since their arrival on these shores.

Intelligence Office and Labor Exchange.

The increasing number of persons demanding the aid and advice of the commission, and the widely extended knowledge of our arrangements for the disposal of laborers, caused the present office accommodation of the Board to become so crowded with emigrants, laborers, and employers, as to render additional accommodations necessary. Accordingly a large double building, Nos. 25 and 27 Canal street, was hired in December last for the purposes of an intelligence office and labor exchange, at which place emigrants desiring work, and persons desiring laborers of any description, have ample opportunity of accomplishing their wishes. Even with the limited means heretofore possessed, useful employment and means of self-support have been procured for over 8,000 emigrants during the past year, through the agency of the commission, and with the additional facilities afforded by the Canal street establishment, it is believed that a still greater proportionate amount of service will be rendered to them, and to the agricultural, manufacturing, and laboring interests of the country. It is highly desirable that the knowledge of this branch of our operations should be as widely extended as possible, that all emigrants who need labor, or laborers, may know where they can most certainly be provided, free of cost to either party.

Agencies have been established in several places in this and other States, through means of which farmers and others have been supplied with laboring hands of both sexes, and it is intended to increase the number of such agencies as circumstances may from time to time require.

Marine Hospital.

This institution does not for the past year exhibit the same accumulation of patients as in former years.

The unusual health of emigrants arriving during the past year, in connection with the law of 1849, which permits admission into this hospital of those persons only who are affected with contagious or infectious disease, has produced this favorable result. During the greater portion of the summer the small hospital buildings have been closed, and the main edifices were alone required for the accommodation of the sick. The Commissioners began to indulge the hope, that the latter would be henceforth sufficient for their purposes. Since the expiration of the last year, however, the number of patients has increased from about 175 to more than 500, and all the hospitals are again in occupation.

Section 3, of the Laws of 1850, authorizes the Commissioners to take charge of the property of infant emigrant orphans whose parents have died on the voyage, or at the hospitals. Many adults die at this institution leaving property of various value, from twenty-five cents upward. The greater part, however, is of sums so small, that if obliged to pass through the hands of the public administrator, it would be entirely consumed in paying surrogate's expenses and commissions of administrator. Considerable time also must elapse before he can settle his accounts and pay over balances, if any, to the next of kin. In the interim those who are entitled to the property and its avails, have proceeded to other parts of the country, and the money belonging to the poorest is thus kept from them and passes into the city treasury. The Commissioners therefore suggest the propriety of conferring upon them the same power over the property of all emigrants dying on the voyage or in the institutions, as they now have over the property belonging to infant orphans.

The Commissioners have caused proceedings to be taken for the recovery of the wharf and ground under water at Staten Island, long used by the Richmond turnpike company, and have every reason to expect a favorable result. The court of last resort has already decided the principle involved in the case. The wharf and ground are of great value, and of importance to the Commissioners.

The greatly decreased proportion of patients at the Marine Hospital since the change of that establishment, from a general hospital for the reception of all who had paid hospital or commutation money, to a quarantine establishment for infectious or contagious diseases, has led the Commissioners to the belief that some economical changes might be made by law, without detriment to the public service.

The number of the assistant physicians is now fixed permanently at four throughout the year, whilst the actual service for a considerable portion of the year can be competently discharged by the chief, with two assistants.

Such a modification of the law respecting the Marine Hospital might be made as to reduce the fixed number of assistants to two, with the authority to employ increased medical aid in case of emergency.

It is also submitted, by a majority of the Commissioners, whether a reduction may not be properly made in the salary of the physician of the Marine Hospital.

An important retrenchment in the expenses of the Commissioners has been made in the past year, in distributing handbills of "Advice to Emigrant Passengers" at Quarantine, on board of vessels as they arrive.

This service, formerly costing some $1,200 per annum, is now made part of the duty of the quarantine boatmen, and which the health officer kindly volunteered to supervise.

Emigrant Refuge and Hospitals, Ward's Island.

After the new organization of the Quarantine Department at Staten Island, under the act of April 11, 1849, which restricted the reception of patients into the Marine Hospital mainly to those afflicted with infectious or contagious diseases, the increase of medical and surgical patients at Ward's Island, frequently amounting to one-half the number of emigrants received there, required a corresponding increase in the medical service of the emigrant hospital on that Island. This demand was at first met, as was stated in our last annual report, by the division of the duties of superintendent from the medical charge, and the appointment of a resident physician in chief, with such medical assistants as the number of patients from time to time might render necessary. This system went into operation in June, 1849, and was continued above a year. But a majority of the Commissioners became gradually convinced that whatever might be the fidelity or ability with which it was administered, it could not supply the efficient service required by a hospital unsurpassed in number, and in variety of cases, by any establishment in this country, containing not less than six hundred patients, and generally from seven to nine hundred, requiring the aid of medical and surgical skill in every department of medical science. For a small sanitary establishment, or in one especially devoted to any single class of maladies, such as insanity, or the diseases of the eye, the plan of a single head, it was admitted, had its advantages and efficiency. But they thought that the variety of diseases, and numerous patients under their charge demanded, in order to receive the full benefit of the present advanced state of professional science, a variety of ability and experience, medical, surgical, obstetrical, or relating to diseases of the eye or other organs, which have within the last thirty years become separate branches of study, such skill as it is impossible to find combined in any one individual.

Even the combination of high medical knowledge, with that superior surgical skill constantly required in a hospital of the extent of that on Ward's Island, is of rare occurrence, and when found, can seldom be commanded for hospital service exclusively at the cost of relinquishing honorable and lucrative private practice. Another practical evil was found in the system of the single physician in chief, in the occasional interruption of the services of that officer by illness, or any other of the casualties of life, when the service was compelled to be supplied by such aid as could be procured on the emergency. Moreover, there are great and obvious advantages to be derived by an unprofessional Board administering the concerns of a large sanitary establishment, from being able to command and rely upon the advice of several men of professional standing and experience, who, by consultation and comparison of opinion, would be likely to indicate the most efficient system of hospital practice, and upon whose opinion in all matters of emergency they might rely with more confidence on their part, as well as on that of the public, than they could upon the views of any single chief physician.

The experience of several of the largest and best managed hospitals of New York, and other great cities, has shown that by appointing a sufficient number of practising physicians and surgeons to divide the higher hospital duties among them in rotation, without sacrificing or abandoning their private practice, professional talent of a higher order in every branch, could be commanded for the service of the poor and destitute. The regular visits of such a body of practitioners, directing the practice in each case, or for the performance of surgical operations, aided by the constant attendance of younger but well-educated physicians, constantly resident in the establishment, would thus secure to the humblest class of patients, a degree of medical care and skill noways inferior to that bestowed on the most opulent patient.

Such is the arrangement which has prevailed, with universal approbation, for more than fifty years in the New York Hospital in this city, and which has been more recently introduced into the Bellevue Hospital. A similar plan has for years been followed in the best institutions of this sort in Philadelphia and Boston, as well as in many of the largest and best governed public hospitals of Paris, London, and Dublin.

When hospitals thus managed are situated in the midst of a great city, or its immediate vicinity, so that the required attendance can be given by physicians without a serious interference with their private practice, it is found that the professional standing given by connection with a great public institution, the experience there gained, and the facilities of public and private instruction afforded, render such places so desirable that they are accepted, and often eagerly sought for, without any direct pecuniary compensation.

After deliberate examination of the operation of this system in several institutions, the Commissioners determined to apply it to the Ward's Island hospital. It was however ascertained, on further inquiry, that the distance of Ward's Island from the city, and the additional delay in crossing to it, would subject the regular visiting physicians and surgeons to some expense, and such a demand upon their time, as to interfere largely with the hours customary for professional visits in private practice, and that, in consequence, the entirely gratuitous attendance cheerfully given to city establishments, could not be relied upon permanently or regularly.

But it was found that this difficulty could not be obviated by offering some pecuniary compensation, not, in the aggregate, much exceeding the expenditure for medical services under the former system (including that paid for occasional services), and which, though small in proportion to the services rendered by each physician and surgeon, would place those attending at Ward's Island, on nearly the same footing with those attending quite gratuitously at the institutions in or near the city.

The compensation was fixed at $600 per annum to each visiting physician and surgeon. The plan was carried into effect by the appointment of the following gentlemen, who commenced their duties on the 1st September last:

Dr. A. E. Hosack, Dr. J. M. Carnochan, Dr. W. S. Bowen, Dr. G. Wilkes, Dr. A. V. Williams, Dr. Wm. Macneven,

Dr. Simon Habel, Dr. H. G. Cox, Dr. Ernest Schilling, Dr. George Ford.

The order of visitation has been so arranged as to give the attendance of at least two physicians and one surgeon every day; the time spent by them must of course vary according to the necessities of the case, but it has thus far been found that the length of time spent in these visits by the three on duty amounts to an average of about thirteen hours a day, or about four hours and a half each. By the careful classification of the patients, the division of the surgical from the medical duties, and the assignment of the lying-in wards and those containing children affected with diseases to which their age and condition are specially subject (as diseases of the eye), to physicians who have specially directed their attention to those objects, it is hoped that all the aid which the present state of medical and surgical skill can contribute, has been secured for the service of this establishment.

Four house physicians and two house surgeons, with a medical assistant to each, have also been appointed, who reside on the island and attend to the practice of the hospital, and the administration of medicines, under the direction of the visiting physicians and surgeons. They receive no emolument other than board and washing, being selected from the younger members of the profession, being however graduates, and recommended to the Commissioners by the Medical Board after examination. The advantages of professional experience to be obtained by attendance on hospital practice on an extensive scale, for a year or two, will unquestionably secure for this hospital, as it has always done in similar establishments, a regular supply of competent and faithful officers.

The visiting physicians and surgeons also constitute a Medical Board for the superintendence of the practice and hygiene of the hospital, and for consultation among themselves, and for advice to the Commissioners or their committees, on all matters relating to the health and physical well-being of the inmates of the institution. In addition to this arrangement for regular professional services, the experience of other hospitals recommended the appointment of some consulting physicians and surgeons, gentlemen of the highest standing and experience, upon whom the Commissioners or the Medical Board might rely for advice when specially consulted. This was carried into effect by the appointment of Drs. Thomas Cock and Edward Delafield as consulting physicians; and Drs. Alexander H. Stevens and J. Kearny Rodgers as consulting surgeons. It is provided by rule that these officers "shall be invited to attend all capital operations; that they shall visit the establishment at Ward's Island when requested by the Commissioners or their committees, and report their opinion as to the state and management of the hospitals, and whenever requested, shall meet the Board for special advice and consultation."

The system as above described went into full operation on the 1st September, 1850, and so far as the experience of nearly five months can test it, the expectations entertained by most of the Commissioners have not been disappointed.

The comparison of the returns of the last four months of 1850 with those of the same period in 1849, shows a decrease in the proportion of deaths of about one-sixth, there being no particular epidemic prevailing at either period. This, however, may be the result of circumstances other than the change of system.

A more satisfactory result has been presented to the Commissioners on the weekly visits of their committees, and the occasional visits of others of them, in the generally improved appearance and service of the hospital wards, and particularly in the great diminution of ophthalmia which had hitherto afflicted the emigrant children, and the entire disappearance of its more malignant form.

The improvements last year in the buildings, and the introduction of the Croton water, have proved highly beneficial, but there is still a deficiency of hospital accommodation sufficient for due classification of disease whenever there comes, as at present, any considerable increase of patients.

Buildings of a more durable material, less combustible, and affording greater comfort, are also extremely desirable.

In connection with the subject of hospital practice it is

proper to add, that during the last autumn certain charges were made, in some city papers, in relation to post mortem examinations and dissections. These were examined by a committee of this Board, and afterwards by the grand jury.

In the opinion of a majority of the committee, which was sustained by this Board, these charges were either groundless or grossly exaggerated, with the exception of one act of some of the younger medical assistants. This was punished by the dismissal or suspension of the offenders.

The decision of the Commissioners was supported by the grand jury, after a deliberate and protracted investigation. The details of this transaction are more fully set forth in the documents herewith submitted. (See Appendix No. 4.)

The Commissioners have endeavored, as far as it might be practicable, to carry out the principle of the law of 1849 regulating the Marine Hospital at Staten Island, which specially appropriates that establishment to the reception of persons attacked by infectious or contagious diseases. This has been done to a very great degree, as to all such diseases, and completely so as to several classes of malignant disease, such as small-pox. But with every precaution, it has been found impracticable to keep Ward's Island free from all malignant diseases, especially from typhus fever.

This frequently makes its appearance amongst persons sent to the Island with the apparent symptoms of other diseases, or from mere destitution, immediately on their arrival in crowded ships. On this account, the number of such patients has been much larger, and the consequent expense of the hospitals (typhus fever patients being of the most expensive class in their proper care) greater than might be estimated. Several wards have been assigned to these diseases.

By an arrangement with the New York Hospital, persons chargeable to this Commission, taken ill in the night, or incapable from any sudden casualty of being removed from the city, are received at that institution, at the charge of the Commissioners, for such time as the nature of the case may demand; all those who can be removed without danger, being sent to Ward's Island or the Marine Hospital without delay.

By an arrangement with the Governors of the alms-house, the insane emigrants chargeable to this fund are received and taken care of at the Asylum on Blackwell's Island.

The spacious brick building for a wash-house, with drying rooms, baths, &c., has been completed. Its original plan has been considerably enlarged, so as to admit of various other uses of the building in the additional apartments.

The carrying the Croton water across the broad and deep channel which separates Ward's Island from Manhattan Island, has been completed, and the expense of the work, although large, has been amply compensated by the numerous advantages of health and comfort which it affords. The superintendence and execution of this valuable and difficult work, was one of the last of the many zealous and useful services rendered to this Commission by our late lamented colleague, David C. Colden.

The Commissioners in their annual report of 1849, informed the Legislature, that some of their buildings on Ward's Island were erected on leased property, and expressed the "hope that by the time the lease of the ground expires, the parties from whom we hold it may be induced either to extend the lease for a long term of years, or sell the land to us at a fair price." This lease has now expired, and the parties owning the land have kindly and generously offered to convey it to the Commissioners in fee, provided the latter will convey to them in exchange a similar quantity of land, so situated as to be satisfactory to the parties interested in the factory property, and upon the Commissioners paying a sum of money sufficient to erect a building similar to the factory, and in the same condition that was, when it was taken possession of by the Commissioners, an allowance of rent or interest being made for the time which will be required to erect such a building.

The Commissioners are now the owners of land upon Ward's Island, which they could spare without serious inconvenience, and which would satisfy, it is thought, the owners of the leasehold premises, who have in view the establishment of a benevolent public institution. The Commissioners, however, are not authorized to sell or exchange lands, and will need that additional power in order to effect the above arrangement. A power to mortgage was given by the Legislature of 1850, subject to the approval of the Governor, Comptroller, and Attorney-General, and the power to sell or exchange might properly be granted under the same limitations.

Receipts, Expenditures, and Financial Concerns of the Commission.

For the accounts of receipts and expenditures of the Commutation Fund for the year 1850, see Table No. VI.

Although the year 1850 was entered upon with an apparent balance of $22,084 in favor of the funds of the Commission, as stated in the last annual report, yet there was a real deficiency at that time, arising from debts for lands bought or contracted for at Ward's Island, to be paid during the current year, amounting to $21,827 ; from the outstanding claims of the counties for reimbursement of their expenses for aliens chargeable to the Commissioners ; and for the unpaid balance for the new buildings then nearly completed on Ward's Island ; and for the cost of introducing the Croton water.

The augmented demand upon the funds during the winter, and the probabilities of progressive increase of the numbers receiving relief from the counties, to be repaid from the commutation fund, induced the Board to represent in their last report, their apprehensions of deficient means for the current expenses of the year, and to remark, that as such deficiency, should it occur, would be caused by the cost of permanent improvements, and a large and valuable addition to the real estate held by this Commission, it would mainly arise from throwing upon the income of the current year the whole expenditures which ought (at least in part) to be borne by succeeding years, and that any serious difficulty would be avoided by enabling the Commissioners to divide these charges amongst the following years which would receive the largest portion of their benefit. They therefore suggested that authority should be given by law to the Commissioners to borrow, under certain restrictions, upon the security of the real estate held by them, such sums as might be necessary to meet the current expenditures.

In conformity with this recommendation, an act was passed March 2d, 1850, giving authority to borrow upon mortgage of the lands held by them, such sums as might, in their judgment, be necessary for the current use of the Commission, upon the certificate of approval of such loan, and of the intended application thereof, by the Governor, Comptroller, and Attorney-General. Under this act an application for permission to borrow on mortgage the sum of $80,000, was made to these officers, and the certificate required by law granted by them.

The sum applied for was much larger than was needed for the immediate wants of the Commission, but it depended upon the amount of the current receipts whether it might not all be wanted, during the year, for the urgent necessities of the establishment at Quarantine and Ward's Island. There was also the inducement of being able to make a single arrangement for the whole sum at once to be taken up, as necessity or convenience might require.

This was effected by a mortgage of a large part of the property held by them for $80,000 to secure the advances to be made; and the sum of $36,000 was received on this account on the 19th July, 1850.

That amount has been found sufficient, together with the current receipts, to meet the immediate expenditure, to be provided for during the year, nor has any further advance been made up to the date of the present report. A part, at least, of the remaining $44,000 will be required for the service of the present year.

But this necessity of borrowing, even although an equal amount in value has been added to the property of the State held by the Commissioners, strongly urges the importance of relieving the emigration fund from all charges not clearly appropriate to its objects, as well of economy in its application.

Amongst the measures of relieving the fund, which can only be attained by means of legislation, are the following:

The Commissioners, in their last annual report, expressed their opinion, which was in conformity with that of the then Attorney-General, A. L. Jordan, Esq., that they were relieved by the acts of the preceding session from the payment of the expenses of the boat, and wages of the boatmen employed by the health officer for the various Quarantine purposes, which expenses had formerly been expressly chargeable upon the Commissioners. But a claim having been made by Dr. Whiting, the last health officer, for the expenses for these objects, advanced by him, the question was submitted to the Supreme Court for this district, in an amicable suit.

Upon the case submitted, the court decided that the former provisions, requiring the payment from the Commissioners, were not abrogated by the subsequent legislation, which did not expressly repeal them. It is now respectfully submitted to the consideration of the Legislature, whether the support of the boat and boatmen used by the health officer, in his visits of inspection, for the general purposes of preserving the public health and enforcing the Quarantine regulations, is not a charge immediately appertaining to the official duties of the health officer, and so remotely affecting the objects for which the commutation fund is constituted, that it should be relieved from this and from any similar claim which may hereafter occur, by a specific enactment that the health officer should not be entitled to any fees or allowances for the duties required by law to be performed by him, or for any expenses incurred in the discharge of such duties, other than the fees now by law specifically allowed.

By the act of April 10th, 1850, the commutation money of $1 50, authorized to be paid, instead of bonds for each alien passenger arriving at this port, is directed to be paid to the Health Commissioner, whose receipt thereof is made a discharge from the requirement of bonds from owners or consignees.

The Health Commissioner is required to pay over, daily, the moneys so received to the city Chamberlain (as the treasurer of the fund), with an account thereof. As a compensation, in lieu of fees and percentage, the Health Commissioner receives by law a salary of $3,500 per annum, to be paid by the Commissioners of Emigration. No other duty in regard to this matter is expressly required of this officer by law; though it may be a legal inference that he should take all the proper precautions and means needed to insure the collection of the sum, for the receipt of which he is so liberally paid.

During the last twelvemonth a loss has occurred to the fund of $3,102 50, by reason of repeated non-payments of commutation for passengers who had arrived in several foreign vessels, consigned to a house which has since become insolvent.

It therefore appears that the intervention of the Health Commissioner, as a receiving officer at a large compensation, adds nothing to the certainty or efficiency of the collection. The other duties of the Health Commissioner relate to the general concerns of the public health, without any immediate connection with the concerns of this Commission.

It is therefore respectfully submitted, whether the rights and interests of the fund, collected for a specific object, under strict constitutional inhibition against its diversion to any other object, would not be consulted by releasing the Commissioners of Emigration from the payment of this officer's salary, and authorizing, by law, the money paid for commutation to be received by some person specially delegated by the Board, and under their immediate inspection.

This duty could be safely assigned to some person charged with other duties, with some additional compensation, so that a saving of near $3,000 might be made to this fund, now scarcely sufficient for its legitimate purposes.

The Health Commissioner's compensation for his other duties, not touching the concerns of this Commission, should be paid from some other quarter.

All of which is respectfully submitted.

G. C. VERPLANCK.
SAMUEL SMITH,
A. R. LAWRENCE,
ROBERT B. MINTURN,
CYRUS CURTISS,
C. S. WOODHULL,
JOHN E. DEVELIN,
ADOLPH RODEWALD.

NEW YORK, *February* 1, 1851.

Fifth Annual Report

FOR THE YEAR 1851.

TO THE LEGISLATURE OF THE STATE OF NEW YORK:

The Commissioners of Emigration respectfully present a report of their proceedings, for the year ending 31st December, 1851, as required of them by law.

The Board in exhibiting a statement of the monetary affairs of the Commission, and the statistics of relief, have, as in former years, deemed it proper to append such other particulars relative to the condition and management of the Institutions intrusted to their care, as appear deserving the consideration of the Legislature.

The most remarkable feature in the immigration of the past year, is its unprecedented increase. The whole number subject to bonds or commutation, who landed at the port of New York, was 289,601, being 76,805 more than in the preceding year, and exceeding by 68,998, the largest number arriving in any one year since the organization of this Department.

Ireland and Germany are the countries which, as heretofore, have chiefly supplied this immense immigration; the former sustaining its precedence, in this respect, being to the latter as five to two, and numerically exceeding the whole number from other countries, by 36,911.

The statistics of immigration to this port for 1851, present the following results:

Number of passengers landed, 326,853. Of these 36,982 were citizens, and 289,601 aliens, viz.: natives of Ireland, 163,256, of Germany, 69,883, of other countries, 56,462. (For particulars see Table A.)

Number of vessels employed in conveying citizen and alien passengers was	1,712	
" conveying citizens only	499	
Total passenger vessels	———	2,211

The statistics of relief afforded to destitute and diseased alien emigrants by the Commissioners, exhibit the following results:

Number in Marine Hospital, Jan. 1st, 1851	234	
" admitted from vessels during the year	1,487	
" " " the city	4,329	
" " " other sources	293	
Total number treated	———	6,343
Number in Emigrant Refuge and Hospital, Ward's Island, Jan. 1st, 1851	1,932	
" born there during the year	493	
" admitted	12,514	
Total number cared for and treated	———	14,939
Number sent from Park Office to Small Pox Hospital, Blackwell's Island	175	
" of sick from do. to New York Hospital	589	
Total cases from Park Office	———	764
Number of lunatic emigrants in City Asylum, Jan. 1st, 1851	75	
" admitted during the year	175	
Total lunatics	———	250
Number supplied from the Park Office with board and lodging		2,649
" of the out-door poor in the city, buried at the expense, in whole or in part, of the Commission.		644
" returned to Europe at the expense, in whole or in part, of the Commission		311
" forwarded to inland places from Park Office, at the expense, in whole or in part, of the Commission		7,080
" temporarily boarded and lodged at the Intelligence Office and Labor Exchange		21,292
of females provided with situations at the Intelligence Office and Labor Exchange	10,203	
of males do.	8,001	
Total number provided with employment at this office	———	18,204

Whole number relieved, forwarded, and provided with employment by the Commissioners of Emigration........	72,486
Number relieved and forwarded, in the several counties of the State, chargeable to the Commission.............	12,550
Grand total relieved, forwarded, and provided with employment, &c., by the Commission, in the city and State of New York....................................	85,036

Number of days spent in Marine Hospital................	179,262	
" " " Hospital and Refuge, Ward's Island	754,748	
" " " in lodging-rooms attached to Intelligence Office and Labor Exchange.........	149,044	
Total in Institutions of Commissioners.......		1,083,054

The beneficial influence of the laws relating to the transportation of emigrants, has been manifested in the generally healthy condition of the passengers who arrived during the past year. Deficient ventilation, crowded ships, bad and insufficient quantity of food, with the consequent disease and mortality so common under former defective regulations, have become less frequent than formerly; and by a vigorous and impartial enforcement of existing laws, these terrible evils, it is believed, may, in future, be prevented in a great degree.

But the large number of passengers who have been received at the Marine Hospital during the last year, attacked by ship fever at the commencement of the year, or again in November, by cholera, either directly from shipboard, or sent down from the city (suffering under these diseases, appearing a few days after their landing), proved the necessity of further precaution. In one day 108 sick were removed from a single ship. The most efficient safeguard, in the opinion of the Commissioners, is one only in the power of Congress to provide, that of requiring by law a still larger proportionate space for each passenger than that now prescribed. In accordance with this view, they have taken measures to urge the subject on the attention of that body.

Many gratifying results have also attended the efforts of the Board, to protect the newly arrived emigrant from the shameless frauds and impositions which had for years been practised with impunity. By diffusing correct information in respect to routes and prices, the employment of faithful agents located at the main points of travel, and the exercise of unremitted vigilance against all infractions of the law, much has been done towards effecting an important reform, which cannot fail to benefit the alien and stranger, who, seeking a home among us, is entitled to the protection of our laws.

Still, with the best endeavors of their officers, and the efficient aid of the mayors of New York, Albany, and Buffalo, the inducements of interest are so strong, that these evils continue greatly to oppress the emigrant.

The immigration of the past year, which has been great beyond all former precedent, has largely partaken of the mixed character of previous years. A far greater part brought with them, not only the means of reaching their respective destinations in our cities, towns, and vast inland, but also what is incomparably more valuable, patient industry and perseverance, those sure elements of prosperity, in a country where the fields for labor and its rewards are abundant. But among the vast multitude who have reached our shores, all are not of the same energetic, independent class. Many of the poor and destitute have been brought hither through remittances of money by friends and relations who preceded them, and on their first arrival found themselves without the means of support; needy, however, as such emigrants on their arrival usually are, being, through the agency of the Commission, brought into connection with their friends, and by them into permanent relation with the industry of the country, they soon cease to be dependent.

There is another description of emigrants, that are undesirable in any country. These are the thriftless and imbecile parish paupers and dependents, who are incapable of gaining their subsistence anywhere, or of taking care of it when earned. On what principle of comity, humanity, or justice, the poorhouses of Europe, and sometimes, the prisons, are emptied on our shores, it is difficult to say. The fact itself is notorious. Ship-loads of these helpless and often vicious persons are sent here, sometimes in the dead of winter, without means or place of destination beyond this city, and become a permanent burden and nuisance, from the moment of their arrival. Such an imposition appears to admit of no conceivable vindication, and should be published abroad, to the lasting disgrace of the perpetrators. It is respectfully submitted that these evils call for the consideration of the Legislature, and for further legislative provision.

But it would be obviously erroneous to measure the effects of immigration among us by the necessitous or worthless few, and overlook the great bulk of directly an opposite character. Adopting the latter as the legitimate test, it might be shown that the vast influx of foreign capital, skill, and labor, through this channel, has been singularly advantageous to this country. It were foreign to the design and limit of this report, to enter upon an elaborate examination of this subject. But from the survey the position of the Board has enabled them to take, they cannot doubt, that notwithstanding the number of those claiming relief, the physical capability, the industry, the skill and wealth of the country, have been greatly and substantially augmented by foreign immigration.

It was to be expected that the number of indigent entitled to assistance, would yearly augment in a ratio corresponding with the annual increase of the whole number arriving, until the termination of the first five years after the time of commutation. As that period will commence on the 5th day of May next ensuing, the number of those requiring aid will probably then reach its highest point; and, after that time, the benefit of the law's limitation of relief, will likely begin to be realized, in the gradual decrease of the dependent. What that decrease, if any, will be, is at present problematical, inasmuch as it will be controlled, both by the number and condition of the immigrants that may arrive in future years, about whom, and other contingencies affecting general results, nothing now can be determined with an approximation to certainty. That the number chargeable to the Commission, is not likely, in future years, to increase under any probable circumstances, may be inferred from the percentage of decrease in previous years, as appears from the following exhibit:

Whole number of immigrants in 1847, 129,062, of whom 11,431 were relieved, which is........................ 8·780 per cent.
Do. in 1848, including the arrival of the previous year, 318,238, and the number relieved, 27,301, or.......... 8·578 "
Do. in 1849, including the two preceding years, 538,841, and relieved, 40,503, or................................ 7·516 "
Do. in 1850, including the three previous years, 751,637, and relieved, 50,250, or................................ 6·685 "
Do. in 1851, including the four preceding years, 1,041,238, and relieved, 72,486*.............................. 6·960 "

If, then, as is manifest, there has been a decrease in relief of nearly 2 per cent. during a period of five years, while the immigrants have more than quintupled, it does not appear within the range of probability, that either the ratio of relief, or the aggregate of the number demanding it, will prospectively increase, when for the next five years, about 20 per cent. of the whole number, previously entitled to aid, will be annually cut off by the terms of commutation.

The same important result, showing that each successive year places a greater proportion of emigrants above dependence, is indicated by the following statement.

There were relieved or assisted at the city establishments, the Ward's Island and the Marine Hospital, during the last year, 16,836. Of which 700 arrived in 1847, 900 in 1848, 1,486 in 1849, 3,514 in 1850, and 10,236 in 1851.

Intelligence Office and Labor Exchange.

This establishment, as heretofore stated, was opened in December, 1850. Being designed for the benefit of all alien emigrants requiring aid, advice, and employment, much was expected from it, and the results have realized the anticipations of its usefulness as an effective auxiliary in carrying out the objects of the Commission. The statistics show, that by the facilities thus afforded, *eighteen thousand two hundred and four* emigrants have, during the year, been temporarily relieved, and provided with the means of self-support, in such kind of labor

* Omitting county relief as in previous years.

as their previous habits best qualified them to perform. The great economy of the establishment, though in itself an important consideration, is not its chief commendation. The advantages it secures to the indigent and unfortunate, beyond what is provided for subjects of public charity, are most manifest. Alms-House relief only meets the present necessities of the needy, without concerning itself to remove the usual cause of dependence among those able to labor, by endeavors to give employment. This Institution, on the contrary, claims the double merit of furnishing both relief and occupation; and by adapting its provisions to the actual condition and wants of the emigrants, fosters in them a spirit of industry and self-reliance, and not of thankless dependence upon others. Such as have relations or friends in this State or elsewhere likely to aid them, are placed in communication with them; if needed, letters are written for them, remittances received, and applied to their use in such a way as to protect the stranger from imposition. The amount thus received from those who have preceded their friends and relations in emigration, bears an honorable testimony to their liberality and family affection, having amounted in 1851, to $9,515.

Though much that is encouraging has already been accomplished through this agency, far more in future, it is believed, may be effected, as a knowledge of its beneficent objects and of its facilities for supplying domestics and laborers becomes more widely diffused among those wanting their services. The large double building appropriated to the purposes of the agency, has of late been found insufficient for the suitable accommodation and orderly control of the multitudes who resort there to avail themselves of its advantages. In order to remedy these deficiencies, the Board have recently leased the premises No. 23 Canal street, adjoining the building before occupied, also a new five-story building, No. 140 Centre street, both of which are exceedingly eligible for lodging-houses. The latter is detached from the others, but not so far as to be inconvenient. Early in the winter much annoyance was felt from the impracticability of preserving proper cleanliness, in consequence of the difficulty of providing suitable water-closets. This could only be remedied by additional yard-room, which was not obtainable, until within the last three or four weeks. The annoyance from this source, however, is now not only removed, but the arrangements for ventilation are greatly improved. With these advantages and additions, the internal regulations of the establishment may now be so controlled as to promote, in a higher degree, the health and comfort of the temporary inmates, and render the management of the entire department more satisfactory and effective.

Still more recently, and whilst this report was in preparation, the Commissioners have been obliged to provide other temporary asylums in different quarters of the city. This necessity has been occasioned by the increasing pressure of newly arrived immigrants in the most destitute condition, in connection with the extreme severity of the winter, which has detained an unusually large number of the needy in the city, and cut off, for the time being, the possibility of regular communication with the islands, as well as the demand for labor either here or in the interior. One of these asylums is in the church, corner of Duane and Church streets, which is now occupied as an immigrant refuge. This edifice will accommodate about seven hundred persons, and with the alterations made in the interior, is well adapted to its present use. The body of the building, being spacious and airy, is used as a dormitory; the basement for cooking, washing, &c., and the whole is under the charge of efficient attendants. The other, on the Third Avenue, corner of Forty-seventh street, is now in course of preparation to meet any future emergency, incident to the peculiar trying circumstances of the present inclement season. The latter building will commodiously lodge from eight to nine hundred persons.

The demand for such assistance during the present month of January, was expected to exceed that of the past year, and preparations, to all appearances, ample, had been made to meet them. But the Commissioners had no reason to expect that these demands would exceed *fourfold* those of the last year.

The supply of laborers now far exceeds the demand. It is also found that large numbers of emigrants arriving here, are instructed by their friends before sailing to throw themselves upon the Commission for support until employment offers, or to be forwarded at the expense of the Board into the interior.

Marine Hospital at Staten Island.

Under the Act of April 11th, 1849, the Marine Hospital, previously open to all classes of disease, was specially devoted to the reception of patients affected with contagious or infectious disorders, and was placed under the charge of a physician-in-chief, appointed by the Governor and Senate. By the Act of July, 1851, that office was abolished, and the Commissioners were authorized to require the health officer of the port to perform, as heretofore, those duties. Under the former law, Dr. F. Campbell Stewart continued to perform those duties, until July 31st, 1851, when he resigned. The new law was then carried into effect, and Dr. A. Sidney Doane, the health officer, was requested to take charge of the Marine Hospital as its medical chief, and was also appointed by the Commission their superintendent, for the administration and supervision of the other concerns of the institution. He discharged those duties during the remainder of the year to the entire satisfaction of the Commissioners, and entered, in full health and activity, upon the labors of the present year. On the 15th of January he was attacked by ship fever, of which he died on the 27th.

During a brief period, the Commissioners have had to lament the loss of Drs. Alden, Cameron, and Curtiss, assistant-physicians at Quarantine, who have successively fallen victims to ship fever, contracted in the faithful and intrepid discharge of their professional duties. To the honored list of men who have fallen victims to a sense of duty and the cause of humanity, is now added the name of Dr. Doane. The Commissioners can but imperfectly express their high appreciation of his character and services.

Bringing to the management of the extensive sanitary establishment at the Marine Hospital, medical acquirements and abilities of a high order, he has acquitted himself in a manner most advantageous to the institution, and satisfactory to the Commission. His untiring zeal and fearlessness in the dis-

6

charge of his perilous duties, entitle him to distinction, as a faithful, energetic, and efficient public officer.

At the first meeting of the Board, subsequent to the decease of Dr. Doane, the following resolutions respecting his character and services, were passed unanimously :

"*Resolved,* That the Commissioners of Emigration are deeply sensible of the public loss sustained by the death of Dr. A. Sidney Doane, from disease contracted in the fearless discharge of public duty, and the service of humanity.

"*Resolved,* That his professional acquirements, his talents, energy, devotion to duty and intrepidity in its discharge, were peculiarly and constantly displayed in his relation to the Commission as health officer of the port of New York, and physician-in-chief to the Marine Hospital."

Dr. Doane was engaged, when first attacked by his fatal disease, in preparing the following report to the Board, made at the request of some of its members, showing the details of the medical administration and condition of the hospital, but which was left incomplete by his sudden illness and lamented death :

"*To the Commissioners of Emigration :*

"GENTLEMEN :—During the early part of 1851, strong westerly gales prevailed on the Atlantic, causing long passages of European vessels. In many cases ships were seriously damaged, and obliged to return to port, and passengers, after being a long time at sea, were compelled to return to Europe, and embark anew upon another boisterous voyage, before recruiting from the effects of the first—hence, sickness and death.

The longest passage in 1851, from Europe to New York was.....	106 days.
The shortest (the Baltic)....................................	10 "
The number of passengers, foreign and native, inspected at Quarantine in vessels from foreign ports in 1851 was............	318,968
The number of children born on the Atlantic in 1851, in vessels arriving at this port, was..................................	534
The number of deaths was..................................	1,879
The largest number of deaths on board of any one vessel was.....	50

"The shipment of persons from the public asylums of Europe, and the payment of passages by landlords, has continued the past year, and to a greater extent than ever before. On board of one British vessel, the whole number of passengers, 230, was derived entirely from this source ; of this number 220 were females between the ages of 16 and 30. As may readily be imagined, much destitution has been witnessed at the Quarantine.

There remained at the Marine Hospital, Jan. 1st, 1851....	234	
Admitted during the year..........................	6,109	
Total treated..........................	——	6,343
Of these were discharged..........................	4,932	
Died..........................	894	
Remaining Jan. 1st, 1852..........................	517	

(For particulars of diseases and mortality, see Table B.)

"The largest number of sick received from one vessel in 1851, was 108. On reference to the statistics of the hospital, we find that even these figures have been exceeded, for in 1842, 120 sick were taken from the 'Eutaw.' In 1837, 158 from the 'Ann Hall,' and as early even as 1802, 188 from the 'Flora,' 220 from the 'Nancy,' and 259 from the 'Penelope,' most of which were cases of *ship fever*—showing conclusively, that this disease is *by no means of recent origin.*

"Of the whole number admitted to the Marine Hospital the past year, 4,329 came from the city. Many of these have resided in New York for months—others, on feeling the influence of unhealthy locations, &c., in other States, have returned to the city for medical treatment. A considerable portion becoming unwell soon after arrival—in good health when inspected at Quarantine,—the change from a *ship* to a *shore diet,* a free indulgence in articles considered as luxuries in Europe, but abundant and cheap here, and other causes, frequently produce sickness in a few days after landing.

"During the early period of 1851, the principal disease at the Marine Hospital was ship fever, brought by vessels, and occurring from causes already stated. It extended, in many cases, to the nurses. Even the physicians were not spared, and the names of *Alden, Cameron* and *Curtiss,* must be inscribed on the register of those who have fallen victims to their sense of professional duty—a duty which finds no adequate compensation in pecuniary recompense, but which is satisfied by the proud consciousness of devotion to suffering humanity.

"In November, the Asiatic cholera appeared most unexpectedly, in the lower hospital. The persons affected arrived in healthy vessels, and some of them had been inmates of the hospital for several days. A cholera ward was immediately established and insulated—in a few hours the other sick were removed from the building, and the disease was arrested.

"Advantage was taken of this circumstance to introduce certain improvements in the lower hospital, by the removal of partitions, &c., and throwing several small rooms into one, to secure better ventilation, and a more thorough oversight over the sick."

This communication to the Board, being abruptly broken off by the decease of the writer, and at the advanced period of time allowed by law for the annual report, the details in respect to the Marine Hospital must be more briefly and generally presented, than they would have been under happier circumstances.

The result of the practice of this hospital, presents a ratio of deaths to cases treated, of 14 per cent., a proportion greater than that of Ward's Island, or the city institutions, but not larger than might have been expected under the circumstances of the year.

The shipment of persons from the public asylums of Europe, and the payment of passages by landlords to a greater extent than in any previous year, often filled the ships with a destitute and unprovided multitude, many of them broken down by age or former disease. Some judgment may be formed of the state of health which prevailed amongst this class of passengers on landing, from the fact, ascertained by the careful examination of the late Dr. Doane, that during the year, 1,879 deaths had occurred on the Atlantic on board vessels which arrived at the port of New York. Fifty of these were on board one vessel.

In consequence of this state of things, the prevailing disease at the Marine Hospital, during the first months of 1851, was ship fever, in its most aggravated character.

The principal hospital buildings are generally good in relation to their several purposes, and afford sufficient accommodation for the average number of patients. Still they are now found insufficient to meet the sudden pressure of augmented emigration and accompanying disease, and preparations are now making for additional buildings to be in readiness for such emergencies.

Emigrant Refuge and Hospitals, Ward's Island.

In order the more effectually to carry out the object of the Legislature, the Commissioners have, from year to year, made such additions to their grounds by purchase, as opportunity and the great and expanding interests intrusted to their care, were deemed to require. They held, on the 1st January, 1852, in fee simple, on Ward's Island, ninety-five acres, three roods, six perches; with some re-leases of water-rights, all which cost $63,818 83; also on lease, eleven acres, one rood, thirteen perches, in all, one hundred and six acres, four roods, nineteen perches. The leased land was, from its contiguity and position, so necessary to the different branches of the establishment, that they were induced to make large additions and improvements to the building thereon, with the expectation that the parties owning it would either renew the lease for a long term of years, or sell it for a fair consideration.

But this leased land having been originally bought as a site for an intended public institution, and held as an honorary trust for that ultimate object, it could not be purchased by the Commission; but the owner early expressed his willingness to exchange this tract for other land held by this Commission on Ward's Island, fitted for the same purpose. The Commissioners having no legal authority to sell or exchange the land held by them, could not take advantage of this offer, until after the passing of the Act of 11th July, 1851, giving them authority to convey any of the land purchased by them, on the approval of the Governor and other State Officers. The Commissioners, with the consent of the lessor, have referred the whole matter of the exchange to Ex-Commissioners, Messrs. William F. Havemeyer and Andrew Carrigan, whose award will be conclusive. It is proper to state, that the Commissioners have been permitted to occupy the property by paying only the interest on its original cost.

The buildings now occupied for the objects of the Commission, on Ward's Island, are as follows :

I.—The Refuge, *Proper.*

This consists of a large, substantial five-story stone edifice, which, with a brick addition of forty feet, is one hundred and seventy feet long, and forty wide. It is chiefly appropriated to feeble and destitute females, who are either incapacitated for labor, or cannot find employment. It contains four hundred beds, offices, dining and sleeping rooms, cutting and sewing apartments, store-house and kitchen. The culinary arrangements and apparatus are probably unsurpassed in any similar institution. It contains two ranges, made by Janes, Beebe & Co., and nine boilers of Hoe's patent, of eighty gallons each. The boiler which generates the heat, is twelve feet long and three feet in diameter, producing a pressure of steam equal to twenty-five pounds on the square inch, and consumes daily about five hundred pounds of coal. The arrangements to economize heat are such, that the exhausted steam is employed in warming water for washing and in heating several apartments. The main building was originally designed for a manufactory, but with the enlargements and improvements to which it has been subjected, it is well adapted to its present purposes. Its chief defect is, that it affords insufficient office room, to remedy which, and also to meet the prospective demand of accommodations for a larger number of inmates, the Board have under consideration the expediency of making another brick addition to the building, when the funds at their command shall justify the undertaking.

II.—The Male Refuge.

This consists of two, two-story wooden structures, filled in with brick. One is connected by a covered way in the rear with the Refuge, and parallel thereto, being one hundred and seventy feet long by twenty wide ; the other is four hundred and seventy feet long, having a wing of the same breadth, one hundred and six feet in length. They are, as was originally designed, principally occupied by indigent male emigrants, who, by age, infirmity or other causes, are temporarily or permanently unable to support themselves ; also by convalescent patients and chronic cases, not requiring rigid hospital attendance. They are of that temporary kind of buildings that have been hastily erected, to meet the unforeseen demands for the accommodation of the feeble and destitute. The structures, however, are well arranged, not only for heating, light, and ventilation, but for division into compartments, so as to admit of a classification that will promote the health and comfort of the inmates.

III.—The Female Hospital.

This is a neat wooden structure, filled in with brick, and has already been described in page 21.

IV.—The Nursery.

This edifice is uniform in size, structure and exterior, to the Female Hospital, having a centre building with wings. The windows are large, so as not only to admit light and pure air, but have on two sides the healthful influence of the sun's direct rays. It has two circular baths, each ten feet in diameter, supplied with cold and warm water for bathing, also contrivances for washing, which prevents the possibility of any two using the same water. The whole interior arrangement is well adapted to its objects, and contains besides apartments for the accommodation of nurses, spacious dormitories which will comfortably lodge four hundred children, a large dining-room, play-room, and school-room, and chapel. The grounds around it, though not yet much improved, are ample and pleasant, affording a wide range for recreation and amusement.

V.—The Male Hospital.

This consists of twelve buildings of the temporary class, contemporaneously erected in 1849, to meet the pressing demand of sick and destitute emigrants. They are wood structures of the simplest kind, consistent with the comfort and proper medical care of the inmates; severally one story, one hundred and twenty-five feet long by twenty feet wide, ceiling thirteen feet high, filled in with brick, lathed and plastered. Each building will accommodate fifty patients, and admit of such compartments as a judicious classification of the sick, in a well-regulated sanitary establishment, requires. They run east and west on parallel lines, twenty-five feet from each other, and at a sufficient distance from other buildings, for all purposes of convenience.

VI.—Bakery and Wash-House.

This is a spacious, substantial brick edifice, consisting of a main building one hundred feet by forty-four, and three wings, each seventy-six feet by twenty-five, and three stories high. The main building is chiefly occupied as a Wash-House and Bakery; the former having steam apparatus, drying rooms, and extensive appliances for washing; and the latter, every arrangement for baking which convenience and economy require. The basement of the south wing is occupied as a store, and the upper part for hospital purposes; the north wing contains reception and probation rooms, sixteen baths, disinfecting apartments, and other conveniences; the east wing, which is fitted up for the accommodation of the resident physicians, contains sleeping and sitting apartments, dining-room, and kitchen with suitable appendages.

VII.—The Surgery.

This building, during the past autumn, was constructed out of a small frame out-house. The necessity of a suitable surgical operating room, of convenient access, effectually separated from the apartments occupied by the patients, had long been felt, and has thus been very economically provided.

VIII.—New Hospitals.

It might have been supposed that the tide of emigration had reached its height during the year when political agitations and famine and pestilence combined to drive so many from their native land. But it appears, on the contrary, to have been retarded by these causes, and to have acquired new strength, by a period of comparative quiet. The Commissioners had effected all that their limited means would allow, in anticipation of a gradual increase of dependent emigrants, so that they were prepared for very considerable augmentation of numbers, but not to the extent the extraordinary influx required. The unexampled increase in the amount of emigration, of more than *thirty per cent.* during the past year, had already crowded their hospital apartments to overflowing; and as there were strong probabilities of a progressive increase of needy subjects during the winter and early spring months, who would inevitably suffer without suitable accommodations, they have been induced to contract for the immediate erection of four new hospital buildings, each to be one hundred and twenty feet long, two stories high, to contain four hundred additional patients. These structures are to be of wood, filled in with brick, lathed and plastered, and to be completed early in February, at a cost of seven thousand nine hundred dollars.

IX.—Warden's Dwelling.

This is a small wooden dwelling-house, with a barn belonging thereto, occupied by the Superintendent of the Institution. There is also another barn and stable for farming uses.

The various buildings are supplied with water from the Croton Aqueduct, through a three and an half inch pipe, beneath the bed of the river. The cost of introducing it was about seven thousand dollars.

The buildings and their contents are insured in fifteen different offices, for $88,400.

Contemplated Improvements.

The supply of Croton water is abundant for the present ordinary and prospective demands of the Institution. But as now used, with no facilities for accumulation, the quantity at command is insufficient for extinguishing fire, in case of a conflagration, or for drenching sewers, vaults, and other purifying purposes, which require a large volume of water. And, if in case of accident to the main conduit, the regular supply should be interrupted or cut off, there being no other resource, great suffering would be the inevitable consequence. To insure, therefore, an adequate supply for all demands, and prevent the disasters a failure would occasion, a *Reservoir* is, in view of the Commission, indispensable. One of sufficient capacity, for all special uses, could be replenished during the night, when the water is not required for other purposes, without interfering with the daily consumption, or diminishing the usual quantity for ordinary demand. Such a provision being absolutely necessary, both for the security and proper sanitary condition of the Institution, its construction is only deferred until funds shall justify a prosecution of the work.

The law of April 11th, 1849, provides, that all alien passengers arriving at the port of New York, for whom bonds have been given, or commutation paid, who are affected with any infectious or contagious disease, shall be sent to the Marine or other Hospital, and shall there be detained until discharged or removed by a permit in writing from said officer. This provision has been found useful against the spreading of pestilential diseases; but, by thus restricting the Quarantine Department to the reception of patients mainly of this class, there has been a material increase of medical and surgical cases at Ward's

Island, requiring a corresponding increase of hospital arrangements. It is found, moreover, that great numbers of emigrants, in apparent health on their arrival, are, in consequence of their previous exposure and privations on shipboard, or from the sudden change of diet or climate, and indulgence in unaccustomed sorts of food, subsequently liable to early attacks of fever, often very severe, and need all the advantages of skilful and well-regulated medical attendance, to recruit their health. Hence it follows, that those sent to Ward's Island, not only require far better care, and a much more liberal and nutritious diet than is usual in ordinary alms-houses, but a large majority of them need the best of hospital accommodations. But while it is matter of gratulation that the hospital for females attached to the Institution, is probably unsurpassed in its arrangements and general excellence by any other, it is an occasion of regret that the male hospitals are, for the reasons before given, principally of a cheap, temporary structure. As the latter should, therefore, in the judgment of the Board, be superseded by the erection of an hospital edifice of a substantial character, with accommodations commensurate with the present and prospective demands on the Institution, they have advertised for plans for one of this description, to contain five hundred beds, and that will admit of a symmetrical enlargement for the reception of one thousand.

Improvement of the Grounds.

The Emigrant Refuge and Hospital Department, occupy an admirable site on the west side of Ward's Island, overlook-Harlem River. The grounds forming a gentle declivity to the water, are still chiefly in a state of nature, and require improvement. Levelling, grading, sewerage, &c., are now in progress, which, when completed, will be of considerable utility and beauty. Various other improvements are projected, and will be carried on, as circumstances favor their accomplishment.

The Board before leaving this branch of their charge, would briefly refer to the school for children, connected with the Nursery. It consists of boys and girls of suitable age, who are in care of a male and female teacher, of excellent qualifications and experience, aided by competent assistants. The average attendance in the former part of the year, was *one hundred and forty-three;* but during the last six months, the number had increased to *two hundred and four.* The same course of instruction is pursued as in the City Public Schools; and the discipline and order maintained, as also the improvement of the pupils in their respective studies, it is believed, will favorably compare with any of them. The Board, regarding the young, impressible children as a peculiarly interesting and hopeful portion of their charge, have spared no exertions to render these means of instruction as beneficial as the circumstances admit.

They would observe, moreover, in this connection, that a primary class has also been formed, and is in charge of a carefully selected instructress, for the benefit of young children, five years of age, and under. Being without maternal care, their tender age required such a guardianship as this provision is designed to supply. Having an apartment to themselves, nothing needful to their comfort is withheld; while by appropriate exercises of body and mind, the health and vigor of both are promoted. Recitations, interspersed with singing, marching, and other agreeable recreations suited to their years, will doubtless, in their case, as experience has shown in others, tend to their present enjoyment and lasting advantage.

From the rapid succession of children in these schools, and the comparatively short period they remain there, the system of instruction cannot be carried so far, ordinarily, as in the larger Public Schools of the State. But for the same reason, this instruction, so far as it goes, reaches a greater number in proportion to the number there at any one time, and is found of much value in habituating children to order and attention, and preparing them to derive immediate benefit from other schools, whenever they leave the island.

The cost of maintaining these schools has been hitherto defrayed from the income of the Emigration Fund.

As all these children are part of the population of the State, and destined to become its citizens, there seems no reason why they should not partake of the general benefits of the liberal provision made by the State for public education. On the contrary, it seems right that the Emigration Fund, limited in amount in comparison with the large demands upon it, should be relieved from every charge which does not of necessity fall within its objects. The Commissioners have had it under consideration to have their schools, on Ward's Island, organized under the authority of the Board of Education, on the footing of a ward school. But on further consideration and consultation with the officers of the Board of Education, various difficulties presented themselves as to such an organization, the requirements of the law transferring the property and control of such schools to other hands, whilst the efficiency and good order of the establishment required that the teachers resident and employed in the Emigrant Refuge, should be subject to the appointment and authority of the Commissioners, and their officers.

The Commissioners, therefore, respectfully submit to the Legislature the propriety and justice of placing the schools in the Emigrant Refuge, on the same footing with those of the New York Public School Society, the Orphan Asylum, and the Half Orphan Asylum, the Institution for the Blind, and the School of the Mechanics' Society, all of which, with some others, are, by law, authorized to receive a proportional share of the school moneys, on compliance with the general system of instruction, and being subject to the visitation and inspection of the Board of Education. The immediate control and government would then remain with the Commissioners, as they do with the Trustees of the several above-named institutions in relation to their own schools.

Many of the children have been provided, as heretofore, with places during the year, and others, being orphans, have been transferred to one or other of the orphan asylums. Six, whose cases demanded it, have been supported at the cost of the Emigrant Fund, at the Institution for the Blind.

A question touching the support of a portion of the children maintained at Ward's Island, seems to require the consideration and perhaps the interposition of the Legislature.

A large number of the children have been born in this country, chiefly in the Lying-in Hospital, at Ward's Island. These are all the children of alien mothers, who have emigrated to this country with the intention of permanent residence. They are, therefore, native citizens of the United States. The impossibility of separating them from their mothers, for months after birth, and the inhumanity of doing so at all, as long as they in any way require maternal care, necessarily throws the whole burden of the present support upon the Emigration Fund. In strictness, however, they are entitled to all the relief provided by our poor laws for other native children. It is therefore respectfully submitted, that the whole cost of support of both mother and child should not be thrown upon this fund, already burdened to its utmost capacity, and that the Commissioners should be allowed by law, reimbursement from the counties which would otherwise be charged with the support of these infants, so far as may be equitable under the circumstances.

The benevolent principle on which the Institution is founded, also required, that the religious instruction of the people should not only be provided for, but differences of faith respected. Accordingly, two chaplains are employed, a Protestant and a Roman Catholic, both of them conversant with the English and German languages. These respectively attend to the subjects of their charge during the week, and in turn conduct religious services in the chapel, on Sunday.

All the above-described buildings have been erected in the brief period of four years and a half. The extent, however, of this department, imperfectly indicates the magnitude and complexity of the trust confided to the Commission.

To trace out, detect, and correct errors and abuses in previous modes of relief; to institute a new system better adapted to its objects; and to provide, with inadequate funds, an asylum for the sick and indigent emigrants, who have been poured upon our shores in constantly augmenting numbers, since the appointment of this Commission, has proved a vast and difficult undertaking in every stage of its progress. With what fidelity and success it has been prosecuted, the results must determine.

But, in respect to this establishment on Ward's Island, the Board may be allowed to remark, that if, owing to the suddenness of the claims upon them, and the scantiness of their resources, they have not always been able to make the arrangements for present relief consistent with their own anticipations of the future, yet, in no instance, they believe, have the health and comfort of the sick and diseased suffered from considerations of economy.

Medical and Surgical Administration of the Hospital on Ward's Island.

In their last year's report, the Commissioners set forth the change of the plan of medical and surgical attendance in the Ward's Island Hospital, which was commenced on the 1st of September, 1850, together with the favorable results of that alteration so far as they could be tested by four months' treatment. Previously to that date, the establishment had been under the charge of a single resident physician, with several subordinate medical assistants. But a majority of the Commissioners were led to the same conviction which had recently induced the Governors of the New York Alms-House to change the similar plan of medical service in the institutions under their care.

The reasons which led to this conviction, were stated in the last year's report of this Board. It was believed that whatever might be the skill or fidelity of a single medical chief, with assistance necessarily of an inferior professional standing, they could not supply the efficient service constantly required by an hospital, unequalled in number and in variety of cases, by any in this country, containing generally from seven hundred to twenty-five hundred (the present number), and requiring the aid of medical and surgical skill of all sorts. For a small sanitary establishment, or to one devoted wholly or chiefly to a single class of maladies, as insanity or ship fever, the plan of a single head has its advantages ; but the variety of diseases, and the number of patients in the Emigrants Refuge, demanded, in order to obtain the full benefit of the present improved state of professional science, a variety of skill, medical, surgical, obstetrical, or relating to the diseases of the eye (which had hitherto been a scourge to this and other public establishments), such arrangement as it is impossible to find combined in one individual. Even the combination of superior medical ability, with that skill in operative surgery constantly demanded in this hospital, is of rare occurrence, and when found, could not be obtained for hospital service at the cost of relinquishing the honors and gain of private practice. There were, moreover, occasions, some of which had already occurred, as in the emergencies of epidemic disease, when the consultation and comparison of opinion of a larger professional body would give to the Commission an aid and a confidence in action, which they could not often derive from the advice of a single resident.

Many years experience, as was then stated, of several of the largest and best managed hospitals of New York and other great cities, had shown that, by appointing a sufficient number of practising physicians and surgeons to divide the higher hospital duties among them in rotation, without sacrificing or abandoning their private practice, professional talent of a higher order in every branch could be commanded for the service of the poor and destitute. The regular visits of such a body of practitioners, directing the practice in such case, or for the performance of surgical operations, aided by the constant attendance of younger, but well-educated physicians, constantly resident in the establishment, thus secure to the humblest class of patients a degree of medical care and skill no ways inferior to that bestowed on the most opulent patient.

The system, soon after its adoption, was carried into effect, and began on the 1st September, 1850, under the charge of the physicians and surgeons named in the last year's report. During the present year, Drs. Hosack and Wilkes have resigned, and the medical and surgical duties are now discharged by the following gentlemen :—

Dr. A. V. Williams, Dr. W. S. Bowen, Dr. Simon Habel. Dr. H. G. Cox, Dr. J. M. Carnochan, Dr. Wm. Macneven, Dr. Ernest Schilling, Dr. George Ford.

Of the Board, Dr. Williams is President, and his residence

in the vicinity of Ward's Island, enables him to keep a regular and constant supervision of the hospital, besides taking the exclusive charge of the obstetric wards.

The consulting physicians, during the year, have been Dr. Cock and Dr. Edward Delafield ; the consulting surgeons, Dr. A. H. Stevens and the late Dr. John Kearney Rogers, who was cut off near the close of the year, in the midst of a career of professional eminence and public usefulness.

The hospital is divided into three general departments :

1*st.* The Lying-in hospital, and for diseases of women and infants.

2*d.* The medical wards for fevers, pulmonary complaints, and miscellaneous medical diseases, and the Children's hospital.

3*d.* Surgical department for ophthalmic and general surgery.

The various departments are under the immediate charge of the eight visiting physicians, five of whom, in their term of duty, visit the hospital daily, and examine into the cases, and direct the necessary treatment for each patient, which is strictly carried out by the resident medical staff, who are always on duty.

The resident medical staff is comprised of twelve graduates in medicine, authorized to practise their profession by the laws of the State. Before their appointment by the Commissioners, their testimonials have been examined, and themselves subjected to an examination by the Medical Board, as is done in the army and navy of the United States.

The Commissioners and the Medical Board take pleasure in testifying to the ability, zeal, and fidelity of these gentlemen, most of whom have in turn been prostrated by fever, acquired in the performance of their labors. Since the close of the year, one of them, Dr. Wilsher, has died from ship fever.

The Lying-in department is under the sole supervision of Dr. Williams, who visits the hospital daily in company of one of his assistants, upon whom it is incumbent, not only to attend him, but also to visit each patient both morning and evening, and at all other times when their services are required. The personal attendance of one of the medical assistants attached to the Lying-in department is also insisted on at each delivery, and in all preternatural cases, as well as in those requiring the use of instruments, the visiting physician, if not present, is sent for.

This institution is the largest of the kind in this country, and enjoys ample advantages for the comfort and convenience of the peculiar condition of the patients for whom it was intended.

Women, during all periods of gestation, are received at the Emigrants' Refuge, in large and well ventilated wards, and enjoy those indulgences and privileges to which their parturient state entitles them. Here they remain until the premonitory symptoms of labor appear, when they are transferred to the Lying-in ward, and receive immediate attendance of one of the resident physicians of this department ; upon one of whom it is obligatory to attend in all such cases, or in event of any serious difficulty occurring, to request the aid of Dr. Williams.

After delivery, the patient remains in the hospital until convalescence is completely established, when, their infants having been vaccinated, they are transferred to other wards appropriated to infants of this tender age, where they still continue to be under the control of the physicians of the midwifery department.

The diet of lying-in women, during the first week after delivery, consists of farina, milk, weak tea, broths, and other light articles of this nature, unless circumstances call for a more stimulating course. During the second week more substantial food is allowed, as beef, or chicken tea, bread, tea or coffee, and small quantities of solid animal food. Thus they are permitted gradually to return to their regular mode of living.

Women who have been but lately delivered, either privately or otherwise, and who have not recovered from its debilitating effects, or such as are suffering from puerperal or other diseases peculiar to the female, are, on application, received into this division of the hospital.

Connected with the Lying-in department, and under the same medical control, are the Nursery and Infants' wards, both of which receive daily attendance from the visiting and resident physicians. The latter consists of two large well-ventilated wards, each capable of accommodating sixty mothers with infants. In the former are the Orphans' ward, and one appropriated to the reception of all diseases of the scalp and skin occurring in children.

The health of this hospital during the year was moderately good. On several occasions, however, during the winter and spring, the puerperal fever appeared to prevail endemically, for, notwithstanding every care and regard were taken to insure a perfect ventilation of the wards, sixty-seven cases of this malignant disease occurred. Of this large number but seventeen proved fatal.

The wards for the treatment of fevers, miscellaneous medical diseases, and Children's hospital, are arranged into three divisions :

1*st Division*—Drs. Cox and Macneven, visiting physicians, with two resident assistants.

2*d Division*—Drs. Schilling and Habel, visiting physicians, with two resident assistants.

3*d Division*—Drs. Bowen and Ford, visiting physicians, with two resident assistants.

As previously stated, three of the visiting physicians visit these wards daily, and spend several hours each in attendance on the patients, under their respective charges. In these visits they are accompanied by their assistants, (who besides regularly visit their wards at least morning and evening,) who state all the occurrences since the previous visit, take down all prescriptions, and see that all directions given are carried into effect.

Typhus, with its various complications, phthisis, with other diseases of the respiratory organs, together with diseases of the bowels, made a large part in the list of diseases ; the great bulk of the mortality is made up from these maladies, and from young children, many of whom, as well as adults, are frequently brought in extremely exhausted, and sometimes in a dying state.

The Surgical department, comprising ophthalmic and general surgery, together with fractures, wounds, and every variety of syphilitic affection, is under the charge of Drs. Williams and Carnochan, with two resident and two assistant house surgeons.

Dr. Carnochan visits the hospital daily, and prescribes the treatment for the patients under his charge, and has also performed many and difficult operations, with a degree of success, both in the operative and curative part, highly satisfactory to the Commissioners, and honorable to his professional skill.

The statistics of admissions, cases treated, births and deaths in the Emigrant Refuge Hospital, present the following results for the year 1851 :

Remaining in Hospital Jan. 1st, 1851	852	
Admitted during the year 1851	10,928	
Born	493	
Total	——	12,273
Discharged cured, or relieved	9,793	
Died	1,324	
Total	——	11,117
Remaining Jan. 1st, 1852		1,156

The general mode of calculating the rate of mortality in the reports of sanitary establishments, appears to be in the proportion of deaths upon all cases under treatment during the year. Adopting this mode as the most convenient for comparison, the ratio of deaths to cases under treatment for the year is something more than 11 per cent. No deduction is made on this estimate (as is sometimes done in similar cases) for the deaths of persons brought into the Hospital Refuge in a dying or almost dying state.

The number of deaths in 1851 was largely swelled by the fatal character of the typhus or ship fever, with which nearly one-sixth of the whole number under treatment were attacked. These were nearly all persons very recently from shipboard, in whom the disease did not manifest itself before their arrival, but in whom it soon after appeared in its most fatal form. There were 2,009 cases of this disease. Deducting these cases, admitted from necessity, though heretofore generally provided for at the Marine Hospital, and deducting also the number of deaths from the same cause, (427,) the proportion of deaths to all other cases treated in 1851 is 9½ per cent., a ratio of mortality about equal to that of the best managed institutions, receiving very few cases of typhus fever and enjoying superior advantages of hospital building, and medical attendance of the highest reputation. Thus, in that excellent institution, the New York Hospital, where infectious and contagious diseases are expressly excluded, no cases known to be incurable are admitted, and as few ship fever cases as possible received, the total number of cases admitted during the ten years ending January, 1851, was 46,713, with a mortality of 4,463, showing a ratio of deaths of very nearly 9½ per cent.

The circumstances of 1851 having crowded that hospital with typhus cases, it is understood that the ratio of deaths has risen to nearly eleven per cent. for the year.

The proportion of deaths from typhus may also seem large, yet so fatal is that disease, that on comparison with the medical statistics of such other hospitals as the Board have at present the opportunity of examining, the practice at Ward's Island has been among the most successful.

These results give evidence of the efficiency of the present system of medical attendance corresponding with the results of the similar change made by the Board of Governors of the New York Alms-House, and showing, as there, a diminished ratio of mortality as compared with former years under the old system of administration. If the ratio of death is still large, it must be remembered that the mass of patients are persons broken down, not a few by age, many by protracted suffering, and destitution of the common necessaries of life in their own countries, and others bringing with them from shipboard or from the other side of the Atlantic, the seeds of fatal diseases, such as ship-fever, contracted on board, or incurable phthisis from Europe. No less than 172 of the deaths were from *phthisis*, or consumption, most of them being of persons who had arrived within the year, and in many of whom the disease must have been already seated incurably, before they left their native country.

That terrible disease of the eyes, purulent ophthalmia, to which children are particularly exposed, often ending in total loss of sight, and which had formerly spread through the Emigrants Refuge, has disappeared as an epidemic disease, and the few cases occasionally brought to the hospital, have been cured without spreading amongst the other inmates of the Island.

The want of a spacious and commodious hospital building, less subject to danger of fire, less affected by extremes of temperature in the great vicissitudes of our climate than the present wooden buildings, in which a large number of the patients are received, and combining all the valuable recent improvements in warming, ventilation, and interior arrangements, is severely felt, and presents no small impediment to the entire success of the present medical organization. A small temporary increase of the amount of commutation, as recommended under the financial head of this report, would supply the deficiency.

The Commissioners have also to regret the want of a convenient separate building, suited for the reception and care of insane patients. By an arrangement with the Governors of the Alms-House, the insane chargeable to this Commission, who have been found thus afflicted in this city or its vicinity, or landed from shipboard, are received and supported at the charge of this Commission, in the Asylum on Blackwell's Island. A number of others are scattered throughout the poor-houses of the counties, and for whose support allowance is also made from the emigrant fund. On various accounts, and especially from the want of accommodation for such patients, in most of the counties, it is very desirable that either provision should be made for the reception of such alien insane in the State Asylum, on the same footing with those charged to the towns or counties, or else that this Commission should be enabled to erect a building under their own control at Ward's Island. The increase of commutation recommended, should the emigration to this port during the next two or three years increase, might enable them also to effect this object.

The subject of diet, and other hospital details have occupied from time to time the attention of the Board, and wishing to avail themselves of the experience of other institutions, they united with the Governors of the New York Alms-House department in engaging the services of the Hon. John S. Gould, of Columbia County, a gentleman whose rare qualifications eminently fitted him for the work, to visit the principal public establishments in the United States, in order to obtain practical information, relative to their economies, dietaries, and general management. The result of his labor is a treatise on these topics, both suggestive and practical, which, as it is believed, will supply a desideratum long felt, the two Boards have resolved to publish. As the work contains valuable statistics, and many important tables on dietaries and alimentary principles, it will, doubtless, be regarded as an important acquisition by those interested in eleemosynary and penal establishments, and it is trusted will tend to useful improvements in the administration of the institutions under the charge of the Commissioners of Emigration.

It is proper to add, that the dietary of the Hospitals and Refuge had already been arranged with great care, after a thorough examination of the best-regulated institutions; and Mr. Gould, after his inspection, reported that in no other place did he find a more judicious system of diet.

County Indemnities.

Under the unequal operation of former laws relating to emigrants, the fund created by the capitation tax, the commutation of special bonds, and the infraction of alien laws, was expended for the exclusive benefit of the city and county of New York, thus leaving every other part of the State without indemnity, for expenses incurred in the relief of recent emigrants, who for any cause became a public charge. That laws so obviously partial and unjust, found no advocates out of the city and county of New York, is not surprising, nor yet, that a modification of these laws, so as to indemnify counties for the relief of such emigrants, should receive the approbation of the representatives of other counties.

The pecuniary claims of the counties for this object, since the Act of April 5th, 1847, have annually augmented in number and amount, as the needy have increased, and found their way into the interior, until the aggregate of this class chargeable to the Commission, during the past year, amounted to twelve thousand five hundred and fifty persons, and the expenditure for their benefit, to the large sum of eighty thousand dollars.

That the country is a gainer in many respects, by the operations of the present law, is most manifest. First, it saves the people of the State from an onerous tax for the support of recent emigrants, equal in amount to the sum refunded by the Commission. Second, it relieves them from a large proportion of the beggary and vagrancy, to which, under the continued operation of the previous law, they would have been exposed. Third, its results are peculiarly favorable to destitute aliens, inasmuch as aid is less likely to be deferred or withheld, when there is a fund for their relief provided by themselves, than if such fund was derived from a local tax. Every tax-payer, therefore, and all opposed to the manifold evils of vagrancy, in their respective towns, cities and counties, within the jurisdiction of the State, and all friendly to the protection and welfare of unfortunate emigrants, have a deep, abiding personal interest, in a law so beneficial in its results.

Although the Board, in view of the many advantages of this mode of indemnity, have been constrained to speak in its commendation, yet they may be allowed to say, that no department of the vast interests intrusted to their charge, has required of them closer scrutiny and care, than the system under consideration. Nor are the embarrassments and difficulties which have been experienced, the less real, because not admitting of legislative relief. Some of these are probably inseparable from any system for the same object; and others can only be removed by improved management in the counties. The motive to the exercise of rigid economy and careful discrimination in relief, appears to be sometimes weakened by the idea of its being derived from a gratuitous fund. Benevolence under such circumstances becomes inconsiderate, and often overlooks the imminent danger of creating more pauperism than it prevents, by indiscreetly aiding the physically able, instead of giving them employment, or sending them where it can be obtained. Serious evils necessarily result from such management on the part of poor-house officers, and others having charge of emigrants in county alms-houses; and *thus*, whilst funds that would otherwise be usefully applied, are wasted on improper subjects, a spirit of pauperism is thereby engendered, which hereafter will powerfully react, to the great annoyance and detriment of the community. It therefore concerns the people of the several towns, cities, and counties in the State, not less than it concerns the Commissioners, to economize this fund, for the benefit of the really helpless and dependent, for whom it is especially designed; and to urge upon all capable of labor, the obligations to self-support, while no proper exertions should be spared in providing them employment. In no other way can they aid in carrying out the beneficent objects of this Commission; or guard their respective communities from the intolerable evils of vagrancy and pauperism.

For particulars of the annual disbursements, see Table E.

Receipts, Expenditures, and Financial Concerns of the Commission.

The funds of the Commission are still, as in former years, mainly derived from the payment of $1 50 from each alien passenger, in commutation for the securities required by the Act of April 1849. But the amendments to that Act, passed July 11, 1851, have given much greater efficacy to the former provisions for special bonds in cases of helpless persons sent from the poor-houses of Europe, merely for the purpose of throwing them upon public relief in this country, and also in cases of lunatics, idiots, and others, who must, of necessity, immediately become a public charge.

Such bonds have, with a few exceptions, been commuted by the ship-owners, or consignees, at such rates as the Commissioners judged sufficient to meet the probable expenses which would be incurred by the support of such persons. The whole amount received, under the similar but less efficacious provisions of the former Act, during the year 1850, was but $81 35; the amount received during 1851 (chiefly in the half year since the enactment of July, 1851), rose to $9,628 69. There is also reason to believe that these enactments have had some effect in lessening the number of aged and infirm shipped to this country by the local authorities of Europe. The provisions of the law in this respect were immediately printed by the Commissioners in several of our papers of the largest circulation, and a circular analyzing the restrictions of the laws, and expressing the determination of the Commissioners to carry out the intention of the Legislature to the full extent of their powers, was prepared and widely circulated here and in Europe.

For statements of the receipts and expenditures of the Commutation Fund, for the year 1851, see Table No. VII.

Although the increased income from commutation money in 1851 was necessarily accompanied with a proportionate increase of urgent claims upon the fund, yet the general financial condition of the Commission was, on the whole, better than in any former years. The outstanding debts to the counties, which, at the close of 1850, were very large, have been paid, and these accounts mostly settled to the 1st December, 1851, some of them to the close of the year; and there was nothing of any amount then due for the ordinary support of the establishments at Quarantine or on Ward's Island.

Since the 1st January, 1852, the great number of destitute persons chargeable on this fund, (many of them recently arrived,) and the great severity of the winter, have created sudden and expensive demands, absorbing all the means at the disposal of the Commissioners.

In their report of 1850, the Commissioners stated, that under the provisions of the Act of March 2d, 1850, giving authority to borrow upon mortgage of some of the lands held by them, upon approval thereof by the Governor, Comptroller, and Attorney-General, an arrangement for a loan of $80,000 on such mortgage had been made with the New York Life and Trust Company, to be advanced in such sums as might be required. These were to be applied for the lands and buildings purchased or erected on Ward's Island, or in reimbursement of the moneys advanced from the ordinary income for such purposes. These have cost above $150,000, an amount too great to be met by the current income of one or two years. In 1850, there had been received on this account $36,000. During the last year an additional sum of $14,000 was advanced on the same security, making the debt $50,000 in all. The remaining $30,000 is reserved with a view to future enlargements of the Ward's Island establishments, or as a resource in any unexpected emergency.

The amount reported last year, as a loss caused by reason of the non-payment of commutation moneys by a house which became insolvent, has been refunded in 1851, by the Comptroller of the State, out of the moneys in the State Treasury, due to the said insolvent house under the Act of April, 1851, for return of commutation moneys paid under protest.

The amounts of moneys received and expended by the Commissioners undoubtedly appear large, but a comparison of their expenditures with the extent of the claims upon the fund, or with the disbursements for any similar object by local authorities, will prove that these sums have been economically applied. For example : the number of alien emigrants who might become chargeable on the Commission, (were all living who have been entitled to its aid,) exceeded one million at the end of 1851, (1,000,033,) or about double the population of the city of New York. As the greater part of them are of the more recent arrivals, a deduction of ten per cent. for deaths since May, 1847, would be about the probable proportion. This would leave 900,000 who might be chargeable on this Commission, or about 70 per cent. more than the population of the city.

If the per cent. of the needy and the cost of relief for those claiming it, were in the ratio of the percentage and cost of the Alms-House poor for the city population, the annual expense of the Commission for relief would far exceed that of the Corporation outlay for the destitute ; but the results show that instead of being that much larger, they do not exceed them. The Board in thus referring to the city expenditures for this object, would not imply that they are indiscreetly made, or extravagant in amount ; on the contrary, under the present able and efficient administration of the Alms-House Department, they believe them to be wisely and economically disbursed. This is merely designed to show that, taking into view the number and condition of those who are entitled to relief from the Commission, the ratio of expenditure *per capita* is probably below that of our best-regulated municipal charities.

The experience of nearly five years has shown that the moneys received for commutation and special bonds, are sufficient, with due economy, to meet the current charges upon the Commission, and to indemnify the counties for the expenses incurred by them for the support of foreign poor. But whatever may be the economy of administration, it is impossible to defray out of the same fund all the appropriations for permanent objects, as lands, buildings, &c., which the well-being of the Refuge and emigrant hospitals require. Since May, 1847, the aggregate sum of above $267,000 has been laid out in lands, (which could now be sold at a much higher price than the cost), buildings, wharves, or in lasting articles of furniture, such as iron bedsteads, &c. Of this amount, $60,000 was received from the State Treasury, and $50,000 from a loan on mortgage, leaving the remaining $157,000 as defrayed, from current income. This expenditure was of absolute necessity, yet it has seriously encumbered the means of the Commission, and limited them in their operations.

But it should be further observed, that the receipts from commutation were interrupted, in part, for nearly a year, and wholly for some months in 1848, '49, by the constitutional objections to the law as it then stood, which were sustained by the United States Supreme Court. The grant of $60,000 from the State Treasury was intended, and was applied to meet the exigency thus created, and ought not strictly to be taken into account.

In another part of this report, the urgent necessity of a larger, permanent, and more commodious hospital on Ward's Island, has been shown. But the erection of such an edifice, with its furniture and other appurtenances, and of such size and character, however simple, as would, in its style and construction, meet the necessities of the increasing number of emigrants, is far beyond the means now at the disposal of this Commission.

It is therefore respectfully, but urgently, submitted to the

Legislature, that an additional amount of twenty-five cents commutation for each passenger be required for the next two years, for the object of creating a permanent hospital on Ward's Island.

In conclusion, the Commissioners beg leave to remind the members of the Legislature, that this Commission is not in the situation of most other official administrators of relief for the poor or diseased, who, whilst they are bound to apply their funds with due economy, are yet also required to make every useful expenditure, with the certainty of being supplied with the necessary means, but, on the contrary, the Commissioners of Emigration are directed by law to apply a limited fund to meet, as far as may be, vast and pressing demands.

In the confidence of having applied the means at their command conscientiously, and to the best of their ability, they respectfully submit the above Report.

G. C. VERPLANCK,
ROBERT B. MINTURN,
CYRUS CURTISS,
ELIAS HICKS,
CHAS. H. MARSHALL,
FERDINAND KARCK,
A. C. KINGSLAND.

NEW YORK, *February* 12, 1852.

Sixth Annual Report

FOR THE YEAR 1852.

TO THE LEGISLATURE OF THE STATE OF NEW YORK:

The year 1852 has been the most important in the history of the Commission, for the number of diseased and destitute emigrants thrown under the charge of the Commissioners during a winter of uncommon severity and duration.

Not only were the Marine Hospitals at Quarantine, and the Hospital and Refuge buildings at Ward's Island, together with such additions as could be prepared or procured, crowded with the severest forms of disease, but it was also for a long time necessary to provide shelter and partial support in the city for a greater number than ever before, of recently arrived foreigners, without means of support, and unable to find present employment in this city or its neighborhood, whilst the length and severity of the winter cut off the ordinary facilities for procuring employment in the interior.

The arrivals from Europe at the close of 1851, and during the winter of 1852, brought typhus fever of the most malignant character, which not only proved fatal to numbers of newly-arrived emigrants, but extended its ravages amongst all in attendance upon them. Physicians, officers, and nurses were attacked by the disease, of whom, some fell victims, and others recovered only after a long and dangerous illness. Cholera and small-pox also made their appearance at the Quarantine and Ward's Island, and continued during the summer after the ravages of typhus fever had ceased.

All the means at the disposal of the Commissioners, as well pecuniary as in buildings and supplies for the sick and destitute, were insufficient to meet these emergencies without the aid of such credit as could be obtained for the time, and such buildings as could be procured on lease or otherwise.

The approach of summer gradually lessened these demands, and the closing months of 1852 happily brought no returns of the excess of disease and destitution which had prevailed in the preceding part of the year. The present year has opened much more favorably, and, at the close of January, 1853, there has been no repetition of the disease, mortality, and distress which marked the end of 1851 and the beginning of 1852.

The statistics of the emigration from Europe to this port, and the relief afforded to aliens under the operation of this Commission, present the following results:

Number of vessels employed in conveying citizens and alien passengers, was	1,662	
" conveying citizens only	528	
Total passenger vessels	——	2,190

Number of passengers landed, 340,144. Of these 39,152 were citizens, and 300,992 aliens; of the latter 118,131 were natives of Ireland, 118,611 of Germany, and 64,250 of other countries. (For particulars see Table A.)

The statistics of relief afforded to destitute and diseased alien emigrants by the Commissioners, exhibit the following results:

Number in Marine Hospital, Jan. 1st, 1852	517	
" admitted from vessels during the year	1,240	
" " " the city	6,751	
" " " other sources	379	
Total number treated	——	8,887
Number in Emigrant Refuge and Hospital, Ward's Island, Jan. 1st, 1852	2,106	
" born there during the year	523	
" admitted	12,553	
Total number cared for and treated	——	15,182
Number of sick sent from Park Office to New York Hospital	87	
" " " do. to St. Vincent's Hospital	159	
Total cases from Park Office	——	246

Number of lunatic emigrants in City Asylum, Jan. 1st, 1852...	135	
" admitted during the year..........................	220	
Total lunatics cared for......................	——	355
Number supplied from Park Office with board and lodging....		20,339
" of out-door poor in the city buried at the expense, in whole or in part, of the Commission............		763
" temporarily boarded and lodged at the Intelligence Office and Labor Exchange to July 31st...........		97,229
" returned to Europe, at the expense, in whole or in part, of the Commission...........................		433
" forwarded to inland places from Park Office, at the expense, in whole or in part, of the Commission....		4,168
Number of females provided with situations at the Intelligence Office and Labor Exchange.....................	8,796	
" of males, do....................................	6,175	
Total number provided with employment.......	——	14,971
Whole number relieved, forwarded, provided with employment, &c., by city institutions................................		162,573
Number relieved and forwarded, in and from the several counties of the State, chargeable to the Commission..........		18,432
Grand total relieved, forwarded, and provided with employment, &c., by the Commission, in the city and State of New York............		181,005
Number of days spent in Marine Hospital..................		209,029
" " " Hospital and Refuge, Ward's Island..		766,022
Total in institutions of Commissioners.........		975,051
Number of letters written from Canal street Office, to friends of recently arrived emigrants............................		1,586
Amount received thereto in reply.........................		$5,879 33
" " by the Irish Emigrant Society from friends of recently arrived emigrants..........................		$11,322 00

These returns show that greatly as the emigration to this port in 1851 went beyond that of any previous year, it has been exceeded in amount by that of 1852. The excess of last year's immigration above that of the year preceding is 11,391. This arose mainly from the augmented emigration from Germany, which has risen to more than double the average of the preceding four years, and is an excess of 48,728, or about 70 per cent. over the number of 1851. The Irish emigration was

8

45,119 (or nearly ¼) less than that of 1851, but still is larger than in any other previous year. The emigration from England gradually increased, though not rapidly, and formed last year, as it has for some time done, something more than a tenth of the whole.

The attention of the Legislature has been heretofore called to the facility of evasion of the provisions of law as to bonds, commutation and other requirements, by captains of vessels not having any resident owners or consignees, and leaving this port for some other destination immediately after landing passengers.

The importance of giving every legal facility to guard against these evasions is evident from the following statement of the number of passenger vessels that arrived at this port, having no resident consignees.

Number of vessels conveying passengers that arrived at the port of New York during the year 1852, which had no resident consignees, were 42 ; of which 18 were American, 18 of Great Britain, and 6 of other nations.

The aggregate number of alien passengers landed from said vessels was 6,082.

It is therefore not a matter of surprise that so large a number have claimed relief either at the establishments of the Commissioners in New York or in the counties. In the last year, as in former ones, much the larger proportion of those so relieved or aided, were of the arrivals of the current twelve months, whilst comparatively few of those who landed here, three or four years ago, are to be found seeking aid from the commutation fund.

Thus making the largest allowance for deaths and for transit to distant States, still each successive year appears to place a larger proportion of emigrants in a situation above dependence on public assistance.

Intelligence Office and Labor Exchange.

TEMPORARY RELIEF, ADVICE AND PROTECTION.

It has been the general policy of the Commissioners, from the beginning of their operations, not to make food and shelter or temporary aid at home in the city, an object of reliance to persons unfit or unwilling to be sent to Ward's Island as patients, or as wholly unable to earn their own support.

Occasional aid or food in cases of apparent, absolute necessity, was granted as an exception, not as the ordinary plan of relief. Until 1851, the large building on Canal street, used for the purpose of an Intelligence Office or Labor Exchange, by the Commissioners, with occasional use of the cheaper emigrant boarding-houses, was sufficient to give shelter to all whose immediate necessities required such aid and shelter for a few nights. Crackers and some other food were also, at very inclement seasons, given at the Commissioners' office, to such destitute strangers. But from the middle of November, 1851, until near May, 1852, the crowd of destitute persons, many aged, many with children, thrown upon our shores in a season of an unusually early and severe and protracted winter, made much larger temporary provision for this sort of relief, imperatively necessary ; large additional buildings on Canal and on Centre streets were procured on hire or lease, and fitted up for the reception of such applicants for aid. Before the end of January, these were found insufficient, and a very large unoccupied church on Duane street was procured for four months, as also a spacious brick building on the Third avenue beyond the thickly built parts of the city. A number amongst those thus received and taken care of for week after week, were doubtless persons who might have taken care of themselves. But it was impossible to discriminate such persons amongst the numerous cases of women, children, old or infirm, and others recently landed, quite destitute, and for whom there was no alternative but to be left in the streets or police station-houses, or to be provided for by the Commissioners for the present.

The condition and habits of many thus received, as well as their state of health, were often such as to prove a subject of annoyance or alarm to the neighborhood of all the establishments of this Commission in the thickly populated parts of the city. Every exertion was made to preserve cleanliness and to prevent such annoyances, yet this could be effected but partially. The interruption by ice of regular communication with

Ward's Island, added to this accumulation in the city; and the condition of many destitute emigrants, either broken down by previous illness or attacked by new and violent disease, often required medical assistance in the city. This was provided for by regular physicians assigned to the Third avenue houses and to one of the Centre street buildings. These arrangements proved of great benefit to the distressed persons for whom they were made, however unpleasant to any neighborhood, and improper for permanent use.

The difficulties pressing upon the Commission may be realized from the single fact that the claims of these strangers, just arrived in a strange land at a bitter season, and quite destitute, were nearly six times as numerous as in any former year. Above 117,500 persons of this class received such temporary relief of food, shelter, or other aid, in the city, nearly all in the first four months of 1852. Every effort was made to relieve these demands by procuring employment in the city and neighborhood, and by providing the means of transportation to different parts, where the emigrants had friends, or where employment could be procured for them.

Much was effected in this way, but it was not until the approach of spring that these numbers were sensibly diminished.

The Commissioners are fully sensible of the evils likely to result from any extensive indiscriminate assistance afforded in the manner above stated, or in similar ways, if habitually provided. It was resorted to only from unavoidable necessity, and the several buildings used for the purpose were closed as soon as practicable. Happily no necessity has occurred of again providing such establishments; and half the present winter has been passed without any recurrence of the pressure of the last.

The system of the Intelligence Office in procuring employment, writing letters to friends for the ignorant, and receiving and communicating the answers, providing passages into the interior, as stated in former reports, has been continued with many beneficial results. 14,971 persons were thus provided with places or employment.

The frauds and impositions practised on newly arrived foreigners (such as stated in former communications from this Commission, and in the evidence before committees of the Legislature) continue to be very frequent subjects of just complaint. Something has doubtless been effected to check such evils by former legislation, and the exercise under them of the power given to the municipal authorities. The officers and agents of the Commission have, it is confidently believed, been zealous and active in procuring legal aid, and in giving advice and information. But their exertions, however beneficial in many cases, have been quite insufficient to put an end to these abuses.

The Commissioners again present the subject to the renewed examination of the Legislature.

Marine Hospital at Quarantine, on Staten Island.

The effects of the severity of the last winter, both here and on the Atlantic, and the wretched and enfeebled state of many of the passengers who arrived at this port after the tempestuous and inclement passages of December, 1851, and the first four months of 1852, were strongly manifested in the hospital at Quarantine, by the great increase of patients who were landed from shipboard suffering under infectious or contagious diseases, or sent down from the city attacked by such diseases, contracted on shipboard and developed in a few days after landing. A larger proportion than usual, of these cases, were of a malignant character, and many terminated fatally.

The number of patients on the 31st December, 1851, was 517, received during the year 1852, 8,370, making the whole number under treatment during the year, 8,887.

This is a greater number than in any preceding year, even including the years before the Marine Hospital was specially appropriated to the reception of infectious or contagious diseases, and received many patients sent from the city for diseases of a milder type. The number for 1852 exceeds that of 1851 by 2,544, or above 40 per cent.

The greater part of these were thrown upon the charge of this Commission between the beginning of January, 1852, and the month of April, so that the average number of patients under treatment at the same time were more than doubled, it having risen from 517, at the end of 1851 (a number much above the ordinary average), to 1,062, from Jan. 24th, to April 24th, 1852. The number of patients was even at one period as high as 1,409. On the 1st July, 1852, it was reduced to about 500, and it has since gradually lessened to 318 in the last week of the year.

This increase of the number of patients was accompanied by an augmented severity of disease and corresponding mortality. Ship fever in its worst forms was the prevailing disease during the winter. The whole number under treatment for typhus fever during the year, was 3,040, far the greater part of whom were received between the 14th January and the middle of April. Out of these 513 died; and the ravages of this infection extended widely amongst the officers and others employed at the hospital.

In our last annual report we announced the then recent death of the accomplished and able health officer of the port, who then acted as the medical head and the superintendent of the Marine Hospital. Dr. Doane died on the 27th January, 1852, from typhus fever contracted on the 14th. His death was soon after followed by that of Lewis B. Butler, the steward of the establishment, from the same cause. He was an active and intelligent officer. On the 4th of May, one of the assistant physicians, Dr. George H. Kingsbury, died of typhus erysipelas, contracted in the same manner. Scarcely any of the physicians or nurses who came new to this hazardous service escaped infection, and several of the subordinates thus employed fell victims.

The number of patients having thus exceeded any previous estimates, was much more than could be provided for in the regular hospital accommodations, including the shanties erected by the Commissioners on the hospital grounds. The Commissioners had therefore to resort to the use of adjoining stores of the United States government, which not being required for the revenue purposes, were placed at their disposition by the Secretary of the Treasury, through the recommendation of the Collector of the port.

These buildings for about two months contained an average of 300 patients. Their situation is not favorable, and their construction was of necessity but badly suited for the purpose of a hospital, to which purpose they would be but imperfectly adapted; they were, therefore, used no longer than urgent necessity compelled. As soon as the pressure upon the establishment decreased, the patients were transferred to the regular hospitals.

During the summer the Quarantine Hospitals were visited by Asiatic cholera. This occurred at a time when, happily, the ravages of typhus fever had been stayed, and many of the convalescents discharged, so that the inmates in the hospitals had been reduced to less than half the number which had crowded them during the winter and early spring. From this cause, and from the skill and watchful attention of the medical officers in charge of the establishment, the dreaded disease was prevented from spreading beyond the Quarantine grounds, and was checked, to a considerable degree, within them. It broke out on the 4th July, on the person of a recent emigrant, who had been admitted with rheumatism, and was convalescing. The disease could not be traced, as to its origin, beyond the Marine Hospital, and, with very few exceptions, was confined to it. It continued to prevail, with short remissions, until towards the end of October, and, notwithstanding all efforts to separate without delay those attacked from others, it carried off 131 persons, all or nearly all of whom had been enfeebled by other diseases. Indeed, both of these scourges, the typhus and cholera, as well as other diseases of a malignant type, were more than ordinarily fatal, from the feeble condition of a large number of emigrants, especially those who had suffered during long and tempestuous passages. As the Commissioners are directed by law to receive into the hospital all cases of infectious and contagious disease, whether from shipboard or sent by authority of the Board of Health from the city, these always constitute a large proportion of the cases there treated, and during the last year that proportion, as well as the actual number of such cases, was augmented. At different periods small-pox prevailed extensively amongst the recent emigrants from the continent of Europe. These were received in a large and commodious hospital for some time devoted to this object, and insulated by its elevation and distance from the other hospital buildings. It was frequently crowded; 678 cases of *variola*, either immediately from shipboard or sent to the hospital soon after their arrival, were treated there.

The whole number of deaths in 1852 at the Marine Hospital, was 1,561, a proportion to the cases treated larger than is found in sanatory establishments filled chiefly with ordinary disease or surgical cases, but to be accounted for here from the previous state of the patients, their unusual number, and the fact that 708 out of 1,561 deaths, or 45 per cent. of the whole, were from Asiatic cholera, or ship-fever, or were else brought in from shipboard in a dying state from some other cause. (For particulars see Table B.)

The Act of 11th July, 1851, having authorized the Commissioners of Emigration, in their discretion, to require the health officer of the port to perform the duties of physician-in-chief of the Marine Hospital, and also of superintendent thereof, the late Dr. Doane, the health officer, was appointed to discharge these duties. After five months of service in this capacity, in 1851, he entered upon the last year in full health and vigor. On the 15th January he was prostrated by typhus fever, contracted in the inspection and landing of about an hundred emigrants suffering with that disease, from on board a vessel which had just arrived. He died on 27th of January, 1852.

Although the zeal and energy of Dr. Doane had prevented any inconvenience being felt from the union of the duties of the chief physician of the hospital with those of the superintendent of its police and fiscal concerns, and those of the health officer, yet it was judged by the Commissioners most expedient now to resort to the other discretionary power given by the Act of 11th July, 1851, "to appoint a superintendent, physicians, and other officers, as they should judge necessary, for the management and care of the Marine and other Hospitals used for Quarantine purposes." They accordingly resolved to place the medical treatment under the charge of a chief physician, assisted by a sufficient number of salaried physicians, employed by the year, for the regular duty, with such additional temporary medical aid as necessity might require.

A separate office of superintendent was also established, with the general authority and supervision of the external concerns, grounds, property, and police of the establishment.

Dr. John W. Sterling, who had for several years been employed as an assistant physician in the Marine Hospital and had given evidence there of his will and conscientious fidelity, was appointed chief physician at an annual salary of $1,600.

Captain Thomas B. Vermilye was appointed superintendent. Dr. Henry B. Fay (deputy health officer) examining officer ; Drs. B. R. Masters, E. J. Prendergast, William O'Donohue, J. Herzka, were appointed assistant physicians, and during the winter others were temporarily employed.

The greater part of the past year was a period of unusual labor and personal exposure to infection, at the Quarantine, to all those in the employment of the Commission, and especially to its physicians and their assistants. The Commissioners have great pleasure in attesting to the faithful, fearless, and conscientious discharge of their duties by the officers of the establishment during many weeks of danger, labor, and anxiety.

During the year a considerable expenditure has been required for repairs and improvements to meet the immediate pressing emergencies. Several of the wooden buildings, formerly erected, have been filled in with brick, and otherwise made more comfortable and convenient. The Secretary of the Treasury having, at the request of the Commissioners, granted a lease, at a nominal rent, of a brick store-house on the wharf, adjoining the hospital grounds, it has been fitted up for a washing and drying-house. The peculiar character of the Quarantine Hospital, in relation to the diseases received there, together with the quantity of used and infectious clothing from patients from shipboard, render a very large and efficient establishment of this kind of absolute necessity, and fully justify, in the opinion of the Commissioners, a large outlay for the purpose, although in a building not owned by the State.

The Quarantine dock has also required and received a very thorough repair at a cost of about $2,000.

Emigrants' Refuge and Hospital on Ward's Island.

The Commissioners of Emigration hold in fee in trust for the State, as heretofore reported, ninety-five acres, three roods, six perches of land, on Ward's Island, together with nearly all the water rights adjoining, and which, independently of the buildings since erected, and other improvements, is now worth, and could be sold for, above $100,000 ; and indeed, taking the rate at which lands on the same island have been recently sold, might be estimated at $150,000.

They also hold on lease a little more than eleven acres, on which some of their most important buildings are erected.

Having long felt the necessity of procuring the fee of the eleven acres now leased, the Commissioners agreed to the liberal offer of Mr. R. B. Minturn, the owner, to refer the terms upon which the fee of the land should be sold to them, or exchanged for other lots, to the decision of two former members of this Board, Messrs. William F. Havemeyer and Andrew Carrigan. These gentlemen have awarded $14,000 as the price of the land, the improvements having been chiefly made by the Commissioners. This award has been accepted by both parties ; the present pressure on the pecuniary means of the Commission has prevented as yet the payment being made, and the title perfected.

The character of the buildings for hospital, refuge, nursery, &c., has been set forth in full in the last report. Some improvements have been made in these, but the principal alteration arises from the destruction by fire, during last August, of a long wooden building, used for the dining-rooms for the Refuge, with nursery rooms above. This was totally destroyed with all its furniture, but no other inconvenience or injury was sustained. The amount of insurance received was $4,750 55. This sum, though less than the original cost, has enabled the Commissioners to erect a more commodious building in another location, which, with some changes in the larger edifices, has improved the comfort of the Refuge.

The additional wooden hospital buildings, mentioned as under contract in the last report, have been finished, after an unexpected delay, and found serviceable.

But experience has convinced the Commissioners of the necessity of some hospital edifices of a superior class, of a more permanent character, and less exposed to the risk of fire.

They accordingly advertised a premium for such plan of a single hospital as they might adopt. Various plans, some of them of high architectural and constructive merit, were submitted. These were all for a single, very spacious, and expensive building. But the deficiency of their means, arising from the extraordinary pressure of the emigration from 1st November, 1851, to May 1852, and the constant current expenditure, together with some other considerations of expediency, induced the Commissioners to lay aside all these plans, and to substitute several separate brick hospital buildings parallel to each other, each being 150 feet long by 25 in width, of one lofty story above a high basement. Four of these were contracted for last October at an expense of $4,221 each. They are now in process of erection. As their building and occupation must belong mainly to the history of the current year, the details of their structure are passed over. But the Commissioners will merely observe that these separate wards will have the great advantage of entire insulation from each other, and of the most perfect ventilation, thus guarding against the spread of malignant infection to which the Ward's Island Hospitals are peculiarly exposed, as well as of erysipelas which is often generated in large hospitals, and also against the danger of fire. They moreover present a plan capable of indefinite enlargement as circumstances demand and permit, though complete for immediate use in their present number and extent.

The supply of water from the Croton aqueduct by means of pipes passing under the bed of the broad and deep inlet, has continued to be ample and regular. But the possibility of an occasional temporary interruption, which would produce the most serious inconveniences, and the value of having a large body of water on the Island to guard against such a contingency, and also for the extinguishment of accidental fires, for drenching sewers, and several other purposes requiring a great body of water, suggested the construction of a reservoir to be kept filled from the Croton. This was for some time under consideration. It has been completed during the last summer, under the supervision of Benj. M. Clark, who had before superintended the introduction of water into the Island. It was built in great part by the labor of the inmates of the Refuge. It is computed to hold 1,099,583 gallons of water, and the estimated cost about $2,500.

The plan of instruction for the children has been carried on, as reported in the preceding years, with excellent effect as to the order, discipline, and morals of the children, and as far in other respects as the tender age of nearly all of them will permit. The Commissioners respectfully renew two of their former recommendations on the subject of these children.

A large number of the children have been born in this country, chiefly in the Lying-in Hospital at Ward's Island. All of these are the children of alien mothers, who emigrated to this country with the intention of permanent residence. They are, therefore, native citizens of the United States. The impossibility of separating them from their mothers, for months after birth, and the inhumanity of doing so at all, as long as they require maternal care, throws the whole burthen of their present support upon the Emigration Fund. In strictness, however, they are entitled to the relief provided by our poor laws for other native children. It is, therefore, respectfully submitted, that the whole cost of the support of both mother and child should not be thrown upon this fund, already burdened to its utmost capacity, and that the Commissioners should be allowed by law, reimbursement from the city of New York, or any other county which would otherwise be charged with the support of these infants, so far as may be equitable.

Medical and Surgical Department on Ward's Island.

The medical and surgical service at Ward's Island, including both the regular practice of the Hospital and also attendance on the numerous cases occurring in the Refuge among its inmates, not requiring regular hospital nursing, continues under the charge of the medical board of eight visiting physicians and surgeons, and the assistant resident medical staff, as fully detailed in the last annual report of this Commission.

Although a much larger proportion than in 1851, of the recent emigrants suffering under disease, were received at the Marine Hospital or attended at the temporary establishments in the city, yet the admission to both departments at Ward's Island exceeded by 242 those of the preceding year.

Of the 15,182 persons in the Refuge and hospital during the year, or some portion of it, 10,966 were received and cared for in the hospital; but disease, requiring medical and surgical aid, was by no means confined to those whose cases required the regular care and nursing of the hospital proper, the wards of which were filled, for the first six months of the year, to the utmost limits of their accommodation. Numerous cases requiring medical care constantly occur in the Refuge, so that in fact the whole establishment becomes one vast hospital. There were 7,321 cases thus treated in the Refuge department, many of them, however, of persons, who had been in the hospital, or were afterwards transferred there.

It was hoped that after the Acts of 1849 and 1851 had specially provided for the reception of contagious and infectious diseases at the Marine Hospital, the institutions at Ward's Island would have been in a great measure free from these scourges. But the frequency and the malignity with which typhus fever, contracted doubtless on shipboard, develops itself some days after landing, among emigrants who at the Quarantine inspection appeared in perfect health, or to suffer only under some light and non-infectious disorder, compelled the reception of many of such patients at Ward's Island. Some of these were sent from the city at seasons when the crowded state of the Marine Hospital or some accidental cause prevented their being sent down to Staten Island. In others, admitted for some chronic disease or as merely helpless and infirm, the disease manifested itself after admission. 1,203 cases of typhus fever thus came under the hospital treatment at Ward's Island.

Asiatic cholera also made its appearance on the Island during the summer. Its attacks were chiefly confined to persons feeble and broken down in constitution by previous disease, and to young children. Prompt measures were taken to arrest the spreading of the infection by opening two separate wards in insulated buildings, with all the necessary arrangements for effective treatment and entire separation. After a few weeks the disease disappeared as unaccountably as it had appeared, but not until it had attacked 132 patients, of whom 71 died.

Taking the hospital department proper, its statistics for 1852 present the following results :

Cared for in the hospital during the year............	10,966
Of whom there died................................	1,201
Discharged, cured or relieved........................	8,942
Remaining at the end of the year...................	823

(For particulars of diseases and mortality see Table C.)

Taking the ratio of mortality on the principle of the last year's report, and as is common in hospital statistics, upon all the cases under treatment in the hospital, this gives the ratio of about $10\frac{9}{10}$ per cent., being about a half per cent. less than during 1851. Taking the ratio of deaths upon the Island on all the cases treated, 18,287, the proportion is $8\frac{5}{12}$ per cent. The deaths in the hospital include all those from typhus fever and other diseases complicated with it, and those from cholera, and no deduction is made of those who died soon after their arrival. As usual, in this establishment, a very large number were extremely prostrated when received, having suffered from exposure, privation, and during the winter, or in long and tempestuous sea voyages. Many of the deaths were of patients who entered in a hopeless state from incurable disease. Thus phthisis was the cause of death in 211 cases. The surgical cures comprised many of injuries and fractures, and many of an acute character. A large number of capital and difficult operations were performed, and with gratifying success.

The beds in the hospital changed occupants, on an average, every forty days ; and the average time spent in the hospital by patients who died, was $33\frac{4}{5}$ days.

Various accidents have combined to delay both the commencement and the completion of the brick hospital edifices before mentioned, and the patients were received during the year in the buildings described in the last year's report. These, though roomy, and, in most respects, comfortable, yet, having been erected with limited means and often in haste, from time to time, as urgent need of more hospital accommodation arose, are not such as are desirable for several classes of patients. The new buildings now in progress will, it is trusted, supply all such deficiencies.

There remains one class of patients, now becoming very considerable in number, for whom this Commission has no suitable establishment under its own immediate control. These are the insane. The proportion of persons thus afflicted, is large amongst recent emigrants, from various causes, amongst which may be mentioned the change of circumstances, of country and climate, separation from friends, high excitement, and sometimes disappointment.

Those of them thus afflicted, who come under the charge of the Commissioners, are provided for at a stated price paid from the Commutation Fund at the City Asylum on Blackwell's Island. The whole number thus supported by this Commission is 353. Some others are scattered about the counties temporarily. Did the pecuniary means of the Commissioners authorize a sufficient outlay for this object, an additional hospital or asylum building on Ward's Island, detached and distant from the other edifices, would be attended with many advantages, and probably some economy.

Financial Concerns, County Bills, &c.

The aggregate receipts of the Commissioners of Emigration from all sources, during the year 1852, amounted to............	$572,529 59
The total expenditure of the year was.................... ...	569,516 74
Leaving a balance in bank of.................	$2,812 85

During the year a mortgage of $80,000 to the New York Life and Trust Company on the lands held by the Commissioners was paid off, and another of $150,000 was authorized, according to law, by the Governor and State officers. The loan was obtained from the Mutual Life Insurance Company, and $130,000 thereof was received; the remaining $20,000 having been reserved to meet the probable contingencies of the winter, has not yet been taken. $30,000 of the first named loan having been received (as well as paid off) during the last year, the whole amount of additional debt on loan or mortgage, included in the above aggregate of receipts, was $80,000.

There was paid during the year for reimbursement to the several counties for their expenses in the support of emigrants chargeable to this Commission, $64,763 90.

To the Governors of the New York Alms-house for the care of insane and a part of the small-pox patients, during a part of the year, $10,912 97.

To other hospitals and institutions, as the Blind Asylum, Hospitals at New York, Buffalo, &c., $12,755 08.

(For particulars of above claims, see Table E.)

The county bills were generally paid up to July, and some small sums to a later period, leaving the county charges at the end of the year nearly six months in arrear. The New York Alms-house had been paid only to May. For some years the short receipts and heavy expenses of the winter have caused a regular increase of indebtedness to the counties during that period, which the larger receipts and lighter expenses of the summer always enabled the Commissioners to pay off, so as to leave but two or three months' charges from the counties unsettled at the end of the year. In the last year the expenses of the long winter, from the causes above stated in this report, went so far beyond the current expenses that the Commissioners were obliged, reluctantly, to postpone the claims of the counties, in great part, until summer. The excess of summer receipts was not sufficient to reduce these bills with the ordinary rapidity, though the sum of $64,700 was thus applied. The chief increase of expense was in the Marine Hospital, where greatly increased numbers, with increased severity of disease and prolonged continuance in the hospital, and with a rise of prices in many articles of consumption, almost doubled the expenses of the year preceding. These were expenditures in which the whole State was interested. The expenses in the temporary establishments in the city were also doubled for more than five times the former number of applicants:

The debt to the counties amounted to, on Jan. 1st, 1853........	$55,104 94
There was due to the Governors of the New York Alms-House..	19,200 68
The aggregate debt Dec. 31st, 1852, was, therefore, including the loan on bond and mortgage of.........................	130,000 00
	$204,305 62

This will probably be increased under the same heads by April to the sum of $225,000, including therein a payment of $14,000 for the lands awarded on Ward's Island, which will add as much to the value of the real estate held by the Commissioners.

This debt, though immediately contracted during the last year, is, in fact, the gradual accumulation of the five preceding years since the beginning of the operations of this Commission, May 5th, 1847, including a period of above a year in 1848 and 1849, when the current income was nearly cut off by the constitutional defect (as it was decided by the United States Supreme Court) of the original law. This deficiency was inadequately supplied by the grant of $60,000 from the State treasury.

During this period the Commissioners have expended on the purchase of lands, the erection of buildings, wharves, water supply and other permanent objects, about $300,000.

For hospital purposes this property is probably now worth little less than its actual cost, the rise of the real estate in a considerable degree compensating for the wear and tear of buildings, &c.

During the same period one million seven hundred thousand emigrants have arrived at this port, and become entitled to relief from this Commission when needed, and probably more than twelve hundred thousand of these persons are still living. Those of them who are diseased and destitute, are entitled to relief from the commutation fund. Thus for nearly six years the cities and counties of the State have been relieved from the burden of supporting the large proportion of the poor and helpless amongst this multitude, whilst the whole amount of debt on that account, at the close of the period, is less than the amount expended on hospital accommodation for future use, and not greatly exceeding what might be realized from the sale of the real estate acquired by the Commission.

Under this view of the history and present condition of their pecuniary affairs, the Commissioners see no cause for regret or apology for the financial administration of the present members or those of their respected former predecessors or associates. It leads, however, to the conclusion, that had the lands and buildings since purchased or erected, been originally supplied, or the means of such supply then furnished, the current income would have sufficed for the support of the Quarantine and Ward's Island establishments, and the regular reimbursement of the counties in full, and without delay. On the other hand, it is evident that at present, without some additional income, the actual debt must continue to augment each year, slowly, it may be hoped, but inevitably. Under this state of things the Commissioners have come to the conclusion, which several of them, and of their former colleagues, have for some time entertained, that it is expedient that an addition be made to the present rate of commutation, not exceeding fifty cents a head.

A suggestion has been made by a committee of experienced county officers of the poor, that the receipts from this additional sum should be reserved as a separate fund until the end of each year, to be applied until then to the reimbursement of the current bills of the counties for the support of emigrant poor; the surplus to pass over each year to the general purposes of the Commission.

No objection is perceived to this provision, and it will effectually relieve the Commissioners from much unpleasant, though unavoidable delay, in settling the accounts of the county officers. They therefore respectfully recommend such an addition to the rate of commutation, subject to the limitation of the special application of the funds thus reserved to the purposes and in the manner above stated.

For statements of receipts and expenditures of Commutation Fund for the year 1852, see Table No. VIII.

General Management of the Business of the Commission.

The executive business of the Commission has been heretofore performed by the Secretary, acting, also, as general agent, and much of it by the Commissioners personally. During the last year, an important alteration has been made in these arrangements. The accumulation of business became so great, that it could be but imperfectly performed by a single salaried officer, combining the duties of an in-door secretary, at the head of an office, with those of general superintendence, requiring frequent absence on visits to Staten Island, Ward's Island, or more distant places. Much of the executive business was thus thrown upon the Commissioners, either in committees or individually. So far as such business related to the general inspection and regulation of their concerns, and the management of their financial concerns, the Commissioners considered this an appropriate and useful duty. But the labor of managing and examining many details was not only daily becoming more oppressive, but required a promptness and regularity of action, which could only be expected from a single officer devoting his whole time to these objects. It was therefore determined to appoint a salaried officer, who should have the superintendence of all the daily concerns and business of the Commission, should attend at all meetings of the Board, and take charge of all matters referred to him, as well as act as the chief executive officer in all matters which might arise, not requiring the decision of the Board. The title of vice-president was assigned to him, to mark his office as having the authority of the president, during the recess of the Board.

The committees of the Board continue to exercise their former duties of inspection, direction, and regulation. The office of secretary was continued as a separate station, for corresponding, keeping minutes, and for a large range of office duties, especially with owners, consignees, and masters of vessels, fully sufficient to occupy his whole time.

James L. Morris was appointed to the office of vice-president on the 1st May, which he filled until 9th December, 1852, when he resigned the station in consequence of his election to another important place in a private corporation. During this time he discharged the duties assigned to him with great fidelity, ability, and energy, and satisfied the Commissioners of the value of such an officer, when competent to the various duties of the place.

Capt. Eleazer Crabtree, long connected with the navigation and the foreign commerce of this port, was elected as his successor, 15th December, 1852, and is now in the discharge of the duties of the office.

Mr. William A. Bayley having resigned the office of secretary of the Board, Bernard Casserly, who had been in the employment of the Commission from its origin, was elected secretary, July 7th, 1852.

During the past year, Robert B. Minturn has been compelled by ill health to resign his seat in the Board, of which he had been a member since its organization in May, 1847. His benevolent zeal, energy, and untiring devotion to its duties, at a great personal sacrifice of his time and other interests, and often at personal hazard, cause his resignation to be deeply regretted by his associates.

Elias Hicks, jr., was also compelled by ill health to resign in November, 1852. This was shortly afterwards followed by his death. Mr. Hicks had taken great interest in the concerns of the Commission, and rendered all the services which the state of his health would permit. His loss is deeply felt by his associates in this Board, as well as by the large community in which he was honorably known.

All of which is respectfully submitted.

G. C. VERPLANCK,
CYRUS CURTISS,
C. BARSTOW,
A. C. KINGSLAND,
CONKLIN BRUSH,
GEORGE W. BLUNT,
C. H. MARSHALL,
JOHN C. ZIMMERMANN, SEN.,
JAMES KELLY,
GREGORY DILLON.

NEW YORK, *February* 7, 1853.

Seventh Annual Report

FOR THE YEAR 1853.

To the Legislature of the State of New York:

The year which has just closed has happily not been marked by those incidents of severe disease and extreme destitution and distress, prevailing extensively amongst recently arrived emigrants at this port, such as occurred in the winter of 1852, and in several other preceding years since the organization of this Commission. Nor was the demand for temporary assistance from healthy persons not yet able to obtain employment and support for themselves, at all approaching that which has been shown in several former reports. The number of persons affected with contagious or infectious diseases, and landed at the Marine Hospital, or sent there from the city, was also much less than in either of the two preceding years.

On the other hand, the aggregate number of the diseased, infirm, and helpless received at the Hospital and Refuge on Ward's Island; and of those otherwise relieved or assisted at the charge of the funds of this Commission, has increased since last year from the number of infirm and destitute persons who had landed here in former years, added to the proportion of the same class who arrived during the year 1853.

The whole number of aliens who arrived at the port of New York, and for whom commutation money was received, during the past year, was 284,945, being 16,047 less than in 1852, and 4,656 less than in 1851, but exceeding the emigration of any other preceding year. The emigration from Germany still goes on increasing, being 1,013 more than in 1852, and doubling the average of the preceding years. That from Ireland has decreased, being 5,447 less than in 1852, and 50,566 less than in 1851.

The statistics of the emigration from abroad to this port, and of the relief and assistance afforded to aliens under the operation of this Commission, present the following results:

Number of vessels employed in conveying citizens and alien passengers, was	1,618	
" do. conveying citizens only	481	
Total passenger vessels	——	2,099

Number of passengers landed, 335,259. Of these 50,314 were citizens, and 284,945 aliens; of the latter, 119,644 were natives of Germany, 113,164 of Ireland, and 52,137 of other countries. (See Table A.)

Number in Marine Hospital, Jan. 1st, 1853	318	
" admitted during the year	4,478	
Total number of patients treated	——	4,796
Being 4,091 less than in the year 1852.		
Number in Emigrant Refuge and Hospital, Ward's Island, Jan. 1st, 1853	2,201	
" born there during the year	644	
" admitted	11,517	
Total number cared for and treated	——	14,365
Number of sick sent from Park Office to New York Hospital (including 14 remaining there Dec. 31st, 1852)	212	
" of sick sent from do. to St. Vincent's Hospital (including 42 remaining there Dec. 31st, 1852)	138	
Total cases from Park Office	——	350
Number of lunatic emigrants in City Asylum, Jan. 1st, 1853	117	
" admitted during the year	185	
Total lunatics	——	302
Of which there left the Asylum, viz.:		
Number discharged cured	103	
" " improved	17	
" died	22	
Total discharges	142	
Number of lunatic emigrants in City Asylum on 1st Jan., 1854, chargeable to the Commission	160	

Number temporarily relieved in this city	20,197
" supplied temporarily with board and lodging in the city	24,317
" forwarded to various places inland	2,991
" sent back to Europe at own request	271
" of out-door poor in the city buried at the expense of the Commission	500
" of persons supplied with situations at the Intelligence Office in Canal street	14,334
" relieved or forwarded in or from the several counties of the State, by or at the expense of this Commission.	9,351
Grand total of persons relieved, assisted, and provided for, &c., by this Commission in the State of New York	91,774
Number of days spent in Marine Hospital	138,123
" in Hospital and Refuge, Ward's Island	920,626
" of letters written to friends of recently arrived emigrants	1,668
Amount of moneys received at the Office in reply thereto	$5,876 17
Amount of moneys received at the office of the Irish Emigrant Society from friends of recently arrived emigrants, and applied to the forwarding of emigrants chargeable to the Commission	$17,496 78

These last sums were applied to the use of such emigrants in forwarding or shipping them to the place of their destination through the agents of this Commission.

No part of the arrangements of this Commission has been more gratifying in the results, than the means provided for the last five years for giving facilities to emigrants to take care of themselves, by procuring for them places and employment in the city and country, by writing and receiving letters for the uneducated, providing the means of conveyance to distant places where they had friends or prospects of support, and in other ways advising and assisting the newly arrived strangers.

The bestowing of out-door and temporary relief has always been found a subject of extreme difficulty, requiring the greatest caution and economy in its exercise, as it is open to constant abuse from imposition, or, even in cases where no fraud is practised, is subject to the danger of fostering habits of reliance upon other means than industry or economy for support. Yet, in severely inclement seasons, when the ordinary demands for labor are cut off, and intercourse with the interior more or less impeded, cases of temporary destitution occur which neither humanity nor justice can allow to be refused assistance. Such, when in urgent need, have been aided with small allowances of money, food or fuel ; or in case of sickness, which it was not necessary to remove to a hospital, such persons were visited and prescribed for at home by the physician employed for the examination at the office of applicants for hospital relief. The whole number of families thus assisted during the year was 3,123 ; the most of them, however, to very small amounts. In special cases of distress, ampler aid was given ; persons have been sent to the Deaf and Dumb Institution, and to that for the Blind. Arrangements made in former years, were continued with the New-York Hospital, for the temporary reception of cases occurring in the night, and for the care of persons chargeable to the Commission, suffering from such accidents or sudden disease, as would prevent their removal to the Ward's Island Hospital without injurious consequences.

The experience of 1853, notwithstanding the increased numbers received in the Hospital and Refuge, still confirms the opinion expressed by the Commissioners in former reports, that, making the largest probable deduction for mortality and for transit to other States and territories, each successive year appears to place a larger proportion of emigrants above dependence on public aid. Large as the whole number is of those who, during 1853, were relieved or aided at the establishments of the Commission, or at its charge in the counties, the proportion to the whole number of survivors of the last five years' emigration, is much less than it was to those entitled to similar aid in the former years of the Commission ; whilst, as in the preceding year, far the largest part of those thus relieved were of the emigration of 1852 and 1853, and comparatively few of those who arrived previously.

No necessity has occurred during the last year for providing special and spacious places of reception for the temporarily destitute, as was required in 1851 and in the winter of 1852. This has somewhat contributed to increase the inmates of the Refuge, at Ward's Island, but not in the same proportion of number or of cost.

The Commissioners are happy not to have to report, as in several former years, the loss of any of their officers from contagion or infection contracted in the exercise of their duties, though some have been severely and dangerously attacked, but have recovered.

They have, with great regret, to record the loss of M. O'K. Reedy, M.D., who died from pulmonary or bronchial disease, possibly aggravated or hastened by the nature of his duties amongst the emigrant poor. Dr. Reedy had been in the service of this Commission since 1851, in different situations, and was, during the last two years, the examining physician, in the city, of patients applying to be sent to the hospitals of the Commission. He was also extensively employed in visiting and prescribing for the sick emigrants in their several places of residence about the city whom it was not advisable to remove. Dr. Reedy was a physician of high education, of great skill and experience, and of exemplary diligence and attention to his duties among the poor, where the results of his practice were eminently successful.

During his last illness, for three months, his place was supplied by Dr. Cleaveland, who discharged these laborious duties with great ability and diligence, and to the entire satisfaction of the Commissioners. Dr. Cleaveland declined being a candidate for the place made vacant by Dr. Reedy's death.

Dr. J. W. Sterling, formerly chief physician of the Marine Hospital, was appointed to succeed Dr. Reedy, and has been, since December, 1853, in the discharge of these duties.

Captain Eleazer Crabtree, who was elected Vice-President of the Board, on the 15th December, 1852, has continued to discharge, diligently and satisfactorily, the duties of chief executive officer of the Board during the past year.

The Marine Hospital and Quarantine at Staten Island.

The number of patients under treatment at the Marine Hospital, whether landed from shipboard or sent from the city, as affected with contagious or infectious diseases (to which the legislation of 1849 has specially devoted this hospital), was

4,796 during the last year. This number is little more than half that received in 1852 (8,887), and considerably below the average since 1849. It was not until the latter part of the year that cholera, to any extent, manifested itself in the arrivals from Europe, nor did the disease ever spread itself in the hospitals among patients, attendants, and physicians in the fearful manner which it was the painful duty of the Commissioners to record in former years.

The following summary of the monthly reports of the Marine Hospital, shows the aggregate results of its operations for the year. (For particulars see Table B, and accompanying reports.)

Number remaining Jan. 1st, 1853	318	
" received during this year	4,478	
Total treated		4,796
Of whom were discharged	3,741	
" died	731	
		4,472
Remaining Jan. 1st, 1854		324

The Marine Hospital was under the charge of Dr. J. W. Sterling, as chief physician, appointed by the Commissioners of Emigration under the law then in force, from the first January, 1852, to 15th July, 1853. The Act of April 13th, 1853, having placed the establishment under the charge of a chief physician appointed by the Governor and Senate, Dr. Alex. F. Vaché was appointed to that office, and entered upon its duties on the 15th July, 1853.

The Act of April, 1854, having vested the nomination of the assistant physicians of the Marine Hospital in the chief physician, subject to the approval of the Commissioners, who are also empowered to fix the rate of compensation, Drs. Darling and Prendergast were nominated by Dr. Vaché, and confirmed by the Board. Their salaries were fixed at $1,300 for the first assistant, and $1,200 per annum for each of the others. In one instance, the Commissioners withheld their assent to a nomination made by the chief physician. The gentleman nominated was, in the judgment of the Commissioners, every way qualified for the station, as he had formerly shown in the same service. Their assent was withheld on the sole ground that the large proportion of German emigrants constantly received at the Marine Hospital, demanded that at least one of the physicians should be conversant with their language and habits. This has been since provided for, by the nomination of Dr. Theodore Walser, who was approved by the Board.

The recent law having directed that the chief physician should also discharge the duties of Superintendent without additional compensation, Dr. Vaché entered upon that office, and has continued to exercise the general superintendence and authority over the establishment at Quarantine, and the persons there employed.

For the purpose, however, of discharging various duties under the direction of the Commissioners, and of attending to many details which might interfere with the more important avocations of the chief physician, the office of warden was created. He is directed to act under the general direction and orders of the Superintendent, to assist him, and to attend generally to economical and police arrangements and discipline, and the erection, repairs, and improvements of buildings, wharves, and grounds. Captain Thomas B. Vermilye, who had discharged similar duties under the former organization, was appointed to fill this place.

Whilst the Commissioners cheerfully acknowledge the professional skill and experience of Dr. Vaché, and his general talent, they have not changed the opinion, expressed by them last year, and in former years to the Legislature, that the Marine Hospital would always be best administered by vesting the appointment of the chief physician and his assistants in this Commission, and not making him or them independent of this Board.

Sundry repairs and improvements of the buildings, wharves and grounds held and used by this Commission at the Quarantine, have been made during the present year, at a cost of $1,971 66. Other improvements, and especially the carrying out a system of sewerage through the grounds, with the introduction of a copious supply of water sufficient to clear out the sewers, and carry off all the deleterious substances which accumulate in such establishments, have been under consideration. A survey and plan for this purpose were prepared under the direction of the late Vice-President, Mr. Morris ; but the disposable funds of the Commission above the necessary current expenses, have all been required for the payment of former arrearages.

During the last months of the year 1853, several vessels filled with emigrant passengers have arrived, on which Asiatic cholera unexpectedly broke out during the voyage. This occurred in different degrees, but in some cases to an alarming and fatal extent. The subject has properly attracted the attention of the Congress of the United States, as well as of your own legislative bodies. The remedy, so far as the causes can be traced to any state of things on shipboard, such as defective ventilation, bad or insufficient food, or too large a number of passengers crowded together, can only be reached by the legislation of Congress, in the exercise of their constitutional jurisdiction over commerce and navigation. The Commissioners have taken measures to collect and lay before the committees of Congress on this subject, all the information which is accessible to them. The subject of the generation or manifestation of this terrible disease on shipboard deserves, and will doubtless receive, extensive and deliberate investigation.

The health officer under the direction of the Board of Health of this city has, in such cases of vessels arriving after losing part of their passengers or crew by cholera, or other infections breaking out at sea, ordered the landing and detaining of all the passengers at Quarantine, though apparently in good health, for the purpose of cleansing them and their baggage, and cleaning and purifying the vessels themselves, which are then permitted to proceed to the city.

The effect has been beneficial, in preserving the city from the spread of infection, which has reached it in a very few instances only, and in no case has been communicated beyond the persons who brought it with them. But the passengers have been left to be provided for at the expense of the funds of this Commission, during their temporary detention at Quarantine. There does not appear to be any legal authority for the use of the Commutation Fund for the general Quarantine precautionary purposes, or for the receiving and supporting at its charge, persons not sent to the Marine Hospital as actually affected with an infectious or contagious disorder ; nor indeed would that fund, even with its present increase, be adequate for such objects, should unhappily the Asiatic cholera, or any other pestilence, become extensively epidemic abroad during the whole year.

The " Act relating to the public health," Sect. 22, provides that " all passengers under Quarantine, who shall be unable to maintain themselves, shall be provided for by the master of the vessel in which they shall have arrived, and if the master shall omit to provide for them, they shall be maintained on shore at the expense of such vessel, and such vessel shall not be permitted to leave Quarantine, until such expense shall have been repaid." The power of thus enforcing payment is confined to the health officer, and should he refuse or neglect to do so (as has already occurred), the Commissioners must either assume the responsibility of the refusing to receive and feed such persons,—a measure hard, and it may be inhuman and dangerous to the public health,—or they must apply the means in their hands to the Quarantine purposes, for which the law does not design them. They have thus far, up to the 1st of January 1854, received and fed for an average of 48 hours each, over 17,000 persons, at a cost of about $8,000, with an addition of expenditure of the same sort, still occurring during the present month of January. For the re-imbursement of these charges (if indeed it can be obtained at all), they must look to the equity of the Board of Health, or to the responsibility of the health officer, or of ship-owners ; all of them doubtful and unpleasant alternatives.

The whole matter is respectfully submitted to the Legislature, in the hope that such legislative direction may be given, as to leave no difficulty in enforcing the intention of the law, or otherwise providing for such expenditures, whenever they may become necessary.

Emigrants' Refuge, and Hospital on Ward's Island.

It was incorrectly stated in a former report, that the Commissioners also own all the water rights adjoining their property along the shore. The water rights for one hundred and fifty feet around the Island, were originally granted by the Commissioners of the Land-Office to four joint proprietors of the island, and the present ownership of this Commission is limited to the proportion held by the respective proprietors, from whom they purchased their upland, and who re-leased all their several rights in the adjoining water rights, being generally one undivided fourth. They also still hold under lease a tract of about eleven acres, which lies in the centre of their property, and on which is their largest building (originally a factory building), and their only wharf. An arrangement, long pending, and delayed by accidental causes only, has been made with the owner, on the most liberal terms on his part ; he to re-lease in fee the lands now leased to the Commission, and to receive in exchange about an equal quantity of their unimproved lands, at the extremity of their possessions, together with an allowance for the building as it originally was, to be valued by two of the former Commissioners. Some small inequalities as to water right and extent were submitted to the decision of the present President of the Board. This transaction requiring by law the assent of the Governor, Attorney-General and Comptroller, its final completion has been delayed by accident, the assent not having been signed before the close of 1853.

The four additional hospital buildings, each containing one large ward, mentioned in the last year's report, as commenced during the year 1852, were completed in the spring of the present year, and were immediately occupied. They are of brick, of a single story, above a high basement, being 150 feet in length by 26 in breadth, placed parallel to each other, but entirely separate. This plan provides most effectually for ample ventilation, and against the danger of fire ; but is still more valuable in preventing the generation of erysipelas, which is the constant scourge of large and crowded surgical wards, as well as the spreading of the contagion of cholera, or any other pestilential disease, to the accidental introduction of which this hospital is peculiarly liable whenever any pestilential epidemic prevails either here or abroad. Such an arrangement of buildings, though simple and unpretending, is probably the best principle of construction of hospitals where economy of ground space is not an object. Some of the best hospitals of modern construction are understood to have been built on this plan, a fact of which the Commissioners were not aware when they adopted it. The experience of their physicians and surgeons has already confirmed the expectations formed of the beneficial results likely to result from these improved hospital accommodations. Large classes of patients, when removed to these wards from the smaller and imperfectly ventilated buildings first erected, were found to recover in little more than half the time which such cases had before required, and there was a great diminution of the quantity of medicine needed to procure the desired effects.

During the summer two additional brick buildings were erected in a different location, and differing only in plan by having two stories. They are 150 feet long by 26 wide, and were completed at a cost of $10,301. They are occupied as a lying-in hospital, and their benefits are already seen in the diminution of puerperal fever, as appears in the present year's reports.

A spacious and substantial dead-house, built of stone, and fitted up for necessary *post-mortem* examinations, but secure against any illegal removal of bodies, has been erected, chiefly by the labor of the inmates of the Refuge.

The next and most desirable addition to be provided is that of a proper and permanent building for an operating-room for surgical cases, such operations now being compelled to be made in too near a vicinity to other patients, though out of their sight.

The Refuge department proper receives, as heretofore, the helpless and chronically infirm, pregnant women waiting childbirth, and others not requiring hospital treatment. But the whole establishment on the island is, to a great extent, one vast hospital, and its inmates are constantly passing from one of the departments to the other; those of the Refuge on access of disease to the Hospital proper, and those in the Hospital often, on recovery, to the Refuge. Thus the aggregate of admissions to each would considerably exceed the total number of inmates for the year in the two.

The following summary gives the aggregate results of the whole Ward's Island establishment for the year, from January 1st, to 31st December, 1853 :

Number of inmates in institution on Jan. 1st, 1853..........	2,204	
" admitted during the year........................	11,517	
" of births do.	644	
Total number cared for......................		14,365
Number discharged during the year.......................	10,493	
" of deaths during the year, in Refuge and Hospital....	1,108	
		11,601
" remaining on Dec. 31st, 1853....................		2,764
Number of days spent in Hospital.........................409,928		
" " " Refuge.........................510,698		
Total number of days spent in both...........		920,626
Number of small-pox cases sent to Marine Hospital.........	22	
" " " " Blackwell's Island.......	3	
		25

The Hospital proper has increased in the number of its admissions, over the last year. On the last day of 1853, it had 1,224 patients against 823 of the corresponding period in 1852.

The statistics of the Hospital department present the following results, which it may be satisfactory to compare with those of the two preceding years, as showing the ordinary operations and constant extent of the establishment :

	1851.	1852.	1853.
Cared for in the Hospital during the year.......	12,273	10,976	12,261
Of these there died...........................	1,324	1,201	822
Discharged, cured or relieved..................	9,793	8,942	10,215
Remaining at the end of the year..............	1,166	823	1,214
Born in the Hospital in the several years........	492	529	644

Thus it will be seen that, though temporary causes, such as prevailing epidemic disorders, the severity of seasons, the special condition of emigrants when landed, or their state on embarkation, cause considerable fluctuations in the numbers and rate of mortality of patients, still the general average of patients remains very large, being about 12,000 in each year, which is rather likely to increase than to diminish; so that the hospital will continue to be, as it has already become, the largest sanitary establishment in our country, and outnumbered by very few in the civilized world.

The year was exempt from any visitation of cholera at this Hospital, but the admissions and deaths were swelled by a number of the emigrant laborers who had been employed on the Panama Railroad, and returned affected with fevers, some of a very malignant character. Typhus fever prevailed at one period. In the autumn there was much of dysentery and diarrhœa, proving fatal in many cases of broken-down constitutions and feeble infants. Pulmonary consumption was the cause of death in no less than 253 cases out of 474 admissions.

The percentage of mortality on this whole number was 4½ per cent.

The surgical practice (chiefly in the new hospitals) has been peculiarly successful. By a report made up for the year ending 1st September, 1853 (see the details in the New York Medical Gazette for November, 1853), it appears that the percentage of deaths of cases treated (4,168), including incurable and patients operated upon, was *two* per cent., which is somewhat less than the proportion of mortality in the city, including sick and well.

Other details of the hospital administration will be found in the tables of diseases and medical report in Table C.

The system of medical and surgical visitations and practice, set forth in former reports for 1851 and 1852, has been continued. Dr. Williams, who has served in this department for the last three years, with acknowledged skill and ability, as President of the Medical Board, with the special charge of the obstetric wards, resigned on the 2d March, 1853. He was succeeded by Dr. Cox in the same duties.

Small-pox has appeared very extensively during the year amongst newly-arrived emigrants; those who showed symptoms on landing, or in the city, were sent to the Marine Hospital immediately; or, where it appeared on Ward's Island, they were sent either to the Quarantine, or to the City Small-Pox Hospital on Blackwell's Island. The insane chargeable to the Commission are provided and paid for by the Commissioners at the Insane Asylum on Blackwell's Island. The hope of establishing an independent Insane Asylum connected with the Hospital or Refuge, at some future, but not distant period, is still entertained.

Charles Riddle, who was appointed Warden at Ward's Island in December, 1852, has continued to discharge the duties of that station with fidelity, zeal and energy. These duties involve the control and superintendence of the police, discipline and economy of the whole establishment. Much useful work has been effected under his charge, by the abler bodied inmates, in grading and draining the grounds. These improvements are still in progress ; they already contribute much to the convenience, health, cleanliness and comfort of the establishment. It is also due to Mr. Riddle to state that, by his care, articles often wasted in similar establishments, formerly neglected to a considerable extent in this, such as bones, soap-fat, ashes, &c., have been sold to the amount of $2,965 60.

Financial Concerns.

In the spring of 1853, the financial concerns of the Commission were in a situation of considerable embarrassment. The debts which had gradually accumulated during the six years' operation of the Commission, for necessary lands, buildings, Hospital and Refuge furniture, the extraordinary but unavoidabl expenditure of 1852, at the Marine Hospital (in consequence of the numbers landed infected with cholera, ship-fever, and small-pox), and the large claims for temporary relief in the city from recently landed emigrants, during the severe seasons of those years, had produced a large indebtedness, the gradual result of the excess of expenditure above income for some years. The ordinary support of the establishments requiring prompt payments, these had been met, first by the mortgage of the lands acquired by the Commission, to the amount of $150,000, and afterwards by means of the postponement of the just claims of several counties for reimbursements for their expenses for the emigrant poor, chargeable to the commutation fund. Thus, in April, 1853, the undisputed bills from the counties and others, for such objects, were more than six months in arrear, besides several unadjusted demands, due at least in part. All these amounted to about $77,461 50.

The sum of $22,775 89 was also due to several institutions and hospitals, and to the Governors of the New York Almshouse, for the care of the insane, and for interments of emigrants. On this last debt the Commissioners claimed a considerable deduction, on account of their support of the native children cf alien mothers, taken care of at Ward's Island. The other debts demanded, were entitled to prompt payment. The Commission was also indebted to the Mechanics' Bank on an overdraft of $36,070 17, which would indeed be speedily repaid by the summer receipts over expenditure, but at the hazard of further delay of other just demands. That excess, under the ordinary receipts, and former rate of commutation, would have also extinguished some of the old debt, but only by incurring new arrearages, and exposing the Commission to the augmented expenses of the approaching winter, with an empty treasury and impaired credit. These difficulties had been anticipated and set forth in the last annual report, as on former occasions, and they were effectually, and it is trusted permanently relieved by the Act of 13th April, 1853, adopting the recommendations of the Commissioners, and adding fifty cents per head to the commutation money, to be applied quarterly to the reimbursement of the several county bills for the relief of emigrant poor, leaving the remaining income free for the other uses of the Commission.

Notwithstanding a somewhat diminished summer emigration, and the late period of the legislative session at which this act was passed, so as to apply only to a little more than eight months of 1853, the debts for supplies and overdraft were promptly paid off, and three quarterly payments, all much in advance of the time allowed by law, were made to the counties and towns for the nine months ending 13th January, 1854, amounting to $122,135 16, and discharging all the bills up to the 1st November, 1853, with the exception of a few special charges reserved for further examination Of this amount the sum of $57,228 60 was for the arrearages of 1852. The debts of other institutions have also been paid off, and that to the Governors of the New York Alms-house reduced to the sums actually in question between the two Boards, and to be adjusted by suit or arbitration. The Commissioners were, therefore, at the close of last year, free from all debts, other than those arising weekly or monthly for current uses, except that on the mortgage, which is now $130,000. It is true that this large and rapid discharge left the Commission, at the beginning of the present year, with funds insufficient to meet any extraordinary expenditure which might be required during the winter period of diminished income from commuted emigrants.

But whatever temporary necessity of debt may thus occur, it is confidently trusted that the income of the year will be sufficient to meet all just and proper demands upon the commutation fund, and to make further additions and improvements to the hospitals.

It is proper here to add to this view of the financial condition of this Commission, that its disposable fund for winter expenditure has been unexpectedly reduced above $10,000, by the unavoidable necessity of making certain advances at the Marine Hospital for Quarantine purposes, which, in the opinion of this Board, are not properly chargeable upon the Commutation Fund, and should be repaid from some other quarter. This is more particularly stated under the head of the Marine Hospital.

The expenditures of the last summer also embraced the erection of substantial brick hospital wards on Ward's Island, and improvements, &c., of real estate, and wharves, the whole amounting to the large sum of $24,636, the greater part of which was for permanent and valuable additions to the property held by the Commission.

The aggregate receipts of the Commission from all sources throughout the year 1853, were........................	$594,464 77
The total payments for expenses of the current year and arrearages of the preceding, were..........................	586,859 09
Leaving a balance in the Mechanics' Bank, Jan. 1st, 1853, of..............................	$7,605 68

In both the above amounts of receipts and of expenditure is included the sum of $20,000, being a portion of $150,000 borrowed from the Mutual Life Insurance Company on mortgage of the real estate held by the Commission, which mortgage had been approved according to law by the Governor, Comptroller, and Attorney-General in 1852. Of this amount $130,000 had been received and expended in or before 1852; the remaining $20,000 was received and applied to the urgent wants of the winter of 1853, and the same amount was repaid to the company in November last, under the arrangement that should it be specially needed in the present winter, the loan should again be made up to its original amount. It has not yet been required, but may be temporarily needed for special expenditures during the winter.

The whole amount of debt at the close of 1853, was the debt on mortgage	$130,000 00
The unadjusted bills of the Governors of the New York Alms House, and some unaudited bills of the counties, chiefly received since Jan. 1st, 1854, making about	20,000 00
	$150,000 00
Balance in bank	7,605 68
Total amount of debt on Jan. 1st, 1854	$142,394 32
The amount of debt due Jan. 1st, 1853, as stated in the last annual report, was	$204,301 00
The cash balance then on hand	2,812 85
Leaving an indebtedness of	$201,488 15
To this sum may be added the sum of $50,000, which was obtained and used during 1852, by increasing the prior mortgage on real estate	50,000 00
	$251,488 15

It will be perceived that, with the aid of the increased commutation for eight months only of the year, the result of the financial condition of this Commission at the end of 1853, as compared with that at the end of 1852, shows a balance of $109,086 in favor of the year just expired, and warrants the expectation that the probable future income of the Commission will not only suffice for the prompt payment of all legitimate current expenditures here and in the counties, but will provide for durable improvements, especially in additional permanent hospital edifices, and ultimately for the liquidation of the present debt on mortgage.

For statement of receipts and expenditures of Commutation Fund, for the year 1853, see Table IX.

During the year, two of the former Commissioners retired from the Board, Caleb Barstow on the expiration of his term and the appointment of a successor, and Cyrus Curtiss by resignation in November, 1853.

Mr. Barstow's period of service was short, but he entered with much zeal and efficacy into the duties of the Commission, and rendered to it valuable services, by his advice and co-operation.

Mr. Curtiss had been since June, 1849, a member of this Commission, and had discharged for a long time with conscientious fidelity the laborious and responsible duties of chairman of the Ward's Island committee, as well as of a member of most of the other committees of the Board; his services were unremitting, judicious, and always effective, and the Commissioners deeply regret the retiring of so valuable and excellent a colleague.

All of which is respectfully submitted.

G. C. VERPLANCK,
CHARLES H. MARSHALL,
GEORGE W. BLUNT,
CALEB BARSTOW,
CYRUS CURTISS,
JOHN C. ZIMMERMANN, Sen.,
JACOB A. WESTERVELT,
JAMES KELLY,
JOHN A. KENNEDY,
EDWARD A. LAMBERT,
THOMAS DUNLAP.

New York, *February* 6, 1854.

Eighth Annual Report

FOR THE YEAR 1854.

To the Legislature of the State of New York:

The year 1854, being the eighth of the operation of this Commission, was marked by many circumstances and events highly unfavorable to the multitude of emigrants who arrived here during that period. Their number much exceeded that of any former year. The prevalence of disease in the countries they had left, and which often broke out on shipboard, or immediately after their arrival—the uncommon number of shipwrecks and accidents at sea, casting the passengers in a state of destitution upon our shores—the appearance of contagious disease in this and other cities—the failing of the customary demand for labor from the derangement of business, as well as the high price of provisions from the short crops of the year, and the unusually early and severe commencement of the present winter, all combined to throw upon this Commission a vast amount of labor, responsibility, and expenditure.

Similar circumstances in the years immediately previous to the formation of this Commission, and also in the first years of its operation, when it was unprovided with hospitals and other means of assistance, and its funds were embarrassed by refusal to pay commutation, and consequent litigation, (although the immigration at this port was then hardly half of that of the last year,) were productive of intense distress among the emigrants, and the spreading of disease and alarm in all directions, not only in this city and its neighborhood, but along all the great lines of internal communication throughout our land. It is mainly due to the effect of the present laws of the State relative to alien passengers arriving in the port of New York, that, whatever may be the imperfection of the system, or the defects or errors of its administration, yet the evils which must have otherwise existed to an incalculable extent, have been checked or alleviated; that the approach and spread of pestilential disease was long averted, and when it appeared, that ample provision was made for the largest class of sufferers without burden to the city treasury, as well for reimbursement to the counties when the duty of providing for this class of poor fell first and immediately upon them. Crowds of destitute persons, who would otherwise have swarmed as beggars in our streets, or filled our Alms-Houses, were forwarded to distant places where they found employment and support, whilst the diseased and entirely helpless were provided for and relieved without adding to the taxation of city or country.

The Commissioners have great satisfaction in laying these facts before the Legislature, not by any means as claiming the merit of them as the effect of their own services, but as proving the value and efficiency, and showing the practical operation of the wise and beneficent system, the administration of which has been confided to their trust.

This will appear from the following statistics of the amount and nature of the emigration to this port, and of the relief and assistance afforded to aliens at the city of New York, and elsewhere throughout the State, under the operation and authority and from the funds of this Commission.

The emigration to this port in 1854 was much greater than in any former year. The whole number of alien passengers who arrived here, and for whom commutation money was received during the year, was 319,223, being 34,278 more than in the year preceding, and even exceeding the emigration of 1852 (the largest on record) by 18,231. This increase was occasioned entirely by the augmented number of German emigrants being 57,342 (or about one-half) more than in 1853, and about three times the average of preceding years. The number of emigrants from Ireland continued to decrease, being, in 1854, 30,862 less than in the year preceding, and 80,954, or nearly one-half less than in the remarkable year of Irish emigration, 1851. The emigration from the other countries of Europe has also increased, but not in any large proportion, except that from Switzerland, which has risen from 4,604 in 1853, to 8,883 in 1854.

The number of patients affected with contagious or infectious diseases, and received in the Marine Hospital at Quarantine, was less than in the two preceding years ; but a larger proportion suffered under the attacks of Asiatic cholera and other severe diseases. On the other hand, the aggregate number of the diseased or helpless received at the Hospital and Refuge at Ward's Island still increased, as it had for some years past, being about one-tenth more in 1854 than in 1853. This arose partly from the larger emigration of the year, and in part from the number of infirm or destitute persons who had become entitled to the benefits of the Commutation Fund during the last five years.

Number of vessels employed in conveying citizens and alien passengers, was	1,566	
" conveying citizens only	525	
Total passenger vessels	——	2,091

Number of passengers landed, 367,354. Of these, 48,131 were citizens, and 319,223 aliens ; of the latter, 176,986 were natives of Germany, 82,302 of Ireland, 30,578 of England, and 29,357 of other countries. (See Table A.)

Number in Marine Hospital, Jan. 1st, 1854	324	
" admitted during the year	4,438	
Total number of patients treated at M. Hospital	——	4,762
Number in Emigrant Refuge and Hospital Ward's Island, Jan. 1st, 1854	2,762	
" born during the year	701	
" admitted	12,487	
Total number cared for and treated	——	15,950
Number of sick sent from Office to the New York Hospital	128	
" of do. sent from Office to St. Vincent's Hospital	1	
Total cases sent from Park Office	——	129
Number of lunatic emigrants supported in City Asylum, Jan. 1st, 1854	160	
" admitted during the year	100	
Total lunatics	——	260

Of which there left the Asylum, viz.:		
Number discharged	101	
" died	47	
Total discharges	148	
Number of lunatic emigrants in City Asylum on 1st January, 1855, chargeable to the Commission	117	
" persons temporarily relieved in this city by food, money or lodgings		17,516
" forwarded to various places inland, at expense of Commission		4,164
" supplied temporarily with board and lodging in the city		51,569
" of out-door poor in the city buried at the expense of the Commission		1,632
" sent back to Europe, at the charge of the Commission, in whole or in part		444
" of males supplied with situations at the Intelligence Office in Canal street	4,968	
" of females	8,996	
		13,964
" relieved or forwarded in or from the several counties of the State by or at the expense of this Commission		10,504
Grand total of persons relieved or assisted by this Commission in the State of New York		120,894

Number of days spent in Marine Hospital	88,239
" " " Hospital and Refuge, Ward's Island	1,171,398

Number of letters written to friends of lately arrived emigrants	1,512
Amount of money received at the Office in reply thereto	$3,601 24
" " received at the office of the Irish Emigrant Society from friends of recently arrived emigrants, and applied to the forwarding of emigrants chargeable to the Commission	$12,530 90
Reported from the office of the German Society as applied solely to the relief of emigrants, who would have been otherwise chargeable to the Commission	$18,917 70

The sick reported as received at the New York Hospital were so received by a contract with that corporation, now continued for several years, by which persons chargeable to this Commission, suffering from such sudden casualties as would not permit removal to the Emigrant Hospitals out of town, were there received at the charge of this Commission. Cases occurring at night, in the city, of such persons are also received until they can be conveniently removed. The Institution for the Blind has received and instructed persons at the charge of the Commissioners.

The number of persons for whom places of permanent employment in city and country were procured, was 370 less than during the past year ; this was caused by the vexatious interruption of the duties of the office, by an injunction which closed it for the first two weeks in May, the most important period in the year for this purpose. The injunction was then dissolved. Had the operation of this part of the establishment not been thus suspended, the number so provided for would probably have exceeded that of last year, by more than a thousand.

The moneys received from friends of the emigrants for their use, were applied to the expenses of sending them from this city to the several places of their ultimate destination, under the protection of the agents of this Commission here and in Albany, and along the lines of internal communication. When the several sums were inadequate to the whole expense, the remainder was advanced by the Commissioners, upon satisfactory proof that the party was otherwise unable to make up the deficiency.

The experience of another year again confirms the opinion heretofore expressed in preceding reports, that no part of the arrangements of this Commission has been of more practical value than those (now in the sixth year of successful operation) for aiding emigrants to take care of themselves, by procuring labor or places of employment in city or country, by writing and receiving letters for the uneducated or those ignorant of our language, by providing those entirely destitute of the means of conveyance to distant places where they had friends, or the means of support offered to them, and in numerous other ways assisting and protecting the newly arrived stranger.

During the greater part of the year there was comparatively little demand or necessity for temporary out-door assistance in the city, but the severity with which the winter set in at an early period, when the city was filled with emigrants just landed, produced many claims of this nature during the last six weeks of the year 1854, which could not be rejected. The bestowing of such relief is open to continual abuse from imposition, and even where there is no ground to suspect intentional deception, is subject to the general objection of fostering habits of relying upon public or private charity for support, to the neglect of industry and economy. Yet in severely inclement seasons, and, in times like the present, when the ordinary demands for labor are suddenly diminished, many cases will occur which neither humanity nor justice can suffer to be left unaided, and which may be aided with more economy, and with a better effect on themselves, in other modes than by sending them to a Refuge or Alms-House. Such have been aided by small allowances of various kinds, and by temporary provision for lodging destitute emigrants for a night or two. In cases of urgent distress, larger aid has been given, and many such are visited and prescribed for at their homes by the physician of the office. The whole number of families thus assisted in 1854, was 4,574.

The winter has thus far proved very unfavorable in this respect, and the expenditure so caused has drawn heavily on the funds of the Commissioners. Since the first of January it has been found necessary to appoint special salaried visitors for the winter, to prevent imposition, and secure as efficacious and economical an application of the means of relief as possible. It is hoped and trusted that this state of things will be of no long duration.

During the year the attention of the Commissioners has been repeatedly called, through the vigilance of their officers, to the fact of cargoes of helpless and broken-down paupers having been shipped to this port by the local authorities of the cities or villages in Europe upon which they had been a charge. Occasionally too, there appeared sufficient evidence that convicts for crimes dangerous to society, had been sent out by the governments or other authorities abroad. It would be most desirable to return to their own countries all of the latter class, and most of those of the former; but this direct power is not granted by the existing laws of this State, and is, perhaps, a regulation of the intercourse with foreign nations not within the competence of State legislation. The subject has been brought before the Congress of the United States, where it is trusted that a remedy will be furnished for this great evil. But the Commissioners have not been negligent in applying the powers already given to them by the laws under which they act, in requiring the full bonds, and enforcing the penalties now provided in certain cases of this class, or of commuting them at a rate sufficient to provide for the probable expense of the support of such paupers, or on condition of returning such persons (especially if convicts) to their own country. Should no more stringent remedy be provided by Congress, it is submitted whether an enlargement of the present powers of the Commission, confided to their discretionary exercise, both as to the amount of bonds and penalties and the class of persons (especially convicts for offences other than political), might not be expedient.

In connection with the subject of the general office business of the Commission, and the legislative aid it may receive, the Commissioners respectfully call the attention of the Legislature to another point, which appears to deserve their consideration and assistance.

The public edifice in the Park, belonging to the city, and where were the apartments occupied under lease by the Commissioners, for the ordinary business of their officers, was destroyed by fire, on the 19th of January, 1854. Temporary arrangements were made for the accommodation of part of this business, and the rest was carried on, though with great inconvenience and exposure, in the basement rooms of the dilapidated buildings, which still remained comparatively capable of occupation. But it was important to provide permanent and convenient locations and buildings for these purposes, with as little delay as might be, and two suitable houses were procured under lease, in convenient situations ; one in Canal street, for the receiving applications for employment, advice or similar aid, as above stated ; the other in Franklin street, for the meetings of the Board, the offices of their vice-president and secretary, the attendance of their examining physicians, and the receiving applications for relief, or admission to the hospitals.

An alarm as to the apprehended danger of spreading contagion through the neighborhood soon arose as to both locations, and this was increased by the fear of the owners of real estate in the vicinity, that such a use would deteriorate the value of their property all around. An injunction was applied for and granted, as to both offices ; but after an injurious and unfortunate interruption of more than two weeks, this was dissolved as to the Canal street office. The other building in Franklin street continued to be used only for the meetings of the Commissioners and their financial business, until the decision of the question. Upon the complaint and answer, the Judge finding in them several issues of fact, thought these proper to be passed upon by a jury, and the points to be submitted for their finding were settled by him. Before, however, these could come to trial, the cholera made its appearance in the city, and the almost vacant Franklin street office was taken possession of by the Board of Health, as a Cholera Hospital. In the meanwhile, the business of the offices was, of necessity, carried on in the basement of the Park building, and in temporarily hired rooms elsewhere, with very great inconvenience to the emigrants and the officers and clerks of the Board, as well as much detriment to the efficiency of the establishments.

Towards the close of the year an opportunity occurred of hiring, on lease, a large unoccupied building in Anthony street, erected and lately used as a church edifice, and in a location where little or no danger could be apprehended to a neighborhood, even if the fears which had been excited as to the former locations, had been well grounded. The same building was also selected and designated, as one of their offices, by the Commissioners of Health, under whose authority the Commissioners act, in sending persons affected with contagious disease from the city to the Quarantine Hospital. The question as to the occupation of the Franklin street building, being no longer of any consequence as to that location, has not been brought to trial, though, as the principle involved in it is important to be settled, for the guidance and protection of the Commissioners hereafter, it may still be expedient to have a final judicial decision on it.

The Commissioners respectfully submit to the Legislature, whether it might not be proper to modify the general law of procedure in the nature of injunction, in cases of State officers acting in good faith and within the bounds of their official authority. Their duties may now be suspended, to the great public inconvenience, or even injury, by the authority of a single Judge, selected out of a number by interested individuals, and acting mainly or wholly upon *ex parte* and *prima facie* evidence. The final decision, as in the present case, may be protracted to a distant period. If in such cases no process of this nature could be granted unless upon due notice to the officers in question, and a hearing before a full Court of competent jurisdiction, ample protection would still be afforded to all private rights, and any delay might be obviated by giving precedence to all such motions and arguments.

If, however, in the judgment of the Legislature it should not appear advisable so to modify the general provisions of law, then it is respectfully submitted—whether it would not be proper to protect the particular public interests confided to the Commissioners, by exempting them from any such interference as to the location of their hospitals, wharves or offices, upon such location receiving the approbation of the State officers, or of some special legal tribunal or body designated by law, or of the Commissioners of Health in the city of New York, as to the Legislature may seem most advisable.

The Marine Hospital and Quarantine.

The number of patients under treatment at the Marine Hospital, whether landed from shipboard or sent from the city, as affected with contagious or infectious disease (to which the legislation of 1849 has specially devoted this hospital), was 4,762 during the last year. This number is little more than half that received in 1852 (8,887), considerably below the average since 1849, and 36 less than in 1853. But the proportion of severe and ordinarily fatal diseases was unusually large—there having been no less than 650 cases of Asiatic cholera, or nearly one-seventh of the whole number of patients under treatment during the year; many of them were beyond the reach of medical aid, when received, in consequence of the time lost between the first attack of the disease and the reaching of the hospital—either from the shipping or from the city. There were sixty-five yellow fever cases from shipboard. 168 others were landed in a dying state; thus indicating with other things a greater prevalence of disease on shipboard than has lately occurred.

The report of the Marine Hospital shows the aggregate results of its operations for the year. The details stating the nature of the diseases and other particulars, will be found in Table B.

The proportion of deaths to cases under treatment appears to be $19\frac{1}{10}$ per cent., a larger proportion than has been usual, but which is to be accounted for from the malignant character of diseases, and perhaps the prevailing influences of a generally unhealthy year.

The hospitals proper have at no time been overcrowded, and some of the wooden buildings erected by the Commissioners to receive the overflow of patients in 1851 and 1852, were seldom or but partially occupied.

The contagion did not, as in those years, reach any of the physicians or superior officers, and but few of the nurses were so attacked.

The hospital has been under the direction of Dr. Vaché, as chief physician appointed by the Governor and Senate, and two assistants, Drs. William Darling and Theodore Walser, nominated by him, and approved by the Commissioners. Dr. Vaché has also discharged the duties of Superintendent, and Capt. Vermilyea those of Warden, as stated in the last year's report.

Dr. Vaché, whilst independent by law of the Commissioners, has acted in harmony with them, and they cheerfully bear witness to this as well as to his professional skill and experience; yet various circumstances confirm them in the opinion they have expressed to the Legislature in former years, that the efficiency and economy of the Marine Hospital would be promoted by vesting the appointment of the Physician-in-chief and his assistants in the Commissioners, and not making him an independent authority.

In their last annual report, the Commissioners made a statement of certain difficulties occurring and likely to occur under the laws concerning the public health. A repetition of similar occurrences during the year 1854, induces them again to present the subject to the Legislative consideration.

During the last months of 1853, and again repeatedly in 1854, vessels filled with emigrant aliens arrived, in which Asiatic cholera had broken out during the voyage.

The health officer, under the direction of the Board of Health of this city, has in such cases of vessels arriving after losing part of their passengers or crew by cholera or other infection breaking out at sea, ordered the landing and detaining of all the passengers at Quarantine, though apparently in good health, for the purpose of cleansing them and their baggage, and cleaning and purifying the vessels themselves, which are then permitted to proceed to the city.

The effect has been beneficial in preserving the city from the spread of infection. But the passengers have been left to be provided for at the expense of the funds of this Commission, during their temporary detention at Quarantine. There does not appear to be any legal authority for the use of the Commutation Fund for thegeneral Quarantine precautionary purposes, or for the receiving and supporting at its charge, persons not sent to the Marine Hospital as *actually* affected with an infectious or contagious disorder; nor indeed would that fund, even with its present increase, be adequate for such objects, should unhappily the Asiatic cholera or any other pestilence become extensively epidemic abroad during the whole year.

The "Act relating to the public health," Sect. 22, provides that "all passengers under Quarantine, who shall be unable to maintain themselves, shall be provided for by the master of the vessel in which they shall have arrived, and if the master shall omit to provide for them, they shall be maintained on shore at the expense of such vessel, and such vessel shall not be permitted to leave Quarantine until such expense shall have been repaid." The power of thus enforcing payment is confined to the health officer, and should he refuse or neglect to do so, the Commissioners must either assume the responsibility of the refusing to receive and feed such persons, a measure hard, and it may be, inhuman and dangerous to the public health, or they must apply the means in their hands to the Quarantine purposes, for which the law does not design them.

Some of the expenses thus incurred have been voluntarily refunded by the ship-owners ; in other cases a previous stipulation has been made by the health officer as the condition of not detaining the ship, but allowing her to go to the city after landing the passengers at Quarantine. In many other cases where no reimbursement of the expenses could be obtained from the vessels, it was considered as an equitable claim against the Board of Health, and this claim is now pending before them, a favorable report having been made by a committee of the body. But the reimbursement of such expenditures seems to depend contingently upon the view taken of the subject by the Board of Health, the health officer, or the ship-owners, as the case may be, and the whole matter is again respectfully submitted to the Legislature, in the hope that such legislative direction may be given as to leave no difficulty in enforcing the intention of the law, or otherwise providing for such expenditures, whenever they may become necessary.

Emigrants' Refuge and Hospital, Ward's Island.

The whole of the land occupied by the Commissioners on Ward's Island, is now held by them in fee. The arrangement for an exchange of a part of their unimproved land at the extremity of the tract, for a release of the land held by them under lease (as heretofore reported), and authorized by law and the approbation of the State Officers, has been finally consummated. The buildings originally on the premises held under lease having been valued, the sum of $8,500, including an allowance for the supply of water, was paid, together with a grant of eleven acres of vacant land at the south end of the island, as the consideration for the release in fee of the eleven acres in the centre of the property held by the Commission, on which are erected their only wharf and the largest building, originally a factory, now used for various valuable purposes.

The exchange considered merely as a matter of property is fair and equal, whilst for all the objects and purposes of the Commission it is highly advantageous.

About two acres surrounded by the lands of the Commission having been offered them, these were also purchased for $2,188 75.

The Commissioners have proceeded on the plan laid down by them and acted upon during the last three years, of substituting as their means would admit, more spacious, substantial, and convenient brick buildings for the single story wooden structures erected in haste to meet the exigency of the first years of the Commission. They have adhered to the general principle on which their first brick hospitals were erected, as stated in the report for 1853 ; that of entirely separated buildings, not wider than is convenient for a single ward, lighted on both sides, and of various sizes, but all of considerable length ; they have varied from their original plan only in not limiting their hospital edifices to a single story. Their experience has already fully confirmed the opinion expressed by them last year, that where there is no reason for economy of ground, this plan provides more effectually than any other for constant and ample ventilation, and against the danger of fire, and the spread of infection, in case of any pestilential epidemic (as cholera), and also against the generation of erysipelas, which breaks forth unaccountably and often very fatally in crowded hospital wards.

The effect of this simple but efficacious arrangement was strikingly manifested during the last summer by the fact, that in this populous establishment, so peculiarly exposed to the ravages of cholera, from the constant arrival of persons from shipboard or infected localities, in whom this disease did not manifest itself at first, it never spread very widely over the hospital at the same time, and several of these insulated wards entirely escaped.

The buildings erected or undertaken during the year, are the following :

Two large substantial brick buildings 25 by 125 ; one of these is a two-story building and the other of three stories. The first floor of the two-story building is one large hospital ward, capable of accommodating 60 adults ; the upper part of the building is divided into three apartments, one a hospital ward, another intended for preparations of morbid anatomy and copies of such in wax-work. The third is the surgical amphitheatre. This was planned with great care, so as to afford the best light for operations, and all other conveniences which the experience of similar establishments has pointed out as conducive to the purposes in view. In this, also, divine service is performed on Sundays, both in English and in German.

In the three-story building there are three spacious and well ventilated hospital wards, large enough to accommodate sixty patients in each ward.

There are now in course of erection three more large brick buildings, commenced in 1854, which will be completed about the middle of March. The first is of three stories and basement, intended for the accommodation of the resident physicians and others. The second is of three stories, 56 feet front and 125 feet long, in which there will be three spacious well ventilated wards, large enough to accommodate sixty patients in each ward. The third is of three stories and basement, 56 front and 125 feet long, with four large and well ventilated wards, capable of accommodating sixty patients in each ward.

The cost of these buildings is estimated at $32,821, of which 17,105 22 has been paid during the year.

In addition to these structures, much useful work has been done during the year under the direction of the Superintendent in levelling the grounds, grading them in front of the main buildings down to the shore, in part filling up to low water mark near the wharf, and protecting the made land by a sea-wall. A good deal of draining has also been done to good effect. In this work, the labor of the more able-bodied inmates of the Refuge was usefully employed. The Commissioners have long had it in view to construct an Asylum for the Insane under their charge, instead of leaving them, as they are at present obliged to do, to be taken care of at their charge in the Asylum under the care of the Governors of the New York Alms-House, and in the counties, according to such means as may be there provided. With this object in view hereafter, and in order to give present employment to those more capable of such labor, they have commenced the getting out stone from a quarry of material suitable for such buildings, on their land on Ward's Island.

The erection of a proper Asylum edifice will require a larger immediate outlay than can well be spared from the present current income of any year, and must therefore be a work of time. No plan has, as yet, been prepared and decided upon.

The Refuge department proper receives, as heretofore, the helpless and chronically infirm, pregnant women waiting childbirth, and others not requiring hospital treatment. But the whole establishment on the Island is, to a great extent, one vast hospital, and its inmates pass from one of the departments to the other; those of the Refuge on access of disease to the hospital proper, and those in the hospital often, on recovery, to the Refuge. Hence the aggregate of admissions to each considerably exceeds the total number of inmates for the year in both. The discharges show the same result.

The reports showing the results, with details stating the nature of the diseases and other particulars, will be found in Table C.

The hospital proper has increased in the number of its admissions over the last year. On the last day of 1854, it had 1,349 patients against 1,224 of the corresponding period in 1853. The number of days passed by patients in the hospitals was above one-fourth more than in the year preceding, being 530,288 in 1854, against 409,928 in 1853.

The statistics of the Hospital department present the following results, which it may be satisfactory to compare with those of the three preceding years, as showing the ordinary operations and constant extent of the establishment:

	1851.	1852.	1853.	1854.
There were cared for in the Hospital during the year	12,273	10,976	12,261	15,861
Of these there died	1,324	1,201	822	1,438
Discharged, cured or relieved	9,793	8,942	10,215	13,074
Remaining at end of the year	1,166	823	1,214	1,349
Born in the Hospital in the several years	492	529	644	701

Thus it appears that, though temporary causes, such as prevailing epidemics, the severity of seasons, the special condition of emigrants when landed, or their state on embarkation, cause considerable fluctuations in the numbers and rates of mortality of patients, still the general average remains very large, being from nearly 11,000 to nearly 16,000 in each year ; so that the hospital itself has become the largest sanitary establishment in our country, and is outnumbered by few in the civilized world.

But in addition to the amount and variety of practice afforded in the Hospital department to the students of medicine and surgery, the adjoining Refuge department is filled with chronic cases, or less serious ailments, not requiring regular hospital treatment, yet demanding more or less professional assistance. During the year 13,805 such cases were there treated, thus making an aggregate of 29,667 cases of various kinds coming under examination or observation.

The consequent value of the Ward's Island establishment as a school of medical improvement, has become widely known, and the places of assistants have been eagerly sought for by young physicians from all parts of the State. The certificates of having satisfactorily performed a term of duty in that capacity, granted and signed by the Commissioners and their Medical Board, are received in our merchant and packet service, and in other employments, as among the best evidences of professional knowledge and skill which a young physician or surgeon can produce.

The emigration of the year 1854 was, under many very unfavorable circumstances (stated in the beginning of this report), and their influence, and that of the prevailing tendency to disease throughout the country, of course severely felt in the Hospital department. A much larger proportion than in the preceding year were landed from shipboard in a diseased or very debilitated state ; many of these came with phthisis already seated incurably, whilst dysentery and diarrhœa were unusually frequent, severe, and fatal. In June, Asiatic cholera appeared, and though arrested by change of diet, and thorough cleansing of the wards, reappeared repeatedly until October.

From these and other causes, both the number and the proportion of deaths was much enlarged. It is, however, worthy of remark, as showing this increase to arise from general causes, and of diseases assuming an epidemic character, and not from any thing peculiar to the Ward's Island establishment, that the proportional increase of mortality, as compared with the last year, is less than the average increase of that in the city of New York in 1854, as compared with 1853.

The percentage of mortality on the whole number of cases treated in the hospitals proper alone, was a little above 9 per cent., the increase above last year being on those diseases which were epidemic, and fatal in this and other ports, and on shipboard during this year.

The surgical practice during 1854, has been extensive and successful. The new surgical wards, by their improved comforts and ventilation, have contributed much to the more rapid progress of the curative part of the practice, and the operating room, finished and put into use during the summer, has removed many serious inconveniences heretofore experienced. The statistics of the year show 4,574 patients under treatment, among which were a number requiring the most difficult and delicate operations of surgery: 89 died, and 4,079 were cured and discharged. This proportion of deaths is about two per cent., being lower than that prevailing in the whole city of New York.

Other details of the hospital administration will be found in reports accompanying Table C.

The system of medical and surgical visitation and practice, set forth in former reports for 1851 and 1852, has been continued.

The Commissioners have to report, with great regret, the death of Dr. Wm. James Macneven, who had served as one of the visiting physicians, and a member and secretary of the Medical Board since the organization of this system. Dr. Macneven's scientific and professional acquirements were of the highest order; his attention to his special duties at Ward's Island was exemplary and unremitting, and his practice skilful and successful. He died in January 1854, of pulmonary consumption. Dr. Th. Addis Emmet, who had formerly served as an assistant physician, to the entire satisfaction of the Commissioners, was elected his successor.

Several of the officers and employees of the Commission were attacked by cholera during the summer, which in some instances was fatal. Amongst the deaths was that of one of the assistant physicians, Dr. Joseph Dennis, who had given evidence of professional ability and probable future success, and had gained the confidence of this Commission and of the Medical Board, by his estimable qualities and his devotion to his duties.

Financial Concerns of the Commission.

The former annual reports of the Commissioners present the record of a constant struggle with inadequate means and financial difficulties, from the organization of the Commission until the summer of 1853. These difficulties limited the efficiency of the system, compelled the erection of cheap and merely temporary buildings, which it is now found necessary to replace by buildings such as it would have been desirable to erect at first; and though these difficulties were surmounted, it was by contracting temporary debts, by delay in reimbursing the counties, and by large permanent loans on mortgage, as well as at the cost of much vexation and trouble to those to whom at different times was confided the administration of the Commutation Fund. In the first years of the Commission, these difficulties specially arose from the intended revenue having been reduced more than half, by the constitutional objection to the law of 1847, and consequent litigation, and afterwards from the inadequacy of the rate of commutation, not only to provide for the current expenditure of supporting the destitute aliens here, and reimbursing the counties, but also for the cost of lands and buildings which were wanted for an efficient and economical administration.

From these embarrassments the Commission was rapidly, and, it is trusted, permanently relieved by the Act of April 1853, raising the commutation to two dollars per head, and appropriating the additional fifty cents to the reimbursement of the county charges in the first instance. The immediate relief thus given, and the large reduction, in 1853, of the gradually accumulated debt of some years, were set forth in the last annual report. The necessary expenditures of 1854 were much raised by the high price of all necessary articles most entering into the consumption of the establishments at Ward's Island and the Quarantine, by many unexpected and unusual claims upon the Commission for aid, and by the increased burthen thrown upon the Hospital and Refuge ; the number of inmates being ten per cent. larger than in 1853, whilst their average sojourn in the wards was longer, the aggregate number of days there spent by the patients and infirm (as has been shown) having risen from 928,626 in 1853, to 1,171,398 in 1854. This was not counterbalanced by the small reduction in the average of the Marine Hospital.

The income of the Commissioners from commutation, penalties, compromises, &c., has nevertheless enabled them to meet all the ordinary and extraordinary claims upon them, to make their regular quarterly reimbursement to the counties in full for all bills and demands then audited and allowed (settling the county bills in full to October 1st, 1854), and also to lay out $27,973 97, in the erection of permanent hospital edifices, and the procuring a release in fee for the land and building on Ward's Island, formerly held by them at a rent under lease, with the purchase of two additional acres.

It was mentioned in last year's report, that $20,000 had been repaid on account of the principal of the loan on mortgage of $150,000, from the Mutual Life Insurance Company, under the express understanding that should the possible necessities of the winter require it, the sum would be returned, and the mortgage raised to its original amount.

The unexpected necessities of the winter, at a time when the ordinary income was nearly suspended, compelled the Commissioners reluctantly to avail themselves of this arrangement, and the $20,000 was drawn in February, 1854, and applied to the current expenditures. They were also obliged to resort to a temporary overdraft on the Mechanics' Bank, where their accounts are kept.

The latter was made good at the first return of the spring income, and in October the sum of $40,000 was paid to the Mutual Life Insurance Company in reduction of the principal of their mortgage. But in view of the possible exigencies of the approaching winter, it was deemed advisable to procure the same stipulation as in the previous case, to which the Company liberally assented.

This money has not yet been required, and probably will not be, at least to the whole amount. It is hoped that the debt on mortgage is now in a train of permanent reduction. It is due to the former Commissioners, under whom the debt was contracted, to repeat that it arose from the purchase of lands, and the erection of buildings now held and used by the Commission, in which, alone, $300,000 were expended prior to 1852.

The aggregate debt due by the Commission on 1st January, 1852, including that on mortgage and deducting cash in bank, was	$201,417 99
The balance due on 1st January, 1853, was..................	142,391 42

The year 1854 offers the following comparison, and presents a more favorable result than, under the circumstances of the year, the Commissioners had anticipated :

The amount of debt at the close of the year 1854, on bond and mortgage, was.................	$110,000 00	
Unadjusted bills of the Governors of the New York Alms-House, and unaudited bills of the counties for October, November, and December, 1854..	35,000 00	
		$145,000 00
Balance in bank, January 1st, 1855...............		61,192 46
Total amount of debt on Jan. 1st, 1855		$83,807 54

The portion of the above sum of $35,000 which consists of the amounts due the several counties other than New York for reimbursement, is in part estimated, and in part the charges of bills rendered since the last quarterly payment to the counties, as prescribed by law, made December, 1854. These charges will be duly liquidated at the next quarterly payment. The rest consists of the claim of the Governors of the New York Alms-House for the support of insane persons chargeable to the Commutation Fund. In the view of the Commission, this amount is subject to considerable deductions, and a large offset for the support of native children born of emigrant mothers, and taken care of in the Nursery department at Ward's Island, for which they have not been able to make any arrangement with the New York Alms-House department. The Commissioners have proposed and are anxious to adjust these and other differences which have arisen between the two Boards, by an arbitration or amicable suit. The nature and grounds of these differences will be found in the annual reports of this Board for 1852 and 1853, and in the report of a committee made to the Commissioners, which is herewith communicated. (See Appendix, No. 5.)

The expenditures, and the sources and several amounts of income for the year 1854, will be found in Table No. X.

During the last year the vigilance of the officers and agents of this Commission has been constantly and often effectually exerted as heretofore, for the protection of emigrants against the frauds to which they are specially exposed. The nature of these impositions has been fully set forth in former years in the reports of committees and of this Board, to be found in the legislative documents for the several years last preceding. They have not altered in character nor extent, though in many instances they were detected and punished, and the injured parties reimbursed by the aid of the law.

One of the most effectual means of protection that could be applied, is that heretofore repeatedly mentioned in the reports of the Commissioners, the exclusive possession and occupation of a wharf or pier by them, for the landing of newly-arrived emigrants. In a former year, such a pier, in an insulated situation, was procured, but its use for the purposes contemplated was instantly prevented by the process and decision of the courts, enjoining such a use as hazardous to the health and injurious to the comfort of the neighborhood. No reason appearing to the Commissioners why the same result should not take place as to any other location which they have had offered to them, they have refrained from again attempting to exercise this power, though expressly conferred upon them by statute. The subject is again respectfully recommended to the attention of the Legislature.

In the month of February, 1854, occurred the death of Gregory Dillon, President of the Irish Emigrant Society, who had, in that capacity, been an *ex officio* member of this Commission from its first organization.

Mr. Dillon was one of our oldest and most respected adopted citizens, and had for years devoted himself with zeal and energy to the welfare of emigrants from his native land. In the service of this Commission he extended the same benevolent zeal to the destitute from all nations who came under its care, and his attention to his different duties was unremitting and faithful.

He was succeeded by James Mathews, Esq., a well-known citizen, of great worth and benevolence. His services were interrupted by his death, after a short illness, in April, 1854. He was succeeded as President of the Irish Emigrant Society, and *ex officio* Commissioner of Emigration, by Andrew Carrigan, formerly one of the appointed members.

On 1st March, 1854, John C. Zimmermann, sen., retired from office as President of the German Society, and an *ex officio* Commissioner of Emigration, after two years of valuable services and wise counsels to the Commission. He was succeeded in the Board by R. A. Witthaus, the present President of the German Society.

On 21st June, 1854, George W. Blunt retired from office as a Commissioner, on the appointment of Elijah F. Purdy, by the Governor, as his successor.

All of which is respectfully submitted.

G. C. VERPLANCK,
JAMES KELLY,
ANDREW CARRIGAN,
JOHN A. KENNEDY,
R. A. WITTHAUS,
ELIJAH F. PURDY,
THOMAS DUNLAP,
EDWARD A. LAMBERT,
JACOB A. WESTERVELT.

NEW YORK, *January* 31, 1855.

The signature of CHARLES H. MARSHALL does not accompany this report, in consequence of his absence in Europe.

Ninth Annual Report

FOR THE YEAR 1855.

To the Legislature of the State of New York:

The year 1855, being the ninth of the operation of this Commission, is remarkable in its history for the sudden and very great falling off of the number of alien emigrants arriving at the port of New York. It has also been remarkable, during the latter part of the year, for a nearly corresponding diminution of the number of the diseased and destitute claiming and receiving relief from the funds of the Commission.

The number of alien emigrants who landed at the port of New York in 1854, had exceeded that of any preceding year, and an unusually large proportion of these arrived in the last quarter of the year. Various circumstances, as stated in the last annual report, conspired to throw upon this Commission an unusual amount of responsibility and expenditure at the close of the year 1854, which extended through the whole of the last winter until April last. Amongst the unfavorable circumstances specially operative were (as then stated): the prevalence of epidemic or other contagious diseases in the parts of Europe which these emigrants had recently left, and which frequently broke out on shipboard, or soon after their arrival at this port; the unusual number of shipwrecks, or other accidents at sea or on our coast, casting the passengers in a state of destitution upon our shores; the failing of the customary demand for labor from the derangement of business, and the excessively high price of provisions from the short crops of the year, and the immense demand for foreign consumption. To these causes were added the unusually early and severe commencement of the winter of 1854–'55, and its long continuance. The very great emigration of the immediately preceding years, though the far greater part had found occupation and self-support, had yet left a large and gradually accumulated remainder of the helpless and diseased of their number in the establishment at Ward's Island, and elsewhere throughout the State, to be provided for from the means of the Commission.

Thus, although comparatively few alien emigrants arrived during the winter and early spring, the Hospital and Refuge at Ward's Island were crowded to their full extent of accommodation, and the impossibility of procuring immediate employment for the number of recently arrived persons in this city, compelled a resort to the bestowing temporary or out-door relief to an extent very far beyond the ordinary former practice of the Commissioners, always subject to more or less misuse and imposition, and to be justified only, in the view of the Commissioners, by the extreme urgency of the case.

To secure an efficient and economical application of the assistance afforded in the city, it was found necessary to appoint salaried visitors, conversant with the languages and habits of the emigrants, who were employed until April 1st.

The cost of meeting these unusual demands, both for out-door relief and hospital support, was increased by the rise in price of the necessaries of life, which were all much dearer than in the preceding year, and averaged from a third to a half more than in the earlier years of the Commission.

This state of things continued until the end of March, when the need of external and temporary aid diminished, and that system of relief was discontinued. The number of the Hospital patients at Ward's Island gradually lessened, and many of the persons received into the Refuge department were discharged, as means of useful occupation were obtained for them. But for more than the first eight months of the year, the number remaining chargeable to the Commission was larger than ordinary.

The number of alien emigrants who arrived during the winter, was, as already stated, smaller than common, but not enough so to lead to the expectation of the great diminution of the usual summer and autumnal arrivals that actually occurred. The total number of alien passengers who arrived at this port during 1855, and for whom commutation money was paid, or special bonds demanded, was 136,233, being less than half the average of the five preceding years, and little more than two-fifths of the numbers in 1854, which were 319,213.

This decrease of emigration from Europe was not confined to arrivals at the port of New York, but was general throughout the ports of the United States, and it extended to those of British America. Various causes have been assigned or suggested for this change, some of them general and others relating to particular countries or classes. As to the correctness of these views, the Commissioners offer no opinion; they would merely mention one cause falling immediately under their observation, which, though it may not be the principal, is yet operative to a considerable extent, and will so far be durable in its effects. It is the effect of the recently enacted laws, on both sides of the Atlantic, regulating the transportation of passengers, securing them against many abuses, but diminishing the number of persons who can be carried in any one vessel, and adding to the cost of transportation. The influence of this cause and probably of others, has been already, and will continue to be, felt chiefly in lessening the number of the most indigent and helpless class of emigrants.

Those who arrived during the last summer and autumn, appeared generally to be of the class and character most able to take care of themselves, and to add to the productive means and industry of the country. The evidence of this fact appeared both in the lessened number of applicants for relief, which was much less than the mere proportion of less emigration, and also from the means of inspection and inquiry afforded to the Commissioners and their officers, by the recent establishment of Castle Garden, as the exclusive landing-place of alien emigrants.

The beneficial effect of this establishment, together with the other circumstances just stated, enabled the Commissioners to carry out many changes in the economy of their establishments rendered necessary by the unexpected reduction of their income from commutation of bonds, as will be stated in another part of this report.

The number taken care of under the immediate charge of the Commission is now little more than half the usual average, and the current expenses have been about met by the current receipts ; but the affairs of the Commission are severely embarrassed by the remains of former debt, partly contracted for lands and buildings and other causes set forth in former reports, and still more by the late necessary heavy expenditures during the last winter, which were not reimbursed, as has been the case for the last six years, by the surplus income of the summer.

The number of patients received at the Marine Hospital, at Quarantine, either directly from shipboard, or sent from the city during 1855, was less than half the number received either for 1853 or in 1854, thus corresponding with the reduced number of foreigners arriving at this port, during the year. This class of persons has always constituted by far the greater part of the patients at the Quarantine Hospitals, although they are not expressly devoted to them, but receive all persons affected with contagious or infectious diseases, sent there by the health officer of the port, or under the authority of the Board of Health, from the city.

The statistics of emigration to this port, and the relief afforded to destitute and diseased aliens under the operation of this Commission, present the following results :

Number of vessels employed in conveying citizens and alien passengers, was	1,626	
" conveying citizens only	607	
Total passenger vessels	——	2,233

Number of passengers landed, 182,939. Of these 46,706 were citizens, and 136,233 aliens ; of which 43,043 were natives of Ireland, 52,892 of Germany, and 40,298 of other countries. (For particulars see Table A.)

Number in Marine Hospital, Jan. 1st, 1855	295	
" admitted during the year	2,107	
Total number treated	——	2,402
Number in Emigrant Refuge and Hospital, Ward's Island, Jan. 1st, 1855	3,168	
" admitted	9,092	
" born there during the year	641	
Total number cared for and treated	——	12,901
Number of sick sent from Office to New York Hospital during the year 1855	227	
" of sick sent from Office to St. Vincent's Hospital	8	
Total cases from Office	——	235
Number of lunatic emigrants in City Asylum on Jan. 1st, 1855,	112	
" admitted during the year	86	
Total number of lunatic emigrants	——	198
" discharged from the Asylum,	63	
" died	14	
" whose term of five years has expired	20	
Number of lunatic emigrants in City Asylum, Jan. 1st, 1856, chargeable to this Commission	101	
" of persons sent back to Europe at their own request.		570
" forwarded to various places inland by the Commission		4,426
" temporarily relieved in this city with money		34,405
" temporarily supplied with board and lodging		59,520
" of out-door poor in the city buried at expense of the Commission		374
" of females provided with situations at the Intelligence Office and Labor Exchange	6,047	
" of males, do.	9,104	
Total number provided with employment at this Office	——	15,151
Whole number relieved, forwarded, and provided with employment, &c., from city Institutions		130,182
Number relieved and forwarded, in and from the several counties of the State, chargeable to the Commission		12,175
Grand total relieved, forwarded, and provided with employment, &c., by the Commission, in the city and State of New York		142,357
Number of days spent in Marine Hospital		51,616
" " " Hospital and Refuge, Ward's Island,		990,007
Total in both institutions		1,041,623

Number of letters written from the Labor Exchange to friends of recently arrived emigrants........................	1,301
Amount of moneys received at Office in reply thereto.......	$5,275 25
Amount of moneys received at the Office of the Irish Emigrant Society from friends of recently arrived emigrants and applied to the forwarding of emigrants, chargeable to the Commission..................................	$5,847 84

The comparison of the above statistics with those contained in the former annual reports of this Board, will show that during the whole year the number receiving aid from the Commission, and the amount of relief extended, was above the average of former years ; at the same time, from obvious causes, the cost of furnishing such aid was much higher, whilst the income relied upon to meet these charges fell off more than half.

The Marine Hospital and Quarantine at Staten Island.

The Marine Hospitals on the Quarantine grounds at Staten Island were, in 1849, devoted expressly (instead of partially as before that date) to the protection of the city and State from the introduction of pestilential diseases, by being set apart for the reception of infectious cases, either directly from shipboard, sent by the health officer of the port, or from the city under the authority of the Board of Health. A very large proportion of all those received and treated at the Marine Hospital are alien emigrants, under the charge of the Commissioners, and sent down from the city, in consequence of infectious diseases, either brought with them from abroad or contracted on shipboard, but which were not manifested until some time after landing. This has been observed to occur for some years, and has been repeatedly mentioned in the report of former health officers and physicians of the Marine Hospital.

The arrangements of this Commission, in this respect, have been found an efficient aid in checking the spreading of pestilential disease, which it was impossible to exclude entirely by the first quarantine inspection, however careful.

From the returns of the Marine Hospital for some years, it appears that not more than a fourth of the patients received at the Quarantine Hospital are directly from shipboard; the others are chiefly of the class just mentioned, and attacked on shore by ship fever, Asiatic cholera, small-pox, or other contagious diseases.

During the year 1855, this city and neighborhood have enjoyed a happy exemption from the assault, and even from the alarm of any species of pestilence, which is the more remarkable, considering the prevalence of yellow fever in the Southern cities, and of cholera and other malignant diseases elsewhere.

The very able, careful, and judicious manner in which the important duties of health officer of this port have been discharged by the present incumbent, Dr. Thompson, has been especially instrumental in producing this happy result. The Commissioners have great pleasure in taking this opportunity of also acknowledging Dr. Thompson's uniform aid and cooperation in the management of the Quarantine Hospitals, and in the arrangements for the landing and protecting of emigrants, where his personal and official assistance was most effectual and salutary.

The number of patients in the Marine Hospital, at the beginning of 1855, was 293, and 814 were received during the next three months; but the number of patients was gradually reduced, until only 93 were left at the end of the year. The whole number of cases treated during the year 1855 was 2,402, being about half the number of patients in 1853 (4,798), and in 1854 (4,762), and generally far below the average of former years. The various forms of typhus fever constituted the largest class of cases, being 907.

The report of the Marine Hospital shows the aggregate results of the year. The details as to diseases, and other particulars, will be found in Table B.

The proportion of deaths in an establishment of this nature must be always greater than in any general hospital for non-contagious diseases and surgical cases. It was, for the first six months of 1855, 13·83 per cent., for the last six, 10·33 per cent.; or, for the whole year, upon all the discharges, 13·05, and on the whole number under treatment during the year, 12·98.

This may be regarded as a very favorable result for an institution of this character, where many are received in a dying state, and nearly all the cases are of serious diseases.

The duties of physician-in-chief were discharged with his usual ability and fidelity by Dr. Alex. F. Vaché until July, when he retired on the expiration of his term of office, which he had filled since June, 1853, to the entire satisfaction of the Commissioners. He was succeeded by Dr. Elisha Harris, appointed by the Governor and Senate, who has since discharged the duties of the office. He is assisted by Dr. Theodore Walser.

The hospitals have at no time during the year been full, as they have formerly often held 500 at a time, or even at one period, though inconveniently, 1,400, and now they have seldom had three hundred occupants. But the accommodations they afford, though happily at present required but in part, may at any time be suddenly demanded to their fullest extent. Some necessary repairs and improvements have been made during the summer. The buildings are all in good order, many of them of the most substantial and durable structure, and fully adapted for their several purposes.

Emigrant Refuge and Hospital on Ward's Island.

The Commissioners of Emigration hold in fee, in trust for the State, about one hundred acres of land on Ward's Island, together with water rights, including shore and marsh partly under water. Some part of these last is in process of filling up to low-water mark, by the labor of the inmates, and more is susceptible of advantageous improvement of the same kind at small expense. The whole of the land has been purchased by the Commission from its funds, or money borrowed on mortgage. The buildings (forty-two in number) required for hospitals, houses for the reception of the aged and helpless, for pregnant and lying-in women, nurseries for children, residences for officers and others, with spacious accommodations for washing, bathing, &c., are scattered in proper and convenient situations about the grounds—an arrangement which gives great advantages to all of them, in air, light, security against the spreading of contagion, and of fire.

The buildings erected in the first years of the occupation of Ward's Island were of wood. All erected within the last six years are substantially built of brick. The hospitals are arranged in long single buildings, of from 24 to 54 feet in breadth, but of different elevations. Several of the wooden hospital wards are still in use; others are at present closed.

A large and commodious brick house was erected in the beginning of the year. It is occupied by the Superintendent, but it contains also spacious accommodation for the use of the Commission.

Two other brick hospital buildings, commenced and contracted for during the last year, were completed in the spring of 1855. They are designed to take the place of some of the low wooden buildings, erected for hospital purposes in 1847, 1848 and 1849; which, being originally hastily and slightly built, are beginning to fall into decay. The new buildings are of three stories, 56 by 125 feet, containing each three wards, with nurses' rooms and other conveniencies, calculated to receive, without crowding, sixty patients in each ward. There was paid for these and the building just mentioned, during the last year, $27,734 16, in addition to $15,668 72, paid in 1854, making the total cost, $43,402 88.

Had the diminution of patients and of income in 1855 been foreseen in 1854, these buildings would probably not have then been undertaken; they are, however, among the most valuable improvements which have been made for the comfort and efficiency of the institution.

During the winter of 1854–'55, the whole establishment was crowded to excess, in consequence of the arrival of numbers at a late period of the year, the early severity of the winter, and the prevalence of disease. On the 1st of January, 1855, there were in the hospitals and Refuge 3,168 inmates, a larger number than ever before reported; and 3,164 were admitted during the months of January, February, and March.

During the spring and summer, the institution was gradually thinned out, and, in the autumn, the number of inmates was greatly reduced, so that at the close of 1855 there were but 1,865.

That number is now again somewhat increasing, but is not likely to at all approach that of the preceding year. The number in the last week of January, 1856, is 1,878.

The reports showing the results, with details stating the nature of diseases, and other particulars, will be found in Table C.

In the latter half of the year the diminished number of inmates has enabled the Commissioners to carry into effect a large reduction in the number of persons salaried or on wages in their employment on Ward's Island. These on the 1st of January, 1855, were 218 ; on the 1st January, 1856, there were 85.

The establishment continued under the charge of Charles Riddle, as during the last year, until 1st October, when he relinquished the office. Amos Pilsbury, who has long been distinguished for his efficient and economical administration of the Albany Penitentiary, and previously of the Connecticut State Prison, was selected for this place. He entered upon its duties on the 1st November, and is now in office.

A revision of the rules for the government of the Institution under his charge was made lately ; the leading principle of the changes adopted was, to give greater authority to the Superintendent, and to impose the full responsibility of the local administration upon this officer.

Hospitals at Ward's Island—their Medical Administration and Statistics for the Year.

The Hospital department at Ward's Island has been for several years administered by a Board of Physicians and Surgeons, residing in or near the city, and visiting in rotation, assisted by a number of younger graduates in medicine resident on the island. This system was analogous to that adopted by several other sanitary institutions, and its details will appear more fully in the annual reports of the Board since 1851. In the judgment of a majority of the present Commissioners, there were reasons which rendered this system not well suited to the peculiar situation of these hospitals, though the ability and attention of the visiting physicians and surgeons were not questioned. In July, 1855, the system was abrogated, and another plan was substituted. The medical department proper was placed under the charge of a salaried physician-in-chief, wholly resident on the Island, with as many salaried assistant physicians, also residing there, as might be required. Dr. H. B. Fay was appointed physician-in-chief, and Drs. George Ford, and F. Simrock were appointed his assistants. They entered on their duties on 15th August, 1855, and are now in office.

The surgical department was continued under the charge of John Murray Carnochan, M. D., as surgeon-in-chief, in regard to whose office actual residence was not considered essential. He is required to visit the hospitals at such regular times as prescribed by the by-laws, or when specially needed, and to perform or direct all capital operations. He is assisted by two surgeons, Drs. Darling and Nelken, who reside continually on the Island.

The medical and surgical reports, showing the results and with details as to diseases and other particulars, will be found in Table C.

During the preceding years, 1851, '52, '53, '54, there were in the hospitals 51,314 patients, so that, in consequence of the numbers received in the winter of 1855, the whole number in the year exceeds the average of these years one-tenth. Those left at the end of the year are fewer than in any of the preceding years.

The Refuge department always contains many aged, infirm, or chronically diseased persons, as well as children, not needing regular hospital care, but requiring occasional, and often frequent medical attendance. These often pass into the hospitals, and many convalescents come from them into the Refuge ; so that the whole number, including many counted more than once, of cases receiving medical care exceeds the number of admissions to the whole establishment.

The number of cases treated in the Refuge in 1855, was 10,582, of whom 235 died.

The percentage of deaths in 1855, including both medical

and surgical cases in the hospitals, was, during the first seven and a half months, $9\frac{7}{10}$ per cent. on all treated. For the remaining four and a half months, under the present organization, $4\frac{4}{5}$ per cent.

On the discharges, the rate of mortality was, during the former period, $10\frac{4}{5}$, and for the latter, $6\frac{1}{3}$.

It is, however, due to those who administered the department in the former period, to add, as observed by the present physician-in-chief, in his report, "that this diminished mortality may have been the result of circumstances other than the change of system;" as the statistics of the city and its institutions show a better state of the general health at one of these periods than at the other. The wards which were filled during the winter, with an average of from 1,300 to 1,500 patients, had, in the latter months of 1855, from 700 to 800, and there was no prevalence of any fatal epidemic. This proportionate decrease was least in the surgical wards, which contained 406 in the beginning of the year, and gradually fell off to 333 at the end.

The surgical practice has been extensive and successful, including many of the most difficult and important operations in surgery. Some of the details are set forth in the reports appended hereto. During the year there were under treatment 3,517 surgical cases, of which 64 died and 3,120 were discharged, cured, or relieved—thus showing a proportion of deaths on all cases treated of $1\frac{4}{5}$ per cent., and on all discharged, or who died, of two per cent.

The present condition of the Medical and Surgical departments is in all respects very satisfactory. The improved insulated hospital wards, erected at different times during the last four years, justify the expectations entertained of their superior comfort and salubrity; whilst the Commissioners are happy to attest to the ability and faithfulness of the physicians and surgeons who have charge of these establishments.

The Commissioners had hoped that their means would have enabled them, during the last or present year, to erect an Insane Asylum on their lands on Ward's Island, where there is more than one excellent location for such an establishment. Their insane, to the average number of 220, have been received and taken care of in the asylum on Blackwell's Island, and the several county or town poor-houses. With a little expansion of their medical staff, if there had been a suitable building or buildings, these unfortunate persons could be taken care of, with probably less expense than they are now supported at the best of these establishments, and with very much more comfort and probability of cure to the patients, than they are kept in those counties not provided with the proper receptacles for this class of patients.

In common with those engaged in the care or supervision of the support of the poor throughout the State, the Commissioners have felt deeply the evil suffered in consequence of the inadequate provision for this class of poor, including their own. They therefore respectfully suggest, that unless other means are provided for this Commission, enabling them to take charge of their insane poor, such provision should be made in additional asylum accommodation, under State management, as would receive all the insane chargeable to this Commission, on such terms and under such regulations, enacted by law, as may be judged necessary and proper.

Establishment at Castle Garden for the Landing Place of Emigrant Passengers.

The Act of April 18, 1855, "For the Protection of Emigrants," having conferred additional powers on the Commissioners to enable them to designate a single landing-place in the city of New York "for the landing of emigrant passengers," has been successfully carried into effect.

The Corporation of the city of New York having granted a lease of the premises known as Castle Garden, for five years, from the first day of May, 1854, at an annual rent, to a private party, the Commissioners succeeded in obtaining an assignment of the lease, on favorable terms, and possession was given on the fifth of May last, when the fitting up of the premises, in a manner suitable for the purpose designed, was immediately proceeded with.

Owing, however, to the extensive repairs required, and the obstructions thrown in the way by those who, on different grounds, apprehended injury to their private interests, the place was not in readiness for use until the first of August, when it was formally opened as the *Emigrant Landing Dépôt.*

It is not deemed necessary to allude to the efforts made to obstruct the execution of the law in this instance, further than to state that where that effort was resorted to with the design of rendering nugatory the power conferred, and for the ejectment of the Commissioners from the occupancy of Castle Garden, the courts have sustained the law in its beneficent objects, and the Commissioners in the possession of the premises for the purpose of carrying the law into effect: and that where violence threatened with a strong hand to lay waste and destroy, the police authority of the city, by prudent and decisive action, effectually checked the thoughtless and lawless in their course, and preserved a valuable property from destruction or damage, and the reputation of the State from disgrace.

Two hundred and fifty vessels have landed their passengers at the Dépôt in the five months it has been in operation—bringing, in the aggregate, fifty-one thousand one hundred and fourteen persons, during which period no accident of any kind has occurred. All have been landed safely, without accident to themselves or property. When landed, proper means have been used to secure their comfort and protection. They have been screened from the intrusion of that class of persons who have heretofore abused the confidence of the emigrants, and despoiled them of the means they had provided to convey them to their ultimate destination, and to sustain them after they had reached it,—who have long been in the practice of taking possession of the person and property of confiding emigrants, and seldom permitting them to pass out of their hands without damage: in many cases reducing them from comparative affluence to destitution, and making them subjects for relief by the funds of the Commission; but in a larger proportion crippling their means to an extent which has affected their after life.

Every facility is provided at the Dépôt, for those whose destination is to the interior, to proceed without unnecessary delay;

and without need or pretext for intercourse with the class of persons in the city before mentioned. By this arrangement, much for the benefit of the emigrant, the shipper, the Commission, and the community at large, has been accomplished. Among these benefits may be mentioned :

First.—To the Emigrants. In a more safe and speedy landing of their person and effects : In the greater safety of their effects after having been put on shore, depredators being limited to fellow-passengers, and but slight opportunity existing for successful pillage by them. In relief from the importunities and deceptions of runners and bookers. In being enabled to continue their journey without delay from the same wharf where they had just landed. In relief from all charges and exactions from landing, "baggage smashing" and porterage ; and where they are proceeding to the interior, from cartages. In being enabled to obtain passage tickets at the lowest rates directly from the various transporting companies. In having their baggage accurately weighed ; and in being relieved from excessive charges for that which is extra. In obtaining reliable information relative to the various routes of travel throughout the country. In being relieved from the necessity of transporting their baggage to boarding-houses when exigencies require a temporary sojourn in the city of New York. And thus in being enabled to depart for their future homes without having their means impaired, their morals corrupted, and probably their persons diseased.

Second.—To the shipper. In the greater readiness with which passengers are discharged where freight and merchandise do not interrupt the process. In the ship being relieved of its passengers at once, and immediately on arrival. In the consignee being relieved from the supervision of the landing of the passengers.

Third.—To the funds of the Commission. In the increased facility afforded for the discovery of cases liable to special bond. In the opportunity for ascertaining the means of passengers for support. In the reduction of sickness and distress among Emigrants. In the diminished proportional number that will become a charge to the Commissioners ; and in the means to readily discover paupers and criminals transported hither.

Fourth.—To the statistician. In furnishing reliable data of the fiscal means of emigrants on arrival. In developing the points of individual destination ; thus exhibiting the number of persons who, at the time of arrival, are destined for each State, and the money-means with which they are provided.

Fifth.—To the community in general. In the diminution of human suffering. In the reduction of calls on the benevolent throughout the country ; and in the dispersion of a band of outlaws attracted to this port by plunder, from all parts of the earth.

All these results are stated not as merely probable, but as results actually and permanently obtained, the evidence of which is constantly passing under the observation of the Commissioners and of the merchants, and others immediately connected with the commerce and navigation of the port. Table D. accompanying the reports will show in part the working of this system.

Financial Concerns and Condition of the Commission.

In their last annual report, the Commissioners stated briefly the history and causes of their former financial difficulties, and still existing debts consequent thereon, and expressed a confident hope that such embarrassments were now ended, and that the debt was in a train of permanent reduction. This hope has been disappointed. The causes of much of the present debt arose in the earlier years of the Commission, when, from 1847 till 1850, the tax intended to be provided by law was reduced by refusal to pay on the part of ship-owners and consignees, or payment under protest, on the ground of the unconstitutionality of the tax. Their objections were sustained by the Supreme Court of the United States. In the meanwhile, the moneys under protest having been paid into the State Treasury, or held to meet the issue of the suit, the Commission was without any adequate income. It was partially relieved y an advance from the State of $60,000, being a small portion only of the sum in question. The defects of the law were supplied by the act of 1850, so framed as to avoid the objections of the United States Judiciary to the prior legislation on this subject, and fixing a commutation of $1 50 per head on each alien emigrant arriving in this port, to entitle him to relief by the Commissioners at any time during five years, should his necessities require such aid, and so reimburse the counties for any expense which might be incurred by them for the support of poor of that class. This sum was insufficient for these purposes at the time, especially as it was to provide also for the whole cost of such lands and buildings as might be needed for the efficient and economical administration of a trust of this magnitude. Had an adequate provision for these purposes been originally made, the system would have gone on without further embarrassment; but the debts which were contracted, some still remaining on mortgage, and others paid in part by the substitute of new debts, still hung upon the Commission. But when the Act of April, 1853, raised the commutation to two dollars a head, and appropriated the additional fifty cents to the repayment of the county charges, there appeared good ground to hope that this income would not only meet all current or new expenditures, but gradually liquidate the whole existing debt. But this expectation was founded on the estimate that the average emigration of the last six or seven years would still continue for some time, or at least not decrease suddenly or very greatly. But during the year 1855, as above stated, it did fall off to less than half this average, whilst the demands upon the Commutation Fund for the greater part of the year were larger than ever before, from the causes stated in other parts of this report, presenting more persons requiring and receiving relief, and that for a longer period and at higher prices for supplies, than in any former year.

As soon as the season permitted the discharge of inmates from Ward's Island, a reduction of their number was gradually effected. A rigid system of retrenchment was then adopted. This retrenchment consisted partly in cutting off expenditures and places no longer required for the present emigration, much improved in comparative condition as well as lessened in number; and also by correcting other minor sources of expense which had grown up gradually for temporary purposes, and been overlooked and continued when no longer needed.

These reductions, with economy in other respects, have brought down the current expenses of the last months of the year nearly to a level with the income. Whether this will hold good throughout the winter is questionable—not, however, so much from increase of expenditure, as from curtailment of receipts. At the close of the year 1854, an unexpended balance of $40,000 was applied to the reduction of the mortgage of $150,000 held by the Mutual Life Insurance Company; but this was done, as on a former occasion, with the stipulation that, should necessity require, the loan should be made up to its former amount, which was accordingly done when requested.

The means of defraying other demands beyond the income, and keeping up the efficiency of the establishments, were temporarily provided for by an arrangement with the Mechanics' Bank, where the accounts of the Commission are kept by the City Chamberlain; by this arrangement, permission was given to overdraw from time to time, to an amount not exceeding in all $100,000, secured by a second mortgage on the real estate of the Commission, approved according to law by the Governor and State officers.

The balance due to the several counties on bills audited and allowed, was all paid in full, to the first month of 1855. (For particulars of county claims for the year see Table E.)

In the next quarter, the proportion of the commutation income set apart for the counties, allowed only a payment of 65 per cent. on the bills due to them, and the Commissioners were not able to discharge the balance, as heretofore, from their general funds. No payment to the counties has since been made. The Commissioners feeling the necessity of the case, and the certainty that any suspension of their establishments here would involve far greater inconvenience and expense to the counties than would result to them from delay of payment, reluctantly took the responsibility of applying all the receipts to purposes immediately and imperatively pressing upon them.

The indebtedness, at the close of the year 1855, stands as follows :

Amount of bond and mortgage on real estate................	$150,000 00
Amount due the several counties for expenses of emigrants, as per bills examined and corrected........................	72,047 96
Overdraft (secured by mortgage) on Mechanics' Bank, December 31st, 1855..	63,031 07
	$285,079 03
Amount of bills of Governors of New York Alms-House, for care and support of lunatics, against which the Commissioners claim a set-off of an equal, or nearly equal amount........	$22,302 69

The particulars of the disputed claims between this Board and the Board of Ten Governors of the New York Alms-House, are stated in full in the special report to the Commissioners, for which see Appendix No. 6.

For statements of receipts and expenditures of Commutation Fund, for the year 1855, see Table XI.

From this financial statement, it appears imminent that the present system of emigrant support is in great danger of being interrupted, and thus effectually broken up by its immediate embarrassments, in spite of either economical reductions or possible increase of income, both which can operate only on the future.

The Legislature appears never to have confidently relied upon the commutation money as always fully adequate to meet all expenses chargeable upon it ; the several acts establishing or amending the system having always directed that the moneys, &c., collected, should be applied to the discharge of the expenses incurred for the purposes of the act "as far as may be." Yet, since the act of 1849, which established the Commutation Fund on its present principle (though not then at its present rate), this Commission has been able, without any external aid, to discharge or fulfil the duties committed to it of relieving the State from the cost and support of emigrant poor, and keeping up the Quarantine establishments and hospitals for the protection of public health ; during which period there has been received and expended the aggregate sum of $3,364,907 32.

It has, besides, acquired a property in lands and buildings, which, for sanitary purposes, much exceeds in value as it has done in actual cost, the sums borrowed on mortgage.

In fact, it may be reasonably estimated that grounds and buildings for sanitary and charitable purposes, equal to the Ward's Island Institution, could not be now procured for less than $300,000.

The Commissioners have also, since they received the charge of the Quarantine Hospitals and grounds, purchased lands for a cemetery, and erected a small-pox hospital and other buildings, and greatly improved the old hospitals before erected; adding about $80,000 to their former cost and value for such purposes.

After nearly eight years' experience, at a period when throughout every county of the State the support of the poor forms a large increase of local taxation, this Commission, administering a limited fund, has suddenly found that income diminished more than one-half.

They must therefore look to the Legislature for such aid as may best insure the preservation of the faith of the State to those to whom, on payment of commutation, a pledge has been given that relief will be afforded from some quarter, whenever, during the period of five years from such payment, they might be obliged to resort to public assistance. Such relief would be effectually afforded by an appropriation of $150,000 to these objects.

In looking back at the history of former legislation in this State, imposing hospital money or other commutation for passengers arriving from abroad at the port of New York, it appears that the moneys thus received under different laws and paid by alien emigrants, have much exceeded in amount all the expenditures for the aid and support of such persons. The reports of former comptrollers of the State, for many years back, show that there were annually applied out of the funds thus collected very considerable sums for various objects, such as grants to dispensaries, annuities to the House of Refuge for Juvenile Delinquents, &c. All the objects of these grants were useful and benevolent, but they are either State or local objects, and not with any propriety chargeable to such a fund. Indeed, such an application is directly repugnant to the principles of the decision of the Supreme Court of the United States in the cases on the constitutionality of the first laws providing for the support of this Commission.

The Commissioners have not, at present, at hand all the means of stating this account with precision, but they are satisfied from the printed legislative documents that the amount thus drawn from alien emigrants and applied to State or local objects, quite foreign to the avowed purposes of such payments, is much more than sufficient to make up the present deficiency of the Commutation Fund.

The appropriation, therefore, of a sum required for the present wants of the Commission, would be no more than a re-appropriation to its proper original object of moneys erroneously applied to other purposes.

On the 25th April, 1855, John P. Cumming was appointed one of the Commissioners, in place of Thomas Dunlap.

On May 7th, 1855, E. D. Morgan was appointed a Commissioner, in place of Charles H. Marshall, resigned.

On February 22d, 1855, Gustav Schwab was elected President of the German Society, in place of Rud. A. Witthaus, resigned, and served as a Commissioner, *ex officio*, until the 2d of May, when he resigned, and was succeeded by Rud. Garrigue, as President of the Society and Commissioner, *ex officio*.

All of which is respectfully submitted.

G. C. VERPLANCK,
JAMES KELLY,
ANDREW CARRIGAN,
JOHN A. KENNEDY,
ELIJAH F. PURDY,
JOHN P. CUMMING,
E. D. MORGAN,
RUDOLPH GARRIGUE,
GEORGE HALL.

NEW YORK, *February* 2, 1856.

Tenth Annual Report

FOR THE YEAR 1856.

TO THE LEGISLATURE OF THE STATE OF NEW YORK :

The year 1856 was one of great anxiety and constantly apprehended difficulty to the Commissioners of Emigration. The sudden falling off of the usual income of the Commissioners, during the preceding year, as stated in the annual report for 1855, and other communications to the Legislature during its last session, and the continuance of the same rate of emigration and income from commutation during 1856, had left the Commission embarrassed with debt, and straitened in its immediate means ; whilst they had, at an early period, good reason to apprehend, what actually took place in the summer, the approach of yellow fever, which, if it gained any foothold in the city of New York, would require the most ample means. Under any circumstances, it was necessary to keep up the Marine Hospital and Quarantine establishment in the most efficient manner. The adjournment of the Legislature, without granting that pecuniary aid which the Commissioners had requested, and which they had every reason to expect, had it not been for the peculiar circumstances of the adjournment, increased their apprehensions. These difficulties, under the care of a kind Providence, have been happily surmounted, for the present, without any other serious inconvenience than that of the continued suspension of payment to the towns and counties of the State, of debts justly due to them, and the continued pressure of other debts on their limited and diminished funds.

The number of alien emigrants who arrived at this port, and for whom commutation was paid, or special bonds demanded in 1856, was 142,342, a larger number by 6,109 than in 1855, but, like that year, less than half the average of preceding years, and little more than two-fifths of the emigration of 1854.

Of these emigrants 56,113 were from Germany, 44,276 from Ireland, and 23,757 from England. (See Table A.)

As in 1855, so in 1856, the decrease was not limited to this port, but was general throughout the ports of this continent including those of British America. It must result from some general, and, perhaps, not temporary causes. One of the causes mentioned in the last annual report was doubtless amongst these, though not the only one, nor perhaps the most powerful. It is the salutary effect of the late laws on both sides of the Atlantic, regulating the passenger business on the ocean, and guarding passengers against much hardship and suffering, often resulting in disease and death, to which they were formerly exposed, but adding to the cost of transportation, and diminishing the numbers of the most indigent and helpless class of emigrants.

As in the greater part of 1855, so throughout the year 1856, the emigrants from Europe were generally of the class and character most able to support themselves, and to add to the productive means of this country. This was manifest through the inquiry and inspection which the establishment at Castle Garden of an exclusive landing-place for such passengers, enabled the Commissioners to make through their officers, and which has been conducted with great care and regularity, and very useful results.

This improvement in the state and character of the passengers arriving, was also evident in the comparatively diminished number of those who, soon after their arrival, sought relief from the Commission, or required medical aid.

The number of feeble or chronically diseased persons who had arrived in former years, and were still chargeable on this Commission, increased the numbers and the expenses at the hospitals and Refuge, and in the counties during the last winter, beyond the proportion due to the more recent emigration.

These were gradually reduced during the summer, until the number of hospital patients and inmates of the Refuge was smaller on 31st December than it had been for several years, and less than half the number in January, 1855.

There has been some increase during the month of January, 1857, but there appears no reason to apprehend any increase during the present winter approaching the number of former years.

The number of patients received at the Marine Hospital at Quarantine affected with contagious or infectious diseases, was also much below the average of former years, and one-third less than in 1855, being 1,648 against 2,402 in 1855 ; but this diminution as compared with 1855, and some prior years, arose mainly from the decrease of lighter and more ordinary infectious maladies, whilst the wards devoted to the more serious diseases of yellow fever and small-pox were unusually full. This circumstance added to the expenses of the Marine Hospital during the summer, and to the care and duties as well of the Commission to whom the duty of keeping up this establishment is confided, as of the health officer of the port and the physician of the Marine Hospital, who are intrusted with the professional responsibility.

The number of persons arriving in infected vessels, and though not requiring hospital treatment, yet temporarily detained in Quarantine and provided for, was much larger than usual.

The details of the various operations of the Commission during the year 1856, present the following results :

Number remaining in Emigrant Refuge and Hospital, Ward's Island, Jan. 1, 1856	1,865	
" admitted during the year	5,339	
" born there	406	
Total number cared for and treated	——	7,610
Number remaining in Marine Hospital, Jan. 1, 1856	92	
" admitted during the year	1,556	
Total number treated at Marine Hospital	——	1,648
Number of sick sent from Office to New York Hospital during the year 1856	237	
" of sick sent from Office to St. Vincent's Hospital	5	
Total cases sent to both hospitals	——	242

Number of lunatic emigrants in City Asylum on 1st Jan., 1856		101	
" admitted during the year		70	
		—	171
Of which there left the Asylum, viz.:			
Number discharged cured	53		
" died	11		
" whose term of five years has expired	38		
	—	102	
Number of lunatic emigrants in City Asylum on 1st January, 1857, chargeable to the Commission	69		
" of persons sent back to Europe at their own request.		54	
" of do. and at expense of consignees of vessels		34	
Total number sent back to Europe		—	88
Number forwarded to various places inland by the Commission			501
" temporarily relieved in this city with money			79
" temporarily supplied with board and lodging			11,093
" of out-door poor in the city, buried at the expense of the Commission			668
" of females provided with situations at the Intelligence Office and Labor Exchange		6,251	
" of males do.		3,127	
Total number provided with employment		—	9,378
Whole number relieved, forwarded, and provided with employment, &c., from city institutions			31,478
Number relieved and forwarded, in and from the several counties of the State, chargeable to the Commission			5,261
Number buried in the several counties of the State, chargeable to the Commission			85
Grand total relieved, forwarded, and provided with employment, &c., by the Commission, in the State and city of New York			36,824
Number of days spent in Marine Hospital			32,625
" " " Emigrant Refuge, Ward's Island	243,243		
" " " Hospital, do.	281,323		
		—	524,566
Total days in institutions of Commissioners			557,191
Number of letters written from the Labor Exchange to friends of recently arrived emigrants			1,061
Amount of moneys received at Office in reply thereto			$8,823 94
" " " of Irish Emigrant Society, from friends of recently arrived emigrants, and applied to the forwarding of emigrants chargeable to the Commission			$1,821 42

Marine Hospital and Quarantine Establishment at Staten Island.

Since 1849, the hospitals on the Quarantine grounds at Staten Island have been devoted exclusively to the protection of the cities of New York and Brooklyn, and the vicinity, from pestilential disease, being set apart by law for the reception of infectious cases.

During the last year the number of natives of the United States received under the health laws, chiefly from shipboard, was 210 out of 1,648 under hospital treatment during the year.

In addition to this number, which includes only those actually laboring under disease, it becomes the duty of the Commissioners to provide for the reception and care of the persons arriving in infected vessels, who, though not manifesting symptoms of disease, yet are thought proper to be temporarily detained by the health officer under the authority vested in him for the protection of the public health.

The prevalence of small-pox early in the spring in emigrant vessels, compelled the exercise of this power to a large extent, so that at times the persons in Quarantine, including hospital patients, gave a population of near 1,600 at a time.

The access of yellow fever in July, August and September, again occasioned the exercise of this salutary power to a large extent.

The whole number of hospital patients at Quarantine, as before remarked, was less in 1856 than in former years, being 1,648 ; but the report and tables of the physician-in-chief, show that the decrease was in the lighter maladies of an infectious character, and that, whilst in the city of New York and its vicinity recent emigrants were remarkably free from infectious disease, the arrivals from sea brought numerous cases of pestilence, in their most dreaded form of small-pox, to an unusual extent in the earlier part of the year, and of yellow fever in June, July, August and September.

This last dreaded pestilence appeared in a very malignant type, and spread itself among the employees of the Hospital, and those employed on or near the vessels. Dr. Walser, the assistant physician, was seized with it, but happily recovered. The gate keeper of the Quarantine grounds, and others died. The infection spread along the shores of the harbor, but through the vigilance and decision of the health officer, Dr. R. H. Thompson, it was happily prevented from reaching the city. The Commissioners have pleasure in testifying to the fidelity and ability of Dr. Harris, the physician-in-chief, through this trying period, as well as at other times. Of the 177 cases of yellow fever, many of them received in a dying or desperate state from shipboard, 58 were fatal, which gives a ratio of recoveries above the proportion of former years, and much more favorable than the average shown by the records of this disease in former years, which have been regularly kept in the Marine Hospital at Quarantine.

The Commissioners, on the request and recommendation of Dr. Harris, added to the medical force such temporary aid as he thought necessary. They also acknowledge with gratitude the great value of the counsel and advice, as to the general administration of the Marine Hospital, afforded to them by Dr. J. W. Francis, whose long experience and special study of this scourge of our port in former years gave great value and weight to his counsels.

The report of the physician of the Marine Hospital shows the nature of the diseases treated, the numbers of each class, and of those admitted, with other details. (See Table B.)

The proportion of deaths in this establishment was, during the year, 12·31 per cent. on all cases under treatment, which is a favorable result for any institution of this nature, and the more so at this hospital from the very considerable proportion of patients landed during the year in an advanced and nearly final stage of yellow fever.

No new buildings or enlargement of old ones have been erected during the year, nor any alterations or repairs made but such as seemed of immediate necessity, as for the repair of the sea-wall, wharves, and similar outlays for the preservation of the property.

Emigrant Refuge and Hospital, Ward's Island.

During the last year, the land on Ward's Island owned by this Commission has been increased a little by filling in, and building a sea-wall along the shore, which work was performed by the inmates of the Refuge. The Commissioners have also acquired the fee of a lot of three acres, which they have for some time occupied. This was purchased at a mortgage sale in 1852, and the title perfected during 1856, the total cost being $2,598. The object of the purchase was not the enlargement of the grounds, which were sufficient in extent, but this lot lies surrounded on three sides by the lands of the Commissioners, actually within their enclosures, and capable of being used in other hands to the injury of the police and order of the establishment. The land on Ward's Island now held by the Commissioners is thus about 103 acres, and with its wharf, water privileges, and ample supplies of water, is probably worth, independently of the buildings, at the rate of recent sales, about $200,000.

The whole cost of buildings and improvements on Ward's Island is about $260,349 28.

It was stated, in the last annual report, that the Ward's Island establishments had been placed on the 1st October, 1856, under the charge of Amos Pilsbury. Upon his entering on the duties of Superintendent, a revision of the rules for the government of the Ward's Island establishment was made, making various changes in the system of government, suggested by the experience of the Commissioners, or by that of the new Superintendent. By far the most important of these consisted in placing the responsibility of the order, discipline, and to a great degree, of the economy of the establishment, on the chief officer, and for that purpose clothing him with full power and authority, which had before been either divided, or in part reserved to be exercised by the Ward's Island committee of the Board.

The expectations of the Commissioners have not been disappointed. The economical administration has been exceedingly improved by the great reduction of the number of persons under pay, and by the order and system, and prevention of all waste throughout, as well as by the substitution for many purposes, both in door and out of door, of comparatively light labor of the numerous inmates, to hired labor. This last measure, whilst conducing much to economy, is very beneficial to the health and comfort of the persons thus employed.

For a report from the Superintendent to the Commissioners, made by their direction, showing the workings and present condition of the Ward's Island Refuge and Hospital, see Table C.

The establishments at Ward's Island are under the immediate care and inspection of the Ward's Island committee, consisting of five Commissioners, who frequently visit the Hospital and Refuge, and are familiar with all their concerns. Their especial acquaintance with the details of the Superintendent's administration, and the more general knowledge of the other Commissioners from the evidences of economy and discipline continually brought under their notice, authorize the Commissioners to adopt this report in full as their own statement of the improved condition of the Ward's Island establishments for the relief of alien emigrants.

Various inconveniences having been found to arise from the former system of the school for children under the charge of the Commissioners, an arrangement was made with the "Board of Education" for the organization of a Ward school, under their charge, the Commissioners providing a commodious apartment, and paying for certain special expenses. The change appears to be beneficial, and the present number of pupils is about 150.

Medical and Surgical Administration of the Hospitals at Ward's Island, and their Statistics for the year.

The Hospital department is administered on the system adopted in July, 1855, and in force during the last four months of that year, as reported last year. H. B. Fay, M. D., is the physician-in-chief, and his permanent assistants are Dr. George Ford and Dr. F. Simrock.

The Surgical department is continued under the charge of J. Murray Carnochan, M. D., as surgeon-in-chief. He is assisted by two salaried and constantly resident surgeons, Drs. William P. Cassiday and Hermann Guleke ; the last named is a German by birth, and speaks several European languages. The Commissioners have always been sensible of the importance of having both on the medical staff, and amongst the other employees, persons capable of conversing with the patients and other inmates in their own languages, so that, except in special cases (as Chinese), it has seldom happened that any inmates could not find an interpreter to explain their wants.

The numbers requiring medical or surgical aid have diminished much below the average of former years, though not quite in the same proportion with others chargeable to the Commissioners ; there having been 6,147 cases treated during 1856, against 11,532 in 1855.

These numbers, in both instances, include only the more serious cases requiring regular hospital treatment ; less serious sickness or chronic cases, requiring occasional professional aid only, are treated in the Refuge department, in which, during the last year, 5,131 cases received such aid.

The proportion of diseases, incurable in their nature, admitted during this year is larger than common, but the general results of practice are highly satisfactory.

The lessened number of patients and others, permitted the abandonment of the use of the older wards which are least comfortable or salubrious, and the occupation of one of the larger new buildings for hospital purposes, for which it has been found admirably adapted.

The details, as to the nature of diseases and other matters, will be found as usual in the medical and surgical reports, in Table C.

The percentage of mortality in the hospitals proper was, for 1856, 6·31 per cent. on all cases treated, and calculated on the discharges, a mode of estimation used in some institutions, 7·32.

On all the cases treated in Hospital and Refuge, the percentage of mortality was 4·66.

The surgical practice, as usual, embraces many serious cases, requiring the most important operations, most of which have been successful. The whole number of surgical cases was 1,856, the number cured and discharged 1,401, and of deaths, 53, or about three per cent. on all cases treated.

Many cases of acute and chronic disease of the eye have been received, but epidemic purulent ophthalmia, which in earlier years was a scourge of the nursery wards, and to the visitations of which such establishments are specially liable, has appeared only in rare instances, and has not extended or become epidemic in 1856, or for some time previous. It is trusted that the children under the care of the Commission will not again be exposed to the sufferings and injuries from this cause, which occurred in the first two or three years of this establishment, and of which the former and older present Commissioners have a painful recollection.

There are about 250 insane poor chargeable to the Commission, who are partly taken care of at Blackwell's Island, and a number in the counties.

As stated in previous annual reports, the chief, and perhaps the only pressing defect of the medical provision for disease, on Ward's Island, is the want of an asylum suitably constructed for the care and cure of the insane.

An excellent site, belonging to the Commission, may be set apart for this purpose; a quarry of stone on the ground would lessen the expenses of building, and many of the present provisions of the government and medical care of the hospital, and its other inmates, could be extended to a Ward's Island Asylum with very little increased expenditure.

Nothing but the absolute pecuniary inability of the Commission prevented the commencement of such a building during the years 1855 and 1856.

Should they be relieved from their difficulties by the aid of the Legislature, the first application of any income hereafter above current expenses, should be to such an object.

Landing-place for Emigrant Passengers at Castle Garden.

The establishment at Castle Garden for the exclusive landing-place of alien emigrants, under the authority and direction of the Act of 18th April, 1855, "For the protection of emigrants," continues to fulfil, and even exceed, the just expectations of the Legislature, in this wise enactment.

The decisions of the courts, upon deliberate argument and advisement, having put an end to the legal obstacles attempted to be interposed to this establishment on the part of persons, who on various grounds feared, or thought their pecuniary interests affected by this measure, the opposition has not since extended beyond acts of inferior, but continued annoyance from those who have formerly profited from taking advantage of the ignorance of newly arrived and friendless strangers.

In their last annual report the Commissioners set forth the advantages which had already been manifested, in the short period of five months. The experience of another year has confirmed all that was then said ; and, moreover, the beneficent effects of the system have been shown in the much diminished number and proportion of recently arrived emigrants requiring aid from the funds of the Commission, or applying elsewhere to public or private charity.

As to the details of the management, and its principal good results, the Commissioners respectfully refer to the accompanying presentment of the grand jury of the county of New York, in September last (see Appendix, No. 7), made after a careful personal inspection of the establishment and its operations. This will speak for the establishment, and those who immediately administer it, better than any statement that can be made by this Board.

The report of the Superintendent of Castle Garden, with accompanying tables, exhibits some other interesting and important details, and will be found in Table D.

The number of persons who landed at Castle Garden, was 141,625—arriving in 579 vessels, from 21 different ports ; the difference between that number and the whole number of aliens reported as having arrived at this port in 1856, arises from those landed at Quarantine, and those arriving in mail steamers.

The plan of assisting families destined for the interior, to proceed on their journey without sacrifice of their property, by making small advances on a pledge of baggage, or other portable property, without interest or any additional charge for storage or otherwise, is an example of great good, effected almost without cost. In little more than four months since 22d August, 1856, when the system was regularly organized (it having been in partial operation for some time before), about twelve hundred alien emigrants, in 210 families, were thus assisted, to their very great relief and protection from almost certain imposition, by an advance of only $2,098, of which all but $647 has been repaid before the 1st January, 1857, and the pledges re-delivered. The rest will doubtless be repaid shortly.

The statistics which are collected and preserved at the Emigrant Dépôt, as to the pecuniary means of emigrants, and their nativities and other details, are curious and instructive, and when they have been continued for some time longer, will form a body of most valuable information for legislative and financial uses.

Financial Concerns and Condition of the Commission.

The statements and views to be presented under this head, have been mostly anticipated in the special communication made by the Commissioners to the present Legislature on 29th of January, 1857.

The financial condition of the Commission at the close of 1856, stood as follows:

The indebtedness of the Commissioners of Emigration at the close of the year 1856 was:

Amount of bond and mortgage on real estate................	$150,000 00
" due to the several counties for expenses of emigrants as per bills examined and corrected...............	102,210 67
" due New York Hospital..........................	789 71
" of overdraft (secured by mortgage) on Shoe and Leather Bank, December 31, 1856......................	9,202 75
	$262,203 13
Estimated additional amount of indebtedness to counties to February 1, 1857......................................	4,000 00
	$266,203 13
Amount of bills of Governors of New York Alms-House for care and support of lunatics, part of which is contested and against which the Commissioners claim, as an offset, a large unliquidated amount for support of native children of emigrants..	$30,540 90

To this, in taking into account the necessary expenses of the winter above the amount of the very small income of the winter months, in part already incurred and in part estimated, there should be added, to show the actual financial state of the Commission,

Estimated amount of expenses for support of Institutions at Ward's Island and Marine Hospital, for the months of January, February, and March, 1857........................ $57,000 00

The system of reduction introduced in 1855, and carried out in 1856, except so far as extraordinary causes of expense arising from the approach of yellow fever prevented, enabled the Commissioners to pass through the year without lessening the efficiency of their establishments.

During the period that the support of the Quarantine and Marine Hospital, and the relief of diseased or helpless alien emigrants have been intrusted to the Commissioners of Emigration, they have expended above $3,700,000, and to that amount at least relieved the State and counties from taxation. They have good reason to believe that the operation of their system has produced a large additional saving in preventing pauperism, besides the benefit it has produced to the persons more immediately assisted or protected.

They have bought lands and erected buildings, &c., at a cost of $290,000, and the property thus acquired, partly from income, partly by means of loan on mortgage, is for all purposes similar to the uses to which it is now applied, worth more than the cost; and it would sell, for ordinary purposes, for a sum much above its encumbrances.

The distresses of Europe, from 1849 to 1854, threw upon the Commission numbers of helpless emigrants, many of them diseased, who, on paying commutation, had a claim for relief for five years. In 1855 and 1856, as elsewhere fully stated, the emigration from Europe, and the consequent income of the Commission, fell off more than half, whilst it is only within a few months that the funds of the Commission have found the relief afforded by a better class of emigrants, and the improved efficiency of their institutions, which last advantage is in no small degree to be ascribed to the wise legislation of 1855 and 1856.

The Commissioners are directed by law to reimburse "as far as may be" the several counties, cities and towns, for the expenses they may incur under our Poor Laws for the support of emigrants who have paid commutation, or given bonds. This was done regularly till 1855. The whole amount thus paid (including the partial payments of 1856) was $553,784, varying in different years, but reaching sometimes above $125,000 in a single year.

In 1855, in consequence of the heavy expenses at the hospitals, &c., at Ward's Island and Quarantine under the immediate charge of the Commissioners, they found themselves under the alternative of either breaking up those establishments, in whole or in part, which would have exposed the whole State to danger, besides imposing heavier burdens upon the counties, or else of suspending in great part their reimbursements to the counties and towns. Under the imperious necessity of the case, they reluctantly determined on the latter course. These payments were, therefore, suspended from January, 1855, to the present time, with the exception of one payment of 65 per cent. on these bills from 1st Jan., 1855, to April, 1855, and another of 50 per cent. from 1st January, 1856, to 1st July, 1856.

The Commission, therefore, owe the counties $102,210 67 on bills audited and allowed up to 31st December, 1856, besides a considerable sum for bills not received at that date.

The Commission also owe, as above stated, $150,000 on mortgage, contracted according to law with the official approval of the Governor and State Officers, which debt was contracted for lands and buildings.

They owe besides another debt secured by a second mortgage, similarly approved, to the Shoe and Leather Bank, in which bank, according to law, their accounts through the City Chamberlain are kept. This mortgage is to secure temporary advances made, or to be made, in the form of an overdraft. This debt was on the 1st January, 1857, $9,202 75; but at the present date it has increased to $16,057 25, and must continue to increase until the end of March.

The statement of receipts and expenditures of the Commutation Fund, for the year 1856, will be found in Table XII.

From the financial statement it appears, that though the economies of last year enabled the Commission to make a partial payment to the counties on their current bills, to reduce the floating debt (which the circumstances of a change of their bank of deposit rendered necessary), and to meet all other claims upon them during a season of difficulty, there is no prospect of their being able to pay off their present liabilities out of their diminished income.

Moreover, from the best judgment they have been able to form, there is no probability of any great increase of that income for some years.

If the present indebtedness, in addition to the large mortgage, remains uncancelled, they are seriously apprehensive that the efficiency of all their operations must be greatly impaired, and that in case of any great emergency, such as the access of yellow fever next summer, their means would be wholly inadequate to the urgencies of public service.

If the debts to the counties were spread equally through the State they would be matters of slighter moment, but they are mainly owing to those localities where the pressure of transient emigration chiefly falls. It therefore seems a claim of strict justice that these should be relieved by the State from the burdens which have first fallen upon them, but for which the faith of the State is pledged.

With regard to this Commission itself, it is thought due to ourselves, and still more to our predecessors in office, to call the attention of the Legislature to the fact that the present debt is the result of some years gradual deficiency, under many adverse and unexpected circumstances, with constantly rising prices, and for several years with a rate of commutation which the Legislature itself, in 1853, pronounced insufficient, and raised.

They also feel it their duty to add, that from all the information they have been able to obtain from sources entitled to high authority, that they look with much apprehension to the probability of danger from yellow fever next summer at this port.

A suggestion was made in a conference with your financial

committees, which on full consideration seems to be of great value. It was, that, in addition to a direct grant of $150,000, as recommended in their last report, to be applied first to the reimbursement of the counties, and then, if any surplus remains, to other pressing demands, a contingent additional appropriation of $50,000 be made, to be paid to the use of the Commission only on the order of the Governor, certifying that such payment was necessary for the public service, by reason of the danger or actual prevalence of pestilential disease.

The Commissioners are well satisfied that the grants thus requested are required by the strongest consideration of justice to many portions of the State, and of public policy, involving the interests of the whole State.

But as a mere question of account between the fund they administer and the State Treasury, there is reason to think that the Commutation Fund is entitled to at least this amount, as a balance due to it from the General Fund. On this point, they content themselves with briefly stating the views formerly presented to the Legislature.

All of which is respectfully submitted.

G. C. VERPLANCK,
ANDREW CARRIGAN,
CYRUS CURTISS,
ELIJAH F. PURDY,
JOHN P. CUMMING,
E. D. MORGAN,
RUDOLPH GARRIGUE,
WILSON G. HUNT.

NEW YORK, *February* 13, 1857.

Eleventh Annual Report

FOR THE YEAR 1857.

To the Legislature of the State of New York:

The last annual report of the Commissioners, as well as their special communications to the Legislature and the Executive, made during the last winter and the session preceding it, showed the Commissioners struggling with difficulties, embarrassed with debt, with their ordinary limited income much diminished, and apprehensive of the most serious public calamity, should a season of pestilence occur, whilst the means at their disposal were thus rendered inadequate for the protection of the public health, and for other duties intrusted to their charge. The Legislature of the session of 1857, by granting a postponement, for three years, if required, of the large debts due by the Commissioners to the cities and counties of the State, and by authorizing a loan or advance from the State Treasury of $30,000, for the purposes of the Commission, relieved their anxiety as to the future, and provided the means of guarding against the apprehended dangers and evils. Happily, a kind Providence has granted that these anticipations of danger, well grounded as they seemed to be at the time, were not realized. A season of unusual health here and abroad, relieved the Commissioners from any especial or additional charges or expenditures at the Quarantine establishment; a large increase of emigration and commutation payments relieved their pecuniary embarrassments, without recourse to the aid of the State Treasury; the improved character of the emigration itself, united with the much increased efficiency and economy of all the institutions under their charge, administered by experienced and able officers, diminished the proportion of their expenditures to the income during the year, and enabled the Commissioners, not only to pay off their temporary and floating debt, but to redeem largely their arrears to the counties and towns. Indeed, the whole of this debt, of which the Legislature had authorized a suspension of payment for three years, would have been paid off, or nearly so, during 1857, had not the Commissioners been obliged to pay an instalment of the debt formerly contracted on mortgage for building and for the purchase of lands: and that it was also judged to be of imperative necessity to guard against the possible contingencies of the winter during a period of general pecuniary difficulty, by making ample provisions of supplies, and retaining in hand a sufficient fund for the support of a large increase of claims upon the emigrant fund, under the pressure of the times. The mildness of the winter, and the lessened cost of provisions and other supplies, have thus far enabled the Commissioners to meet these claims, without any renewed increase of debt, even by temporary loan (for which they had also made provision), although the numbers of destitute or diseased, supported or relieved by them since the end of November, 1857, is greater than it has been for some time. Should the present expectations of the Commissioners be realized, of carrying their establishments through the winter upon the means now on hand, without aid or loan, they trust to resume, at an early period, the liquidation of their debts to the several counties, cities, and towns; that debt being now reduced to an amount within their ordinary means of discharging.

The important subject of the removal and permanent location of the Quarantine establishments will demand the serious attention of the Legislature. It is also most desirable, as will be shown in another part of this report, to make some more suitable and efficacious provision for the insane poor falling under the charge of this Commission.

With these exceptions, there is nothing upon which the Commissioners have specially to ask legislative assistance, though there may be some minor points on which the existing legislation may probably be improved.

The number of alien emigrants who arrived at this port in 1857, and for whom commutation was paid or special bonds required, was 183,773, being 41,431 more than in 1856, and 47,540 more than in 1855. But it is worthy of observation that, like the emigration of 1855 and 1856, that of 1857 is still much below that of the preceding years, falling about one-third short of the average of those years.

Of these emigrants, 80,976 were from Germany, 57,119 from Ireland, and 28,622 from England ; the increase for the last year being mainly from Germany and Ireland. (For particulars see Table A.)

During the last, as well as the year immediately preceding, the emigrants were of a class and character superior to the mass of those who arrived during the earlier years of this Commission, and were generally such as appear able to support themselves, and to add materially to the productive means of this country. This was manifest, through the inquiry and inspection which the establishment at Castle Garden as an exclusive landing-place for such passengers, enabled the Commissioners to make, through their officers, and which has been conducted with great care and regularity, and very useful results.

This improved character and condition of the emigration may be ascribed to the co-operation of various causes :

1*st.* To the more stringent legislation, and the action under it, of the officers of the Commission, aided by the co-operation of the consuls and diplomatic officers of the United States abroad, thus excluding, in a great degree, the most worthless class, sent by local or State authorities abroad, to be thrown upon our shores for support, or to live by worse means. 2*d.* By the salutary effect of the legislation, both here and in Europe, guarding passengers on the ocean from much of disease and suffering to which they were formerly exposed, thus landing them here in health and vigor. Finally, much must be ascribed to the character of the emigrants themselves, leaving their homes with better information as to this country, and more distinct ideas of what they might reasonably expect, and of what was necessary for their welfare here.

During the last two months of the year, the number of those claiming relief or assistance increased considerably, in consequence of the sudden interruption of the usual demand for labor, and the derangement of exchanges and business, materially affecting the plans and interests of many of these strangers in our land. In consequence, the inmates in the Hospital and Refuge at Ward's Island, rose from 1,370, which had been the number in January, 1857, and which was above the average during the succeeding months, to 1,915, on the first day of the present year. That number has continued to increase, but there happily appears no reason to apprehend any thing like the amount of disease and suffering recorded in the reports of several earlier years of this Commission.

The number of patients received at the Marine Hospital at Quarantine, affected with contagious or infectious diseases, was 1,856, which was 208 more than during the preceding year, but like that, in number, much below the average of many preceding years, being a fourth less than in 1855. That decrease, however, arose mainly from the smaller number of lighter cases and classes of disease; whilst though yellow fever, and the severe forms of typhus, were diminished in comparison of 1855 and 1856, yet cholera appeared at one period in a threatening form, and the insulated edifice, devoted to the small-pox cases, was often full. The number of well passengers landed and temporarily provided for at Quarantine, from ships affected with cholera and yellow fever, who were detained for a short time by authority of the health officer of the port, until the danger of communicating contagion appeared to have passed, was 3,772, a larger number than usual, being 508 more than in 1856; but their period of detention was generally much shorter, not averaging three days.

All these circumstances added to the expenses of the establishment and the duties of the Commission, as well as to the duties and cares of the medical officers who are intrusted with the professional responsibility.

The general result of these labors, as well on the patients

themselves, as in the exemption not only from the spread of disease, but from serious alarm or interruption to commerce and navigation, has been highly satisfactory throughout the year. The details of the various operations of this Commission during the year 1857, present the following results :

Number remaining in Emigrant Refuge and Hospital, Ward's Island, January 1, 1857	1,370	
" admitted during the year	6,701	
" born there during the year	468	
Total cared for and treated there	——	8,539
Number remaining in Marine Hospital, January 1, 1857	79	
" admitted during the year	1,777	
Total cases treated at Marine Hospital	——	1,856
Number of sick sent from Office to New York Hospital during the year 1857	136	
" of sick sent from Office to St. Vincent's Hospital	18	
Total cases sent to both Hospitals	——	154
Number of lunatic emigrants in City Asylum on Jan. 1st, 1857	52	
" admitted during the year	31	
Total number of lunatic emigrants	——	83
Of which there left the Asylum, viz.:		
Number discharged cured	28	
" died	2	
" whose term of five years has expired	13	
Total discharges	—— 43	
" of lunatic emigrants in City Asylum, on Jan. 1st, 1858, chargeable to the Commission	40	
Number of persons sent back to Europe at their own request	64	
" and at expense of consignees of vessels	104	
Total number sent back to Europe	——	168
Number forwarded to various places inland by the Commission		361
" temporarily relieved in this city with money		303
" temporarily supplied with board and lodging		5,108
" of out-door poor in the city buried at the expense of the Commission		627
Number of females provided with situations at the Intelligence Office and Labor Exchange	6,615	
" of males do	4,318	
Total number provided with employment at this Office	——	10,933
Whole number relieved and forwarded in and from the several counties of the State, chargeable to the Commission		4,253
Grand total relieved, forwarded, and provided with employment, &c., by the Commission, in the State and city of New York		**32,385**

Number of days spent in Marine Hospital.................		32,143
" " " Emigrant Refuge, Ward's Island...	215,901	
" " " Hospital, do. ...	294,544	
		510,445
Total days in institutions of Commissioners....		542,588

Number of letters written from the Labor Exchange to friends of recently arrived emigrants.................	2,007
Amount of money received at Office in reply thereto.......	$10,445 73
" " " " of Irish Emigrant Society, from friends of recently arrived emigrants, and applied to the forwarding of emigrants, chargeable to the Commission..	$2,408 60

The Marine Hospital and Quarantine Establishment at Staten Island.

During the last year the number of natives of the United States received under the health laws, chiefly from shipboard, was 61 out of 1,856 under hospital treatment during the year.

In addition to this number, which includes only those actually laboring under disease, it is made the duty of the Commissioners to provide for the reception and care of persons arriving in infected vessels, who, though not manifesting symptoms of disease, are yet thought proper to be temporarily detained by the health officer, under the authority vested in him for the protection of the public health.

The frequency of small-pox cases in emigrant vessels at various periods, and the appearance of cholera and yellow fever during the autumn, enforced the necessity of exercising this power to a large extent, so that the Quarantine grounds and buildings were sometimes obliged to receive several hundred persons besides the patients.

The efficient means now provided for purifying and ventilating ships and cargoes, and for the care and inspection of passengers and seamen, have, it is believed, rendered this detention as brief and as little burdensome either to commerce or the individuals detained, as practically consistent with the important objects in view. The average period of detention of passengers has not exceeded three days. The whole number of persons, other than those received as patients, thus temporarily landed and detained at Quarantine, in consequence of their arrival in vessels in which cases of cholera, small-pox, or yellow fever had occurred, was 3,772.

There were thirty cases of yellow fever received into the Marine Hospital from vessels from the West Indies. Eight of these were of ship-keepers and stevedores employed here on these vessels when in port. Otherwise the disease did not spread, and was confined entirely to the patients received from shipboard.

On 19th September two cases of cholera were landed from a Hamburg vessel, and on the 28th November the disease appeared among the patients in the hospital who had been admitted with other diseases. It spread rapidly in the hospital for a time, and fifteen died within the next twenty-five days. The whole number of cholera cases during the year was 80, of which 26 died; but this terrible disease was effectually confined within the limits of the Marine Hospital.

Comparatively few cases, and those of a milder form, of typhus fever, were received from shipboard. The diminution of this disease on shipboard, which in former years appeared in such a fatal form and to an alarming extent, may be ascribed under Providence to the improved sanitary regulations and arrangements of passenger vessels, resulting not only from the wise laws on this subject recently passed by the United States and by other maritime powers, but also from the humane care of many masters and owners.

The Commissioners have great pleasure in bearing witness to the fidelity, prudence, and ability with which the affairs of the Marine Hospital have been managed by Dr. Bissell, the physician-in-chief. The medical service of the hospital by Dr. Bissell and his assistant physicians has been to the entire satisfaction of the Commissioners.

The powers and duties of the Commissioners as the trustees and managers of the Quarantine establishment, are closely and intimately connected with those of the health officer of the port, with whom, especially in seasons of disease, they are brought into constant co-operation, and without whose aid much of their labor would be of little avail. They therefore feel themselves bound, as in the last year, to express their acknowledgments to Dr. Thompson, for the harmony and mutual confidence which has marked his action in relation to this Board ; for his sound judgment and advice at all times, especially in seasons of disease or other difficulty, and for his firm and judicious exercise of the large discretionary powers confided to him by law for the protection of the public health.

The report of the physician of the Marine Hospital, shows the nature of the diseases treated there, with other details, and will be found in Table B.

The proportion of deaths in this establishment was, during the year, 11·26 per cent. on all cases under treatment, which is a favorable result for any institution of this nature, and the more so, as this hospital numbered during the year, 45 deaths of persons landed from shipboard in a dying condition, and also 26 deaths by cholera.

No new building or enlargements of old ones have been erected during the year, nor any alterations or repairs made but such as seemed of immediate necessity, as the repair of the sea-wall, wharves, and similar outlays absolutely needed for the preservation of the property, or the immediate uses of the establishment.

The same course has been followed in regard to buildings and improvements at the Marine Hospital during the year 1856, and for some time preceding. In this the Commissioners were governed by their conviction that the public good, as well as the public sentiment, now required a change of the Quarantine location, and that their occupation of the present site of the Marine Hospital could not be of long continuance. The great and rapid increase of population along the shores of the harbor, and throughout the whole of all Staten Island, with the constant and easy communication with the neighboring cities, render the Quarantine laws less and less efficacious, and their strict observance more difficult, whilst the danger of diffusing contagion or pestilence grows daily more threatening.

The Commissioners of Emigration do not believe that any point on Staten Island would meet the requirements and convenience of a proper permanent Marine Hospital for Quarantine purposes, with the necessary appendages of a Quarantine station. Accordingly, at their conference held during the last summer with the Governor and other State officers, they expressed their decided opinion in favor of Sandy Hook, whenever the proper cession of jurisdiction could be obtained from the State of New Jersey. But the Legislature having confided the duty of selecting, procuring, and preparing proper sites and buildings for such hospitals, both temporary and permanent, to another set of Commissioners, this Board did not think it proper to take any further action, or express any further official opinion thereon ; but held themselves in readiness to comply with whatever decision might be made according to law, and to facilitate all measures where their co-operation might be necessary or useful.

The selection of Seguine's Point as a site for a temporary or yellow fever hospital, was not, as they thought, a question for them to pronounce upon, nor have they done so in any way. But when the ground was procured, and the buildings erected there were tendered to them by the other Commissioners, these were found on inspection by a Special Committee of this Board, not to be such in accommodation, in hospital furniture, &c., as would warrant this Commission in placing in them their yellow fever patients, and others who might be placed there by the operation of the law. This judgment of the Commissioners was confirmed by that of the health officer, the physician-in-chief of the Marine Hospital, and of Dr. Rockwell, the resident physician, Dr. Miller, the Commissioner of Health, and J. N. Phillips, the President of the Board of Health of New York. On this point of fitness our own long experience, and that of those public medical officers, had certainly enabled this Board to form a correct judgment ; and it was their duty by law to make proper and effectual provision for the reception of all patients suffering under malignant or contagious diseases. These buildings have consequently never been accepted or occupied for hospital purposes ; but this Board has taken measures to protect them against injury or destruction, as far as possible.

For the grounds and reasons of their action on this subject, the Commissioners respectfully refer to the report of their Special Committee, which was unanimously approved by the Board. That report is herewith submitted, and will be found in the Appendix, No. 8.

The Commissioners of Emigration regret that there should be any collision or difference of opinion between themselves and another Commission acting under State appointment, and having in view the same common and most important objects in regard to the protection of the public health, and of the commerce and navigation of this port. They are themselves conscious of having acted in the business without the slightest bias of personal feeling or interest, and to the best of their judgment ; and without entering further into any detail or argument on the points in which they have appeared to differ with the Commissioners on Quarantine location, they refer to the report just mentioned, which contains all that seems necessary to be said by them in relation to this question.

Great excitement having been manifested by many of the inhabitants of Staten Island, residing near the Quarantine, or near Seguine's Point, against those establishments, one of the buildings at the latter point having been destroyed by incendiaries, and similar threats having been made as to the Marine Hospital, the Commissioners found themselves obliged, in concert with the health officer, to take all the precautions in their own power and those provided by law. Additional watchmen were employed, and the aid of the Municipal Police demanded. The notice provided by statute in similar cases was given with the proper evidence, to the Sheriff of Richmond County, so as to make the county responsible for any injury caused by popular violence. These and other measures, aided by the influence of the more prudent and peaceful inhabitants, have been thus far effectual to the prevention of any violence and the preservation of the public property.

Emigrant Refuge and Hospital, Ward's Island.

The Commissioners now hold in fee one hundred and six acres on Ward's Island, together with appurtenant water rights and marsh partly covered with water.

The purchase of a lot of land containing about two acres, which had been contracted for some time ago, and since occupied, was completed during this year at a cost of $1,408 09. This purchase is considered of great value to the whole property, from its position in the midst of the lands owned by the Commissioners, and in the vicinity of the Hospital and Refuge buildings, which might be exposed to great annoyance if this land were in the hands of other owners.

The buildings, as heretofore reported and described from year to year, as they were successively erected, can accommodate a larger number than now occupy them. On the 1st January, 1857, there were in the buildings 1,370 inmates; the number on 1st January, 1858, was 1,915.

The other buildings for the reception of aged or chronically-diseased poor, for lying-in-women, for the nurseries, for wash and bake-house, for residences for the Superintendent and physicians, all of them plain and simple, are good and convenient for their several purposes, and entirely separate from one another.

The whole number of inmates, whether diseased in the hospital, or infirm and helpless in the other department, during the year, was 8,539, being something larger than have been reported since 1855, and 929 more than in the last year. The average number at any one time was nearly 1,400. The net cost of support of the Emigrant Hospital and Refuge was $108,845 26, but little differing from the cost of the preceding year, which was $109,721. The amount, however, of actual expenditure in 1857 includes the payment for a supply of flour for the present winter, sufficient to last till April, and also $1,418 paid for a purchase of land contracted for in a preceding year, and needed to prevent intrusion within the boundaries of the establishment.

For statistics of admissions to and discharges from the Institutions during the year, see Table C.

Medical and Surgical Administration of the Hospitals at Ward's Island, and their Statistics for the year.

The Hospital department is administered on the system adopted in July, 1855, as reported last year. H. B. Fay, M. D., is the Physician-in-chief, and his assistants are Dr. George Ford and Dr. F. Simrock.

The Surgical department is continued under the charge of J. Murray Carnochan, M. D., as Surgeon-in-chief. His assistants are Drs. J. Carey Selden and Hermann Guleke.

The number receiving medical or surgical aid, though below the average of the years preceding 1856, were more than in the last year, there being 6,893 cases treated in the hospital, against 6,147, in 1856.

These numbers in both instances include only the more serious cases requiring regular hospital treatment ; slighter sickness or chronic cases, requiring occasional professional aid only, are treated in the Refuge department.

The proportion of patients in the hospitals, and of others requiring occasional medical attention in the Refuge, to the whole number of the inmates of the Ward's Island establishment, has been this year unusually large, nearly the whole excess of the number of inmates above that of the year preceding, arising from the increased number of hospital patients. The proportion of incurable diseases appears to have been somewhat less than in 1856, and the general results of the practice, both in the medical and surgical wards, highly satisfactory, comparing advantageously with the statistics of any similar establishments.

The usual diseases of children, as measles, scarlatina, &c., have prevailed, at times, to some extent ; but endemic ophthalmia, that pest of large nursery establishments, which proved a source of constant anxiety in the earlier years of this establishment, is now of rare occurrence here. In the lying-in department, puerperal fever has at no time been epidemic, and the surgical wards have been free from erysipelas. This is justly ascribed, in great part, to the insulation of the several hospital buildings, which affords peculiar advantages, as well for ventilation and cleanliness, as especially for limiting and controlling, as far as may be, the spreading of any infection.

The percentage of mortality in the hospital proper was, for 1857, 5·71 per cent. on all cases treated, and calculated on the discharges, a mode of estimation sometimes preferred, 6·68.

On all cases under treatment in Hospital and Refuge, the percentage of mortality was 4·11.

The Surgical department has received, as heretofore, many intractable cases, produced by malignant diseases and scrofulous *caries.* The ophthalmic wards have received many acute or chronic cases from the city, and the accidents of a busy city contributed many cases requiring serious operations from injuries. Many capital operations have been performed, and the general result of the practice is gratifying. The whole number of surgical cases treated was 1,608, of which 1,286 were discharged cured, and 37 died, showing a proportion of deaths of 2·30 on all cases treated, and 2·79 on all discharged.

The reports of the Physician-in-chief and of the Surgeon-in-chief, with the tables of diseases, &c., thereto appended in Table C, present many valuable and interesting statistics of disease.

During the present year, a committee of this Board has been appointed, and measures taken to procure information, plans, and estimates, for the erection of a fit edifice for the cure of the insane, on Ward's Island. The debt still remaining due to the counties, and which it will be the duty of the Commissioners to discharge (as it is trusted that they will be able to do) during the next summer, may probably absorb any excess of income which might be expected during the year 1858.

But the Governor, in his late annual message, has wisely and humanely urged upon the Legislature the duty of making more ample and effectual provision for the insane poor, now suffering in the various poor-houses and elsewhere throughout the State. Of the number of this class, the insane chargeable to the Commissioners of Emigration form at all times no inconsiderable item. It would, then, seem to be a proper part of the general policy to supply to this Board the means of the care and cure of this class; and it would also be a measure of wise economy, as well as of humanity, to do so. A large portion of the expense of keeping up such an establishment, is already provided in the Superintendent, Physicians, &c., who would need only an addition of proper assistants and nurses. The ground and materials, in part, are also provided, and little is wanted beyond the actual cost of building. If, then, the Legislature would advance, for this specific object, to the Commissioners of Emigration the sum of $30,000, which was appropriated as a loan to them last year in view of probable urgent necessity, which happily was averted, and which sum remains in the Treasury, it would enable the Commissioners to provide for this pressing want without delay, and would put an end to many unpleasant collisions with local authorities. This advance might very properly be directed to be repaid out of the proceeds of the Quarantine lands at Staten Island, whenever the Marine Hospital is removed to a cheaper and better location. Thus this very desirable improvement might be effected almost without cost to the State, and with great advantage to the funds of the Commission, and inestimable benefit to many of the suffering and destitute under their charge.

It would, moreover, considerably diminish the amount required for providing for the county insane in proper asylums, as many insane emigrant poor, though ultimately to be paid for by the Commutation Fund, are now in the first instance secured in the towns and counties, where they may be attacked with disease.

Landing-place for Emigrant Passengers at Castle Garden.

The Commissioners have the satisfaction of again reporting that the experience of a second year amply confirms the opinions expressed by them in their last annual report on the great efficiency and usefulness of the establishment at Castle Garden for the exclusive landing-place of alien emigrants, under the authority and direction of the Act of April 18th, 1855, "For the protection of Emigrants." The establishment continues to fulfil, and even exceed the just expectations of the Legislature, in this wise enactment.

The beneficent effects of this system have been shown, in the much diminished proportion of recently arrived emigrants requiring aid from the funds of the Commission, or applying elsewhere to public or private charity.

The report of the Superintendent of Castle Garden, with accompanying tables, which will be found in Table D., exhibits many other interesting and important details, of which, not the least valuable and important is the statement of the ultimate destination of the alien passengers who arrived in 1857.

The number of persons who landed at Castle Garden was 185,186 (including those not subject to bonds or commutation), arriving in 615 vessels, from 27 different ports.

The experience of the last four months of 1856, of making advances on a pledge of baggage, for the purpose of enabling families destined for the interior to proceed on their journey, showed the great value of this plan, and it has since been continued regularly with the best effect. Thus assistance has been rendered to many who might otherwise have become the prey of fraud, or have fallen into destitution, whilst the character of the assistance was such, as not to lessen the feeling of independent self-reliance necessary to self-support and success in all its callings.

There has been advanced for this object during 1857 the sum of $8,723 88, to 788 families. Of this amount $6,414 50 has been already repaid by 606 of these families. Of $2,098 advanced in 1856, all has been repaid but $290.

The whole establishment has been greatly improved in convenience, by the erection of a spacious, secure, and convenient baggage-house, for the regular reception of the baggage of emigrants, each parcel of which is regularly checked as it is received. As it has actually happened during the present year that an average of near 2,300 passengers a day has landed for six consecutive days, with nearly an equal number of packages, trunks, &c., it will be seen how great an advantage is afforded by a perfect system of order and security, and what protection is thus rendered to the stranger, ignorant of our country and customs, and often of the language.

Many improvements have been introduced into the *discipline* and arrangements of the establishment, as suggested by the experience and ability of its Superintendent.

The general inspection and regulation of Castle Garden is intrusted to a committee of three of the Commissioners, who make almost daily visits to the establishment, and are perfectly familiar from constant observation, with all its operations.

The former annual reports of the Commissioners, and those of successive Legislative Committees, have shown the long, persevering, and too often successful system of imposition upon emigrants in detaining them in this city at charges above their means, and of grossly defrauding them in the purchase of tickets for inland transportation of themselves, their families, and their baggage. Very much had been done by judicious legislation, and by the operation of the Castle Garden establishment, to check these abuses, until the parties in this system of imposition, finding these obstacles in their way in this country, changed the scene of their operations, by opening offices in the seaports of Europe whence the emigrants chiefly embark, and also in cities and towns in the interior of England, Ireland, Germany and Switzerland. The evil effects of many of these agencies and offices were soon manifest, in the numerous cases of suffering falling under the notice of the officers of the Board, or claiming aid from the Commissioners. Families and individuals who had been "booked" in Europe for distant inland points in the United States, were frequently grossly overcharged upon genuine tickets, and often imposed on by fraudulent ones, either wholly so, or conveying them but a small part of their intended journey. They were, in many instances, also consigned to other confederates in this country, and thus exposed to continued depredation.

The Commissioners, in the hope of effectually restraining these abuses, determined to call upon the aid of the Government of the United States to bring these abuses before the view of the governments of those states of Europe which had thus become the scene of these *depredations*. The President of the Board accordingly addressed the Secretary of State of the United States, setting forth the nature and extent of these evils, and requesting that efforts should be made to induce the several European governments to prohibit these practices under which many of their own subjects suffered thus severely. The late Mr. Marcy, who then filled that office, entered zealously and efficiently into the subject, and without delay addressed a circular letter to the diplomatic and consular agents of the United States in those countries of Europe from which emigration chiefly flows hither, instructing them to bring the subject of these communications to the notice of the Governments to which they are respectively accredited, and of the authorities of the places where they reside, and to urge the adoption of such measures as may be required "by the claims of humanity (in Mr. Marcy's words) or the comity of nations."

The Commissioners judged it proper also to send an agent of their own to Europe, to furnish the necessary information in detail to our own diplomatic officers and to the several administrations abroad. He was furnished by Mr. Marcy with ample facilities for the accomplishment of his purpose.

Although all that was desired has not yet been attained, still great good has been effected. Several of the powers of Germany have done all that was asked in the way of legislation, and the officers intrusted with the supervision of foreign emigration in Great Britain and France, have given a hearty and effectual co-operation to the measures of this Commission.

The Commissioners have with pleasure to acknowledge the zeal and interest manifested by our own diplomatic and consular representatives in Europe. Amongst these, it is trusted that it will not be invidious to name specially Mr. Fay, the minister resident of the U. S. in Switzerland, whose official papers and publications in the German language on this subject are calculated to be of eminent service.

The correspondence of the late Secretary of State with the President of this Board and with our diplomatic Agents abroad, will be found in the Appendix, No. 9.

Financial Concerns and Condition of the Commission.

On the 1st day of January, 1857, the books of the Commission presented the following result of their financial condition :

Amount of bond and mortgage on real estate................	$150,000 00
" due to the several counties for expenses of emigrants as per bills examined and corrected...............	102,210 67
" due New York Hospital..........................	789 71
" of overdraft (secured by mortgage) on Shoe and Leather Bank, December 31, 1856......................	9,201 75
	$262,203 13

Under this state of their pecuniary affairs, the Commissioners, entertaining the most serious apprehensions that if the income from commutation of bonds, &c. should not materially increase (of which there then appeared but a very doubtful prospect), and if their necessary expenditures should be augmented, either by a protracted winter and increased numbers needing relief or temporary support, or else by the appearance and continuance of pestilence during the summer, requiring additional aid and expenditure at Quarantine, they might be exposed to insurmountable difficulties in discharging the various duties confided to them by law, urged upon the Legislature the necessity of relieving them in some manner from the then pressing floating debt, and the immediate pressure of the debt due by them to the counties or towns, to reimburse them for the expenses they had incurred under our poor laws for the support or relief of emigrants. They at the same time assured the Legislature that "the experience of several years, with the aid of excellent officers, has enabled the Commissioners to carry into effect many excellent arrangements, greatly reducing the expenses without impairing the efficiency of the establishment, to which reduction the landing-place at Castle Garden materially contributes, by the protection and aid it affords to many who otherwise would have been thrown upon the Commissioners for support."

Under these circumstances the affairs of this Board appeared to them to warrant the well-grounded confidence, that if the Commission were relieved from its floating debt, and the immediate pressure of the county bills, they could, without difficulty, meet all future demands as they arise, as well in the counties as at this port.

The Legislature responded to the application, as set forth in the annual report made February, 1857, by the act of 16th

April, 1857, which provided for the suspension of the payments to the counties for three years, "unless the Commissioners shall be in funds applicable thereto," and also granting a loan of $30,000 for the support of the institutions on Ward's Island and the Marine Hospital.

This act was a wise and prudent measure of precaution, although, happily, the Commissioners have been relieved from availing themselves of its provisions, except partially. The increased income from emigration in the spring and summer, the diminished expenditure from the improvements of the economical administration, the beneficial effect of the exclusive landing depot, and the character of a large portion of the emigration, with the freedom from all causes for extraordinary expenditure, such as the approach of yellow fever and cholera, have combined to leave a constant and considerable excess of income above ordinary expenditure, from April to December, applicable to the liquidation of the indebtedness formerly contracted. Accordingly, the Commissioners did not resort to the loan from the State Treasury, and after paying their floating debt of the winter and the overdraft on the bank in which they keep their account, were enabled to pay several large instalments of their county and town debts.

The total amount of these payments was $85,563 85, leaving the present debt, on that account, so far as bills had been rendered and allowed up to 1st January, 1858, $42,662 29. There has also been paid to incorporated hospitals and institutions at New York, Troy, Buffalo, &c., $6,680 16.

(For particulars of County claims see Table E.)

The debt of $150,000 secured by mortgage on the real estate held by the Commissioners, and contracted, as shown in former reports, for the purchase of lands on Ward's Island and the erection of buildings, was also reduced during the year by a payment of $25,000. The Commissioners would have preferred applying this amount to a further payment to the counties, but this instalment was required according to an express stipulation for gradual reduction, and was accompanied by an agreement on the part of the mortgagee, the Mutual Life Insurance Company, to renew the loan to the original amount, should any urgent necessity during the winter compel a resort to such assistance.

That necessity has not yet arisen, nor is there any probability that this sum will be required.

The amount of debt still due by the Commissioners stands thus on 31st December, 1857 :

Indebtedness at the close of the year 1856, as per annual report, was......................		$262,203 13
The indebtedness of the Commissioners of Emigration at the close of the year 1857, was:		
Amount of bond and mortgage.................	$125,000 00	
" due the several counties for expenses of emigrants, as per bills examined and corrected	42,662 29	
	167,662 29	
Deduct balance in Shoe and Leather Bank to credit of Commissioners of Emigration, Jan. 1, 1858.	32,155 89	
		135,506 40
Being less than at the close of the year 1856.....		$126,696 73

The unsettled account with the Governors of the New York Alms-House, amounting on 1st January, 1858, to $37,548 41, still remains unadjusted, the Commissioners claiming as heretofore a large amount as an off-set to these charges, being for the support of native children of emigrant mothers. The nature and grounds of this claim are fully set forth in the report of the Board for 1855, and the accompanying documents in the Appendix.

The statement of the receipts and expenditures of the Commissioners of Emigration, during the year 1857, will be found in Table XIII.

All of which is respectfully submitted.

G. C. VERPLANCK,
ANDREW CARRIGAN,
CYRUS CURTISS,
ELIJAH F. PURDY,
JOHN P. CUMMING,
E. D. MORGAN,
WILSON G. HUNT,
S. S. POWELL,
RUDOLPH GARRIGUE.

NEW YORK, *February* 8, 1858.

Twelfth Annual Report

FOR THE YEAR 1858.

TO THE LEGISLATURE OF THE STATE OF NEW YORK :

The several annual reports of this Commission, from its organization in 1847, show the widely varying character and numbers of emigrants from abroad, with the various and unexpected incidents and difficulties which have successively arisen in the administration of the trust confided to the Commissioners. The year 1858 has been marked throughout by the greatly lessened number of alien emigrants who arrived during the year in the United States, and especially at this port. There was, indeed, reason to calculate on a very considerable diminution, as compared with former years ; but the actual diminution was much more than could have been inferred from any former experience. The general character and condition of the emigrants were, however, such as to lessen the burden which would otherwise have fallen on the diminished means of the Commission. There was no extensively prevailing epidemic or other disease, either among emigrants from Europe or the passengers who arrived from tropical climates ; and thus the numbers of patients in the hospitals at Ward's Island and the Quarantine were much below the former average. The improvements introduced from time to time, in all the establishments of the Commission, have placed them in a high state of order and efficiency ; and at no time have their affairs been in a better state, either as to practical administration or their financial prospects, than during the first eight months of the last year.

Having carried on their establishments through the winter without aid from the State or from loans, the Commissioners had a reasonable confidence in the speedy payment of their debts to the several towns and counties, and a release, at no distant date, of their debts on mortgage, contracted for buildings and purchases of lands.

These prospects were frustrated by the act of popular violence which, on the nights of the 1st and 2d of September, destroyed the Marine Hospital, by violent assault and fire.

In consequence of this, much labor, expense, and anxiety were thrown upon the Commission during the latter months of 1858. The details of these matters will be set forth in the other parts of this report.

The number of alien emigrants who arrived at this port, during the year 1858, and for whom commutation was paid, or special bonds executed, was 78,589, being 105,184 less than in the year immediately preceding, and 63,753 less than in 1856; whilst the proportion to the average of former years, since 1846, is much less than half.

Of these emigrants, 31,874 were from Germany, 25,075 from Ireland, 12,324 from England, and 9,316 from other countries. (See Table A.)

The whole number of patients admitted to the Marine Hospital was 1,167; the number of passengers and sailors not apparently ill, but detained for a short time at Quarantine by the authority of the health officer until danger of contagion should be past, was 1,025.

The details of the various operations of the Commission and their officers, during the year 1858, present the following results —much smaller in number under most of the heads than in former years, but yet showing a large amount of relief afforded and good effected, without any public charge:

Number remaining in Emigrant Refuge and Hospitals, Ward's Island, January 1, 1858	1,915	
" admitted during the year	4,625	
" born there " "	366	
Total cared for and treated at Ward's Island	——	6,906
Number remaining in Marine Hospital, January 1, 1858	37	
" admitted during the year	1,167	
Total treated at Marine Hospital	——	1,204

Number of sick sent from Office to New York Hospital during the year 1858		53	
" of sick sent from Office to St. Vincent's Hospital		14	
Total cases sent to both hospitals		——	67
Number of lunatic emigrants in City Asylum, Jan. 1st, 1858.		40	
" admitted during the year		53	
Total number of lunatic emigrants treated		——	93
Of which there left the Asylum, viz.:			
Number discharged cured	32		
" died	7		
" whose term of five years has expired	7		
Total discharges	—	46	
Number of lunatic emigrants in City Asylum on 1st January, 1859, chargeable to the Commission	47		
Number of persons sent back to Europe at their own request.		170	
" do. and at expense of consignees of vessels		44	
Total number sent back to Europe		——	214
Number forwarded to various places inland by the Commission			301
" temporarily relieved in this city with money			413
" temporarily supplied with board and lodging			3,731
" of out-door poor in the city buried at the expense of the Commission			85
" of females provided with situations at the Intelligence Office and Labor Exchange		6,744	
" of males do.		2,602	
Total number provided with employment		——	9,346
Whole number relieved and forwarded in or from the several counties of the State chargeable to the Commission			4,200
Grand total relieved, forwarded, and provided with employment, &c., by the Commission in the State and city of New York			26,560
Number of days spent in Marine Hospital			21,322
" " " Emigrant Refuge, Ward's Island		178,766	
" " " Hospital, do.		259,780	
		——	438,546
Total days spent in institutions of Commission.			459,868
Number of letters written from the Labor Exchange to friends of recently arrived emigrants			476
Amount of money received at Office in reply thereto			$4,531 46
" " " at office of the Irish Emigrant Society from friends of recently arrived emigrants, and applied to the forwarding of such emigrants chargeable to the Commission			$1,188 93

Marine Hospital and Quarantine Establishment at Staten Island.

Under this head the Commissioners have to report with sorrow and regret, as the chief and almost the only very important incident, the fact already familiar to the people of the State, of the destruction of the buildings of the Marine Hospital by lawless violence.

The other incidents and statistics of the Marine Hospital, and the Quarantine establishment, so far as this Commission have authority over them, may be briefly stated.

Since 1849, the hospitals on the Quarantine grounds at Staten Island, then set apart by law for the reception of infectious cases, have been devoted exclusively to the protection of the cities of New York and Brooklyn, and the vicinity, from pestilential disease. The patients are either directly from shipboard, sent by the health officer of the port, or else sent from the cities under the authority of their Boards of Health. Many of those treated for such diseases at the Marine Hospital, are aliens who have paid commutation, and are at the charge of the Commissioners. Most of these, during 1858, as in preceding years, were sent from the city, in consequence of infectious diseases brought from abroad or contracted on shipboard, but not manifested until after landing. The arrangements of this Commission in co-operation with and by the authority of the New York Board of Health, have, as in former years, thus proved an efficient check to pestilential and infectious diseases, which, of necessity, often escape the most careful Quarantine inspection.

It is due to the present health officer and his assistant to add, that during his administration of the office, that duty appears to have been always carefully and fearlessly performed.

During the last year, the whole number of patients under hospital treatment, was 1,204, being the smallest number received for many years, and being but half the number received in 1855, 444 (or one-fourth) less than in 1856, and 652 (or one-third) less than in 1857, and very far below the average of preceding years since the Marine Hospital has been under the authority of this Commission.

The average duration of treatment was eighteen days. From the first of January, 1858, to the middle of April, the number was small; small-pox cases among emigrants from shipboard, contributed the largest class of cases. From the 16th to the 20th April, 40 yellow fever cases were landed from the U. S. frigate *Susquehanna*, and from the 8th June to 7th October a number more from shipboard, together with several others from the neighborhood, directly or indirectly connected with or employed at Quarantine, making 210 yellow fever cases in all. Of typhus fever, there were 177 cases admitted during the year, affording on the diminished proportion, even to the diminished number of passengers, as compared with the earlier experience of this Commission, evidence of the great value and efficacy of the improved sanitary arrangements and regulations of passenger vessels and to the humane care of many of our shipowners and masters.

The report of the physician-in-chief, with its accompanying tables from the Marine Hospital, shows the nature of the diseases treated there, the numbers of each class, and of those admitted in each month, with other details, and will be found in Table B.

The proportion of deaths in this establishment was during the year, 8·81 per. cent. on all cases under treatment, which is a very favorable result for any institution of this nature.

In addition to those actually laboring under disease, it is made the duty of the Commissioners to provide for the reception and care of persons arriving in infected vessels, who, though not manifesting symptoms of disease, are yet judged proper by the health officer to be temporarily detained for the protection of the public health.

The frequency of small-pox cases in emigrant vessels at various periods, and the appearance of cholera and yellow fever for about six months, made it necessary to exercise this power quite often, though not to so large an extent as in some preceding years. From emigrant vessels infected with small-pox, 4,004 persons were landed from thirteen different vessels, and detained and provided for at an average of five days. Besides these, 250 officers and crew of the *Susquehanna*, 13 officers and crew of the Spanish steam frigate *Berenguela*, and 159 passengers and 312 sailors from fifty-five other vessels, infected with yellow fever, were detained by the health officer, and provided for by the Commissioners for the same average time of five days ; thus making 4,725 sailors and passengers during the year, quarantined for various periods, but averaging five days each, as a precautionary measure. In some of these cases disease manifested itself ; but, in the great majority, after purification of the vessels, baggage, &c., there appeared no cause for apprehending any danger of infection.

During the spring and early part of the summer of last year, occasional rumors reached the Commissioners of an intention on the part of persons on Staten Island to destroy the Marine Hospital and other buildings at the Quarantine station. Although unwilling to believe that there was any foundation in fact for these intimations, this Board, from time to time, as they became current, gave formal notice to the sheriff of Richmond county thereof. This action was deemed proper in case any damage was done by a mob, to preserve the claim of the State against the county, under the provisions of chapter 428 of the Laws of 1855.

No attempt or demonstration was made against the institution, however, until the night of the first of September last. The day had been a holiday for the citizens of the metropolis, and the residents in the vicinity, who had swarmed to the city to take part in celebrating the successful laying of the Atlantic cable. Scarcely had the sound of rejoicing ceased, when the officers in charge of the public buildings were aroused by the tramp and shouts of a mob, estimated at a thousand strong, who, soon after battering down the walls and bursting open the gates, rushed within the Quarantine enclosure, and in a few minutes fired some six buildings, including the Small-pox Hospital.

The superintendent, physicians, and other officers of the institution, endeavored to keep back the mob ; but were borne before them, and even threatened with death, if they offered any resistance. Dr. Bissell, the chief physician of the hospital, in attempting to protect some property, was felled to the ground by a rioter. Dr. Walser, his first assistant, was assaulted, and a stevedore was shot in the tumult, and died the next day. The officers, with no support, except an unprepared and unorganized corps of employées on the grounds, soon ascertaining that resistance was not only useless, but destruction, turned their attention to the care of the sick, who had been brought out by the mob, from the burning buildings, and laid uncovered and unprotected on the grass. About one o'clock the rioters dispersed, leaving behind them a sad scene of desolation ; but still leaving untouched one of the brick hospitals, the boatmen's and some other dwelling-houses, occupied by the officers and employées, at the station.

As soon as the news of this destruction reached the Commissioners, a meeting was held on the second of September, and a committee immediately despatched to make every necessary arrangement for the care and protection of the patients still there.

Apprehending a repetition of violence, and another attack in which the remaining edifices would be destroyed, Capt. Crabtree, the vice-president of the Commissioners, and Commissioner Jellinghaus, president of the German Society, about noon of the second of September, called upon Mr. Nye, the president of the Metropolitan Police Board, and requested him to send down to Staten Island a force sufficient to prevent further action on the part of the mob. The number of men was fixed at sixty, and President Nye assured Captain Crabtree and Commissioner Jellinghaus, that that number, armed with volcanic rifles (provided by the Commissioners), and their own revolvers, should be detailed and despatched that afternoon to the scene of violence. An order for that purpose was also issued by President Nye.

In the mean time, the Collector of the port, apprehensive lest the stores at Quarantine landing belonging to the United States should be destroyed, communicated with the Secretary of the Treasury, who ordered some marines to be sent down, a detachment of which, to the number of about eighty, under command of Capt. Rich, reached the ground late on the afternoon of the second of September.

Owing to some misunderstanding or informality in the order issued by President Nye, or some other unexplained cause, no police force went down that evening. The Commissioners relying upon the police, and its sufficiency, took no further steps to protect the remaining property.

It is reported that the rioters again assembled about eight o'clock on the night of the 2d September, near the Quarantine walls, but intimidated by the presence of the marines, were quietly dispersing, when information was spread among them that the United States force would only protect the Federal buildings, and would not interfere to protect the State property. Encouraged by this assurance, asserted to have been communicated by persons holding positions under the General Government, the mob in a few moments was within the walls, repeating the acts and violence of the preceding night. The remaining hospital was fired, the dwelling-houses were burned, and even the wash and boat-houses, and the barns and stables and wharves were not spared. The coal piles, containing some 500 tons (just laid in for the winter's use), were set on fire and consumed. The sick were dragged from the hospitals; men, women, and children, some afflicted with typhus, and others with yellow fever, were thrown indiscriminately upon the earth. Not a few were placed between two of the burning buildings not widely distant from each other. The officers of the institution, as on the previous night, exerted themselves in every way to shelter the sick, but their efforts could be productive of but little good. Capt. Rich was requested and solicited to prevent with his force this outrage, but repeatedly declined on the ground that his orders confined his interference to the protection of the Federal property alone. Not a roof was left upon a State building at Quarantine. The few physicians and nurses, without food or sleep for more than thirty hours, were engaged in doing all within their power, and went from spot to spot with almost superhuman zeal and endurance.

In speaking of the alleged conduct of persons holding office under the United States Government, the Commissioners are desirous to be understood as not at all referring to the Collector, or any other superior officer of the Customs in the port of New York.

From Collector Schell they have received uniform aid and support, and through him they obtained from the Treasury Department, at this period of necessity, the privilege of using the unoccupied United States public stores. These were placed at the disposal of the Commissioners for quarantine purposes, for which, indeed, they were, during a time of great peril to the public health, absolutely indispensable.

The Commissioners, though pressed for means, immediately made arrangements to meet the requirements of the station, and to protect the State from the introduction of pestilence. At first tents were spread ; then the Mayor of the city of New York erected a temporary shanty, fit, however, only for summer use. Subsequently the Commissioners contracted for and have completed the erection of six brick hospitals, situated so far within the grounds, and from any houses in the village, as, in the judgment of physicians, selected by reason of their great experience in regard to infection (see certificates in Appendix, marked No. 10), to afford no reasonable cause for apprehension to those dwelling beyond the walls. These hospitals were erected in a great measure from materials of the destroyed buildings, and thus the cost was so much diminished, as but little to exceed the price of temporary wooden buildings. They are pronounced by persons having experience on the subject, both physicians and others, as being unsurpassed in utility by any hospitals for the reception of infectious and contagious diseases. The Quarantine station not having been changed, and all cases of pestilential disease being consigned, by law, to the hospitals at Quarantine, the Commissioners had no alternative but to make such preparation for the reception and care of the sick, as in their judgment would enable them to fulfil the law, and meet the exigencies of the times. This, and only this, in the erection of the new hospitals, have they done. They have also, for the same reasons, caused new offices to be erected for the health officer and physician of Marine Hospital ; but the question of erection of abodes for these and other officers, the

Commissioners deemed it proper to leave open until the Legislature had expressed its will in that regard, and in relation to a change of site for the Quarantine establishment.

Intimately connected with this subject is a point which the Commissioners deem it their duty to lay before the Legislature.

In the year 1847 this Commission was organized, and the Quarantine ground and buildings committed to its charge. It was then an entirely new creation, without lands, buildings, or means; the arriving emigrants were affected with various contagious and infectious diseases, among which the most prevalent were cholera, small-pox, and ship-fever. The number of sick was frightful, and it will be seen by the table (Appendix, No. 11), that in the first eight years of the Commission nearly 50,000 were treated within these hospitals. Since this time, large hospitals on Ward's Island have been erected, and the sanitary character of the incoming emigrants is generally changed and improved, in consequence of legislation on both sides of the Atlantic. Accommodations for nearly all sick emigrants can be afforded at Ward's Island, and the Commissioners therefore think and submit that the reasons for placing the Marine Hospital in their charge have ceased to exist. There are, in addition, positive reasons, enforcing the propriety of a change in this regard. The fund under the charge of the Commissioners, always limited, has been seriously diminished by the decrease of emigration, and is barely sufficient for the maintenance of those who contribute to it, and for the reimbursement of the counties. Under these circumstances, the Commissioners suggest such an alteration in the present laws as will relieve them from the management and expense of this Institution, and place it in charge or under the control of some competent body vested with the proper authority. The Commissioners should, in case of such change, be charged a reasonable amount for such emigrants as they are directed to maintain, who may be sent to the Institution by the health officer; but beyond this, the Commissioners submit that it is unjust to those from whom the Emigrant Fund is collected, to compel that fund to contribute, even incidentally, towards the support of Quarantine, and maintenance of the health laws. The Commissioners desire to be understood as not wishing to escape any personal or official responsibility in regard to the present position of Quarantine affairs; but as the present state of emigration, which will be likely to continue, has scarcely any connection with, or need of, Quarantine, and as considerable amounts are, as before stated, unavoidably paid from an insufficient Emigrant Fund for other than emigrant purposes, the Commissioners have felt it a duty they owe to the contributors to the fund, and to those who have a right to call upon it for aid or reimbursement, to make this representation to the Legislature, and to suggest this alteration in the present laws. They assure the Legislature, nevertheless, of their willingness and desire to assist with their experience, and co-operate with any officers or commission to which the Legislature may deem it advisable to transfer the control and management of the establishment; or they are even willing to continue their present relation and duties thereto, until the proper time arrives for the change to take effect.

In the latter case it is respectfully suggested, that the period for the severance of these two important but discordant classes of duties should now be fixed, to take place at some no very distant period. Under any circumstances, the Commissioners strongly urge upon the Legislature the necessity of also providing by law for the reimbursement to the Emigration Fund of the full amounts which may have been drawn from it, directly or indirectly, under the peculiar situation of that fund, and applied to the general purposes of the Quarantine and the protection of the public health.

Emigrant Refuge and Hospital at Ward's Island.

The Commissioners hold in fee one hundred and six acres on Ward's Island, together with appurtenant water rights and marsh partly covered with water. These lands were purchased, as stated in former reports, from time to time, at prices much less than half of that for which adjoining lands are now sold, and were paid for either from the annual income or from funds obtained on mortgage, with which the property, greatly increased in value in itself, as well as by numerous buildings, is still encumbered.

The tract of land, owned and held in fee by the Commissioners, has been increased somewhat in size and much in convenience and value during the last two years, by the filling in and building a stone sea-wall along the shore, which was performed chiefly by the labor of the inmates. This labor has also been applied by the Superintendent to the grading and levelling the grounds, and other similar improvements conducive to health and convenience.

The buildings, as heretofore reported and described in the several annual reports of this Board, as they were successively erected, can accommodate a much larger number than now occupy them. On the 1st January, 1858, there were in the buildings 1,915 inmates ; the number on 1st January, 1859, was 1,052. Some of the many buildings erected in the earlier years of the Commission were of wood, and, from the pressure of circumstances and want of means, slight in their construction ; some of these have been removed, being a good deal decayed. Those erected since 1850 are of brick, well and durably built, and in perfect order. The hospitals are detached buildings, with a single large ward, with its appendages, on each story, with windows on both sides, and surrounded with large open grounds. They are without architectural pretension, but are believed to be on the very best plan for hospital buildings, whenever there is sufficient ground-space, and are unsurpassed in convenience and comfort, besides having great security against fire, or the communication of any of those infectious diseases which often break out and spread widely in large sanitary establishments.

The other buildings, for the reception of aged or chronically diseased poor, for lying-in women, for the nurseries, for wash and bake-house, for residences for the Superintendent and physicians, all of them plain and simple, are convenient for their several purposes, and entirely separate from one another.

The whole cost of buildings and improvements on Ward's Island is about $260,000. Some portion of this sum, spent in the earlier wooden buildings, which were very useful for the time, may be considered as sunk; but the more important works were economically as well as durably constructed, and it is probable that equal accommodation for the objects of such an institution, exclusive of the price of land, could not now be obtained for a less sum than the whole amount laid out in buildings.

It may be fairly estimated, that an equal accommodation in lands and buildings for any similar sanitary or benevolent purpose, could not be procured in or near the precincts of the city of New York for less than half a million of dollars, which is much above the whole cost of the present Ward's Island establishment.

Since the 1st October, 1855, the Ward's Island establishment had been under the charge of Amos Pilsbury, an officer of long experience in the government of public institutions, and who had been recommended to the Commissioners by his very successful and economical administration of the Albany Penitentiary. He has been invested with the full responsibility of the order and discipline of the Island, and to a great extent, also, of the economy of the Refuge and Hospital. In this administration he continues to give the same ample satisfaction stated in the last annual report. He has been especially successful in the substitution, for many purposes, of labor, both out of doors and within, of the services of the healthy inmates, instead of hired labor from without. This plan, conducing considerably to economy, has been found of decided benefit to the health and spirits of those so employed.

The general care of the establishment on Ward's Island is confided to a standing committee, appointed for the year, who make frequent visits of inspection, and meet regularly for the management of its business. The Island is also visited from time to time by the other Commissioners, and occasional meetings of the Board are held there.

The whole number of inmates, whether diseased in the hospital, or infirm and helpless in the other department, during the year, was 6,906, being 1,633 less than in 1857, and 704 less than in the year preceding. The average number at any one time was about 1,200. The net cost of support of the Emigrant

Hospital and Refuge was $76,243, being $32,602 less than in 1857, and $33,540 than in 1856, and amounting to little more than one-third of the expense in 1855 or in several preceding years. The number provided for was indeed less than in those years; but the economy, with equal comfort and liberality of supplies, was much greater than the proportionate diminution of numbers. The whole number of days spent by the inmates of the Hospital and Refuge during the year in those institutions, being 438,546, gives an average of 1,200 persons throughout the year. It will be seen that the average annual cost of support, including the compensation of physicians and surgeons, the salaries and wages of officers and nurses, and all other expenses on the Island, was nearly $63 50 a head; or, exclusive of these salaries of medical and other officers and wages of subaltern employees, about $43 50 per head for their whole cost for the year, including special hospital expenses. Of the above average of 1,200 persons sustained and aided in the Ward's Island institution, there was about an average of 730 Hospital patients, and 470 in the Refuge department. It is quite difficult to separate the accounts so as to show the relative expense of each class, but the Hospital patients, of course, receive much the largest proportional share.

Abundant supplies of vegetables, as well as of poultry, eggs, &c., are raised on the extensive grounds, and applied to the use of the establishment, thus far lessening the amount of money expenditure.

The diet is generally better than in many similar institutions, and not inferior to the best. The reduced state in which many patients are received, has made it a principle, as well of economy as humanity, to provide the most nourishing food, proper for the case, and which has always been done. The whole cost, including occasional and not expensive clothing, &c., it will be seen is, therefore, during the last year, one dollar and twenty-two cents a head per week.

For statistics of admissions and discharges from the Institutions, during the year, see Table C.

Medical and Surgical Administration of the Hospitals at Ward's Island and their Statistics for the Year.

The Hospital department is administered on the system adopted in July, 1855, as reported in 1857. The Medical department proper is under the charge of a salaried physician, wholly resident on the Island, with as many salaried assistants as the hospital service may require from time to time. H. B. Fay, M. D., was the physician-in-chief, until his resignation in July last, when Dr. George Ford, who had acted as one of his assistants for two years preceding, to the entire satisfaction of this Board, was appointed his successor. He is assisted by F. Simrock, M. D.

The Surgical department is continued under the charge of J. Murray Carnochan, M. D., as surgeon-in-chief, who visits the surgical wards at times fixed by the by-laws, and as often in addition as the surgical service may demand. He performs all important operations. He is assisted by two salaried and constantly resident surgeons, Drs. J. Carey Selden and Hermann Guleke; the last, as well as Dr. Simrock, is a German by birth; both of them speak several European languages.

The number receiving medical or surgical aid was below the average of the years preceding, there being 5,672 cases treated in the hospital, against 6,147 in 1856, and 6,893 in 1857.

The usual diseases of children, as measles, scarlatina, &c., have prevailed, at times, to some extent, but were of a very mild character, and the children's wards were free from endemic ophthalmia, that pest of large nursery establishments, which proved a source of constant anxiety in the early years of this establishment. The ophthalmic wards have been quite free from purulent ophthalmia, with the exception of some cases sent from the city. The surgical wards have continued to be entirely free from those endemic maladies, such as erysipelas, hospital gangrene, &c., which frequently prevail and infect the wards of large hospitals. This is to be ascribed, in part, to the insulation of the several hospital buildings, which affords peculiar advantages, as well for ventilation and cleanliness, as for limiting and controlling the spreading of infection. But it is also due to the Superintendent to add, that the surgeons and physicians bear the strongest attestation to his "scrupulous care in promoting the general hygiene of the hospital;" and that he neglected nothing which could secure to the patients all the advantages and comforts of the best hospitals, with the most perfect order, cleanliness, pure air, and proper diet.

The percentage of mortality in the hospital proper was, for 1858, 6·56 per cent.; on all cases treated, and calculated on the discharges, a mode of estimation sometimes preferred, 7·36.

On all cases under treatment in Hospital and Refuge, the percentage of mortality was 4·79.

The average number of patients in the hospital throughout the year, both medical and surgical, was 730.

The surgical department has received, as heretofore, many intractable cases, and the accidents of a busy city contributed many cases requiring serious operation from injuries. Many capital operations have been performed, mostly attended with favorable results. The whole number of surgical cases treated was 1,329, of which 1,089 were discharged cured, and 28 died, showing a proportion of deaths a fraction more than two per cent. on all cases treated.

The reports of the chief physician and of the chief surgeon, with the table of diseases, &c., thereto appended, which present, as usual, many valuable and interesting statistics of disease, will be found in Table C.

Landing-place for Emigrant Passengers at Castle Garden.

The Commissioners have the satisfaction of reporting, that the experience of a third year amply confirms the opinions expressed by them in their former reports on the efficiency and usefulness of the establishment at Castle Garden for the exclusive landing-place of alien emigrants, under the authority and direction of the Act of April 8th, 1855, "For the protection of emigrants." The establishment continues to fulfil, and even exceed, the expectations of the Legislature.

The Commissioners regret to state, that though the establishment is no longer harassed by legal proceedings, since the decisions of the courts in 1856 and 1857, yet the opposition has continued in constant acts of annoyance, originating with those who have formerly profited by taking advantage of the stranger ignorant of our country, its laws and usages, and often of its language.

The diminished number of those sent from the dépôt to the office in Worth street for relief, or admitted to Ward's Island within a year or two after their arrival, as well as those of this class, falling in the first instance on the charge of the counties, proves the salutary effect of the Castle Garden arrangements.

The report of the Superintendent at Castle Garden, with accompanying tables, will be found in Table D.

The number of persons who landed at Castle Garden was 84,226 (including many not subject to bonds or commutation), arriving in 451 vessels, from 19 different ports.

None of these vessels were crowded with passengers, as often occurred in former years, the average number in each vessel being 187. Register entries have been made of the intended or avowed destination of each passenger, a table of which accompanies this report. Of these, 34,296 reported their intended destination to be the State of New York; 8,630 Pennsylvania and New Jersey; 5,400 to New England; 4,962 to the Southern States; and 30,938 to Ohio, Indiana, Illinois, Michigan, Wisconsin, Iowa, Minnesota, and California.

The experience of the last year showed the great value of this plan, and it has since been continued regularly with the best effect. Thus assistance has been rendered to many who might otherwise have become the prey of fraud, or have fallen into destitution, whilst the character of the assistance was such as not to lessen the feeling of independent self-reliance necessary to self-support and success in all callings.

There has been advanced for this object, during 1858, the sum of $4,873 to 425 families. Of this amount $3,759 has been already repaid by 346 of these families.

Of the whole amount advanced since this plan was adopted in August, 1856, viz., $15,693 50, there remains due $2,179 75 by 162 families.

Some improvements have been introduced. Amongst these, the more perfect arrangement of the department for letters and messages for the emigrants, has been of excellent effect. Since June 30th of this year (when an additional clerical force was given to the department), to 1st January, 1859, there were 1,376 letters written for newly-arrived passengers, to which 562 answers were received at Castle Garden, containing $5,315 51. Besides this, remittances amounting to $6,734 62 were also received in anticipation of the arrival of the passengers; and in addition, numerous messages from emigrant societies and from individuals, to inform passengers on their landing, of funds being ready at their disposal when they should arrive, with the necessary information respecting them.

These letters and messages are quite distinct from those mentioned in another part of this report, as written or received at the Labor Exchange and the Commissioners' Office.

The general inspection and regulation of Castle Garden are intrusted to a committee of three of the Commissioners, the presidents of the German and Irish Emigrant Society being generally, as they have been for the past year, two of the number.

The lease under which Castle Garden is held by the Commissioners expires in May. The title of this property, with the building, wharf, &c., is in litigation between the State and the city of New York, and the case is now before the Supreme Court. Whatever may be the decision as to the legal ownership, in the judgment of the Commissioners, the renewal of this lease is important for the protection of the helpless emigrant, and the best interests of humanity.

Financial Concerns and Condition of the Commission.

On the 1st January, 1858, the books of the Commission presented the following results of their financial state :

Amount of mortgage........................	$125,000 00	
" due the several counties for expenses of emigrants, as per bills examined and corrected	42,662 29	
		167,662 29
Deduct balance in Shoe and Leather Bank to credit of Commissioners of Emigration, Jan. 1, 1858.		32,155 89
		$135,506 40
Being less than at the close of the year 1856.....		$126,696 73

This was exclusive of the unsettled claim of the Governors of the New York Alms-House, then amounting to $37,548 41, against which the Commissioners claimed a large off-set, nearly or quite equal in amount, for the support of native children of emigrant mothers, as set forth in June reports.

During the year 1857, the original debt, contracted for the purchase of lands and the erection of buildings, secured by mortgage on the real estate held by the Commissioners, $150,000 on amount, had been reduced by a payment of $25,000, accompanied by a stipulation on the part of the mortgagee to renew the loan up to the original amount, should any necessity arise for such assistance. This was happily not required during the winter; the improved economy of the establishments, and the diminution of the claims upon them, making up for the great falling off of income from emigration. But on the Commissioners learning that in the straitened condition of the State Treasury, the sum of $30,000, granted as a loan by the Act of 16th April, 1857, if required for the support of the institutions on Ward's Island and the Marine Hospital, could not be relied on in case of any necessity which might arise, and fearing that the possible recurrence of the yellow fever or cholera might subject them to unusual expense, they were induced to avail themselves of the stipulation, and to increase their debt on mortgage to the same mortgagee. The bank in which the Commissioners keep their account agreeing to receive this sum of $25,000 on deposit on interest, until it was required for special use, no additional interest was incurred. The probable use to which this sum was intended to be applied happily did not occur; but the destruction of the Marine Hospital on September 1st and 2d, having imposed, as is elsewhere stated, the necessity of providing such buildings as might answer the absolute necessities of the public health, it was considered that this sum, having been raised on the security of the real estate on Staten Island and Ward's Island, and not forming any part of the Emigrant Commutation Fund, afforded the most appropriate resource for this contingency, and it was so applied.

The account of its receipts and its expenditures is therefore not included in the general accounts of the Commutation Fund.

The amounts due the several towns and counties for the support of alien emigrants were reduced in the month of July, by a payment of $16,893 16 on account; and several local hospitals, at New York, Troy, Buffalo, and Rochester, which had received special cases, chargeable to the Commission, were also paid up to the amount of $8,002 73.

For particulars of county claims, see Table E.

It was the earnest wish and confident expectation of the Commissioners to have made a second and very considerable reduction, in October or November, of the debt due to the counties, which would have been effected, had it not been for the unexpected expenses accruing from the destruction of the Marine Hospital.

The Commissioners were also disappointed in not receiving, during the year, a considerable sum due from the New York Board of Health, incurred by their authority. From these causes, this debt to the counties, with the addition of that incurred during the year, stands now at $47,687.

The general financial condition of the Commissioners may be thus stated:

Indebtedness at the close of the year 1857, as per annual report, was......................		$135,506 40
Indebtedness of Commissioners of Emigration, at the close of the year 1858, was as follows:		
Amount of bond and mortgage............	$125,000 00	
" of do. increased on Feb. 11th, 1858.....	25,000 00	
" due the several counties for expenses of emigrants, as per bills examined and corrected	47,687 69	
	197,687 69	
Deduct balance to credit of Commissioners of Emigration in Shoe and Leather Bank, Jan. 1, 1859	5,656 28	
		192,031 41
Being greater than at the close of 1857..........		$56,525 01

The Board of Health of this city having, in 1854, taken, for a cholera hospital, one of the buildings rented and used by this Commission, and being also indebted to them for the support of patients affected by contagious diseases, and sent by their authority to the hospital at Quarantine, this indebtedness has been acknowledged by a committee of the Board of Health, but no appropriation has yet been made by the Common Council. This sum, when paid, would reduce the unfavorable balance of the year above $16,000.

The balance of indebtedness is also increased by the sum of $25,000, secured on mortgage on the Ward's Island and Staten Island real estate held by this Commission. The sum would have been applied in full to the reduction of the debts above stated, had it not been for the destruction of the Marine Hospital, and the imperative necessity of providing sufficient accommodation for the Quarantine service, until proper provision could be made by legislative authority.

The Commissioners were unwilling to apply the receipts of the Commutation Fund for this purpose, to which it was not applicable by law, whilst they considered the sum raised on the credit of the Staten Island property—and which could be refunded from the proceeds of that property whenever a sale should take place—as peculiarly proper to be thus applied, so far as it could meet the necessary expenditure, which it has nearly done. This sum of $25,000 having been specially deposited on interest, and distinct from the general account of the Commissioners, has, therefore, been thus applied, and the account of its disbursement kept separately.

The account for this special object shows the following results :

Amount of special deposit to credit of Vice-President, Feb. 11th, 1858, exclusive of interest.....		$25,000 00
" paid as per contract for erection of six one-story brick hospitals, at Quarantine, Staten Island, and being in full therefor..	$16,449 96	
" paid on account of contract for erection of offices for health officer and physician, for warden's house and store, gatekeeper's lodge, and repairing Quarantine wall....	9,201 25	
		25,651 21
Overdraft..		$651 21
There is a balance still due on the last contract of....		$1,368 75
Which will be reduced in amount about six hundred dollars for interest accrued on special deposit.		

The statement of the receipts and expenditures of the Commission, during the year 1858, will be found in Table XIV.

E. D. Morgan retired from the Board towards the close of the year, having been elected Governor of the State. His usefulness as a member of the Commission, and his active co-operation in carrying out, as Chairman of the Ward's Island Committee, various measures referred to in this report whereby great beneficial results were obtained, make his separation a great loss to the Board and to the emigrant.

He was succeeded by A. A. Low, who took his seat January 26, 1859.

All of which is respectfully submitted.

G. C. VERPLANCK,
ANDREW CARRIGAN,
CYRUS CURTISS,
ELIJAH F. PURDY,
JOHN P. CUMMING,
WILSON G. HUNT,
WILLIAM JELLINGHAUS,
SAMUEL S. POWELL,
DANIEL F. TIEMANN,
A. A. LOW.

NEW YORK, *February* 8, 1859.

Thirteenth Annual Report

FOR THE YEAR 1859.

TO THE LEGISLATURE OF THE STATE OF NEW YORK:

The year just ended, like that immediately preceding it, was distinguished from all the other years during which the Commissioners of Emigration have discharged the important trust committed to them, by the greatly diminished number of emigrants who arrived at this port (as well as elsewhere in the United States), and, also, by their generally improved state as to health, means, and general condition. There was no severe or general epidemic disease prevailing among emigrant passengers, either on shipboard or after landing. The number of patients, or of entirely destitute and helpless persons in the hospitals, or otherwise obtaining relief from the funds of this Commission, has continued to diminish, even below the lessened number of 1858, whilst the improvements gradually introduced by the experience of the Commissioners and their officers, have placed all the establishments under their immediate charge in a state of order and efficiency. Thus the immediate cares and labors of the Commissioners have been materially diminished, and although the decreased numbers of persons paying commutation continued to keep down the income of the Commission much below that of former years, the improved economy of their establishments, and the lessened demand upon them for relief, enabled them to meet the current expenditure of the year, and to diminish considerably the debts contracted in former years, including those to the counties for the support of emigrant poor.

Their labors and responsibilities have also been lessened by the operation of the last law in relation to the removal of the Quarantine. The details of the subject, and their views in relation to it, will be found in a subsequent part of this report.

The number of alien emigrants who arrived at this port during the year 1859, and for whom commutation was paid, or special bonds executed, was 79,322, being 733 more than in 1858, but 104,451 less than in the year 1857, and 63,020 less than 1856; whilst the proportion to the average of former years, since 1846, is much less than half.

Of these emigrants, 32,652 were from Ireland, 28,270 from Germany, and 18,400 from other countries. (See Table A.)

The whole number of patients admitted to the Marine Hospital from January 1st to June 25th, was 243.

The details of the various operations of the Commission and their officers during the year 1859, present the following results —much smaller in number, under most of the heads, than in former years, but yet showing a large amount of relief afforded and good effected, without any public charge:

Number remaining in Emigrant Refuge and Hospitals, Ward's Island, January 1, 1859	1,052	
" admitted during the year	3,048	
" born there " "	261	
Total number cared for and treated	——	4,361
Number remaining in Marine Hospital, January 1, 1859	31	
" admitted to June 25th	243	
Total cases treated	——	274
Number of sick sent from Office to New York Hospital during the year 1859	54	
" of do. to St. Vincent's Hospital	10	
Total cases sent to both hospitals	——	64
Number of lunatic emigrants in City Asylum on Jan. 1st, 1859,	45	
" admitted during the year	44	
Total number of lunatic emigrants treated	——	89

Of which there left the Asylum, viz.:

Number discharged cured	29
" died	7
" whose term of five years had expired	12
Total discharges	48
Number of lunatic emigrants in City Asylum, Jan. 1st, 1860, chargeable to this Commission	41

Number of cases of small-pox chargeable to the Commissioners of Emigration admitted to Small-pox Hospital, Blackwell's Island, during the year 1859, from June 24th....			28
Of which were discharged cured..........................	24		
Number remaining on 1st of January, 1860, chargeable to the Commissioners of Emigration.......................	4		
Number of persons sent back to Europe at their own request.		68	
" of do. and at expense of consignees of vessels......		31	
Total number sent back to Europe...........		——	99
Number of persons forwarded to various places inland from Castle Garden, at expense of Commission......		54	
" forwarded to various places inland by agents......		23	
Total number so forwarded..................		——	77
Number of persons temporarily relieved in this city.........		21	
" " " " " by agent at Buffalo.		701	
Total number so relieved...................		——	722
Number of persons temporarily supplied with board and lodging in this city............................		3,274	
" temporarily supplied with board and lodging by agent at Buffalo............................		586	
Total number boarded and lodged...........		——	3,860
Number of out-door poor in the city buried at the expense of the Commission...........................		42	
" of interments from institutions on Ward's Island in City Cemetery at expense of this Commission..		262	
Total number buried.......................		——	304
Number of females provided with situations at the Intelligence Office and Labor Exchange............		4,420	
" of males, do. do. do...........................		2,329	
Number of both sexes provided with employment by agent at Buffalo................................		401	
Total number provided with employment.....		——	7,150
Whole number relieved and forwarded, in and from the several counties of the State, chargeable to the Commission.			2,407
Grand total relieved, forwarded, and provided with employment, &c., by the Commission, in the State and city of New York..........			19,435
Number of days spent in Marine Hospital from January 1st to June 27th............................			5,400
" of days spent in Emigrant Hospital, Ward's Island..		163,219	
" " " Refuge, do.....		83,539	
		——	246,758
Total days spent in institutions of Commission			252,158

Amount of money received at Office for recently arrived emigrants..	$1,848 77
Amount of money received at office of Irish Emigrant Society from friends of recently arrived emigrants, and applied to forwarding of such emigrants, chargeable to the Commission..	$1,826 84

The Quarantine, Marine Hospital, &c.

The Commissioners of Emigration have stated, in their last annual report, the arrangements and expenditures which they judged it to be their duty to make immediately for the protection of the public health, after the destruction of the hospitals and other buildings of the Marine Hospital at Staten Island, on the 1st September, 1858. Under the state of things at that time, and as the laws stood, it was evident that whatever might be the decision and enactments of the Legislature, no effectual provision for the uses of the Marine Hospital could be made and carried into operation for several months, during which period it was quite possible that ship-fever or other infectious cases, during the winter (as occurred formerly), and cases of yellow fever, early in the summer, might possibly endanger the public health and general welfare,—considerations which demanded immediate provision for the reception and care of patients. Such provision as was thought adequate, was made with as little delay and as much economy as practicable, and in such a manner as to place as few obstacles as could be in the way of any alteration by the Legislature, of the Hospital and Quarantine system and location under the existing laws.

The Commissioners, though pressed for means, immediately made arrangements to meet the requirements of the station, and to protect the State from the introduction of pestilence. At first tents were spread; then a temporary shanty built. Subsequently the Commissioners built by contract six brick hospitals, situated so far within the grounds, and from any houses in the village, as to afford no reasonable cause for apprehension to those dwelling beyond the walls. These hospitals were constructed chiefly from materials of the destroyed buildings, and thus the cost was so much diminished as but little to exceed the price of temporary wooden buildings. They were completed and in part occupied in January, 1859.

The report of Dr. Jerome, who as Physician-in-chief, had the care of these hospitals from that time until the patients were removed in June, with accompanying tables, will be found in Table B.

During the year, from January 1st to June 25th, the whole number of patients under hospital treatment, was 274, being the smallest number received for many years, and being but one-fifth of those received last year, when the number was one-third less than what it had been in 1857, and very far below the average of preceding years since the Marine Hospital has been under the authority of this Commission.

The average duration of treatment was nineteen and two-third days.

The proportion of deaths in this establishment was, during the year, 9·12 per cent. on all cases under treatment.

In July last the Quarantine Commissioners, appointed under the Act of 1859, gave notice to this Commission, that a Floating Hospital for the reception of infectious and contagious diseases was completed. The language of the Act of 1859, taken in connection with other unrepealed provisions of law, in relation to the temporary Quarantine establishment for the care of the sick, appeared to admit of contradictory interpretations. Yet it seemed to the counsel and committees of this Board that, under these enactments, either the Quarantine Commissioners or the Commissioners of Emigration, acting in good faith and with the concurrence of the other Commission, might legally maintain and administer the temporary Floating Hospital, or a Marine Hospital, or Quarantine Institution.

The Commissioners of Emigration, after much deliberation, and acting with the best understanding and full conference with the Quarantine Commissioners, and their officers, came to the determination that it was not advisable for this Board to take charge of this hospital, and that it could be administered as the law then stood, and with regard to all circumstances, more efficiently, and with better results as to the public service, under the authority of the other Commission who had planned and prepared the establishment. The Commissioners of Emigration agreed to support at their charge, either on the Floating Hospital, or at the Small-Pox Hospital (according to the disease), all patients chargeable to the Cómmutation Fund, and also to provide and pay for most of the current expenses of the Floating Hospital, leaving to the other Commissioners the appointment of officers, and the authority and direction of the hospital administration.

The papers, reports, &c., herewith submitted, which passed between the said Commissioners in relation to this subject, will exhibit all the details of these transactions, and will be found in Appendix, No. 12.

In a strict construction of all the laws applicable to this subject, still in force, it would seem at least doubtful whether any of the commutation income could be properly applied to purely quarantine objects ; and the very limited income of this year made it hazardous to other important interests, to encroach at all upon funds collected and set apart exclusively for the aid and support of alien emigrants. But from the urgent necessity of the public service in regard to the most important interests of the commerce and the health of the whole State, the Commissioners of Emigration were induced to go as far in the advance of funds as their means would permit.

The patients were all removed from the Marine Hospital on Staten Island in July last, and the results during the year have been in all respects satisfactory. But all the arrangements and understandings between the two Boards of Commissioners are of course temporary, and the future permanent administration and government and support of the Quarantine Hospitals call for the most deliberate consideration of the Legislature.

A considerable part of the amount advanced at different times during the present year, by the Commissioners of Emigration, for the support of the Marine Hospital, appears to this Board to be a just claim in favor of the Commutation Fund raised from emigrant aliens, and for their uses. The sale of the very valuable lands lately occupied by the Marine Hospital, as provided by law, will furnish a fund above the debts now directly charged upon it, out of which all such advances may be properly refunded, without injustice or inconvenience to the other funds of the State Treasury.

In relation to the general subject of Quarantine and its Hospital, much consideration and years of experience of the Marine or Quarantine Hospital system, under different forms of administration, have led the Commissioners of Emigration to the conclusions stated in respect to this question in their last year's report, and which the occurrences of the last two years more strongly confirm, and induce them again to press upon the attention of the Legislature.

Emigrant Refuge and Hospital, Ward's Island.

A small parcel of land, consisting of three lots, which is entirely enclosed by the former purchases of this Board, but had never been owned in fee by them, though in their use and occupation, was purchased during the year, at a cost of $1,000. From its peculiar situation, it is an important acquisition.

The tract has also been enlarged in size, convenience, and value during the last three years, by filling in and building a stone sea-wall along the shore, which was performed chiefly by labor of the inmates. This labor has also been applied by the Superintendent to the grading and levelling the grounds, and similar improvements conducive to health and convenience.

The buildings, as heretofore reported and described in the several annual reports of this Board as they were successively erected, can accommodate more than double the number that now occupy them. On the 1st January, 1859, there were in the buildings 1,052 inmates; the number on 1st January, 1860, was 764.

Since the 1st October, 1855, the Ward's Island establishment had been under the charge of Amos Pilsbury, an officer of long experience in the government of public institutions, and who had been recommended to the Commissioners by his very successful and economical administration of the Albany Penitentiary. He was invested with the full responsibility of the order and discipline of the Island, and, to a great extent, of the economy of the Refuge and Hospital.

In his administration of these important duties, from his entrance on office, he has given the most entire satisfaction to this Board, and it is due to him to state, that it is in a great degree owing to the economy, system, and efficiency which he has introduced into the whole Ward's Island establishment, that the Commission has been enabled to surmount the most serious embarrassments and difficulties. He resigned his office, July 1st, 1859, on being appointed General-Superintendent of the Metropolitan police. The Commissioners appointed as his successor, Louis D. Pilsbury, who now fills that office. He had been trained under the former Superintendent in similar places, and had since been employed as deputy-superintendent on Ward's Island.

The whole number of inmates, whether diseased in the hospital, or infirm and helpless in the other department, during the year, was 4,361, being 2,545 less than in 1858, and 4,178 less than in the year preceding. The average number at any one time was about 676. The net cost of support of the Emigrant Hospital and Refuge was $54,890 40, being $21,352 50 less than in 1858, and $53,954 85 than in 1857, being only one-half the expense of that year, and amounting to little more than one-third of the expense in 1855 or in several preceding years. The number provided for was indeed less than in those years; but the economy, with equal comfort and liberality of supplies, was much greater than the proportionate diminution of numbers. The whole number of days spent by the inmates of the Hospital and Refuge during the year in those institutions being 246,758, gives an average of 676 persons throughout the year. The average annual cost of support, including the compensation of physicians and surgeons, the salaries and wages of officers and nurses, and all other expenses on the Island, was nearly $81 20 a head, or, exclusive of these salaries of medical and other officers, and wages of subaltern employées, about $50 96 per head for their whole cost for the year, including special hospital expenses. This increased ratio of cost over that stated in the report for 1858 is mainly due to the less number of patients, the number and compensation of physicians remaining the same, with some diminution only of subalterns. Of the above average of 676 persons sustained and aided in the Ward's Island institution, there was about an average of 446 hospital patients, and 230 in the Refuge department. It is difficult to separate the accounts so as to show the relative expense of each class, but the hospital patients, of course, receive much the largest proportional share.

For statistics of admissions to and discharges from the Institutions during the year, see Table C.

Medical and Surgical Administration of the Hospitals at Ward's Island, and their Statistics for the year.

The Hospital department is administered on the system adopted in July, 1855, as reported in 1857. George Ford, M. D., who has had the advantage of several years' practical experience on a large scale, in various medical positions in the hospitals of this Commission, during periods when the wards were filled with the greatest number of patients and varieties of disease, was, in July, 1858, appointed Physician-in-chief at Ward's Island, and has discharged the duties of that station with fidelity and success, to the satisfaction of this Board. He resides on the Island, and devotes himself exclusively to the service of the Institution. The lessened number of patients has not required the services of more than one resident medical assistant. This place has been filled during the year by F. Simrock, M. D., who is a German by birth, and both he and Dr. Guleke (one of the assistant surgeons) speak several European languages.

The Surgical department is continued under the charge of J. Murray Carnochan, M. D., as surgeon-in-chief. He performs all important operations. He was assisted by two salaried and constantly resident surgeons, Drs. J. Carey Selden and Hermann Guleke.

Dr. Selden resigned his station on 1st January, 1860. A successor will be appointed whenever an increase of patients in the surgical wards may require additional aid.

The number receiving medical or surgical aid was below the average of the years preceding, there being 3,668 cases treated in the hospital, against 6,147 in 1856, 6,893 in 1857, and 5,067 in 1858.

During the past year the Hospital and Refuge were quite free, as they have been for a number of years, from any prevailing epidemic. There were some sporadic cases of scarlatina and measles, and a larger proportion of typhus fever cases, and of a severer character than for several years, were admitted. But none of these diseases spread among the patients, or the other inmates of the establishments.

The percentage of mortality in the hospital proper was, for 1859, 4·85 per cent. on all cases treated ; and calculated on the discharges, a mode of estimation sometimes preferred, 5·55.

On all cases under treatment in Hospital and Refuge, the percentage of mortality was 3·74.

The average number of patients in the hospital throughout the year, both medical and surgical, was 446.

Many of the most serious operations of surgery have been performed successfully, and in some instances, at least, there is reason to trust that the science itself has been improved in its means of relieving human suffering. The number of surgical cases treated was 1,029, of which 875 were discharged cured, and 11 died, showing a proportion of deaths a small fraction more than one per cent. on all cases treated—a proportion the more remarkable and gratifying from the consideration of the broken-down constitutions of many of the patients.

The reports of the chief physician and of the chief surgeon, with the table of diseases, &c., thereto appended, will be found in Table C.

Landing-place for Emigrant Passengers at Castle Garden.

The Commissioners have again the satisfaction of reporting, that the experience of a fourth year confirms the opinions expressed by them in their former reports, on the efficiency and usefulness of the establishment at Castle Garden for the exclusive landing-place of alien emigrants, under the authority and direction of the Act of April 18th, 1855, "For the protection of Emigrants." The establishment continues to fulfil all the expectations of the Legislature.

Making ample allowance for the less number of emigrants, yet the still diminished number of those admitted to Ward's Island, or otherwise relieved within a year or two after their arrival, as well as those of this class falling on the charge of the counties, may be properly ascribed in no small degree to the salutary effect of the Castle Garden arrangements.

The report of the Superintendent at Castle Garden, with accompanying tables, which will be found in Table D, exhibits many interesting and important details, of which not the least valuable and important are the statements of the relative proportions of sailing and steam vessels, bringing passengers, the increased proportion of steamers in the business, their respective national flags, and the ports from which they sailed.

The number of persons who landed at Castle Garden was 85,602 (including many not subject to bonds or commutation), arriving in 437 vessels, from 19 different ports.

None of these vessels were crowded with passengers, the average number in each vessel being 196. According to the registered entries made of the intended or avowed destination of each passenger, 40,923 reported their intended destination to be the State of New York; 9,991 Pennsylvania and New Jersey; 8,510 to New England; 5,066 to the Southern States; and 15,790 to Ohio, Indiana, Illinois, Michigan, Wisconsin, Iowa, Minnesota, and California, and 5,322 to Kansas, Nebraska, New Mexico, and Canada, &c., &c.

There was advanced on baggage of emigrants going into the interior, during 1859, the sum of $2,345 50 to 239 families. Of this amount, $2,031 50 has already been repaid by 211 of these families.

Of the whole amount advanced since this plan was adopted in August, 1856, viz., $18,039, there remains due $1,650 25, by 132 families.

During the year 1859, there were 1,564 letters written for newly-arrived passengers, to which 789 answers were received at Castle Garden, containing $6,283 76. Besides this, remittances amounting to $6,825 19 were also received in anticipation of the arrival of the passengers.

Financial Concerns and Condition of the Commission.

On the 1st January, 1859, the books of the Commission presented the following results of their financial state :

Amount of mortgage..........................	$150,000 00	
" due the several counties for expenses of emigrants, as per bills examined and corrected	47,687 69	
		197,687 69
Deduct balance in Shoe and Leather Bank, to credit of Commissioners of Emigration, Jan. 1st, 1859..................................		5,656 28
Indebtedness of Commission on 1st Jan., 1859....		$192,031 41

This was exclusive of the unsettled claim of the Governors of the New York Alms-House, then amounting to $40,770 19, against which the Commissioners claimed a larger offset, which will more than balance the account in amount, for the support of native children of emigrant mothers, as set forth in the reports of former years.

But another account of long standing between the city of New York, represented by their Board of Health, and this Commission, has been finally amicably settled and closed during the past year. This consisted of the claims by this Commission, stated in former reports, for the support of patients afflicted with contagious diseases and sent by the Board of Health from the city to the Marine Hospital, for damages for the taking and using in 1854, for a cholera hospital, a building rented by the Commissioners, and other items, which the Commissioners claimed as proper offsets to the rent of Castle Garden for some years. All these were settled by mutual agreement, and the balance allowed by this Commission paid over to the city.

The debt on mortgage on the land held at Ward's Island and at the Marine Hospital, remained at the close of the year as at the close of 1858, the interest having been duly paid.

The amounts due the several towns and counties for the

support of alien emigrants, were reduced by a payment of $23,535 75 on account; and several local hospitals, at New York, Troy, Utica, Buffalo, and Rochester, which had received special cases, chargeable to the Commission, were also paid up to the amount of $6,380 21.

(For particulars of county claims see Table E.)

It was hoped to make a second reduction of the debt still remaining due to the counties, but the necessity imposed on the Commissioners by the peculiar circumstances of the case, of supporting in great part the Quarantine establishment, together with the diminution of their income from the commutation of emigrants, compelled them to delay for the present any further payment.

During the present fiscal year, in January, 1860, a further payment was made to the counties of $17,890 31. Unless some unforeseen and unexpected circumstances should cause the necessary expenditure of the winter to much exceed what is now anticipated, it is hoped that a payment to the counties in full up to 1st January, 1860, can be made in the spring.

The general financial condition of the Commission may be thus stated:

Indebtedness at the close of the year 1858, as per annual report, was		$192,031 41
Indebtedness of Commissioners of Emigration, at the close of the year 1859, was as follows:		
Amount of bond and mortgage	$150,000 00	
" due the several counties for expenses of emigrants, as per bills examined and corrected	37,559 75	
Overdraft against Commissioners of Emigration, in Shoe and Leather Bank, Dec. 31st, 1859	11,653 16	
		$199,212 91
Being greater than at the close of 1858		$7,181 50

The unsettled account with the Governors of the New York Alms-House, amounting on 1st January, 1860, to $43,846 98, still remains unadjusted, the Commissioners claiming as heretofore a larger amount as an offset to these charges, being for the support of native children of emigrant mothers.

The statement of the receipts and expenditures of the Commissioners of Emigration, during the year 1859, will be found in Table No. XV.

All of which is respectfully submitted.

G. C. VERPLANCK,
ANDREW CARRIGAN,
CYRUS CURTISS,
ELIJAH F. PURDY,
JOHN P. CUMMING,
WILSON G. HUNT,
WM. JELLINGHAUS,
SAMUEL S. POWELL,
A. A. LOW.

NEW YORK, *February* 8, 1860.

Fourteenth Annual Report

FOR THE YEAR 1860.

TO THE LEGISLATURE OF THE STATE OF NEW YORK :

The year 1860 presented the same striking contrast, stated in the last annual report of this Commission, in respect to 1858 and '59, compared with all the preceding years since 1847, during which the Commissioners of Emigration have discharged the important trust committed to them, in the greatly diminished number of emigrants who arrived at this port (as well as elsewhere in the United States), and in their improved state as to health, means, and general condition. There was no severe or general epidemic disease prevailing among emigrant passengers either on shipboard or after landing. The number of patients, or of entirely destitute and helpless persons, in the hospitals, or otherwise obtaining relief from this Commission, has seldom risen much above the lessened number of 1859, whilst the improvements introduced by the experience of the Commissioners and their officers, have placed all the establishments under their immediate charge in a state of great order and efficiency. Thus the cares and labors of the Commissioners have been materially diminished, and although the decreased numbers of persons paying commutation continued to keep down the income of the Commission much below that of the years preceding 1858, yet the improved economy of their establishments, and the lessened demand upon them for relief, including county claims, enabled them to meet the current expenditure of the year, and to extinguish the debts reported in former years, with the exceptions of the debt secured by mortgage on their real estate, and contracted principally in the purchase or improvement of their lands.

Their labors and responsibilities have also been lessened by the operation of the last law in relation to the removal of the Quarantine. The details of the subject, and their views in relation to it, will be found in a subsequent part of this report.

The whole number of passengers landed at this port during the year 1860, was 155,371. Of these 50,209 were citizens, or persons not subject to bonds or commutation ; and 105,162 were aliens for whom commutation was paid, or bonds executed, showing an increase in alien emigrants of 25,840 more than in 1859, and 26,573 more than in 1858, but being 78,611 less than in the year 1857, and 37,180 less than 1856 ; whilst the proportion to the average of former years, since 1847, is much less than half.

Of these emigrants, 47,330 were from Ireland, 37,899 from Germany, and 19,933 from other countries. (See Table A.)

The Commissioners have much gratification in stating that while the number of alien emigrants arrived during the year shows an increase over the years 1858 and 1859 of some 22 per cent., yet the number of destitute and diseased chargeable to the Commission in their institutions on Ward's Island and temporarily furnished with board and lodging in the city, and relieved and provided for in the various counties, shows no increase over the year 1859, and is nearly 6,000 less than in 1858, and less than in any previous year.

The general supervision of all the extensive and varied business of the Commission continued, during the first part of the year 1860, to be discharged by the late Vice-President, Eleazer Crabtree, Esq. In the month of August last, this excellent officer and esteemed and honored citizen died, after a short illness, from ship fever, contracted in the discharge of duties to which he was prompted by his usual active benevolence and humanity. His death was felt as a public loss, not only by all connected with this Commission either officially or from their course of business, but by the larger class of our citizens by whom he had long been known and esteemed. His services to this Board, and the thousands who have fallen under its care or protection during his executive administration of much of its concerns, were rendered more acceptable to the public by his high and honorable character, and his uniform courtesy and amiable deportment.

After much consideration of the subject, the Board determined on restoring the office of General Agent, as it existed in the first years of this Commission, united with the office of Secretary. The long experience and tried ability of the present Secretary, Bernard Casserly, seemed, in the judgment of the Commissioners, to qualify him eminently for this position, and he has discharged its duties to their entire satisfaction.

Cyrus Curtiss, Esq., has been elected Vice-President, to preside and discharge the duties of the President in case of his absence or inability, but without any of the office or executive duties of the former Vice-President, all of which are now discharged by the Secretary.

The details of the various operations of the Commission and their officers during the year 1860, present the following results :

Number in Emigrant Refuge and Hospital, Ward's Island, Jan. 1st, 1860		764	
" admitted during the year		3,701	
" born there " "		264	
Total number cared for and treated		——	4,729
Number of sick sent from Office to the New York Hospital during the year 1860		67	
" of do. to St. Vincent's Hospital		5	
Total cases sent to both hospitals		——	72
Number of lunatic emigrants in City Asylum, Jan. 1st, 1860		41	
" admitted during the year		41	
Total number of lunatic emigrants		——	82
Of which there left the Asylum, viz.:			
Number discharged cured	23		
" died	2		
" whose term of five years had expired	16		
" transferred to Emigrant Lunatic Asylum, W. Island	27		
Total discharges	68		
Number of lunatic emigrants in City Asylum on 1st January, 1861, chargeable to the Commission	14		

Number of cases of small-pox chargeable to the Commissioners of Emigration admitted to Small-pox Hospital, Blackwell's Island, during the year 1860....			115
" discharged cured..............................	88		
" died..	5		
Total discharges..........................	93		
" remaining on 1st of January, 1861, chargeable to the Commission................................	22		
Number of persons sent back to Europe at their own request		67	
" of do. and at expense of consignees of vessels......		33	
Total number sent back to Europe...........		——	100
Number of persons forwarded to various places inland from Castle Garden at expense of the Commission...		206	
" forwarded to various places inland by agent at Albany		27	
" do. by agent at Buffalo.........................		56	
" do. " " Rochester......................		12	
Total number so forwarded....................		——	301
Number of persons temporarily relieved by this Commission at residences of parties, too sick to be removed to the hospital............................			122
" temporarily supplied with board and lodging in the city..		3,242	
" temporarily supplied with board and lodging by agent at Buffalo............................		1,476	
" do. by agent at Albany........................		397	
Total number so relieved..................		——	5,115
Number of out-door poor in the city buried at the expense of the Commission...........................		30	
" of interments from institutions on Ward's Island in City Cemetery at the expense of this Commission		228	
Total number buried.......................		——	258
Number of males provided with situations at the Intelligence Office and Labor Exchange..................		2,220	
" of females......................................		4,401	
" of both sexes provided with situations by agent at Buffalo		684	
" do. do. by agent at Albany......................		412	
Total number provided with employment.....		——	7,717
Whole number relieved and forwarded in and from the several counties of the State, chargeable to this Commission			2,104
Grand total of destitute alien emigrants landed at the port of New York during the past five years, who were relieved, forwarded, and provided with employment, &c., by this Commission in the State and city of New York during the year 1860.....................			20,715

Number of days spent in Emigrant Hospital, Ward's Island..	173,649	
" " " " Refuge, do. ..	89,752	
Total number of days in both...............		263,401

Amount of money received at Office for recently arrived emigrants.......................................	$2,864 96
Amount of money received at office of the Irish Emigrant Society from friends of recently arrived emigrants, and applied to the forwarding of such emigrants chargeable to the Commission................................	$3,219 49

The Quarantine, Marine Hospital, &c.

In their annual report for 1859, the Commissioners of Emigration stated the difficulties, arising from the obscurities and apparent contradictions, under the several acts relating to their duties and rights, and those of the Quarantine Commissioners, and the doubtful legal and constitutional right of applying any part of the income collected from alien emigrants by commutation, for their support and assistance, to the general purposes of the protection of the public health. They then hoped and expected, that the Legislature of 1860 would not only clear up all such difficulties, but relieve this Board, according to the views they have repeatedly expressed to the Legislature, from all care and responsibility as to the Quarantine and Marine Hospital. But the Legislature adjourned without any decisive action on any of the bills introduced, for the permanent regulation of the Marine Hospital. Happily for the public welfare, the good understanding between the highly respectable and efficient Quarantine Commission and this Board led to the continuance of arrangements similar to those of the last year, which effectually attained the great objects of both Boards, in respect to the Marine Hospital and the public health.

In relation to the general subject of Quarantine and its hospital, much consideration and years of experience of the Marine or Quarantine Hospital system, under different forms of administration, have led the Commissioners of Emigration to the conclusions stated in respect to this question in their last year's report, and which the occurrences of the last two years more strongly confirm, and induce them again to press upon the attention of the Legislature.

There having been no amendment of these laws in 1860, from the necessity of the case the same plan of adjustment and administration was continued during the last year. Had the year been marked by wide-spread and dangerous pestilence from abroad, it is possible that the most serious difficulties might have arisen, as to the means and funds for carrying on the system. But the year was comparatively free from such dangers, and no such difficulties occurred.

This Commission was convinced that, in an equitable construction of all the laws applicable to their permanent rights and duties, the Commutation Income should not be applied to merely Quarantine purposes. But for the immediate necessities of the case, as affecting the public health and the most important interests of commerce, they were then induced to go as far in the advance of funds as their means would permit. But this was done in the full expectation, which they still confidently entertain, that their advances would be repaid either directly from the State Treasury, or, as they then suggested, from the probable ample proceeds of the sale of the lands of the State Marine Hospital at Staten Island.

But the Commissioners of Emigration were anxious to avoid, during the summer of 1860, as far as possible, any further diversion of the Emigrant Commutation Fund from its legitimate objects. They accordingly joined in an application to the Board of Health of the city of New York, to induce them to assume the responsibility, or at least to advance the means of supporting the establishment for the protection of the health and commerce of the port. This request was rejected in an argumentative report, which came to the conclusion of imposing the whole liability upon the funds of this Commission from the commutation of alien passengers. This Board could not assent either to the argument, or the conclusion; but, fortunately, they had within their reach another alternative, which was free from all objection except the possibility and indeed the apparent probability that the amount might not be adequate to the needed expenditure.

About fifty acres of land, at Seguine's Point, had been purchased in 1858, with a view to the purposes of a Marine Hospital for pestilential or infectious diseases, by the former Commissioners for the removal of Quarantine. It had been abandoned as to those objects from various causes which have been stated to the Legislature, but remained under the charge of this Board; the legal title, as in respect to the other real estate held by them, being vested in the Commissioners of Emigration in trust for the people of the State of New York. The property having been purchased for the purposes of Quarantine and paid for from an appropriation from the State Treasury, it seemed perfectly proper to apply whatever sum could be raised by sale or mortgage to the support of the present Floating Hospital. Application was made accordingly to the Governor, Comptroller, and Attorney-General, for their approval, as by law provided, of a mortgage on the premises, the proceeds to be applied exclusively to the support of the Floating Hospital and other arrangements for the protection of the public health. The sum of $7,500, being the highest amount which could be obtained, was borrowed on this security from the New York Life Insurance Company. It was paid over from time to time to the Quarantine Commissioners, as their requirements demanded; and the judicious economy of their expenditures, together with the general favorable character of the season as to our foreign commerce, rendered these means nearly adequate to the important uses for which they were required. These means are, however, now exhausted, and it is confidently hoped that the Legislature of the present winter will put an end to the recurrence of any difficulty similar to those of 1859 and 1860.

The Commissioners take the liberty of again repeating and urging upon the consideration of the Legislature the reasons which have long impressed them with the conviction, that they and the fund specially intrusted to them should be relieved from all connection with the government or expenses of the Marine Hospital and Quarantine. As stated, in substance, in former reports, this Commission was organized in the year 1847, and the Marine Hospital, with its grounds and extensive buildings, committed to its charge. The Commission was then an entirely new creation, without lands, buildings, or means; the arriving emigrants were affected with various contagious and infectious diseases, among which were widely prevalent cholera, small-pox, and ship fever. The number of sick was appalling, so that in the first eight years of the Commission nearly 50,000 were treated within these hospitals. Since that time large hospitals on Ward's Island have been erected, and the sanitary character of the incoming emigrants is greatly changed and improved, in consequence of legislation on both sides of the Atlantic. Accommodations for all sick emigrants other than those arriving with infectious diseases can be afforded at Ward's Island, and the Commissioners, therefore, think and submit that the reasons for placing the Marine Hospital in their charge have ceased to exist. There are, in addition, strong positive reasons, enforcing the propriety of a change in this regard. The fund under the charge of the Commissioners, always limited, has been seriously diminished by the decrease of emigration, and is now barely sufficient for the maintenance of those who contribute to it, and for the reimbursement of the counties. These considerations compel the Commissioners to advise such an alteration in the present laws as will relieve them from the management of the Quarantine or Marine Hospital, wherever located, and the salary of its chief, and to place the establishment in charge or under the control of some competent Board or officers vested with the proper authority. The Commissioners should, in case of such change, be charged a reasonable amount for such emigrants as may properly be chargeable to their fund, and who may be sent to the Institution by the health officer. But beyond this, the Commissioners submit that it is unjust to those from whom the Emigrant Fund is collected, to compel that fund to contribute, even incidentally, towards the support of Quarantine and maintenance of the Health Laws. The Commissioners desire to be understood as not wishing to escape any personal or official responsibility in regard to Quarantine affairs ; but as the present state of emigration, which will be likely to continue, has scarcely any connection with, or need of, Quarantine, and as considerable amounts are, as before stated, unavoidably paid from an insufficient Emigrant Fund for other than emigrant purposes, the Commissioners have felt it a duty they owe to the contributors to the fund and to those who have a right to call upon it for aid or reimbursement, to make this representation to the Legislature and to urge this alteration in the laws now regulating the duties of the Commissioners of Emigration and those relating to the Quarantine and the Public Health.

The Commissioners have also to report under this head, that the government and immediate administration of the temporary or Floating Hospital having been conceded to the Quarantine Commissioners, and the patients all removed, or no longer received at the former Marine Hospital on Staten Island, according to the directions of the law of 1858, this Commission discharged, as soon as practicable, the various officers in their employment at that station for whose service there was no longer any occasion.

But the late physician of the Marine Hospital continued his residence on the grounds without the request or authority of the Board, and has claimed a compensation of $5,000 a year. The Board being advised by counsel that, the duties of the office having been abolished by the Act of 1858 for the Removal of Quarantine, the office itself was by necessary implication of law also abolished, declined to pay the demand. The late physician thereupon appealed to the Courts, and the Supreme Court of this district has the case now under advisement for decision.

But the Commissioners respectfully request that, whatever may be the result as to the present claim, all future difficulty should be removed by a repeal, without delay, as recommended by the Governor in his annual message, of the provisions of law establishing this office, and the Emigrant Fund be relieved from a serious burden, always of doubtful justice and constitutionality.

Emigrant Refuge and Hospital, Ward's Island.

The buildings and lands on Ward's Island, as heretofore reported, have been described in the several annual reports of this Board, as they were successively erected and purchased. On the 1st January, 1860, there were in the buildings 764 inmates; the number on the 1st January, 1861, was 1,068.

Louis D. Pilsbury filled the office of Superintendent of Ward's Island from July 1, 1859, to July 31, 1860, when he resigned.

Mr. Pilsbury succeeded his father, Amos Pilsbury, to whose economy, system and efficiency our former reports have been witness.

Upon the resignation of Mr. Pilsbury, the Commissioners selected for the office James P. Fagan. Mr. Fagan was well known to most of the Commissioners from many years of former faithful and efficient service in their employment, though for the last two years he had been engaged in other avocations. He immediately entered upon the duties of the office, and has fulfilled the expectations confidently entertained of his fidelity and fitness for the station.

The whole number of inmates, whether diseased in the hospital, or infirm and helpless in the other department, during the year, was 4,729, being 368 more than in 1859, and 2,177 less than in the year preceding. The average number at any one time was about 722. The net cost of support of the Emigrant Hospital and Refuge was $58,913 41, being $4,023 more than in 1859, but $17,330 less than in 1858, and $49,932 less than in 1857, amounting to little more than one-half the expense of that year, and one-third the expense in 1855, or in several preceding years. The number provided for was indeed less than in the earlier years; but the economy, with equal comfort and liberality of supplies, was much greater than the proportionate diminution of numbers. The whole number of days spent by the inmates of the Hospital and Refuge during the year in those institutions being 263,401, gives an average of 722 persons throughout the year. The average annual cost of support, including the compensation of physicians and surgeons, the salaries and wages of officers and nurses, and all other expenses on the Island, was nearly $81 60 a head; or, exclusive of these salaries of medical and other officers, and wages of subaltern employées, about $58 per head for their whole cost for the year, including special hospital expenses. This increase of proportional cost over that of 1858 and 1859 is mainly due to the necessary expenses attending the opening of new wards for the reception of typhus fever cases and the expensive treatment of that disease. Of the above average of 722 persons sustained and aided in the Ward's Island institutions, there was an average of 476 hospital patients, and 246 in the Refuge department. It is difficult to separate the accounts so as to show the precise expense of each class, but the hospital patients, of course, receive much the largest proportional share.

The whole cost, including in many cases not expensive clothing, &c., it will be seen, is, therefore, during the last year, one dollar and fifty-seven cents a head per week.

The following summary gives the aggregate results of the whole of these establishments, including the hospitals proper as well as the Refuge department:

Number of inmates in institution on Jan. 1st, 1860	764	
" admitted during the year	3,701	
" of births in " "	264	
Total number cared for and treated		4,729
Number discharged during the year	3,433	
" of deaths " "	228	
Total number		3,661
" remaining on 31st December, 1860		1,068
Number of days spent in Hospital	173,649	
" " " Refuge	89,752	
Total number of days		263,401

Medical and Surgical Administration of the Hospitals at Ward's Island, and their Statistics for the year.

The Hospital department is administered on the system adopted in July, 1855, as reported in 1857. The Medical department proper is under the charge of a salaried physician, wholly resident on the Island, with as many salaried assistants as the hospital service may require from time to time. George Ford, M. D., who was, in July, 1858, appointed Physician-in-chief, continues to discharge the duties of that station with fidelity and success. The lessened number of patients has not required the services of more than one resident medical assistant. This place has been filled during the first part of the year by F.

Simrock, M. D. He was succeeded by Dr. Guleke, long an assistant surgeon in this establishment.

The Surgical department is continued under the charge of J. Murray Carnochan, M. D., as Surgeon-in-chief, and who performs all important operations.

The number receiving medical or surgical aid was below the average of the years preceding, except 1859, there being 3,863 cases treated in the hospital, against 6,147 in 1856, 6,893 in 1857, 5,067 in 1858, and 3,668 in 1859.

These numbers, in both instances, included only the more serious cases requiring regular hospital treatment ; slighter sickness or chronic cases, requiring occasional professional aid only, are treated in the Refuge department.

Although the numbers received in the establishment were less, yet the proportion of patients in the hospitals, and of others requiring occasional medical attention in the Refuge, to the whole number of the inmates of the Ward's Island establishment, has continued to be this year, as well as in the three years preceding, larger than formerly. The results of the practice, both medical and surgical, compare advantageously with the statistics of any similar establishments.

During the first half of the year, the patients were fewer than they had ever been for any equal period of time ; but during the last six months of 1860, the admissions increased so as to exceed the number under treatment at any time last year, though still far below the rate of many former years.

The establishment, generally, was kept free from any prevailing epidemic or infectious disease ; though, in July last, circumstances compelled the admission of many cases of ship-fever. Separate and insulated wards were appropriated to these patients, and there was no single instance of the disorder being communicated on the Island.

Of this class of patients there were 305, many of whom were received in a moribund state, which somewhat increased the ratio of mortality over that of last year.

Toward the close of the year, measles and scarlatina have appeared.

The following summary gives the aggregate results of the

practice, both medical and surgical, during 1859. The details, as to the nature of diseases and other matters, will be found, as usual, in the medical and surgical reports appended to this report :

Cared for in the Hospital during 1860 (including 461 remaining on 1st January, 1860), together with 264 births	3,863
Number discharged cured or relieved	3,014
" died	190
" remaining on 31st December, 1860	659

In the Refuge department, which is regularly visited and inspected every day by the Physician-in-chief or an assistant, there were 2,924 cases treated. There were 36 deaths of infants in the Refuge, and 43 in the hospitals proper, the deaths of many of whom are to be attributed to the deaths or sickness of the mothers, or their inability to afford the natural nourishment.

The percentage of mortality in the Hospital proper was, for 1860, 4·91 per cent. on all cases treated ; and calculated on the discharges, a mode of estimation sometimes preferred, 6·30.

On all cases under treatment in Hospital and Refuge, the percentage of mortality was 3·10.

The average number of patients in the Hospital throughout the year, both medical and surgical, was 480.

The Surgical department continues to receive a larger proportion of patients, than the other departments of the Ward's Island establishment. During the year many capital operations were performed in this department : as amputations, resection of bones, exsection of joints, generally with a successful result. The number of surgical cases treated was 1,078, of which 817 were discharged cured, and 18 died, showing a proportion of deaths, about 1·66 per cent. on all cases treated.

The reports of the chief physician and of the chief surgeon, with the table of diseases, &c., thereto appended, which will be found in the Appendix to this report, present, as usual, many valuable and curious statistics of disease.

That serious defect of the provision for disease on Ward's Island repeatedly mentioned in former reports—the want of a properly constructed Asylum for the Insane, has, happily, been at length remedied, though not in time for occupation during 1860.

A spacious and substantial brick building of three stories, with a high basement, had been erected in 1854, with a view to various purposes required for the uses of the establishment with the number of inmates which were then under the charge of the Commission, and which, it was thought probable, would not be materially lessened for some years. The diminished number, during the last three years, rendered the building no longer necessary for its original objects, and it was thought that it might, at a comparatively moderate expense, be converted into an asylum, sufficient for all the purposes of this Commission. Plans were procured and approved, and the necessary alterations of the building commenced in October, 1860. They were nearly completed during the past year, and the establishment will be ready for the inspection and examination of the Supervisors of the county (whose approval of all insane asylums is required by law), by the end of February, 1861. By means of additional brick work within for the division of the wards and rooms, with external staircases to the several stories, a very effectual classification can be obtained, with accommodations in all respects convenient and comfortable. The building is situated at a sufficient distance from the other hospitals and edifices, and is surrounded by the lands of this Commission, of which it is intended to devote an ample space adjoining the Asylum to separate yards and grounds for the male and female patients. Though without some of the advantages of larger and more costly establishments, it is believed that nothing will be wanting to the comfort and recovery, if possible, of the patients who may become chargeable to this Commission. In its situation, its grounds, water, and general salubrity, it will bear comparison with the best establishments of the kind.

During the past year, the insane chargeable to this institution, who could be safely kept in the wooden buildings temporarily fitted up for them, were received and treated there by the medical staff of the Island. There were 204 under treatment during the year, of whom 87 remained at the end of the year, and 57 were discharged cured or relieved to the city ; 27 were removed to Blackwell's Island in consequence of unsuitableness of the buildings for their peculiar state, 21 were transferred for other maladies to different wards, 5 eloped, and 3 died.

This necessity of removing violent or other peculiar cases from want of proper accommodation, it is trusted, will henceforth be effectually obviated.

Landing-place for Emigrant Passengers at Castle Garden.

The establishment at Castle Garden for the exclusive landing-place of emigrants, under the authority of the Act of 1855, for the protection of emigrants, has now had its utility confirmed by the experience of a fifth year.

The able and efficient Superintendent, John A. Kennedy, who first organized this department, and to whom we are indebted for much of its usefulness, continued to discharge the duties of this station until June last, when he resigned on accepting the appointment of superintendent-general of the police of the Metropolitan district. The duties of his station have been transferred to the Secretary and General Agent, by whom they have since been efficiently performed. It may be observed, that the combination of these duties with others of the General Agent is now made more practical, by the removal of all the offices of the Commission in the city to Castle Garden.

The report of the Superintendent and General Agent, with accompanying tables, appended to this report, will be found in Table D.

By comparison with former years, it is shown that the number of steamers landing passengers at Castle Garden, has increased from 22, bringing 5,111 passengers in 1856, to 109, bringing 34,247 passengers in 1860. The relative proportion of passengers in steamers, as compared with sailing vessels, is even more striking than in 1859. In that year, the average number brought by steamers was about 230 against about 184, showing a difference in favor of the former of 49 persons; the average number brought by steamers last year was 314 against 199 by sailing vessels, showing a difference in favor of the steamers of 115 passengers per vessel.

The statistics collected and preserved at the Emigrant depot, as to emigrants, their nations, and their destination in this country, with other details, are curious and instructive, and gradually form a body of valuable information for legislative and financial uses.

The number of persons who landed at Castle Garden was 108,682 (including many not subject to bonds or commutation), arriving in 482 vessels, from 14 different ports.

None of these vessels were crowded with passengers, as often occurred in former years, the average number in each vessel being 225. Register entries have been made of the intended or avowed destination of each passenger, a table of which accompanies this report. Of these, 56,131 reported their intended destination to be the State of New York; 12,926 Pennsylvania and New Jersey; 10,776 to New England; 4,938 to the Southern States; and 16,828 to Ohio, Indiana, Illinois, Michigan, Wisconsin, Iowa, Minnesota, and California; and 7,083 to Kansas, Nebraska, New Mexico, and Canada, &c., &c.

There has been advanced to emigrant families, destined for the interior, on a pledge of baggage, without interest or any charge for storage or otherwise, during 1860, the sum of $1,756 to 173 families. Of this amount, $1,658 50 has already been repaid by 168 of these families.

Of the whole amount advanced since this plan was adopted in August, 1856, viz., $19,795, there remains due $1,541 75 by 131 families. The table in the Appendix shows the annual amounts since 1856.

A considerable quantity of baggage unclaimed and unredeemed, has accumulated in the store-rooms at Castle Garden, appropriated for baggage-rooms, much of which, from the length of time, is deteriorated, or has, indeed, become already of little value, and is becoming an incumbrance to the establishment. It is respectfully suggested that the Commissioners should be allowed, in their discretion, with such guards as the law might provide, to dispose of, by public auction, such baggage left in pledge or remaining unclaimed after a stated term. The proceeds should be applied to liquidate the advance, and the excess, if any, as also the proceeds of the unclaimed effects, held for the benefit of the owner, whenever he might appear.

The arrangements of the department for letters and messages for the emigrants, have been of excellent effect. During the year 1860, there were 1,867 letters written for newly-arrived passengers, to which 713 answers were received at Castle Garden, containing $7,654 45. Besides this, remittances amounting to $7,133 79, were also received in anticipation of the arrival of the passengers, not including the two several amounts of $2,864 96 and $3,219 49, mentioned in page 271 of this report as having been received at this office, and at the office of the Irish Emigrant Society, and applied to the forwarding of recently arrived emigrants. In addition, numerous messages were received from emigrant societies and from individuals, to inform passengers on their landing, of funds being ready at their disposal when they should arrive, with the necessary information respecting them.

Financial Concerns and Condition of the Commission.

On 1st January, 1860, the books of the Commissioners of Emigration presented the following results of their financial state:

Indebtedness at the close of the year 1858, as per annual report, was........................		$192,031 41
Indebtedness of Commissioners of Emigration, at the close of the year 1859, was as follows:		
Amount of bond and mortgage..................	$150,000 00	
" due the several counties for expenses of emigrants, as per bills examined and corrected	37,559 75	
Overdraft against Commissioners of Emigration, in Shoe and Leather Bank, Dec. 31st, 1859.....	11,653 16	
		199,212 91
Being greater than at the close of 1858..........		$7,181 50

The large amount due the counties, for reimbursement of expenses of emigrants, who had become chargeable upon them during the last three years, according to the bills then audited and allowed, besides others of a later date not then audited, and the overdraft in the Bank, where the accounts of this Commission were kept by the Chamberlain of the city, whilst there was no prospect of any large augmentation of income exceeding expenditures, induced the Commissioners to apply to the Governor and State officers, for permission to increase the amount of their mortgage, for the purpose of finally extinguishing the long accumulation of debt. The approval required by the law was granted, and an addition of $50,000 was obtained on mortgage on their property, now greatly increased in value. The counties were paid up in full to 1st Nov., 1860, to the amount of $51,113 59. The further sum of $7,755 49 was also paid to several local hospitals at New York, Troy, Utica, Buffalo and Rochester, in discharge of their bills, for special cases chargeable to the Commutation Fund, relieved by them.

A further loan on mortgage, for the special use of Quarantine, of $7,500, as above stated, was also made and paid over to the Quarantine Commission. The accounts of the Commission, at the beginning of the present year, present the following comparative statement:

On the 1st of January, 1860, the books of the Commission presented the following results of their financial state:

Amount of bond and mortgage..................	$150,000 00
" due the several counties for support of emigrants, as per bills examined.....	37,559 75
" of overdraft on Shoe and Leather Bank..	11,653 16
Indebtedness at the close of the year 1859.......	$199,212 91

The indebtedness, at the close of the year 1860, is as follows:

Amount of bond and mortgage..................	$207,500 00	
" due the several counties and institutions in this State, as per bills examined and corrected................................	3,029 94	
	210,529 94	
Deduct balance in bank, Dec. 31, 1860..........	71,750 39	
Indebtedness at the close of the year 1860.......		138,779 55
Being less than at the close of 1859.............		$60,433 36

As the above last-mentioned debt on mortgage of $7,500 was incurred for the general public service, and was expended entirely by other public officers, it ought not, in strictness, to be taken into account in respect to the financial administration or condition of this Commission. With the additional deduction, it will be seen, that, notwithstanding the increase of the mortgage, the actual reduction of the debts of the Commission, during the last year, was $67,933 36.

It is proper, however, to add, that the necessary expenses of the winter, with increased numbers in the Ward's Island establishment, and, probably, of persons in the several counties chargeable, much exceeding the diminished winter income, have lessened considerably the funds on deposit, and will doubtless continue to do so until after the beginning of April.

The Commissioners, under the Act of the last session, for assessing on the county of Richmond the damages resulting, from the late riotous destruction of the Marine Hospital edifices, to this Commission and others, assessed the sum of $107,251 79 as compensation to this Commission, for the injury to their real property from the destruction of buildings, and that of $14,347 60 for loss of personal property, as hospital furniture, stores, &c. No portion of this award has yet been received.

The Commissioners respectfully recommend the sale of the former Marine Hospital lands, containing about thirty acres of land, with valuable water rights. This has now become of great value, and, in its present state, is of some expense and inconvenience to the Commission. It is encumbered by a mortgage for $200,000, which sum is very far short of the price which it would bring when judiciously sold. The relieving this Commission from the annual interest would place their financial concerns hereafter on a secure footing; whilst the amount of the principal, so paid from the proceeds of the sale, would only in part indemnify the Commutation or Alien Emigration Fund, for advances in former years for the protection of the public health, and, in some prior years, for other general purposes.

It is also advisable, that the lands at Seguine's Point should be sold, as there is no probability that they can be turned to account for hospital purposes, for which they were originally purchased, or, indeed, any other public use.

A piece of ground of about four acres on Staten Island, about three miles from the former Marine Hospital, was purchased by the Commission in 1849, for a burying-ground. It can no longer be used for that purpose, and should also be sold. As the land was paid for from the general Commutation Fund, it is but equitable that the proceeds of the sale should also be refunded to the Commissioners on the same account.

The unsettled account with the Governors of the New York Alms-House, amounting on 1st January, 1861, to $46,959 47, still remains unadjusted, the Commissioners claiming as heretofore a larger amount as an offset to these charges, being for the support of native children of emigrant mothers. The nature and grounds of this claim are fully set forth in the report of the Board for 1855, and the accompanying documents in the Appendix.

The statement of the receipts and expenditures of the Commissioners of Emigration, during the year 1860, will be found in Table No. XVI.

All of which is respectfully submitted.

G. C. VERPLANCK,
ANDREW CARRIGAN,
CYRUS CURTISS,
ELIJAH F. PURDY,
JOHN P. CUMMING,
WILSON G. HUNT,
WM. JELLINGHAUS,
A. A. LOW,
S. S. POWELL.

NEW YORK, *February* 25, 1861.

APPENDIX,

WITH TABLES AND REPORTS CONNECTED WITH THE

ANNUAL REPORTS

OF THE

COMMISSIONERS OF EMIGRATION.

Table A,

Showing the Numbers and Nativities of alien Emigrants for whom Commutation and Hospital Moneys were paid or Bonds executed, according to the Act of May 5, 1847, *and for whom Commutation Money was paid or Bonds executed according to the Acts of April* 11, 1849, *and July* 11, 1851, *and April* 13, 1853, *who arrived and were landed at the Port of New York, from May* 5, 1847, *to December* 31, 1860.

COUNTRY OF BIRTH.	1847.	1848.	1849.	1850.	1851.	1852.	1853.	1854.	1855.	1856.	1857.	1858.	1859.	1860.	Total Nationalities.
Ireland	52,946	91,061	112,591	117,038	163,306	118,131	113,164	82,302	43,043	44,276	57,119	25,075	32,652	47,330	1,107,034
Germany	53,180	51,973	55,705	45,535	69,919	118,611	119,644	176,986	52,892	56,113	80,974	31,874	28,270	37,899	979,575
England	8,864	23,062	28,321	28,163	28,553	31,551	27,126	30,578	22,938	23,787	28,622	12,324	10,375	11,361	315,625
Scotland	2,354	6,415	8,840	6,772	7,302	7,694	6,456	4,909	4,240	4,723	5,170	2,718	2,325	1,617	71,535
France	3,330	2,734	2,683	3,462	5,964	8,868	7,470	7,986	4,174	2,984	3,069	1,786	1,532	1,549	57,591
Switzerland	1,947	1,622	1,405	2,380	4,499	6,471	4,604	8,883	3,273	2,559	2,454	1,315	791	1,422	43,625
Holland	3,611	1,560	2.447	1,174	1,798	1,223	1,085	1,466	822	1,666	1,734	348	261	440	19,635
Wales	472	1,054	1,782	1,520	2,189	2,581	1,182	1,288	1,118	1,376	887	566	500	811	17,276
Norway	882	1,207	3,300	3,150	2,112	1,889	377	81	203	438	62	3	36	53	13,793
Sweden	139	165	1,007	1,110	872	2,005	1,630	1,859	304	918	619	237	318	361	11,547
Italy	197	321	602	476	618	359	553	785	667	690	596	669	399	542	7,474
Belgium	551	....	118	230	475	82	34	398	1,201	850	444	253	57	76	4,769
Spain	101	253	214	257	278	471	659	646	457	330	263	146	234	228	4,537
West Indies	299	392	449	554	575	265	....	11	19	225	330	344	416	523	4,402
Denmark	95	52	159	90	229	157	94	102	174	469	453	284	493	495	3,346
Poland	26	79	133	188	422	188	186	169	346	142	245	88	114	80	2,406
Sardinia	....	....	172	165	98	69	72	148	67	426	405	324	164	89	2,199
South America	....	31	33	104	121	120	175	111	112	163	66	92	138	110	1,376
Portugal	34	57	287	65	26	37	237	205	24	30	93	27	45	19	1,176
Nova Scotia	....	....	151	164	81	73	6	128	9	30	40	18	81	23	804
Russia	10	28	38	18	23	33	39	55	20	56	42	19	69	61	511
Canada	....	....	59	61	50	48	....	2	64	57	30	17	25	25	438
Mexico	....	12	23	41	42	23	51	34	20	19	11	13	13	22	324
Sicily	....	....	21	28	12	42	37	58	18	10	26	19	1	4	276
China	....	2	9	11	22	14	53	20	18	8	11	15	4	13	200
East Indies	23	....	34	32	10	18	....	....	5	....	....	7	....	4	133
Unknown	....	95	....	....	....	....	....	....	....	....	....	....	....	....	95
Greece	....	1	6	4	1	11	1	7	3	3	8	2	6	2	55
Turkey	1	....	6	4	4	5	10	6	2	4	....	6	3	3	54
Arabia	....	....	8	....	....	....	....	....	....	....	....	....	....	....	8
Annual Totals	129,062	189,176	220,603	212,796	289,601	300,992	284,945	319,223	136,233	142,342	183,773	78,589	79,322	105,162	2,671,819

Table A.

Statement of Vessels with Emigrants that have arrived at the Port of New York, in the Year 1849, *showing the whole Number of Passengers, including Citizens, the Number of Sick on arrival, the Number of Deaths and Births, and the ratio of each.*

Nation of Vessel.	Number of Vessels.	Passengers.	Sick.	Deaths.	Births.	Ratio of Sick.	Ratio of Deaths.	Ratio of Births.
American,..................	594	134,657	921	1,556	113	61·100	1,16·100	9·100
British,..................	371	62,463	475	658	76	76·100	1,5·100	12·100
German,..................	85	10,966	66	87	11	60·100	79·100	10·100
French,......	12	1,779	1	1	1	6·100	6·100	6·100
Belgian,..................	8	810	....	4	....	....	49·100	....
Swedish, Norwegian, &c...	581	13,718	18	41	10	....	....	....
Total,.............	1,651	224,393	1,481	2,357	211			

Table B.

Admissions into the Marine Hospital, Staten Island, showing the number of Cases of each Disease admitted annually, from January 1st, 1847, to June 27th, 1859, when the Marine Hospital was closed by act of the Legislature.

Years.	Simple fever.	Typhus fever.	Yellow fever.	Remittent fever.	Intermittent fever.	Scarlet fever.	Measles.	Small-Pox.	Erysipelas.	Diarrhœa.	Dysentery.	Cholera.	Pneumonia.	Pneumonia Typhoides.	Phthisis P.	Moribund.	Other diseases.	Total.	Number of deaths.
1847*	....	5,740	1	28	28	1	47	125	18	160	193	...	15	16	8	..	552	6,932	874
1848	42	4,413	24	165	130	5	22	640	28	218	347	73	17	..	26	..	1,961	8,111	1,181
1849	290	2,201	..	24	45	21	17	305	32	105	414	352	65	39	20	..	1,624	5,563	923
1850	260	1,408	..	4	55	13	18	171	26	62	146	25	55	70	19	..	736	3,068	391
1851	680	2,857	..	4	50	9	34	507	209	215	198	8	89	192	38	..	1,019	6,109	894
1852	1,203	3,237	1	10	122	24	62	678	50	319	220	175	67	118	82	..	2,002	8,370	1,561
1853	358	1,284	44	28	436	33	63	400	44	206	57	384	38	70	43	36	954	4,478	731
1854	315	948	45	305	156	24	78	805	..	106	38	625	24	42	60	118	749	4,438	909
1855	323	790	12	79	89	32	42	145	..	35	38	6	16	46	40	55	359	2,107	312
1856	193	269	177	64	64	29	41	325	33	32	24	4	19	6	13	37	226	1,556	203
1857	196	356	30	15	88	79	164	298	18	42	40	80	14	7	9	45	396	1,777	209
1858	56	173	210	55	33	9	66	267	19	37	8	...	14	..	5	15	200	1,166	106
1859	23	49	....	8	4	5	15	49	13	6	2	...	6	9	4	..	50	243	25
	3,939	23,725	544	789	1,300	284	669	4,715	490	1,543	1,725	1,732	439	615	367	306	10,828	53,918	8,319

Recapitulation.	
Contagious Diseases, or regarded as such.	
Typhus fever.......	23,725
Yellow "	544
Scarlet "	284
Measles.............	669
Small-pox	4,715
Erysipelas	490
Acute Dysentery...	1,543
Cholera Asphyxia...	1,732
	33,702
Non-contagious Diseases.............	20,216
Total	53,918

* The apparent discrepancy between the above report and that of the Commissioners of Emigration for the year 1847, is owing to the circumstance of its commencing on the 1st of January, 1847, whereas the report of the Commissioners dates from the 5th of May of said year, the time when the Board was organized.

Table B.

ADMISSIONS INTO THE MARINE HOSPITAL.

Showing the relative number of patients annually sent from Shipboard by the Health Officer, and from the City of New York, and from other sources.

	Number received from Vessels.	Number received from City.	Number received from other Sources.	Total.
From Jan. 1st to Dec. 31st, 1847	3,983	2,802	147	6,932
" " " 1848	3,587	4,167	357	8,111
" " " 1849	1,215	4,281	58	5,554
" " " 1850	622	2,241	205	3,068
" " " 1851	1,487	4,329	293	6,109
" " " 1852	1,240	6,751	379	8,370
" " " 1853	1,805	2,432	240	4,477
" " " 1854	1,861	2,288	289	4,438
" " " 1855	410	1,607	100	2,117
" " " 1856	578	843	135	1,556
" " " 1857	810	925	42	1,777
" " " 1858	595	498	74	1,167
" " " 1859	66	173	4	243
	18,259	33,337	2,323	53,919

By Legislative Act of April 11th, 1849, the Marine Hospital at Staten Island was specially restricted to the reception of contagious and infectious cases, and placed under the separate charge of a physician-in-chief; notwithstanding which, it will be perceived by reference to the Table on the opposite page, that the number of non-contagious and non-infectious cases admitted, rather increased than diminished from the time of the passage of said Act. This circumstance may, in a great measure, be attributed to another provision in the enactment, whereby the physician of the Marine Hospital was obliged to receive all cases sent down by agents of the Board of Health of the city of New York to said hospital, in consequence of which, as appears from the above Table, out of 53,919 admissions, 33,337 cases were sent from the city, of which total 20,216 were non-contagious diseases at the time of admission.

ANNUAL REPORTS

OF THE

PHYSICIAN OF THE MARINE HOSPITAL,

Accompanying the preceding Tables, commencing with the year 1853, *and ending with* 1859, *during which year the Hospital was closed.*

MARINE HOSPITAL, QUARANTINE, S. I., *Jan.* 1, 1855.

TO THE COMMISSIONERS OF EMIGRATION:

It will be remembered, that I entered on the duties of Physician (in chief) of the Marine Hospital, on the 15th July, 1853. The percentage of deaths for the last six months of the year, was 16·71. It will also be seen by this report, that the percentage for 1854 is 19·10, making an increase of 2·39; but when it is taken into consideration, that 650 were cases of Asiatic cholera, many of which beyond the reach of medical aid, owing to the time lost between the invasion of the disease and the reception of the patients from the shipping in the harbor, and from the city of New York; and that 109 of those attacked, were inmates of the institution, already prostrated by typhus fever, small-pox, etc., etc.; that 45 were landed with yellow fever, in a deplorable condition; that 118, with unknown maladies, were admitted in a dying state; and that 68 were in the advanced state of consumption,—the mortality will not appear surprising.

Excluding the cases of diseases referred to in this note, those of ship fever, Chagres fever, small-pox, and all other maladies in the Table, present a percentage of 10·53.

ALEX'R F. VACHÉ, *Physician, Marine Hospital.*

Summary Report of Percentage of Deaths at Marine Hospital, of deaths to discharges, and of deaths to total cases, treated during the year 1854.

Percentage of deaths from January 1st to July 1st	13·83
" " " July 1st to December 31st	10·33
" " to discharges	13·05
" " to total treated	12·68

MARINE HOSPITAL, QUARANTINE, S. I., *Jan.* 9, 1856.

TO THE COMMISSIONERS OF EMIGRATION:

Gentlemen:—Having entered upon the duties of my appointment as Physician-in-chief of the Marine Hospital in July last, it becomes my duty to make to your Board the accompanying statistical report of the establishment for the year 1855.

It will be observed that the number of patients treated at the Marine Hospital, during the past year, bears to the numbers of former years a ratio very nearly corresponding to the diminished rate of immigration to the port of New York. It would appear from the Tables that less than one-fourth of the total number was received directly from shipboard; yet the majority of the sick admitted here are recent immigrants, many of whom are transferred to this hospital immediately or soon after disembarkation in New York. These patients are the cases of typhus and the eruptive fevers.

The cases of remittent and of intermittent fever were received from coasting vessels, and were generally of an aggravated character, and placed in the hospital under Quarantine order. Of the cases of yellow fever, ten were received from vessels, and two from the city, the latter patients having reached New York by railroad from Norfolk, Va. The cases of small-pox have been received about equally from the city and from shipboard. The mortality from this malady has been remarkably low, being less than four and a half per cent. on the cases received.

It will be observed that the rate of mortality of patients in the Marine Hospital, during the past year, has been much lower than in former years. As will be seen in the Tables, the average percentage of mortality on all cases received has been less than 13 per cent.; and for the last six months of the year only 10·33 per cent.; and if, as is customary, we exclude all cases that were received in a moribund or dying condition, and also deduct the cases of phthisis which are sent to this hospital only in the last stage of that disease, the percentage of mortality is diminished still further, being for the last six months only 5·04 per cent. But the Quarantine Hospital, receiving, as it does, only such diseases as are supposed to be infectious and malignant, can never exhibit an absolutely low percentage of mortality.

In closing this annual report, I desire to bear testimony to the generous and humane spirit which has been uniformly evinced by the Commissioners of Emigration in the ample and excellent provision which they promptly make for all the requirements of this great sanitary establishment, and especially for every necessity and every interest of the sick, who, though placed in this lazaretto for the isolation of infectious and dangerous maladies, are as well supplied with all that can contribute to their happiness and recovery as the patients and their friends could desire, or humanity dictate.

Respectfully, your obedient servant,

ELISHA HARRIS, M. D.

Marine Hospital, Quarantine, S. I., *Jan.* 14, 1857.

To the Commissioners of Emigration:

Gentlemen:—I herewith present to you the Statistics of the Marine Hospital for the year ending December 31, 1856.

These tables of statistics have been compiled and arranged with great care and accuracy, and they afford a condensed view of as many facts as can conveniently be exhibited by figures alone, respecting the diseases and the results of medical service at this institution.

It will be observed that while these statistics exhibit pleasing evidence of a remarkable decrease in the lighter and more common infectious maladies provided for at the Marine Hospital, and also show that during the past year there has been enjoyed an unusual degree of immunity from infectious diseases among recent immigrants, in the city and vicinity of New York, as well as on shipboard, those sections of the tables devoted to yellow fever and to small-pox furnish impressive testimony to the fact, that two of the direst forms of pestilence have, during the past season, made their unwelcome advent at the very portals of our great commercial metropolis.

It will be observed that, notwithstanding the very large number of cases of small-pox and yellow fever which have been treated at the Marine Hospital during the last season, the average percentage of deaths in the institution, during the year, has been lower than in the previous years.

All cases admitted to the hospital are reckoned in the tables as having been under medical treatment; but it may be observed that 38 persons were, when received into the hospital, in a moribund or dying condition from various diseases of which it was not important that specific record should be made; and none of these were subject to, or susceptible of, medical treatment. Besides this class of moribund patients, we received nearly fifty other persons in a dying condition, and which admitted of no other than such ministrations as would assuage the pangs of death; but the maladies, from which they were dying, were of such importance to our records, that they were classified under the proper heads. This class of moribund patients consisted principally of yellow fever in an advanced stage of black vomit, typhus fever, and pneumo-typhus. If we could strike out the record of all these cases, together with the cases of phthisis, which seldom reach this hospital except in the last stage of that malady, the average ratio of deaths to cases *actually treated* would be truly gratifying. But, in the discharge of a physician's duties, the melancholy pleasure of alleviating the anguish of the dying, and performing for those who depart the last offices of humanity, is not the least of rewards which a true physician receives.

I would here remark, that the cemetery of the Marine Hospital is kept and guarded with care, and the dead are buried with propriety.

The percentage of deaths from yellow fever was necessarily large, but it is below the ratio of previous years, and considerably lower than the average of the records of this malady at the Marine Hospital for the past fifty-seven years,—the period since the establishment of the institution.

The total number of cases of typhus fever admitted to Marine Hospital during the past year, was less than one-third the number admitted in 1855; and, although for the sake of uniformity in the records, I have included two very distinct forms of fever under this one head, it is proper to remark that very few cases of the common typhus or ship fever have been received into the hospital during the year; the prevailing type of what in the table is denominated typhus, being what is known as "abdominal typhus," or *typhoid disease*. This form of fever is seldom, if ever, infectious, and although as fearfully fatal as the simple typhus fever, its presence on shipboard and in the crowded tenements of poverty is not, like typhus, a source of great danger to the public health.

As the records of the hospital are now kept, the cases of typhoid disease will in future be recorded distinctly from the cases of typhus fever.

The cases of remittent and of intermittent fever have been received principally from southern coastwise vessels, and these patients were mostly seamen, admitted to Marine Hospital by order of the health officer. In most of these cases the fever was of a severe and malignant type, such as to preclude the idea of removal to the Seamen's Retreat of such as were really the proper subjects for the care of that institution. There was but one death among this class of our patients. I refer to this fact to illustrate the difference between this form of fever and that scourge of the tropics which has recently made us such a threatening visitation, and also to call attention to the fact that the specific remedy, viz., quinia, which is the indispensable agent of cure in the former case, is principally expended on seamen for the care of whom your honorable Board receives but three dollars per week, which is not sufficient to pay the cost of medicine and nursing.

I would respectfully suggest that the expense incident to the care of seamen at the Quarantine Hospital might with great propriety be paid from the United States General Hospital Fund. If the subject were properly represented to the General Government, there can be no doubt that the Seamen's Fund and Retreat of the State of New York would at once be relieved of the burden of this expense. It certainly would seem just and proper, after the State of New York has done so much to provide for the vast number of sick seamen who now find at the Retreat such unrestricted hospital privileges as they find nowhere else in the United States, that the seamen sent to Marine Hospital by the health officer, suffering as they do from acute diseases contracted in a commercial service that is of general interest to our nation, should be provided for from the general Hospital Fund of the Federal Government.*

* According to the Report recently made by a special committee appointed to examine into the present condition of the United States Seamen's Hospital Fund, it appears there is a sum due to seamen from that fund, amounting to one million five hundred and thirty-six thousand three hundred and seventeen dollars ($1,536,317).

The total amount of money collected from seamen by the United States Government, in the

The whole number of seamen admitted to Marine Hospital during the past year was 253, of which number 39 died, and 214 were discharged as soon as they could with safety to themselves be transferred to the Retreat. Thirty-eight of the deaths among seamen were from black vomit. A considerable proportion of these were in a moribund condition when they reached the hospital. The total number of seamen admitted with yellow fever, was 107. The total number of days spent in the hospital by seamen during the year, was 2,370; and the average number of days for each patient of this class was 9·36.

I have thus particularly referred to the facts relating to this class of our patients, because of the importance of the questions and interests involved in providing for sick seamen in the Marine Hospital.

The public safety, as well as the economical interests of the Seamen's Hospital Fund, require that seamen sick with infectious or suspicious maladies should be placed under treatment and quarantine surveillance at the Marine Hospital, and it would seem proper that the expenses incident to the care of such patients should be provided for as here suggested.

The number of cases of small-pox treated at this institution during the year was 355, of which 27 died. Notwithstanding an unusually large proportion of confluent and severe cases, the deaths occurred principally in a class of children too feeble to recover from any acute disease.

Early in the spring small-pox began to prevail extensively on emigrant passenger vessels, and previous to June 10th, five such vessels had landed eighty patients with small-pox, and had, under Quarantine order, disembarked and placed in the hospitals under our care two thousand two hundred and sixty-four passengers, who remained at an average of a little less than a week on the hospital grounds.

At one time these companies and the sick gave to the establishment a population of nearly 1,600, which number occupied all our available room, and was through your prompt liberality provided for without any embarrassment.

At the close of the past unusual and trying year at Quarantine, we have the pleasure of believing that there was not, during the entire season, a single instance of successful infraction of Quarantine regulations or the rules of the institution on the part of any one who was placed in the official keeping of the Marine Hospital; and no article of infected clothing or baggage delivered into the custody of the institution has in a single instance left the establishment until it was thoroughly disinfected.

It will be observed that several cases of Asiatic cholera have been admitted to the hospital during the past year. The first company—three persons from Nicaragua—was received June 1st, when the weather was warm and

year 1851, was $105,972 72; which was applied to the relief of 9,748 seamen, 8,150 of whom were inmates of hospitals.

The amount of United States hospital money collected from seamen arriving at the port of New York, as appears from the New York Custom House records, averages about $34,000 annually; and of this sum only about $17,000, or one-half, is applied to the relief of seamen at this port.

the atmosphere humid. Every precaution was taken to keep these patients completely isolated and free from any possible communication with the wards occupied by other patients, believing as I do in the contingent communicability of that fearful malady. No cholera, nor any tendency thereto, had occurred in any of our wards during the season, until the eighth day after the reception of these patients, all of whom were in collapse. The malady then made its advent very suddenly, and threatened to sweep through the wards: The first victim, a strong man, died within six hours from the first symptom of the malady, and during the three succeeding days a large number of patients presented the preliminary symptoms; but the scourge was providentially averted.

On two other occasions cases of cholera have been received from shipboard, but they were so provided for as to nearly preclude the possibility of any danger to the hospitals.

Unpopular as is the doctrine of the communicability of this Oriental scourge, it nevertheless is true, and the malady is provided for accordingly at the Marine Hospital. (See Report of Marine Hospital for 1855, Senate Doc., No. 104, p. 8.)

It would afford me pleasure to embody in this brief report, were it possible, a sketch of the origin and progress of yellow fever as it appeared at Quarantine during the past season; but as I shall soon present to you a complete memoir on this interesting and important subject, I will in this place only advert to a few of the events which were of special interest to the hospital.

Early in the month of April we received from an Havana vessel, one well-marked case of yellow fever, and on the 18th of June the malady made its appearance for the season, the schooner "Julia M. Hallock" having arrived on that day from St. Jago de Cuba, with three malignant cases of the fever.

July 21st, the ship "Jane H. Gliddon" arrived from Havana with a large company of sick and dying, and from that date to the 6th of October we continued to receive cases of yellow fever from the West India and Charleston vessels.

The time at which the West India vessels were principally laden, and the circumstances under which the cargoes were received, owing to the unprecedented lateness of the sugar crop, with the very malignant type of the fever as it appeared from the first, strongly portended the fearful events which followed.

It early became evident that this pestilential malady was being communicated with unusual facility, both on shipboard and on shore; and as no officer but myself was protected from the fever by a previous attack, I anticipated events with no little anxiety. On the 23d of June, my assistant, Dr. Walser, was seized with the fever, from which he fortunately recovered after but a few days' illness. He contracted the malady on board the "Julia M. Hallock."

July 14th, we began to receive into the hospital the stevedores and lightermen that contracted the infection which inhered in the cargoes and vessels they were engaged in unloading.

The total number of cases occurring among this class of laborers, and admitted to the Marine Hospital previous to September 1st, was 32. These persons were mostly citizens and residents of Staten Island.

On the 22d of July, the pestilence suddenly made its appearance in a fearful form in the dwellings near the waterside on the Quarantine grounds. The son of the matron of the institution was reported ill with yellow fever, and one of the employées of the institution was, on the evening of the same day, suddenly stricken to the earth, and died in a few hours of black vomit; and immediately followed three of the family of this man, and the venerable gate-keeper and his wife. Twenty-five of the employées were seized with the fever, and of these five died.

Though some who witnessed these trying and afflictive events may have been panic-stricken, it gives me pleasure to report that all the officers and employées of the institution vied with each other to aid me in the care of the sick and in the execution of my wishes. I wish here to mention, with special commendation, the intelligent co-operation and untiring faithfulness of Dr. Theodore Walser, assistant physician, and the efficiency and industry of Mr. F. C. Gilmore, the steward and clerk of the hospital.

It affords me pleasure to refer in this place to the self-denying faithfulness of the chaplains of the institution, Rev. Gordon Winslow, D. D., and Rev. Mark Murphy, D. D., both of whom heroically continued daily to minister the consolations of our holy religion to the sick and the dying in the hospitals, when the pestilence was in our midst walking in darkness and wasting at noon day.

Gentlemen, in closing this report, I would cordially thank you for all the kindness you have shown me personally and officially, and I desire particularly to thank you for the promptness with which all requisitions from the Marine Hospital have been honored by your Board.

I have the honor to remain your obedient servant,

ELISHA HARRIS, M. D.

MARINE HOSPITAL, QUARANTINE, S. I., *Jan.* 1, 1858.

To HON. G. C. VERPLANCK, President of Commissioners of Emigration:

Sir:—With the present, I have the honor to transmit to your Board the statistics of the Marine Hospital for 1857—the accompanying Tables exhibiting the number of patients remaining since the previous year, the number admitted, and total treated, of each disease, during 1857; the number of discharges and deaths, and the percentage of deaths to discharges.

On entering upon the discharge of the duties of Physician of the Marine Hospital, on the 1st May last, I found the hospital in an unusually healthy condition.

Comparatively very few typhus cases were admitted, either from vessel or from the city, during the year, and these of a milder form.

Among the 30 cases of yellow fever were 8 sailors from different vessels from the West Indies, 8 shipkeepers, and stevedores employed on those vessels, and 14 passengers from the "Illinois,"—the disease being confined entirely to admissions from shipboard.

September 19th, the first 2 cases of cholera came from a Hamburg vessel; the 25th of November the disease made its first appearance among the patients of the hospital admitted with other diseases—very few remained exempt, and 15 died of the malady within twenty-five days.

The number of well passengers landed and provided for at Quarantine from cholera, yellow fever, and small-pox vessels, amounted to 3,772, at an average remaining three days under observation here.

Although several were ill, no death occurred among the employées of the hospital.

Very respectfully, your obedient servant,

D. H. BISSELL, *Physician, Marine Hospital.*

MARINE HOSPITAL, QUARANTINE, S. I., *Jan.* 1, 1859.

TO HON. G. C. VERPLANCK, President of Commissioners of Emigration:

Sir:—In presenting the statistics for 1858, the usual annual return of the numbers and diseases of the patients treated in the Marine Hospital, during the past year, I have also to reiterate my former report of the destruction of all the buildings vested by legislative enactments in the hands of the Commissioners of Emigration, and in my charge as Superintendent thereof.

During the first three months the number of admissions were comparatively small, even to the largely diminished immigration—small-pox, admitted directly from shipboard, forming the largest number of cases of any single disease. From the 16th to the 20th of April, the first cases of yellow fever, 40 in number, were admitted from the United States ship *Susquehanna*, and from the 8th June to the 7th October, 141 more, directly from shipboard, arriving from infected ports, 19 shipkeepers, stevedores, and lightermen, and 10 from the village—2 of whom, alone, were directly or indirectly connected with vessels or Quarantine, making a total of 210 cases, of whom 44, or one-fifth, died.

I am happy to be again permitted to report not only the entire immunity of the inmates of the hospital from yellow fever, but also that none of the employées, or any of the residents of Tompkinsville, living in the immediate vicinity of the hospital, suffered with any contagious or infectious disease contracted from the Marine Hospital.

4,004 emigrants were landed from 13 different vessels, among whom small-pox had appeared, either during the passage or on arrival here; they were quarantined and provided for, at an average of five days. Besides these, 256 officers and crew of the *Susquehanna*, 157 passengers and 312 sailors from 55 different other vessels infected with yellow fever, were detained for observation for the same length of time.

On the night of the 1st September, when, besides a large number of sick, principally yellow fever cases, 56 passengers detained by the health officer for observation, had retired for the night, a mob of several hundred persons entered the hospital grounds by breaking down the wall of the enclosure, and commenced firing the buildings. They succeeded, after spirited resistance from the inmates of the Institution, in burning ten of the eleven used for the reception and treatment of the sick, together with their contents, the small force under my control being entirely insufficient to protect them.

I regret to say, that at an early period of the attack, one of the inmates was mortally wounded by the discharge of a musket in the hands of some person to me unknown. He was sent to the City Hospital, where he died in a few days.

On the morning of the 2d September, I addressed a note to Capt. Crabtree, Vice-President of the Commissioners of Emigration, informing him of the destruction of the hospitals, and requesting him to send a sufficient force to protect us, as well as the remaining buildings from the threatened vengeance of the mob. To that communication he replied, saying, "That a force of sixty policemen would be sent by the evening boat," but, from some misunderstanding of those having the matter in charge, they were not sent. At an early hour of the evening, however, a large number of United States Marines, under command of Capt. Rich, were landed at Quarantine for the avowed purpose of protecting the United States government property there. The mob had, by this time, collected in large numbers in the vicinity of the hospital, and, learning that no police force had arrived to protect the grounds, they commenced again the work of destruction by setting all the remaining buildings on fire, and battering down the walls surrounding the enclosure.

Early in the evening, I applied to Capt. Rich to furnish me with a detachment of his command, to assist in defending the only remaining hospital building, filled to overflowing with the sick and dying, and to save the unfortunate beings from the fate which seemed to await them. To all my entreaties, he only replied, "That he was sent here to protect the Government property, and nothing else, and that he would not comply with my request." Dr. Walser, the assistant physician, also implored him to protect the sick, our families, and our homes, from the fury of the invaders, but alike in vain. He remained in the vicinity of the burning buildings, and witnessed their destruction without an effort to save them. The sick and the dead were removed from the hospital, previous to its being set on fire, to the open grounds adjacent thereto, where they were compelled to remain until the evening of the 3d September, when they were removed to such other quarters as we could command.

The total number of buildings burned by the incendiaries was forty.

Very respectfully, your obedient servant,

D. H. BISSELL, *Physician, Marine Hospital.*

MARINE HOSPITAL, QUARANTINE, S. I., *Jan.* 1, 1860.

To HON. GULIAN C. VERPLANCK,

President of the Board of Commissioners of Emigration :

Dear Sir :—The accompanying Tables will exhibit the condition of this hospital, for the first six months of the current year. Since which time, as you are aware, I have not been permitted to exercise the functions of my office toward the sick of Quarantine. With sentiments of respect,

I am your obedient servant,

J. H. JEROME, *Phys. and Sup't of M. Hospital.*

Table C,

Showing the number of Admissions to, and Births and Deaths in the State Emigrant Refuge and Hospitals, Ward's Island, under the charge of the Commissioners of Emigration, from the organization of the Commission, May 5, 1847, to Dec. 31, 1860.

Year.	Number Admitted and Classified.					Total Admissions.	Number of Births.	Total Number of Admissions and Births, showing the whole number of Persons cared for and treated.	Number of Deaths Classified.				
				Distribution.					In Hospitals.				
	Adults.	Children between 1 & 12 Years.	Infants under 1 Year.	To Hospital.	To Refuge.				Adults.	Children between 1 and 12 Years.	Infants under 1 Year.	In Refuge.	Total Deaths.
1847	......	......	......	......	....	1,629	29	1,658	164	10	40	......	214
1848	......	......	......	......	......	3,491	177	3,668	194	44	67	......	305
1849	......	......	......	......	......	6,827	346	7,173	740	100	390	......	1,230
1850	......	......	......	7,084	1,014	8,098	384	8,482	429	129	204	132	894
1851	......	......	......	10,928	1,586	12,514	493	13,007	877	197	250	330	1,654
1852	......	......	......	9,336	3,217	12,553	523	13,076	831	220	150	342	1,543
1853	......	......	......	10,794	723	11,517	644	12,161	504	167	151	286	1,108
1854	......	......	......	9,803	2,684	12,487	701	13,188	729	322	387	269	1,707
1855	7,801	949	342	6,349	2,743	9,092	641	9,733	543	202	298	235	1,278
1856	4,402	643	294	3,625	1,714	5,339	406	5,745	229	65	94	138	526
1857	5,499	911	291	4,405	2,296	6,701	468	7,169	224	59	111	125	519
1858	3,967	415	243	3,282	1,343	4,625	366	4,991	205	44	123	115	487
1859	2,660	226	162	2,319	729	3,048	261	3,309	113	18	47	84	262
1860	3,144	382	175	2,662	1,039	3,701	264	3,965	128	19	43	36	226
Total...	....	......	......	......	......	101,622	5,703	107,325	5,910	1,596	2,355	2,092	11,953

NOTE.—The records do not show the ages of the persons admitted previous to 1855, nor the distribution of those admitted during the years 1847, 1848, and 1849.

Table C,

Showing the Diseases of Patients admitted to the State Emigrant Hospitals, Ward's Island, from January 1, 1852 (*when the reports from the Physicians of the Hospitals were first presented in tabular form to, and embodied in the Annual Reports of, the Commissioners of Emigration*), *to December* 31, 1860.

DISEASES.	1852.	1853.	1854.	1855.	1856.	1857.	1858.	1859.	1860.	TOTAL.
Aberratio Mentis,	....	....	....	....	....	5	....	....	....	5
Abortio,	2	5	4	5	1	1	....	....	...	18
Abrasiones,	2	....	....	....	...	....	....	....	....	2
Abscessus,	94	128	119	111	84	68	33	15	36	688
Acne,	1	8	2	2	1	1	....	2	1	18
Adenitis,	15	17	28	22	8	12	9	9	16	136
Adiposis Hepatis,	....	....	1	....	....	....	....	....	....	1
Albugo,	2	....	2	....	....	1	....	....	....	5
Albuminaria,	13	....	....	2	9	2	....	....	....	26
Alopecia,	....	....	2	....	....	....	1	....	....	3
Amaurosis,	17	22	13	17	10	9	3	2	1	94
Amblyopia,	4	5	4	3	....	....	....	....	....	16
Amenorrhœa,	44	34	56	22	17	13	6	1	5	198
Amentia,	2	....	24	....	....	....	....	....	....	26
Amputationis Cicatrix,	....	....	....	....	....	....	....	....	1	1
Anasarca,	12	10	11	8	12	10	3	3	3	72
Anæmia,	8	3	77	39	43	82	101	85	38	476
Anchylosis,	10	9	7	7	....	10	2	3	3	51
Aneurysma,	....	....	3	....	2	1	1	1	2	10
Angina,	....	3	14	5	....	3	....	4	3	32
Anteflexio Uteri,	....	....	....	....	1	1	2	....	....	4
Anteversio "	....	....	1	....	....	1	....	....	....	2
Anthrax,	19	4	8	11	2	7	4	7	2	64
Aphonia,	....	1	....	....	....	....	....	....	....	1
Apoplexia,	10	3	4	1	....	1	....	....	....	19
Apthæ,	14	1	1	....	....	....	....	1	....	17
Arachnitis,	....	....	....	....	1	2	....	....	....	3
Arthrites,	2	7	....	1	1	....	....	....	....	11
Ascites,	45	23	5	11	2	1	....	....	....	87
Asphyxia,	....	2	....	....	....	....	....	....	....	2
Asthma,	9	3	2	1	4	17	9	2	5	52
Atelectasis Pulmonum,	....	2	....	....	....	....	....	....	....	2
Atrophia,	22	55	55	48	1	1	....	8	....	190
Balanitis,	....	....	....	....	....	1	....	1	7	9
Blenorrhœa Glandis,	....	....	....	....	....	1	....	....	2	3
" Oculi,	....	....	....	2	....	....	....	....	....	2
Bleparadenitis,	....	....	....	....	....	....	....	....	6	6
Bronchiectasis,	....	....	2	1	3	1	....	....	2	9
Bronchitis,	665	356	449	362	119	165	116	75	65	2,372
Bronchocele,	....	....	....	5	5	....	....	....	....	10
Bursitis,	....	....	....	4	....	6	2	4	5	21
Cæcitas,	....	....	2	....	....	....	....	....	....	2
Cachexia,	....	....	2	16	4	10	2	....	....	12

TABLE C. (*Of Diseases.*)—*Continued.*

DISEASES.	1852.	1853.	1854.	1855.	1856.	1857.	1858.	1859.	1860.	TOTAL.
Calculus Urinarius, . .	1	....	....	....	....	....	....	....	2	3
Cancer, . . .	9	11	11	17	....	5	4	4	....	61
Cancrum Oris, . .	21	....	....	....	....	....	....	....	....	21
Carcinoma, . . .	7	5	7	....	5	4	4	4	2	38
" Hepatis, .	....	6	24	....	....	1	....	....	....	9
Cardialgia, . . .	....	....	....	....	....	....	....	....	4	4
Caries, . . .	6	9	12	17	5	4	2	2	3	60
Cataracta, . . .	7	14	6	14	7	7	3	6	3	67
Catarrhus, . . .	....	2	69	....	....	35	78	107	32	323
" Pulmonum,	....	20	....	....	....	....	....	3	29	52
Cerebritis, . . .	....	....	....	2	....	....	....	....	....	2
Cephalalgia, . . .	7	2	....	19	7	32	8	12	5	92
Cirrhosis Hepatis, .	....	2	2	....	....	....	3	4	....	11
Chemosis, . . .	2	....	....	....	....	....	....	....	....	2
Chlorosis, . . .	2	4	2	8	38	3	....	....	....	57
Cholera Asiatica, . .	132	....	345	4	3	....	....	....	....	484
" Infantum, .	....	2	7	18	10	3	....	....	....	40
" Morbus, . .	....	1	....	1	10	3	....	....	....	15
Chorea St. Viti, . .	3	6	2	5	7	4	3	1	....	31
Choroiditis, . . .	....	....	....	....	....	....	2	....	....	2
Clavus, . . .	....	....	2	....	....	....	....	....	....	2
Colica, ...	10	7	7	2	2	11	1	4	1	45
" Pictonum, .	12	15	16	7	6	....	8	3	2	69
Combustio, . . .	....	....	....	....	....	....	....	....	6	6
Concussio cerebri, .	2	2	1	3	....	....	....	....	....	8
Condylomata, . .	....	....	....	12	8	9	....	....	14	43
Congelatio, . . .	....	....	....	2	66	46	7	14	20	155
Congestio Cerebri, . .	1	1	....	1	3	1	....	....	....	7
" Hepatis, .	9	....	3	3	....	1	....	....	....	16
" Pulmonum,	....	3	....	3	3	....	....	....	....	9
Conjunctivitis, . .	521	442	628	297	193	134	54	19	13	2,301
Constipatio, . .	13	14	2	14	4	6	2	....	....	55
Contractio Digitorum, .	....	....	....	....	2	1	....	....	....	3
Contusio, . . .	116	112	33	21	58	36	15	14	7	412
Convulsiones, . .	85	32	31	3	1	2	....	....	....	154
Cophosis, . . .	1	7	2	3	....	....	....	....	....	13
Corneitis, . . .	147	123	123	134	98	26	8	2	2	663
Coryza, . . .	....	....	....	1	....	....	....	....	....	1
Coup de Soleil, . .	4	11	4	....	1	....	....	....	....	20
Coxalgia, . . .	....	....	5	6	....	8	....	....	....	19
Coxitis, ...	....	....	....	1	4	4	1	....	....	10
Cryptorrhis, . .	....	....	3	....	....	....	....	....	....	3
Cyanosis, . . .	....	....	3	....	....	1	....	....	....	4
Cynanche Trachealis, .	14	5	15	5	....	1	....	....	....	40
Cystitis, ...	....	1	4	....	1	3	....	....	1	10
Dacryo-cystitis, . .	....	....	....	....	....	1	1	....	....	2
Debilitas, . . .	259	285	226	158	56	84	55	....	25	1,148
Decubitus, . . .	....	....	....	....	....	....	....	....	1	1
Delirium Tremens, .	....	....	16	17	16	25	16	17	4	111
Dementia, . . .	1	18	....	22	6	4	3	23	50	127
Dentitio, . . .	....	22	....	....	....	....	....	....	....	22

TABLE C. (*Of Diseases.*)—*Continued.*

DISEASES.	1852.	1853.	1854.	1855.	1856.	1857.	1858.	1859.	1860.	TOTAL.
Diabetes,	....	3	4	....	....	2	....	....	....	9
Diarrhœa,	992	441	946	372	98	110	113	76	98	3,246
Diplopia,	1	....	....	....	....	....	....	....	....	1
Diptheria,	....	....	....	....	....	....	....	....	3	3
Dislocatio,	4	6	8	5	....	....	3	....	....	26
Distortio,	....	....	....	4	....	2	2	1	10	19
Duodenitis,	....	....	....	....	....	1	....	....	1	2
Dysenteria,	318	251	383	187	125	158	101	58	38	1,619
Dysmenorrhœa,	....	3	7	1	....	1	....	....	1	13
Dysoccorea,	....	....	....	....	....	....	....	....	6	6
Dyspepsia,	16	9	....	3	8	3	1	....	....	40
Dysuria,	2	2	2	5	1	....	....	....	....	12
Ecchymosa	2	1	3	1	....	....	....	....	....	7
Eclampsia,	....	8	....	....	....	....	5	1	....	14
Ecthyma,	16	5	10	9	12	1	3	....	5	61
Ectropium,	4	1	....	....	4	....	....	2	....	11
Eczema,	85	94	157	83	51	59	32	18	9	588
Elephantiasis,	1	1	1	3	....	2	1	1	....	10
Emphyema,	7	1	2	....	1	....	2	....	....	13
Emphysema,	14	5	18	10	4	11	5	4	10	81
Endocarditis,	2	....	20	16	3	3	....	2	2	48
Enteritis,	8	4	11	4	4	....	....	....	....	31
Enterohelcosis,	1	2	2	8	5	1	....	....	2	21
Entropion,	2	2	9	12	....	1	1	....	....	27
Epidydimitis,	....	5	....	2	....	....	....	....	....	7
Epilepsia,	23	39	18	24	22	26	15	18	10	195
Epispadia,	....	....	1	1	....	....	....	....	....	2
Epistaxis,	....	2	....	2	1	1	....	....	....	6
Eruptio,	....	....	....	....	....	....	....	....	3	3
Erysipelas,	124	770	169	59	14	25	54	35	14	1,266
Erythema,	18	....	7	18	1	1	....	....	3	48
Exanthema,	....	....	....	8	....	....	....	....	....	8
Excoriatio,	....	8	8	11	....	5	13	7	16	68
Exhaustio,	....	....	1	....	....	....	....	....	....	1
Exostosis,	....	....	4	....	....	2	....	....	....	6
Exudatio Pleuratica,	....	....	....	....	....	....	....	4	1	5
Febris Billiosa,	....	....	....	....	....	....	....	1	....	1
" Catarrhalis,	171	98	....	....	....	....	....	....	....	269
" Chagres,	....	....	....	....	....	1	....	....	....	1
" Continua,	....	....	....	....	....	2	....	....	....	2
" Ephemeralis,	110	39	19	3	....	....	....	....	....	171
" Gastrica,	249	164	83	7	....	13	8	....	....	524
" Intermittens,	504	1,945	2,045	906	257	346	357	293	64	6,717
" Puerperalis,	124	24	2	....	17	1	7	3	1	179
" Remittent,	38	29	....	1	13	....	1	....	....	82
" Simplex,	....	8	....	9	....	11	1	....	....	29
" Synocha,	4	....	....	....	....	....	....	....	....	4
" Typhus,	1203	376	217	305	64	92	61	68	305	2,691
Fissura Ani,	....	....	....	3	....	....	....	....	....	3
Fistula,	4	2	1	7	2	2	....	....	3	21
" in Ano,	10	13	10	6	5	2	4	4	....	54

TABLE C. (*Of Diseases.*)—*Continued.*

Diseases.	1852.	1853.	1854.	1855.	1856.	1857.	1858.	1859.	1860.	Total.
Fistula Faciei,	....	....	....	....	....	1	....	....	....	1
" Perinæi,	....	....	1	2	....	1	....	....	....	4
" Scroti,	....	....	....	....	2	....	....	....	....	2
" Urethræ,	....	....	....	....	....	2	....	....	....	2
" Vesico Vaginalis,	....	4	4	5	1	1	3	2	....	20
Fracturæ,	50	76	57	41	38	37	33	23	16	371
Fungus Hæmatodes,	1	....	3	2	....	1	....	....	....	7
" Palpebræ,	2	....	....	....	....	....	....	....	....	2
Furunculosis,	29	24	16	20	11	20	32	15	11	178
Gangræna Oris,	....	38	46	21	2	....	....	....	....	107
" Pedis,	....	....	1	3	....	2	....	....	....	6
" Pulm,	4	....	3	....	....	1	4	1	....	13
" Senilis,	....	5	....	....	....	....	....	....	....	5
" Uteri,	....	1	....	....	....	....	....	....	....	1
" Vagina et labiorum,	1	....	....	....	....	....	....	....	....	1
Gastralgia,	....	3	....	17	4	7	9	1	14	55
Gastritis,	....	....	....	67	2	3	3	2	....	77
Glossitis,	....	....	....	1	1	....	....	....	....	2
Gonorrhœa,	146	182	100	148	78	119	90	87	58	1,008
Graviditas,	....	....	....	....	....	....	....	9	2	11
Hæmatemesis,	....	....	1	1	2	3	1	....	....	8
Hæmaturia,	....	....	....	1	....	....	....	....	1	2
Hæmoptysis,	10	2	3	3	1	3	....	1	....	23
Hæmorrhagia,	2	4	....	4	....	....	....	....	4	14
Hæmorrhoides,	21	34	12	29	4	12	10	11	8	141
Helminthiasis,	....	....	6	4	1	1	2	....	....	14
Hemiplegia,	3	7	7	1	10	16	5	1	....	50
Hepatitis,	11	4	11	6	3	8	3	1	3	50
Hernia,	18	13	29	27	13	23	18	4	7	152
Herpes,	4	16	19	6	13	8	4	5	1	76
Hordeolum,	4	3	7	1	....	2	....	....	....	17
Housemaid's Knee,	5	....	....	....	....	....	....	....	....	5
Hydarthrus,	2	....	1	4	4	....	....	....	....	11
Hydræmia,	....	....	17	17	....	8	....	2	....	44
Hydrargyritis,	....	....	4	5	....	....	....	....	....	9
Hydrocele,	3	4	5	2	3	6	1	2	1	27
Hydrocephalus,	....	2	11	1	....	....	....	1	....	15
Hydrops Articuli,	1	....	....	....	....	....	....	....	....	1
" Ovariorum,	3	....	....	....	....	....	....	....	....	3
" Pericadii,	1	....	2	3	....	....	....	....	....	6
" Scarlatina,	....	....	....	....	....	....	....	2	5	7
" Universalis,	....	....	3	....	....	....	....	....	....	3
Hydrothorax,	5	1	6	3	4	5	....	....	....	24
Hygroma,	....	....	....	2	5	1	....	....	....	8
Hypertrophia,	8	....	22	10	2	....	....	....	....	42
Hypochondriasis,	20	6	3	8	2	3	13	13	22	90
Hysteria,	16	18	22	23	26	32	21	14	10	182
Icterus,	30	30	28	27	15	8	11	6	12	167
Ilius,	....	....	2	....	....	....	....	....	....	2
Imbecilitas,	....	....	....	3	5	3	11	6	2	30

TABLE C. (*Of Diseases.*)—*Continued.*

DISEASES.	1852.	1853.	1854.	1855.	1856.	1857.	1858.	1859.	1860.	TOTAL.
Impetigo,	20	72	69	52	3	3	4	....	....	223
Inanitio,	....	....	....	....	....	....	....	5	12	17
Incontinentia Urinæ,	....	3	7	3	....	2	5	1	5	26
Induratio Mammæ,	....	1	....	1	....	....	....	....	....	2
" Uteri,	....	....	1	....	....	....	....	....	....	1
Inflammatio,	15	11	18	29	....	....	....	....	2	75
Injuria,	7	....	203	184	77	129	82	70	61	813
Insanitas,	11	10	....	....	43	35	30	21	13	163
Insuff. Valv. Cordis,	....	....	6	....	....	10	1	....	....	17
Intractibilitas,	....	....	....	....	....	....	....	3	....	3
Intussusceptio Intestinalis,	....	3	2	....	....	....	....	....	....	5
Iritis,	23	13	27	20	16	5	11	9	6	130
Irritatio Spinalis,	3	....	2	1	....	3	....	....	....	9
Ischias,	3	19	....	5	1	5	1	....	....	34
Keloides,	....	....	....	....	1	....	....	....	....	1
Keratitis,	....	....	....	....	....	....	....	2	1	3
Labium Leporinum,	....	....	....	....	....	....	....	....	1	1
Laceratio Perinei,	....	....	....	....	....	....	....	1	....	1
Lachiorrhagia,	....	....	1	....	....	....	....	....	....	1
Lagontomum,	1	....	....	....	....	....	....	....	....	1
Laryngitis,	31	6	17	20	2	12	15	3	2	108
Lepra,	1	1	1	6	1	3	....	....	5	18
Leucoma,	....	1	2	21	7	7	5	1	....	44
Leucorrhœa,	....	26	17	21	7	10	7	5	11	104
Lichen,	....	3	50	3	4	6	....	1	....	67
Lipoma,	....	....	....	....	....	1	....	....	....	1
Lumbago,	11	11	20	23	27	29	17	18	3	159
Lupus,	8	1	2	5	7	4	....	1	1	29
Luxatio,	....	....	....	....	8	1	1	....	2	12
Luxatio Brachii,	....	....	....	....	1	....	....	....	....	1
" Carpi,	....	....	....	....	1	....	....	....	....	1
" Claviculæ,	....	....	....	1	1	....	....	1	....	3
" Femoris,	....	....	4	3	1	....	....	1	....	9
" Humeri,	....	....	2	1	4	....	....	....	....	7
" Ulnæ,	....	....	....	2	1	....	....	....	....	3
Mania,	14	10	5	3	47	35	36	25	1	176
Mania à Potu,	8	19	....	....	2	....	1	....	....	30
Mania Puerperalis,	3	3	1	1	1	8	....	....	....	17
Marasmus,	53	....	2	27	4	3	3	4	....	96
Mastitis,	....	2	....	....	....	....	4	....	....	6
Melæna,	....	....	1	1	....	1	....	....	....	3
Melancholia,	....	....	....	8	23	43	25	....	....	99
Meningitis,	2	3	1	....	....	1	1	4	4	16
Menorrhagia,	6	5	6	5	6	7	4	2	2	43
Meteorismus,	....	1	1	4	....	....	....	....	....	6
Metritis,	9	3	1	2	....	3	3	5	....	26
Micropia,	....	1	....	....	....	....	....	....	....	1
Micturitro Involuntaria,	1	....	....	....	....	....	....	....	....	1
Monomania,	....	....	3	....	15	7	6	2	....	33
Morbus Brightii,	13	7	28	34	26	21	16	10	10	165
" Cordis,	7	35	....	....	18	26	28	11	9	134

TABLE C. (*Of Diseases.*)—*Continued.*

Diseases.	1852.	1853.	1854.	1855.	1856.	1857.	1858.	1859.	1860.	Total.
Morbus Coxarius,	34	27	19	9	6	4	....	7	....	106
" Hydrops Pericardii,	....	6	....	....	....	....	....	....	....	9
" Mercurialis,	....	1	....	....	....	....	....	....	....	1
" Pottii,	3	11	16	11	11	13	5	2	....	72
" Spinalis,	14	....	....	....	....	....	9	....	....	23
Molluscum Vulgare,	....	1	1	....	....	....	....	....	....	2
Moribundus,	....	2	6	2	2	2	....	....	....	14
Morsus Canina,	....	....	....	....	....	....	....	2	....	2
Musculo-patti,	....	....	....	....	....	....	1	....	....	1
Myelitis,	....	....	1	....	....	....	....	....	....	1
Narcosis,	1	....	....	....	....	....	....	....	....	1
Nebula,	1	....	....	....	....	....	....	....	....	1
Necrosis,	44	31	34	16	21	23	9	3	10	191
Nephritis,	3	1	4	2	1	3	....	1	2	17
Neuralgia,	11	10	....	23	23	42	14	4	10	137
Nymphomania,	....	....	....	....	2	1	....	1	1	5
Odontalgia,	1	....	....	4	....	1	2	....	....	8
Odontophia,	17	....	....	....	....	....	....	....	....	17
Œdema,	....	5	10	43	....	8	14	4	5	89
Olophonia,	1	....	....	....	....	....	....	....	....	1
Omarthrocace,	....	....	....	1	....	1	....	....	....	2
Onanismus,	....	....	....	....	....	....	....	....	1	1
Onychia,	....	1	....	....	....	....	....	....	....	1
Opacitas Corneæ,	25	6	8	....	....	2	....	....	....	41
Ophthalmia,	....	....	....	227	....	43	3	14	24	311
" Catarrhal and Muco-pur.,	18	40	103	....	2	....	....	....	....	163
" Gonorrh. and Purulent,	304	396	393	....	34	....	20	....	....	1,147
" Strumosa,	50	....	7	....	....	....	12	....	....	69
" Tarsi,	30	22	19	2	....	....	....	....	....	73
Orchitis,	....	2	....	24	23	6	10	3	7	75
Osteosarcoma,	....	1	4	....	....	....	....	....	....	5
Ostitis,	....	....	....	....	....	1	....	1	2	4
Otitis,	13	8	7	14	10	5	6	4	4	71
Otorrhœa,	....	2	5	2	....	....	....	....	....	9
Ovaritis,	....	4	3	....	5	7	10	2	1	32
Ozæna,	1	....	....	....	....	....	....	1	....	2
Palpitatio Cordis,	....	....	....	....	....	....	1	2	....	3
Pannus,	....	....	....	....	....	....	3	....	1	4
Paralysis,	10	....	7	8	10	7	....	13	4	59
Paraphymosis,	3	....	....	....	....	....	....	1	1	5
Paraplegia,	8	....	13	14	7	....	12	....	....	54
Paresis Generalis,	....	....	....	....	3	....	1	....	....	4
Paronychia,	102	143	157	117	84	88	32	17	42	782
Parotitis,	28	29	15	16	7	13	10	3	4	125
Partus Præmaturus,	....	19	11	6	....	....	....	....	....	36
Parulis,	....	....	....	....	1	1	3	....	....	5
Pemphigus,	26	34	7	7	6	4	7	....	4	95
Pericarditis,	8	4	12	5	4	....	3	....	....	28
Pernio,	41	19	53	83	3	....	....	....	....	199

TABLE C. (*Of Diseases.*)—*Continued.*

DISEASES.	1852.	1853.	1854.	1855.	1856.	1857.	1858.	1859.	1860.	TOTAL.
Periostitis, . .	6	2	3	6	3	3	7	1	1	32
Peritonitis, ...	8	6	9	166	....	8	7	2	2	208
Pertussis, ...	104	69	38	6	5	7	1	....	5	235
Pes Valgus, ...	....	....	....	....	....	....	....	7	5	12
Phagadæna, . . .	....	....	....	....	....	....	....	2	....	2
Pharyngitis, ...	9	5	2	4	1	....	....	....	....	21
Phlebitis, ...	1	....	....	....	....	3	2	....	1	7
Phlegmasia, ...	3	....	4	....	9	11	....	1	....	28
Phrenitis, ...	2	1	....	....	....	....	....	....	....	3
Phthiriasis, ...	....	1	5	....	....	1	4	....	....	11
Phthisis Pulmonum, .	289	474	405	311	166	163	103	127	54	2,092
Phymosis, ...	....	....	....	....	....	....	....	3	....	3
Plethora, ...	....	....	3	1	....	....	....	....	....	4
Pleuritis, ...	55	42	50	35	38	45	47	22	16	350
Pleurodynia, . . .	9	1	....	4	4	4	2	....	1	25
Pleuropneumonia, . .	....	2	....	8	2	4	3	1	8	28
Pneumonia, . . .	360	245	236	159	64	227	63	....	29	1,383
Pneumothorax, . .	....	....	....	2	1	1	1	1	....	6
Polypus Urethræ, .	....	....	....	....	1	....	....	....	....	1
Porrigo, ...	71	205	129	60	45	66	8	1	13	598
Post Puerperium, .	....	....	....	40	55	91	76	44	78	384
Prolapsus Ani, . . .	7	4	9	6	2	1	1	....	....	30
" Uteri, . .	4	6	4	3	2	1	3	1	1	25
" Vesico Vaginalis,	1	....	....	....	....	....	....	....	....	1
Prostatitis, ...	....	....	....	....	....	1	....	....	....	1
Prurigo, ...	5	82	120	57	27	13	....	....	....	304
Pseudarthrosis, . .	4	....	2	....	....	....	....	....	....	6
Psoriasis, ...	23	76	6	18	8	11	15	5	4	166
Pterygium, ...	....	1	1	....	....	....	....	....	....	2
Ptyalismus, . . .	4	8	7	2	3	2	7	....	2	35
Puerperium, ...	580	712	763	715	469	506	403	273	278	4,699
Purpura Hæmorrhagica,	4	12	12	9	11	3	....	1	....	52
Pyæmia, ...	....	1	1	1	....	....	....	3	2	8
Pyrosis, ...	1	....	....	....	....	....	....	....	....	1
Rachitis, ...	1	....	1	1	1	....	....	....	....	4
Ranula, ...	....	....	1	....	....	....	....	....	....	1
Retentio Urinæ and Mensium, ...	....	....	....	2	....	....	1	....	1	4
Retroversio Uteri, . .	1	1	4	2	....	1	1	....	....	10
Rheumatismus, . .	416	532	676	405	192	228	276	158	138	3,021
Roseola, ...	1	2	2	6	....	....	....	....	....	11
Rubeola, ...	332	276	387	173	92	88	56	6	48	1,458
Rupia, ...	4	1	18	9	1	2	1	....	....	36
Ruptura, ...	2	1	1	1	....	....	....	....	....	5
Sarcoma Encephaloides,	....	....	....	1	....	....	....	....	....	1
Scabies, ...	288	246	383	365	222	24	137	48	53	1,766
Scarlatina, ...	23	116	57	29	4	24	22	8	20	303
Sciatica, ...	....	....	....	5	12	11	11	....	....	39
Scirrhus Hepatis, &c., &c.	6	....	4	....	2	3	2	....	....	17
Schirrhosis, ...	....	....	4	....	....	....	....	....	....	4
Sclerotitis, . .	10	7	13	9	1	11	....	4	....	55

TABLE C. (*Of Diseases.*)—*Continued.*

Diseases.	1852.	1853.	1854.	1855.	1856.	1857.	1858.	1859.	1860.	Total.
Scorbutus,	....	9	26	58	....	3	4	6	....	106
Scrofulosis,	....	....	37	27	10	9	23	1	4	111
Senectus,	....	....	....	....	....	....	....	1	5	6
Sequelæ Abortionis,	....	....	....	....	4	....	3	....	....	7
" Amputationis,	....	....	....	4	....	6	4	2	....	16
" Choleræ,	....	....	....	....	....	1	2	4	....	7
" Congelationis,	....	....	....	....	....	1	4	....	....	5
" Fracturæ,	....	....	1	1	7	5	4	6	2	26
" Injuriæ,	....	....	....	1	3	4	3	....	....	11
" Intermittentis,	....	....	....	....	....	....	....	....	1	1
" Luxationis Acromii,	....	....	....	1	....	1	3	....	....	5
" Scarlatina,	....	....	....	....	....	3	3	1	....	7
" Typhi,	....	....	....	18	....	2	9	9	....	38
" Ustionis,	....	....	....	3	....	3	4	....	....	10
Simulatio,	....	....	....	....	....	....	....	....	1	1
Spermatorrhœa,	....	1	6	6	....	2	....	....	....	15
Splenemphraxis,	....	....	2	1	....	....	....	....	....	3
Staphyloma,	10	8	8	6	8	3	1	5	5	54
Stenosis,	....	....	....	....	....	....	....	2	....	2
Stomacace,	....	....	....	7	....	....	....	....	....	7
Stomatitis,	....	2	14	6	2	5	1	2	....	32
Strabismus,	....	....	1	1	....	....	1	....	1	4
Strictura Urethræ,	....	7	6	3	12	7	7	....	5	47
Struma,	....	....	6	....	....	....	....	....	....	6
Subluxatio,	....	58	21	24	4	4	8	3	2	124
Surditas,	....	....	....	....	1	5	1	....	....	7
Sycosis,	....	....	4	4	2	1	1	....	....	12
Synechia,	....	....	....	1	1	1	2	2	2	9
Synovitas,	....	58	68	3	34	39	19	4	13	238
Syphilis Prima,	260	190	329	319	231	290	215	160	109	2,103
" Secunda,	266	259	251	143	93	111	38	45	43	1,249
" Tertia,	4	....	....	....	11	17	47	20	13	112
Tabes Mesenterica,	59	7	....	....	....	....	1	....	....	67
Tænia,	....	1	2	3	....	....	....	....	2	8
Talipes,	....	....	....	13	13	29	29	6	....	90
Tetanus,	1	....	....	1	....	....	....	....	....	2
Tic Doloureux,	....	....	1	....	....	1	....	....	....	2
Tinæa Capitis,	....	....	....	....	....	....	....	....	2	2
Tonsillitis,	65	36	44	34	17	36	28	7	15	282
Torticollis,	2	....	....	....	....	....	....	....	....	2
Tracheitis,	....	....	....	....	5	6	6	3	16	36
Trachoma,	1	8	5	4	....	24	46	61	28	177
Tremor Mercurialis,	....	....	....	1	....	....	2	....	....	3
Tuberculosis,	47	....	90	....	....	....	....	....	....	137
Tumor Albus,	....	2	2	....	....	....	3	1	....	8
" Ovarii,	....	....	....	....	2	2	2	3	2	11
Tumores,	4	....	3	5	....	....	....	....	....	12
Tympanitis,	....	....	1	1	....	....	....	....	....	2
Typhlitis Stercoracea,	....	....	....	....	....	....	1	....	....	1
Ulcera,	366	426	547	430	239	234	141	85	94	2,562

TABLE C. (*Of Diseases.*)—*Continued.*

Diseases.	1852.	1853.	1854.	1855.	1856.	1857.	1858.	1859.	1860.	Total.
Ulcus Cornea, &c.,	2	....	....	....	4	....	11	.....	....	17
Uræmia, . .	.....	....	1	....	....	....	.....	1	....	2
Urticaria, . .	.....	....	6	....	2	2	1	1	....	12
Ustio, . . .	64	66	77	44	32	41	21	1	3	349
Uvula Elongata,	.....	....	....	....	1	....	....	.....	....	1
Vaginitis, . .	1	1	4	....	....	....	.....	.....	....	6
Varicella, .	.....	6	26	2	35	17	.....	4	....	90
Varicocele, . .	.....	....	....	....	1	2	.....	.....	....	3
Varicosæ Venæ,	.....	....	....	....	....	....	.....	11	6	17
Variola, . .	16	10	43	3	18	11	4	4	9	118
Varix, . .	6	22	8	28	7	9	9	2	....	91
Vegetationes, .	.....	5	....	....	2	....	17	7	8	39
Vertigo, . .	.....	1	....	....	....	....	.....	.....	....	1
Vitium Cerebri, .	.....	....	....	....	....	3	.....	3	....	6
" Cordis Valv.	.....	....	39	14	....	....	.....	.....	....	53
" Uteri, .	.....	....	....	....	....	....	3	.....	....	3
Vulnera, . .	65	121	43	14	11	6	8	.....	2	270
Total annual admissions, .	9,336	10,794	13,936	9542	4965	5645	4,303	2,802	3138	64,461

Table C,

Showing the Diseases of Patients who died at the State Emigrant Hospitals and Refuge, Ward's Island, from January 1, 1852, *to December* 31, 1860.

MORTALITY.	1852.	1853.	1854.	1855.	1856.	1857.	1858.	1859.	1860.	TOTAL.
Abscessus,	8	1	8	11	3	4	....	1	....	36
Adenitis,	....	....	....	1	1	....	....	....	....	2
Albuminaria,	6	....	....	....	....	....	....	....	....	6
Anæmia,	5	4	14	7	....	....	....	7	2	39
Anasarca,	1	2	3	....	....	3	....	....	....	9
Angina,	....	....	7	....	....	....	....	....	....	7
Aorteurysma,	....	1	1	....	....	....	1	....	....	3
Apoplexia,	6	7	9	7	2	1	1	2	....	35
Arachnitis,	....	1	....	2	1	....	....	....	....	4
Ascites,	11	8	....	....	....	1	....	....	....	20
Asphyxia,	....	....	2	1	3	3	2	1	4	16
Asthma,	1	....	....	....	1	....	....	....	....	2
Atelactasis,	3	6	4	....	....	6	10	....	....	29
Atrophia,	123	77	135	....	70	75	....	2	....	482
Bronchitis,	24	16	10	35	2	....	1	....	1	89
" et Diarr. et Marasmus,	6	....	....	....	....	....	....	....	....	6
Cachexia,	....	5	....	2	....	....	....	....	....	7
Cancer,	3	22	13	11	2	6	4	2	....	63
Cancrum Oris,	....	3	....	2	4	2	....	....	....	11
Carcinoma,	4	13	....	....	....	....	....	....	1	18
Caries,	2	1	....	1	2	1	....	....	....	7
Cerebritis,	....	....	....	....	3	....	....	....	....	3
Cerebromalacia,	....	1	1	....	....	....	....	....	....	2
Cholera Asiatica,	73	....	173	4	1	....	....	....	....	251
" Asphyxia,	2	....	....	....	....	....	....	....	....	2
" Infantum,	9	2	14	27	23	25	9	7	....	116
" Morbus,	5	....	....	....	1	....	....	....	....	6
Chorea St. Viti,	....	....	....	1	....	....	....	....	....	1
Cirrhosis Hepatis,	....	....	3	2	....	1	1	3	....	10
Concussio Cerebri,	....	....	1	....	....	....	....	....	....	1
Congestio Cerebri,	....	1	....	....	....	1	1	....	....	3
" Pulmonum,	....	1	....	5	2	....	1	....	....	9
Contusio,	....	1	....	....	....	....	....	....	....	1
Convulsiones,	50	46	57	48	30	32	17	....	....	280
Coup de Soleil,	1	....	....	....	....	....	1	....	....	2
Colica,	....	....	....	1	....	1	....	....	....	2
Coxitis,	....	....	....	....	....	....	....	....	1	1
Cyanosis,	....	1	25	....	....	1	....	1	....	28
Cynanche Trachealis,	5	10	7	....	....	....	....	1	....	23
Cystitis and Nephritis,	....	1	1	....	....	....	....	....	....	2
Debilitas,	21	....	9	6	....	....	....	....	....	36
Delirium Tremens,	....	....	1	....	....	....	....	....	....	1
Diabetes,	....	....	....	2	....	1	....	....	....	3

TABLE C. (*Of Deaths.*)—*Continued.*

MORTALITY.	1852.	1853.	1854.	1855.	1856.	1857.	1858.	1859.	1860.	TOTAL.
Diarrhœa,	106	69	151	70	29	20	14	7	....	466
Diphtheritis,	....	....	....	1	....	....	2	....	....	3
Drowning,	....	....	....	....	1	....	....	....	....	1
Dysenteria,	124	83	97	51	31	31	28	14	10	469
Echinococcus Hepatis,	....	1	....	....	1	1	....	....	....	3
Eclampsia,	....	....	....	....	....	....	....	1	....	1
Emphysema,	1	....	7	1	....	....	....	....	....	9
Empyema,	2	5	2	....	2	1	4	....	....	16
Endocarditis,	1	....	2	5	2	....	....	....	....	10
Enteritis,	3	2	2	3	5	1	3	....	....	19
Enterohelcosis,	2	..5	16	28	....	3	1	....	3	58
Enteromalacia,	....	1	2	....	8	....	....	....	....	11
Epilepsia,	1	6	1	1	2	1	2	9	8	31
Erysipelas,	20	11	13	7	1	4	2	1	2	61
Exhaustio,	1	4	8	1	....	2	....	....	....	16
Febris,	115	....	....	....	....	....	....	....	....	115
" Puerperalis,	35	8	2	15	7	....	....	3	1	71
" Typhoid,	....	....	....	....	....	....	....	....	14	14
" Typhus,	151	47	91	109	15	13	6	9	21	462
" " et Pneumonia, &c.,	69	1	1	....	....	....	....	1	1	73
Fractura,	....	....	1	....	....	....	....	....	....	1
" Cranii, &c.,	....	....	2	....	....	....	....	....	....	2
" Cruris Complicata,	....	....	....	....	....	....	....	....	1	1
" Vertebrarum,	....	2	2	....	....	....	....	1	....	5
Fungus Hæmatodes,	1	....	....	....	....	....	1	....	....	2
" Medullare Ovarii,	....	....	....	1	....	....	....	....	....	1
Gangræna,	16	4	38	17	3	5	2	....	1	86
Gastritis,	1	....	....	....	....	....	....	....	....	1
Hæmatemesis,	....	....	1	1	....	....	....	....	....	2
Hæmaturia,	1	....	....	....	....	....	....	....	....	1
Hæmiplegia,	1	....	1	....	....	....	....	1	....	3
Hæmoptysis,	4	1	1	1	1	....	....	....	....	8
Hæmorrhagia,	2	....	....	1	....	....	....	....	....	3
Hæmorrhoides,	1	....	....	....	....	....	....	....	....	1
Helminthiasis,	....	....	....	1	1	1	1	....	....	4
Hepatitis,	1	1	1	1	....	4	....	6	1	15
Hernia,	....	1	....	....	1	....	....	....	....	2
Hydarthrus,	1	....	....	....	....	....	....	....	....	1
Hydatides,	....	1	....	....	1	....	....	....	....	2
Hydræmia,	....	....	1	5	....	....	....	....	....	6
Hydrocephalus,	5	7	21	5	....	3	....	7	....	48
Hydrops,	....	1	1	....	....	....	....	....	2	4
" Ovarii,	....	1	....	....	1	....	....	....	....	2
" Pericardii,	....	....	4	1	....	....	....	....	1	6
Hydrothorax,	1	1	4	....	3	1	1	....	....	11
Hypertrophia,	1	....	4	6	....	....	1	....	....	12
Icterus,	4	....	3	6	....	1	1	....	2	17
Ilius,	....	....	3	....	....	....	....	....	....	3
Inanitio,	....	....	7	34	20	29	....	....	14	104
Induratio Telæ Cellulosæ,	....	....	....	1	....	....	....	....	....	1

TABLE C. (*Of Deaths.*)—*Continued.*

MORTALITY.	1852.	1853.	1854.	1855.	1856.	1857.	1858.	1859.	1860.	TOTAL.
Inflammatio sub cellularis,	3	....	....	....	....	....	....	....	....	3
Injuriæ,	....	....	1	1	....	....	....	....	....	2
Insuff. Valv. Cordis,	....	....	3	....	....	....	....	....	....	3
Intussusceptio Intest.,	1	....	....	....	....	....	....	....	....	1
Laceratio Perinæi,	....	....	....	....	....	....	....	1	....	1
Laryngismus Stridulus,	....	1	....	....	....	....	....	....	....	1
Laryngitis,	....	4	26	5	1	....	....	....	....	36
Mania à Potu,	5	3	....	....	....	....	....	....	....	8
" Puerperalis,	2	....	....	1	....	....	....	....	....	3
Marasmus,	....	....	29	42	23	24	133	78	35	364
Melæna,	....	....	1	....	....	....	....	....	....	1
Meningitis,	3	....	5	4	2	1	10	7	6	38
Menorrhagia,	....	....	....	....	1	....	....	....	....	1
Metritis,	1	....	....	1	....	2	....	....	....	4
Mollities Cerebri,	1	....	3	....	....	3	7	3	....	17
Morbus Brightii,	2	11	23	21	5	19	9	4	7	101
" Cerebri,	....	....	....	....	....	....	....	....	2	2
" Cordis,	2	8	2	....	6	11	10	6	7	52
" Coxarius,	1	2	5	1	4	....	....	....	....	13
" Pottii,	1	1	1	3	3	2	....	2	....	13
Moribundi,	....	8	6	1	2	2	....	....	2	21
Necrosis,	1	2	....	....	....	....	1	....	....	4
Nephritis,	....	....	....	1	....	....	....	....	....	1
Œdema,	....	2	2	....	....	3	1	....	....	8
Osteo-Sarcoma,	1	....	....	....	....	....	....	....	....	1
Ovaritis,	....	....	....	....	....	....	....	2	....	2
Paralysis,	1	1	....	1	....	....	....	1	1	5
Paraplegia,	1	....	....	1	1	....	....	....	....	3
Parotitis,	1	1	....	1	....	....	....	....	....	3
Pemphigus,	1	....	....	....	....	....	1	....	....	2
Pericarditis,	2	1	4	4	2	1	2	....	....	16
Peritonitis,	4	....	4	....	....	....	....	....	2	10
Pertussis,	13	5	3	1	1	9	2	....	1	35
Phagedena,	1	....	....	....	....	....	....	....	....	1
Pharingitis,	....	....	1	....	....	....	....	....	....	1
Phlebitis,	2	5	3	....	2	3	2	....	....	17
Phlegmasia,	1	3	....	....	....	....	....	....	....	4
Phthisis,	211	253	223	116	84	72	70	42	28	1,099
Pleuritis,	8	3	....	9	2	3	5	1	....	31
Pleuropneumonia,	....	3	....	....	2	6	3	....	3	17
Pneuma Typhoidea,	....	....	....	....	....	....	....	....	2	2
Pneumonia,	80	80	112	119	25	29	21	12	8	486
Pneumothorax,	....	....	1	....	....	3	....	1	1	6
Premature Birth,	9	17	25	21	....	....	4	4	2	82
Purpura Hæmorrhagia,	1	4	11	4	2	3	2	1	....	28
Pyæmia,	....	1	5	2	2	6	6	6	6	34
Rachitis,	....	....	....	1	....	....	....	....	....	1
Rheumatismus Chr.,	....	....	....	....	....	....	....	....	1	1
Rubeola, &c.,	74	35	109	52	19	8	27	1	1	326
Ruptura,	....	1	....	....	....	....	....	....	....	1
" Gastrica,	1	....	....	....	....	....	....	....	....	1

TABLE C. (*Of Deaths.*)—*Continued.*

MORTALITY.	1852.	1853.	1854.	1855.	1856.	1857.	1858.	1859.	1860.	TOTAL.
Sarcoma Medulare, .	....	1	1	1	....	....	....	....	....	3
Scarlatina, . . .	9	29	1	16	1	1	2	1	....	60
" Anginosa,	....	....	2	....	1	....	5	1	3	12
" Maligna, .	....	5	1	....	....	....	....	....	3	9
Scirrhus, . . .	....	1	1	....	3	1	....	....	....	6
Scleroma, . .	....	....	....	....	....	....	....	....	2	2
Scorbutus, . . .	....	....	4	3	....	....	5	....	....	12
Scrofula, . .	4	....	....	1	2	....	2	....	....	9
Senectus Ultima, .	2	....	8	2	1	....	....	1	2	16
Septochymia, . .	1	....	....	....	....	....	....	....	....	1
Stomacace, . . .	....	....	....	2	....	....	....	....	....	2
Stomatitis Gangrænosa,	....	....	1	1	....	....	....	....	....	2
Strictura Œsophagi,	....	....	....	1	....	....	....	....	....	1
Suicidium, . .	1	2	....	....	1	....	....	....	....	4
Synovitis, . . .	....	....	....	....	....	....	....	....	2	2
Syphilis Prima, .	....	....	9	1	3	4	....	2	5	24
" Secunda, &c.,	....	....	....	.	2	2	....	1	....	5
Tabes Mesenterica, .	22	9	3	....	3	....	....	....	....	37
Tetanus, . .	1	2	....	3	1	....	....	....	....	7
Tonsillitis, . . .	....	....	7	2	3	....	....	....	....	12
Tracheitis, . .	....	....	7	8	16	1	4	....	....	36
Trismus Nascentium, .	....	....	....	....	....	....	5	4	2	11
Tuberculosis, . .	....	....	90	....	....	....	....	....	....	90
Tumor Ovarii, . .	....	....	....	....	....	....	1	....	....	1
Ulcera, . . .	....	....	3	11	....	3	1	....	....	18
Uræmia, . . .	....	....	2	....	1	....	....	1	1	5
Ustio, . . .	....	1	3	1	2	....	1	....	....	8
Vaginæ Fistula et debilitas, . . .	1	....	....	....	....	....	....	....	....	1
Variola, . . .	1	....	....	....	1	....	....	....	....	2
Vesico-vaginal Fistula, &c., . . .	1	....	....	....	....	....	....	....	....	1
Vitium Cerebri, .	....	....	....	....	....	1	....	....	....	1
" Ventriculi, .	....	....	....	....	....	....	....	2	....	2
Vulnus Capitis et Phrenitis, . . .	1	....	....	....	....	....	....	....	....	1
Total annual mortality,	1,543	1,108	1,707	1,278	526	519	487	262	226	7,656

ANNUAL REPORTS

OF THE

EMIGRANT REFUGE AND HOSPITALS, WARD'S ISLAND,

Accompanying the preceding Tables, marked C, and being from the Superintendent of the Institution for the years 1856, 1859, *and* 1860; *and from the Medical Board of the Hospitals, for the years* 1853 *and* 1854; *and from the Physician-in-chief, from the year* 1855 *(during which year the Medical Government of the Hospitals was changed) to* 1860; *and from the Surgeon-in-chief from the year* 1854 *to* 1860.

Reports of the Superintendent of Ward's Island.

STATE EMIGRANT REFUGE AND HOSPITALS,
Ward's Island, N. Y., Jan. 7, 1857.

TO THE COMMISSIONERS OF EMIGRATION:

Gentlemen:—In compliance with the resolution passed by your Board at the last meeting, I herewith submit my report of the workings and condition of the Emigrant Refuge and Hospitals under my charge, to Dec. 31st, 1856.

It was with feelings of considerable embarrassment and apprehension, that I accepted and entered upon the discharge of the duties of the office with which you had honored me. The character and condition of the institution were far from inviting; yet, the confidence reposed in me by your honorable Board, and the urgent solicitation of many distinguished gentlemen of this city and other parts of the State, determined my acceptance of the appointment, and I assumed the responsibilities of the care and government of the institution on the 1st day of October, 1855.

My first efforts were to establish order where none existed, and to improve the condition of the whole establishment, by disciplinary and moral regulations, for the general government of the subordinate officers, employées, and inmates. Although more than one hundred employées had been discharged from the island, by your action, just prior to my taking charge of the institution, I have, from time to time, dispensed with the services of a large additional number of persons employed and paid by the Commissioners, believing that the duties and labor performed by them could be done by other employées in addition to what they were then doing, or by the inmates, without pay. A large amount has thus been saved in wages and board, while it is believed that the services and labor by them rendered have been more satisfactorily performed than heretofore.

It has been my desire and determination, so far as it depended on me, to have an efficient, humane, but economical administration of the affairs of the institution; to require order and regularity in every department; that, while all necessary and reasonable care and attention should be given to the welfare and comfort of the inmates, no extraordinary expense should be incurred, or unnecessary articles called for or used. I have, therefore, from time to time, introduced and established such measures of reform, retrenchment, and economy, as it seemed to me the diminished income of the commission imperiously demanded, and such as I believed would meet with the approbation of the Commissioners. There has, however, been some increased *average* expense, arising from the diminution of the number of inmates and patients —the small number treated in the several wards, especially in the lying-in, recovery, and some others. In some of these wards there have been treated and cared for only from ten to twenty adult patients, while they are capable of accommodating from forty to sixty patients each. They may be, and no doubt are, more comfortable than if the wards were *full;* but it will be readily seen that the average expense must be much increased over what it would be, were the number in each of the wards double or treble the present number—each of these wards requiring a nurse, fuel, lights, cleaning, and other necessary expenses, as those having a full number of inmates or patients. The facilities, however, for the medical care and treatment of the patients—the good air, extra room, and other advantages for their improvement, favorable to rapid cure and health, may, and perhaps do, outweigh the objection of the extra average expense.

Believing manual labor in the open air (when the weather permits) to be the best means to promote and secure health, as well as habits of industry, calculated to fit them for labor and usefulness on leaving the institution, I have kept many of the partially insane and convalescent inmates at work during the spring, summer, and autumn months, in the garden and fields, in cleansing the grounds and other light labor; while those who have entirely recovered, or were sent here to be put at work, have been employed in blasting rock, building sea-wall, grading the land, whitewashing and keeping the wards and buildings in ordinary repair, &c., all calculated to instil into their minds a spirit of industry, self-reliance, and dependence on themselves, as they go forth from here into this (to many of them) new world.

The following table shows the amount of the vegetable crop raised on the farm, by the labor of the inmates:

Asparagus, ...	678	lbs.	Tomatoes, ...	50	bush's
Spinach, ...	800	bush's	Cucumbers, . .	12	"
Potatoes, ...	1,778	"	Melons, ...	55	"
Turnips, ...	1,800	"	Peppers, ...	6	"
Parsnips, ...	800	"	Radishes, ...	12	"
Beets, ...	400	"	Sweet corn (ears), .	64	"
Onions, ...	87	"	Cabbages, . . .	30,000	heads
Peas, ...	60	"	Lettuce, . . .	5,000	"
Bush Beans, . . .	50	"	Celery, ...	8,030	"
Lima Beans, ...	100	"	Hay, ...	30	tons.

Only one gardener (or paid man) was employed in the cultivation, care, and gathering of the above produce. The labor has been performed by the larger class of boys, and invalids, incapable of taking care or of earning a living for themselves outside.

On the 4th of June last, through Mr. Morgan, chairman of the Ward's Island Committee, I called your attention to the miserable condition of the *eighty* insane persons then on the Island. By the action of your Board I was authorized and directed to send to the Asylum on Blackwell's Island such as were noisy and difficult to control, and to transfer all others to wards more suitable for their proper care and treatment.

I took immediate steps to carry out the wishes of the Commissioners as expressed in their resolution passed on the 9th of June, so far as I was able to do so, with the unoccupied buildings, by fitting up separate wards with yards attached, for both males and females, that should afford more suitable and healthy accommodations, and transferred them from their wretched abode, the old barracks, to their new quarters, as soon as they were in readiness to receive them. And although their condition is much improved, it is not yet such as suffering humanity in the form of "minds in ruin" calls for at our hands. Our accommodations for them, even now, do not afford that comfort they so much need. I can only repeat what I said to you in my communication before alluded to: there are no buildings on the Island properly constructed for classifying, or that would enable us to separate the noisy from the more calm and quiet—the partially insane from those hopelessly so, or the strong and violent from the weak and inoffensive. I cannot, therefore (if this class are to be continued here), dismiss this subject without urging on the attention of the Commissioners not only the importance, but the actual necessity of an insane asylum on Ward's Island, separate from all other buildings, suitable and convenient for the reception and care of this unfortunate class of emigrants—where they may receive all that medical, moral, and physical attention and treatment which their condition entitles them to, and which is so well calculated to bring back and restore the disordered mind to its primitive condition of order and health.

The school, as organized some years hence under the care of a male and female teacher, was continued for several months; but, believing that little or no benefit resulted to the children, either from their instruction or example, by advice of the Committee I discharged them, and for a short time the school was discontinued. It was, however, on the 1st day of August, reorganized as a ward school, and placed under the care and supervision of the "Board of Education," and is now in a most flourishing and prosperous condition. A pleasant and commodious apartment has been fitted up as a general school-room, with recitation-rooms adjoining, affording all requisite accommodations for the welfare and improvement of the children. The principal teacher, Mrs. Spofford, is a lady of excellent character and qualifications, whose experience for several years as principal of the public school at Yorkville, commends her to our highest confidence. She is assisted by two efficient young ladies, competent and well qualified for their respective duties. This change has already proved beneficial. The same course is pursued here as in the other public schools of the city; and the rapid improvement of the children in reading and other studies, in singing, and general deportment, all go to show the wisdom of placing this school under the organization of the "Board of Education." The average number of scholars is about 150, who, apart from school hours, are under the management and control of the superintendent and his assistants, when due consideration is given to their wants and comfort, by allowing them ample time for exercise and various sports, running, marching, &c., in the play-room and open air, designed to strengthen and invigorate both body and mind.

The moral and religious instruction of the inmates has been confided by your Board to two chaplains, Rev. Thomas Cook, (Protestant,) and Rev. A. Manahan, (Catholic.) Services have been held on each Sunday in the two chapels, and in the Protestant in both the English and German languages. The attendance has been large and constant. The chaplains have also visited the various wards and other apartments of the institution on Sunday, and other days of the week, distributing books, cheering and consoling the sick and dying by their advice and ministrations. The Protestant children, from 40 to 60, are collected twice on every Sunday in the chapel, as a Sunday-school, under the charge and instruction of the matron, (Mrs. James,) and Mr. Malignon, who, although not now connected with the Island, has kindly continued to instruct the German children in reading, singing, &c. The Catholic children, numbering from 100 to 150, (able to attend,) are assembled in the Catholic chapel every Sunday morning, under the care and instruction of the assistant matron, Mrs. Browne, and others. Several of the nurses have also rendered valuable assistance in conducting the Sabbath-schools. The Sabbath on the Island the past year has been observed as a day of quiet and order—emphatically "a day of rest."

The present medical system, with competent resident physicians and surgeons, whose duties and powers are confined to the *medical* and *surgical* treatment of the inmates, and the directing of the quantity and quality, mode of cooking and distributing the food to the patients in the hospitals, I consider well calculated to secure the prompt care and treatment of the sick and diseased, and especially so in cases requiring immediate attention and relief.

Notwithstanding the large proportion constantly in the hospitals, the general health of the institution has been good, no contagious or epidemic disease having prevailed during the past year.

Much care and attention has been given to the cleanliness of the buildings and the premises adjoining the same—the different wards being frequently and thoroughly scoured and whitewashed, and the grounds kept cleared and in good order.

A large amount of labor has been performed, all of which it would be difficult to specify; but among the principal items are the following: the grounds between the park and the nursery have been graded and laid out for grass; considerable stone has been taken from the quarry, prepared, and used for walks and for macadamizing the road to the dock; the basements of some of the buildings have been put in good condition and much improved; new sewers have been built, and old ones cleansed and relaid; the chimneys and blinds to the different buildings, which were out of order, have been repaired; the waste water, which formerly collected under and around the wash-house, is now carried off by a sewer; the wagons, ploughs, carts, &c., have been kept in good repair, and some new ones necessary for the use of the Institution have been built by the inmates, by whom are also made all the coffins required for the use of the Institution; the reservoir has been recemented; over two hundred iron bedsteads have been repaired; shoes and clothing for more than seven thousand persons (who have been cared for in the Institution during the past year) have been repaired and kept in order; over thirty tons of hay have been cut. The grading of the land between the old hospital building, containing the offices, and the river, had been begun, as also the building of a sea-wall along the same, which improvements, when completed, (as they probably will be in another season,) will add much to the beauty of the Island; a small wash-house, bathing-room, and shed attached to the new hospital have been built; fifteen hundred tons of coal were received at the dock and carted to the yard; all which labor has been performed by the male inmates, under the directions and orders of the officers of the Institution.

The female inmates of the Refuge Department have assisted the matrons and nurses in caring for the sick, washing and ironing, cooking, cleaning, &c., and have manufactured and made up more than fourteen thousand separate garments and articles of bedding, clothing, &c., for the male and female inmates, and children and infants' use. A large proportion of this kind of work and labor has heretofore been performed by "paid help."

The deputy, clerks, steward, and other officers and employées have devoted their whole time to the discharge of their various duties, and have given me general satisfaction. The worthy matron, Mrs. James, who has been identified nine years with the care and management of the female inmates, has rendered me valuable service, as have also the two assistant matrons, Mrs. Malloy and Mrs. Browne, by their industry and faithful attention to their respective duties.

The annexed tables will show the number cared for during the year—the daily admissions—sex, age, and distribution, nativity, year of arrival, ports sailed from, daily discharges, monthly discharges of males and females, discharges to the Labor Exchange, discharges to the Marine Hospital, and days spent on the Island during the past year by infants born here and in the United States, and admitted to the Institution after birth.

Charged with the care and control of all the buildings and land connected with the Refuge and Hospitals, and the supervision of all the property of every description belonging to the Commissioners, the appointment and dismissal at pleasure, and the government and direction of all the subordinate officers, and of persons employed in the Refuge and Hospitals, or other parts of the establishment on Ward's Island, (excepting the chaplains and physicians,) I have not been unmindful of the responsibilities of the office, nor of my obligation to the Board of Commissioners; and while I have endeavored to discharge the various duties devolving on me fearlessly, independently, and, I trust, conscientiously, I have not been willing that any person should interfere with or assume power delegated to me as chief officer of the Institution, although ready at all times, to receive suggestions, or advice, from those connected with or interested in its welfare.

If the management and condition of the Institution since it has been under my care, has been such as to meet the expectations of the Commissioners and the friends of the Commission, who urged my acceptance of the office, I shall, in a measure, be reconciled to the seclusion of myself and family from society and many of the privileges of life.

All which is respectfully submitted.

AMOS PILSBURY, *Superintendent.*

Ward's Island, N. Y., Dec. 31, 1859.

TO THE COMMISSIONERS OF EMIGRATION:

Gentlemen:—With this I transmit to you the statistics of this Institution for the past year. During that period all inmates admitted upon work-tickets, as well as those discharged from the hospital as cured, (but who preferred remaining on the Island,) have been kept steadily at work, either upon the farm, or in improving the property. The amount of produce from the garden the past summer, with but one hired man, was as follows:

Asparagus, lbs.,	278	Cucumbers, bushels,	12
Spinach, bushels,	360	Tomatoes, "	30
Potatoes, "	830	Peppers, "	25
Turnips, "	1,300	Sweet Corn, "	100
Beets, "	400	Cabbage, heads,	28,000
Parsnips, "	400	Lettuce, "	3,000
Carrots, "	500	Celery, "	2,500
Onions, "	150	Pumpkins,	2,000
Peas, "	32	Squashes,	400
Lima Beans, "	120	Egg Plants,	4,000
Bush " "	25	Hay, tons,	35
Radishes, "	3		

The sea-wall, on the north side of the dock, has been finished, and is nearly completed on the south side. The field adjoining the garden on the east, which has been overgrown by underbrush and briars for many years, has been cleared off, and prepared for planting next summer. Drains have been made, and the grounds between the Nursery Building and the river are now being graded.

Since my appointment as Superintendent on the 1st of July last, I have endeavored to faithfully carry out the discipline and economy established by my father, and trust my efforts have been satisfactory to your honorable body.

The chief surgeon and chief physician, and their assistants, by their hearty co-operation, have rendered to me valuable aid; and it gives me great pleasure to testify to the skill and kindness with which the inmates of the hospital have been uniformly treated.

My thanks are due to the deputy, clerk, steward, matron, and assistant-matrons, as well as all the other employées, for the faithful manner in which they have discharged their respective duties.

All which is respectfully submitted.

LOUIS D. PILSBURY, *Superintendent.*

Ward's Island, N. Y., Jan. 1, 1861.

To the Commissioners of Emigration:

Gentlemen:—I herewith transmit to you the statistics of this Institution, and also an account of the products raised on the farm, for the year ending December 31st, 1860. Respectfully,

JAMES P. FAGAN, *Superintendent.*

Statement of the Produce of the Farm-garden, W. Island, for the year 1860.

Asparagus, lbs.,	300	Cucumbers, bushels,	13
Spinach, bushels,	360	Tomatoes, "	35
Potatoes, "	818	Peppers, "	20
Turnips, "	1,860	Sweet Corn (ears), bushels,	160
Beets, "	400	Cabbages, (heads),	11,000
Parsnips, "	500	Lettuce, "	2,000
Carrots, "	430	Celery, "	3,000
Onions, "	112	Squashes,	300
Peas, "	25	Egg Plants,	400
Lima Beans, "	100	Hay, tons,	35
Bush " "	23	Oats, bushels,	175
Radishes, "	4		

Number of inmates in Institution, January 1, 1860,	764	
" " admitted,	3,701	
" births,	264	
Total number cared for during the year,	——	4,729
Number discharged during the year,	3,433	
" of deaths during the year in both Refuge and Hospital,	228	
Total number,	——	3,661
" remaining on 31st December, 1860,		1,068

Number of days spent in Hospital,	173,649	
" " " Refuge,	89,752	
Total number of days spent in both,	——	263,401

Medical and Surgical Reports of the State Emigrant Hospitals.

Ward's Island, N. Y., Jan. 7, 1854.

To the Commissioners of Emigration:

Gentlemen:—The Medical Board of the Emigrant Refuge Hospitals, beg leave to present the following (with the annexed tabular statement) as their annual report for the year 1853:

By the books of the hospital it will be seen there remained on the 1st of January,	823
There were admitted during the year,	10,794
Born,	644

Thus 12,261 patients passed through the hospital wards.

There were discharged, 10,215; died, 822; in the refuge department, 12,591 were treated; making a total of 24,852 cases of disease treated in the institution; of which, in the refuge department, 286 died. The percentage of mortality on the number treated in the institution is $4\frac{1}{2}$; on the admissions, is $7\frac{5}{8}$; on the discharges, is $8\frac{1}{10}$; which is nearly 4 per cent. less than in the year 1852, 6 per cent. less than in 1850, and 4 per cent. less than in 1848.

The principal diseases were 692 cases of dysentery and diarrhœa; 383 of typhus fever; 474, pulmonary consumption—which latter was the cause of death in 253 cases; a large number of "Panama" and intermittent fever, some of a most malignant type, in laborers who had been employed on the Panama railroad.

In the lying-in department there were admitted 712 women, (including those received from the city immediately after confinement,) and there were born 644 children; 44 deaths occurred during the year among the women; there have been 49 cases of puerperal fever, under which head are included metritis, phlebitis uteri and peritonitis. In 1852, 574 women passed through this department. There were born 523 children; 68 women died, and 124 cases of puerperal fever were reported to have existed during the year. Prior to March last the women were confined in the large hospital building, since which they have been transferred to separate buildings, and whenever puerperal fever has appeared, the ward in which it existed has been immediately abandoned; and this, in connection with other precautions, has arrested its progress.

In the surgical department, there have been the usual extent and variety of diseases. A large number of capital and important operations have been performed, besides many of a minor character, which have terminated with gratifying success.

It may be proper to state that in the apothecary's department, the bill for quinine has exceeded that of the previous year by $738, and for cod-liver oil by $240; there having been many hundred more cases of intermittent fever, among which are classed the grave cases received from Panama, in which the first of these expensive medicines is employed. The cases of pulmonary consumption and scrofulous diseases have exceeded the same year by about 200; in these latter, cod-liver oil enters largely into the treatment; and the whole number of cases treated in the institution has been greater than in 1852. The apothecary, in his report, states, that there remained on hand last year, but a small amount of medicines; at present, there is a stock of $904 77; by deducting the excess of the above two items of drugs alone, with the stock on hand, will make a difference of $818 43 in favor of the present year.

The Medical Board would beg to suggest that, as the two-story hospital frame buildings are becoming somewhat dilapidated, they be replaced as soon as may be by substantial brick structures, as the large number of patients requiring hospital aid will render them necessary for years to come.

There is one feature in this hospital different from that of any other. The large number of feeble and scrofulous children received here, after long sea-voyage, where the food required for children can scarcely be supplied, is decimated by the severe dysentery and diarrhœa with which they are afflicted. Pregnant women are also confined on shipboard, and come to us immediately after having landed; some directly after confinement in the city are received, both mother and child often in a desperate condition; others, but a few days in the country, reach the hospital, and are prematurely delivered of feeble infants, many of which merely breathe and then cease to exist; others linger a few hours or days at most; and in this way they swell our bills of mortality, without being in any way amenable to the physician's skill, or the surgeon's art; they end their sufferings almost as soon as begun, but they are as prominent in the necrology of the hospital as if they had reached adult life.

As there seems to be some misapprehension, or a want of knowledge, as to the manner in which the Medical Board discharge the duties assigned them, it may be well to state that the Board may be denominated a Medical Bureau for advice and counsel, in all matters pertaining to the hospital, while each separate division has its appropriate head to superintend and direct the house physicians and surgeons (all graduates in medicine) in discharging their duties. Five chief, or superintending physicians, are on duty every day, under whose directions the house physicians prescribe and carry into effect their instructions as regards the patients, two of the Board visiting daily through the year, the others alternating every two months; and ten hours on an average are spent in this work of superintending. In addition, in all cases requiring consultation, sufficient counsel can, at any time, be had in those demanding immediate action, without waiting, as is sometimes necessary elsewhere, for a day or more to elapse before the consulting physicians can be brought in; and in this way the emigrant is placed on a better footing than the wealthy private citizen, besides having a physician who speaks the language, and is familiar with the customs and peculiarities of the people of the country whence he has emigrated.

The Medical Board beg to return their thanks to the Board of Commissioners generally for their co-operation in all matters relating to the hospital, and particularly to the president, vice-president, and to the chairman of the Ward's Island committee, the last of whom by his continued visits and frequent personal inspection of every thing connected with the interest of the hospital has been in a position to perceive at once the wants of the institution, which, by his active measures, have met speedy relief.

To the majority of the house physicians the Board feel much praise is due for their fidelity and industry in carrying out their instructions, and discharging their duties for the welfare of the sick, and the Board take pleasure in recording their appreciation of their services.

To the warden and matrons also, the Board bear willing testimony to the prompt and efficient aid which they have received from them, by means of which their labors have been rendered less arduous, and the well-being of the Institution been promoted.

In conclusion, this Board takes the opportunity, at the close of another year, respectfully to tender their congratulations to the Commissioners of Emigration, on the present position of the Emigrants' Hospital—a few years ago unknown beyond the precincts of our city, it now takes rank among the first and oldest of the scientific and humanitarian institutions of the country. And the man of science as well as the philanthropist from other countries where its fame has reached, seek it out and generously and frankly volunteer the assertion that it compares favorably with the richly endowed hospitals of the old world.

It is a haven in which the friendless and destitute emigrant from every clime finds a refuge, where all that humanity can devise is tendered him as freely as it could be were he still surrounded by the old familiar faces of his native home.

HENRY G. COX, M. D., *President.*

THOMAS ADDIS EMMETT, M. D., *Acting Secretary.*

Ward's Island, N. Y., Jan. 10, 1855.

TO THE COMMISSIONERS OF EMIGRATION:

Gentlemen:—The Medical Board of the Emigrant Refuge Hospitals, beg leave to present the following as their annual report for the year 1854:

There remained in Hospital on the 1st January, 1854,	1,254
Admitted during the year,	13,936
Born,	701

By which it will be seen that 15,861 patients were treated in the wards of the hospital. There were discharged 13,074; 1,438 died. In the Refuge Department, in which are included the insane, incurable, &c., 13,806 cases of disease received medical treatment, of whom 269 died. It necessarily happens in the Refuge Department, that patients who have been treated for one malady, and discharged cured, have again been admitted, at a subsequent period, for other diseases.

The percentage of mortality on the whole number of cases treated in the Institution, amounting to 29,667, was $5\frac{4}{5}$, on the admission $9\frac{1}{15}$, on the discharges $9\frac{9}{10}$. It will be noticed, that the increase in the numbers treated, has been 25 per cent.; the mortality has only exceeded the small ratio of last year by 2 per cent.; and, if the cases of cholera be deducted, the percentage will be about the same. The average increase of the city mortality is greater than in this hospital.

Asiatic cholera, of a most virulent form, showed itself in June, and it continued during the summer months to attack patients, both in the Hospital and Refuge Departments; at times becoming considerably mitigated, but without perfect cessation until October. It is remarkable, that although no connection can be traced to them, the first two cases of cholera occurred in persons who had left the Marine Hospital, where it then prevailed, only a day or two before their admission here. The great majority of the cases in which it proved fatal, were in persons who were debilitated by previous diseases, as fever, dysentery, or pulmonary consumption; very few of those who had not already suffered from some grave malady fell victims; but among these the Board feel that more than a passing reference is due to the memory of Dr. Joseph Dennis, (son of the Rev. R. G. Dennis, of Grafton, Mass.,) one of the assistant physicians, who, while convalescent from dysentery, sank after a few hours from an attack of this fatal malady. Dr. Dennis had secured the confidence of this Board by the faithful discharge of his duties, and had given evidence of future professional position, had not the thread of life been thus prematurely severed. As soon as the cholera appeared in the city, a rigid regard to diet was enjoined upon all the inmates of the Institution; thorough ventilation, and general and frequent cleansing of the wards were resorted to, and to these precautions may, in a great measure, be attributed the fact, that some of the buildings escaped without having a case occur in them; also affording proof of the great advantage of separate buildings for so great a number of patients.

The Medical Board have to lament the loss of one their members, in the death of Dr. William H. MacNeven, who died from pulmonary consumption in Charleston, whither he had gone to recruit his health. Dr. MacNeven was a valued member of this Board, a judicious and skilful practitioner, a tried and able counsellor.

The principal diseases treated in the Medical Department of the hospital were cholera, diarrhœa, dysentery, marasmus, (among the children,) phthisis pulmonalis and other affections of the chest, with many cases of Panama, intermittent, and typhus fever.

In the Lying-in Department 894 women were admitted, including some just after confinement, 701 children were born, 35 women died, and there were 19 cases of puerperal fever, under this term being enumerated metritis, peritonitis, phlebitis uteri, &c. Thirteen cases of instrumental delivery (11 by forceps and 2 craniotomy) were effected; thus the number of lying-in women was 182 greater this year than in 1853, while the deaths were 9 less, and the cases of puerperal fever 30 less, and the number of women 320 greater than in 1852, the deaths 33 less, and the cases of puerperal fever 105 less than in that year.

In the Surgical Department, the variety of diseases has been great and interesting; among the many capital and successful operations, may be mentioned the excision of the arm at the shoulder-joint, for a tumor produced by cancerous degeneration of the bone, in size the largest on record; and the exsection, in two patients, of each of the bones of the fore-arm, occasioned by disease of the bones, the hands having been thus saved, and their usefulness preserved. During the last three years anæsthetics have been administered when indispensable, in upwards of 1,000 cases; and in no instance has an accident occurred, or the least bad effect followed their exhibition.

In the Apothecary's Department, the Board remark with satisfaction, that notwithstanding the increase of patients requiring the use of drugs has been 25 per cent. greater than the preceding year, that deducting the excess of the cost of the two items of quinine and cod-liver oil—both of which, owing to the many scrofulous cases, and diseases of a low type, have been largely needed—the entire cost of medicines will be less than that for the year 1853, with the addition of a good stock still on hand, with which to commence the present year.

Among the improvements which have been made during the year, is the addition of the operating theatre, which has supplied a great desideratum, and the patients are no longer operated upon in the wards, in presence of their more fortunate fellow-sufferers, who are thus saved the shock of witnessing scenes which are necessarily distressing, and, in many instances, have exercised a most unfavorable influence upon them.

Before another year has passed, the Board trusts that the buildings now in course of erection, with those contemplated, will be sufficient for all the requirements of the patients, and supply the place of the wooden structures, now beginning to be unfit for hospital purposes.

The Medical Board would beg to express to the Commissioners of Emigration their gratification for the manner in which they have been aided in their efforts for the well-being and comfort of the patients, and the elevation of the hospital as one of the great scientific institutions of the country.

To the assistant physicians and surgeons, the Board take pleasure in according their testimony for their fidelity and faithful discharge of their duties, during the trying season when cholera prevailed, as well as on all other occasions; some of them have suffered, but their places have been at once supplied by those in health. As a proof of the appreciation of the hospital, by the profession and community at large, among the assistant physicians are to be found some who, having been passed by the Army Board as assistant surgeons, have sought places in this Institution; and all give promise, by their scientific acquirements, and the faithful fulfilment of the duties assigned them, of future usefulness and eminence.

From the warden and matrons, the Medical Board acknowledge having received such assistance in the discharge of their duties, as their opportunities have permitted them to afford.

Notwithstanding the fearful epidemic of cholera which visited the hospital during the year, the large numbers of patients (especially children) prostrated by suffering when admitted, and the low type of diseases which have prevailed during the last three months, the hurried manner in which hospital accommodation, as required, has been supplied, the Board feel pleasure in stating that the results in this, the largest hospital in the country, will favorably compare, even under these circumstances, with those in Institutions where all the buildings and arrangements connected therewith are in a state of comparative perfection.

The Medical Board, in conclusion, beg to add, that under all circumstances, the same tender regard and concern have been manifested for patients in this hospital, as in the private sick room. At the same time feeling the obligations which, as members of an enlightened profession, with the opportunities of observing so great a variety of diseases, they owe to the cause of humanity, and the progress of science, it has been their aim, consistent with the above considerations, by their cliniques, discussions on the subjects of the diseases prevailing, and the opportunities afforded for witnessing surgical operations, to contribute their share to the promotion of science, and to present this Institution in its true light, as among the great sources for the improvement of American medicine and surgery, and which, from its magnitude, will hold, in the future, second rank in no respect to any in the country.

HENRY G. COX, M. D., *Pres. of Medical Board.*

THOS. ADDIS EMMETT, M. D., *Secretary.*

Ward's Island, N. Y., Jan. 10, 1855.

TO THE COMMISSIONERS OF EMIGRATION:

Gentlemen:—I have the honor to enclose herewith the annual report of the Surgical Department of the State Emigrant Hospitals, for the year ending December, 1854.

By this statistic, it is shown that the whole number of cases treated during the year was 4,574, the number of patients cured and discharged, 4,079, and the number of deaths, 89, or less than two per cent. on the number of cases treated.

It is deserving of remark, that the mortality among the surgical patients of the hospital is lower than that of the population of the city, including both sick and well.

The cases of death were, for the most part incurables, or children admitted to the hospital in a state of marasmus, existing as a complication of some surgical malady.

In the Eye Department, I can report this year, as well as the last, a total absence of disease of an epidemic character.

The great majority of the surgical patients were restored to health by curative treatment; but still, during the year, the performance of operations was unavoidable, and among these were several of magnitude, in some of which new methods were successfully resorted to for the relief of suffering and the removal of disease.

My assistants on the surgical staff, Drs. Winer, Gould, Robinson, Haggin and Smith, are entitled to my commendation for assiduity and general usefulness, during their past year of service.

J. M. CARNOCHAN.

Ward's Island, N. Y., Jan. 7, 1856.

To the Commissioners of Emigration:

Gentlemen:—I herewith transmit the statistics for the annual report of the Emigrant Hospitals at Ward's Island, for the year ending the 31st of December, 1855; during which period there have been treated in the wards of the hospital, 11,532 patients.

In the Refuge Department, 10,582 individuals have received professional assistance for diseases not requiring hospital treatment.

Making, in all, 22,114 persons who have come under medical observation during the year.

The new organization of a resident physician-in-chief and assistants, entered upon their duties on the 15th of August, 1855, and, as will be seen, the mortality on the cases treated during the last 4½ months of the year is 4⅘ per cent.; on the discharges, for the same period, 6⅛ per cent.

The ratio of mortality for the latter part of the year will compare favorably with the previous months; however, it may have been the result of circumstances other than the change of system.

In the Lying-in Department, there have been 709 admitted; 641 births, and 46 who were received from the city just after confinement, making in all 755 patients.

The surgical practice has been extensive and successful.

In the Apothecary's Department, the requisitions for drugs, medicines, stimulants, &c., have been much curtailed.

The assistant physicians have devoted their whole time to the duties assigned them; and I take pleasure in attesting to the care and attention bestowed on the sick committed to their charge.

Very respectfully,

HENRY B. FAY.

Ward's Island, N. Y., Jan. 1, 1856.

To the Commissioners of Emigration:

Gentlemen:—I have the honor to enclose herewith the annual report of the Surgical Department of the State Emigrant Hospitals for the year ending 31st December, 1855.

By this statistic, it is shown that the whole number of cases treated was 3,517, the number of cases cured and discharged, 3,120, and the number of deaths 64, or less than 2 per cent. on the number of cases treated.

During the year the department remained wholly free from disease of an epidemic character.

Among the capital operations successfully performed were one for congenital elephantiasis, or enlargement of the tongue, on a female patient, aged 15 years, by tying the external carotid artery, and, after an interval, the common carotid on the other side; one for the exsection of the entire bone of the heel, on a male adult, resorted to instead of amputation of the leg, as formerly practised: one for amputation at the shoulder joint, on a male adult, for mutilation by railroad accident.

The assistant-surgeons, Dr. Darling and Dr. Nelken, are entitled to my commendation for their zeal and general usefulness.

Most respectfully,
J. M. CARNOCHAN.

Ward's Island, N. Y., Jan. 7, 1857.

To the Commissioners of Emigration:

Gentlemen:—I have the honor to submit the annual report and the accompanying statistics of the Emigrant Hospitals at Ward's Island, for the year ending the 31st December, 1856.

By which it will be seen that 6,147 patients were treated in the wards of the hospital during the above-mentioned period.

In the Refuge Department, which includes the nursery, 5,131 individuals received professional assistance for diseases not requiring regular hospital treatment.

Making in all 11,278 persons who have come under medical observation during the year.

The ratio of mortality on the cases treated is 6.31 per cent., on the discharges, 7.22 per cent.; this is 3·44 per cent. on the cases treated, and 3·63 per cent. on the discharges less than 1855, and will compare favorably with previous years under any and all systems.

It is deserving of note that the large number of feeble infants received here, who survive a few days, or at most weeks, increase our bills of mortality without being in any way amenable to treatment.

In the Lying-in Department, there has been 469 admissions, 406 births, and 55 who were received from the city just after confinement; in all 524 patients.

In June, the south brick building, 56 feet front by 125 in length, was completed, containing four wards, three of which were occupied, and have been found admirably adapted for hospital purposes.

In July, the insane females were transferred to wards 33 and 34, and in October the insane males to 35 and 36, improving their condition; still a suitable building with the requisite enclosures, would contribute largely to the restoration of this class of patients.

During the year a few cases of small-pox occurred, which were immediately isolated, and transferred to the Marine Hospital.

Ophthalmia, which generally prevails in the nursery department of large institutions, has at no time been epidemic; and it is worthy of remark that its occurrence is rare throughout the Institution.

The apothecary's returns show a diminution of 73 per cent. in the bills for medicines, and 97 per cent. in the amount of wines, brandy, and other stimulants used during the year, with a fair stock on hand; this is a reduction of $12,227 as compared with an average year under the former organization; and it is believed that other departments of the hospital will exhibit similar results.

In conclusion, it affords me pleasure to award full credit for the satisfactory results of treatment in the several departments of the Institution to the assistant physicians, who have at all times shown a commendable zeal and fidelity in the discharge of their duties.

Respectfully, your obedient servant,

HENRY B. FAY.

Ward's Island, N. Y., Jan. 1, 1857.

To the Commissioners of Emigration:

Gentlemen:—I have the honor to enclose herewith the annual report of the Surgical Department of the State Emigrant Hospitals, for the year ending 31st December, 1856.

By this statistic it is shown that the whole number of cases treated was 1,756; the number of cases cured and discharged, 1,401; and the number of deaths, 53, or about 3 per cent. on the number of cases treated.

During the year the department has remained entirely free from epidemic disease; but an unusual number of cases incurable in their nature, either by operation or by therapeutic means, have been admitted. Many of these were from scrofulous caries of the large joints, spinal column, and pelvis.

The Ophthalmic Wards continue to be supplied abundantly from the city with acute and chronic diseases of the eye; the epidemic or purulent ophthalmia, however, no longer exists in the hospital.

As heretofore, many capital operations have been performed, such as trepanning the skull for fractures of the head; the application of the ligature upon the large arteries for the cure of aneurism; amputation of the members; resection of the bones; and operations on the eye, as for cataract, entropion, &c.; most of these have been attended by a successful result.

The invariable co-operation of the superintendent in all matters appertaining to the discipline and hygiene of the hospital has afforded additional facilities in the medical treatment of the patients.

The assistant-surgeons, now in the service of the hospital, Drs. Cassiday and Guleke, the latter of whom is conversant with German and other European languages, are entitled to my commendation for their zeal and general usefulness.

Most respectfully,

J. M. CARNOCHAN.

Ward's Island, N. Y., Jan. 6, 1858.

To the Commissioners of Emigration:

Gentlemen:—The annual report, and the accompanying statistics, of the Emigrant Refuge Hospitals, for the year 1857, is herewith respectfully submitted.

During the above-mentioned period 6,893 patients were treated in the wards of the hospital proper.

In the Refuge Department, which contains many chronic cases, women awaiting child-birth, and includes the nursery, 5,715 individuals received professional assistance for diseases not requiring regular hospital treatment.

In all, 12,608 persons have come under medical observation during the year.

The ratio of mortality on the cases treated in the hospital is 5·71 per cent. On the discharges, 6·68 per cent. In the whole institution, 4·11 per cent. This is less than 1856, and compares favorably with any year since the institution was organized.

The deaths occurring in the Refuge Department were children under two years of age. A large proportion of them being nursing infants, who, from various causes, were deprived of a mother's care.

In the Lying-in Department there have been 506 admissions, 468 births, and 91 who were received from the city just after confinement—in all, 597 patients. The mortality in this division has been remarkably low, but four deaths having occurred from causes the sequel of parturition.

The usual diseases of childhood, such as measles, scarlatina, &c., have prevailed to some extent; but ophthalmia, that former pest of the nursery, is of rare occurrence throughout the institution.

In the Lying-in Department, puerperal fever has at no time been epidemic, and the surgical wards have been remarkably free from erysipelas. This, in a measure, is due to the insulation of the hospital buildings, which, in an institution of the class and magnitude of this have particular advantages, not only for ventilation, cleanliness, &c., but in the facilities for limiting and controlling, as far as may be, the spread of infectious diseases.

The transfer of the insane to the wards at present occupied, has proved beneficial; still there is a deficiency of accommodation sufficient for due classification, which is regarded by those having large experience as the primary requisite of hospital treatment. Yet, when the patients have been received at an early period of the disease, the result, in a large proportion of the cases, has been highly favorable. I trust that the building long contemplated for this class of patients, may be commenced at an early day. Remaining last year, 66. Admitted since, 144. Discharged during the year, 96. Died, 10. Remaining, 104.

In the Apothecary's Department, the bill for drugs, medicines, &c., is $1,762 40. This, notwithstanding there has been a large increase in the number of inmates requiring the use of medicines, is less than last year, with a fair stock remaining on hand, and it will be recollected that the bills of 1856 were 73 per cent. less than in 1855.

With the increase in the number of patients, there has been an increase in the number of those said to require the use of stimulants. The total amount for brandy, wine, ale, &c., is $301 20, a small item when compared with previous years.

Whilst every reduction has been made in the hospital requisitions consistent with the welfare of the patients, it is believed that in no instance has the health and comfort of the sick suffered from considerations of economy.

The assistant physicians are entitled to commendation for the care and attention bestowed upon the sick committed to their charge, as the satisfactory results of treatment in the several departments of the institution attest; and it is gratifying to state that a harmony, never for an instant interrupted, has characterized the entire period of our connection.

The duties devolving upon the apothecary and hospital clerk have been performed in a manner highly satisfactory.

I have the honor to be, with great respect,

Your obedient servant,

HENRY B. FAY.

Ward's Island, N. Y., Jan. 1, 1858.

To the Commissioners of Emigration:

Gentlemen:—I have the honor to enclose herewith the annual report of the Surgical Department of the State Emigrant Hospitals, for the year ending 31st December, 1857.

By this statistic, it is shown that the whole number of cases treated was

1,608; the number of cases cured and discharged, 1,286, and the number of deaths, 37, or about two and a half per cent. on the number of cases treated.

The department has remained entirely free from epidemic disease; but, as heretofore, there has been a number of intractable cases, produced chiefly by malignant disease, and by scrofulous caries of the large joints and bones, and of the spinal column, and pelvis.

The city continues to supply the ophthalmic wards with acute and chronic cases. The department, however, remains free from endemic or purulent ophthalmia.

Many capital operations, followed by success, have been performed during the year, such as the application of the ligature upon the large arteries, amputations of the members, resection of the bones and joints, trepanning the skull, as well as operations on the eye, as for cataract, entropion, &c.

I have continued to derive great advantages from the solicitous co-operation of the superintendent in all matters appertaining to the discipline and hygiene of the hospital.

The assistant-surgeons, Drs. Güleke and Selden, have shown unremitting attention to their duties, and are entitled to my commendation for their general usefulness.

Most respectfully,

J. M. CARNOCHAN.

Ward's Island, N. Y., Jan. 5, 1859.

HON. G. C. VERPLANCK, President of Commissioners of Emigration:

Sir:—I respectfully beg leave to submit the subjoined statistics of the hospitals for the past year, by which it may be seen that there have been treated 5,672, of which there were discharged, 4,695; died, 372; and remaining on the 1st of January, 1859, 605 patients.

In the Refuge Department, which might for medical purposes be termed the Dispensary Department of the hospital, 4,487 received medical advice and treatment, of whom 115 died, who were all infants under one year old, artificially nursed, having no mother to afford them their natural sustenance.

The ratio of mortality	on the	cases	treated in hospital, .	6·56
"	"	"	discharged, . .	7·34
"	"	"	Refuge and Hospital,	4·79

In the Obstetric Department there were 403 births, of which 37 were still-born; there were 76 admissions after confinement: in all 479. Of these 14 died, 6 from peritonitis and 1 from eclampsia, the remainder from diseases unconnected with parturiency.

I am happy to congratulate the Commission on our freedom from epidemics during the past year, except those incident to childhood, such as scarlatina, measles, &c., which have been of an unusually mild character.

As my appointment of chief physician took place in July last, I deem it unnecessary to enter into any comparative statement of the medical administration of the hospital for the last year, except to say that I have endeavored (with a due regard to the requirements of the sick) to carry out the system of economizing the drug and medical stores, so successfully inaugurated by my predecessor, Dr. Fay.

Before concluding, I feel bound to express to the superintendent, Capt. Pilsbury, my acknowledgments for the willingness always manifested by him in carrying out my views with regard to the sick, and in most cases anticipating them. From my long connection with the Institution, I am able to state with confidence, that cleanliness, order, and discipline (the primary requisites of an hospital) were never better observed than at present, and which is entirely owing to his unceasing care and attention.

The zeal and efficient services of my assistant, Dr. Simrock, are deserving of all praise. The apothecary, Mr. Dwyer, merits my approbation for the correct and careful administration of his department.

I have the honor to be, your obedient servant,

GEORGE FORD, M. D.

Ward's Island, N. Y., Jan. 1, 1859.

To the Commissioners of Emigration:

Gentlemen:—I have the honor to submit the annual report of the Surgical Department of the State Emigrant Hospitals, for the year ending Dec. 31, 1858.

The whole number of cases treated was 1,329; the number of cases cured and discharged, 1,089; and of deaths 28, or a fraction more than 2 per cent. on the number of cases treated. The past year has been favored by immunity from any general epidemic disease, and also from those endemic maladies, such as erysipelas, hospital gangrene, &c., which sometimes prevail and infest the wards of large hospitals.

I have also the satisfaction to state that the Ophthalmic wards have been free from purulent ophthalmia, with the exception of some cases introduced from the city.

The capital operations performed in the department were mostly attended with favorable results.

I was efficiently aided by the Superintendent in the discharge of my duties, and express with satisfaction my appreciation of his scrupulous care in promoting the general hygiene of the hospital.

Dr. Guleke and Dr. Selden, my assistants, are entitled to special commendation for their intelligent zeal and alacrity.

Most respectfully,

J. M. CARNOCHAN.

Ward's Island, N. Y., Jan. 1, 1860.

To the Commissioners of Emigration:

Gentlemen:—I have the honor to submit the following, as my report of the State Emigrant Hospitals, for the year ending 31st Dec., 1859:

In hospital, January 31, 1859,	605	
Admitted since,	2,802	
Born,	261	
Stillborn, 19 } Abortion, 1 }		
Total treated,		3,668
Discharged,	3,029	
Died,	178	
		3,207
Remaining, January 1st, 1860,		461

In the Midwifery Department, 273 women gave birth to 116 girls and 145 boys, making a total of 261 living, and to 7 girls and 12 boys (total, 19) still-born—in all, 280 births. There were 7 twin cases. Six women died; one from Eclampsia, and three from Puerperal Fever, early in the year, but, owing to the facilities we have in this Institution of changing wards, the spread of this dangerous disease was checked immediately by so doing.

In the Insane Department, 100 females and 82 males came under treatment, of whom there were 56 females and 47 males discharged, and 2 females and 4 males died. There was one case of suicide. I beg to remind your Honorable Board, that in this Division we still labor under the same disadvantages which have been so often represented to you.

It may be seen by the annexed Table that 113 adults and 65 children died, making a total of 178. Of the latter, 47 were under one year, whose deaths are generally to be attributed to the sickness or inability of the mothers to afford them their proper care or nourishment.

The mortality on the cases treated and discharged will compare favorably with any former year.

In the Refuge or Dispensary Department, 3,326 came under observation, of whom 84 children died, owing to the various causes assigned in last year's report.

In the whole Institution there were 6,994 treated, of whom 262 died, giving a percentage of mortality on cases treated of 3·74.

During the past year we have been visited by no particular epidemic, with the exception of those few cases of Puerperal Fever which have been already noticed. There were some sporadic cases of Scarlatina and Measles, from which a few deaths resulted without extending to the inmates; neither did Typhus Fever, though we admitted a proportionally larger number, and of a graver character, than in former years, in consequence of the abolition of the Quarantine Hospital. On the whole, the general hygiene of the Institution continues favorable.

To the Superintendent, Louis D. Pilsbury, I am indebted for his ready response, at all times, to my representations regarding the sick, as well as for a continuance of the personal courtesy and kindness I always received from his predecessor, Capt. Amos Pilsbury.

I have again with pleasure to express my acknowledgments to my assistant, Dr. Simrock, for his unremitting and faithful care of his patients, as well as for his invaluable aid and advice when necessary.

The apothecary, Dr. Dwyer, continues to merit my highest approbation for his efficiency and strict attention to his department.

The hospital clerk has discharged his duties to my entire satisfaction.

Very respectfully, your obedient servant,

GEORGE FORD, *Chief Physician.*

Ward's Island, N. Y., Jan. 1, 1860.

To the Commissioners of Emigration:

Gentlemen:—I have the honor to inclose herewith the annual report of the Surgical Department of the State Emigrant Hospitals, for the year ending 31st December, 1859.

By this statistic, it is shown that the whole number of cases treated, was 1,029; the number of cases cured and discharged, 851; the number of cases transferred to the medical wards, 24; and the number of deaths, 11 = 1·06 per cent., or a small fraction more than 1 per cent. on the number of cases treated. There remain under treatment, 143.

It will be observed from this statement, that the percentage of deaths has been remarkably small, particularly when the broken-down and cachectic constitution of those admitted is considered.

Since the last report, the Department has remained entirely free from epidemic disease. There have been admitted, however, a number of severe chronic diseases, such as scrofulous caries of the large joints, spinal column, and pelvis, as well as many cases of aggravated syphilis.

As in previous years, many capital operations have been performed, such as resection of the bones and of the joints, the ligation of large arteries, amputations, &c., as well as some of the important operations on the eye and its appendages. I may, also, mention the introduction, for the first time, into the hospital, of an original operation for the cure of reducible hernia, which, judging from the cases already treated, is likely to be attended by the most beneficial results to those affected by this malady.

The co-operation of the Superintendent in all matters appertaining to the hygiene and discipline of the hospital, has afforded me additional facilities in the medical management of the patients.

The assistant surgeons, Drs. Guleke and Selden, are entitled to my commendation, for their zeal, intelligence, and general usefulness.

Most respectfully,

J. M. CARNOCHAN

Ward's Island, N. Y., Jan. 1, 1861.

To the Commissioners of Emigration:

Gentlemen:—I have the honor to submit my annual report for the year 1860:

In hospital, December 31, 1859,	461	
Admitted since,	3,138	
Born,	264	
Total treated in hospital,		3,863
Remaining in hospital, Dec. 31st, 1860.		659

In the early part of the year, the hospital was in a remarkably healthy state, and the number of patients considerably lower than at any previous period; but for the last six months the admissions have increased, and exceed now the number in hospital two years ago, while the general character of the diseases has been far more serious than ordinarily.

In July last, we received a large accession of ship fever; and I became apprehensive that it would extend among the inmates. To prevent such consequences, I appropriated suitable wards for its exclusive treatment; and, to avoid the necessity of opening additional ones, I distributed the non-contagious diseases which they contained, through the other general wards of the hospital, and, I am glad to say, that in no instance has it been communicated to any one who had not been exposed to its influence before admission. Ship fever includes both typhus and typhoid. More than two-thirds of the cases were of the latter type. Of this class of patients, 305 came under treatment, some of them admitted in a moribund state; 36 died: making a mortality of about 11 per cent., whilst in the whole hospital (these included) the percentage was only 4·91; in both Hospital and Refuge, 3·10. A very favorable result, considering the class of patients treated.

Early in December, a case of small-pox made its appearance; and several others having since occurred, I deemed it necessary, as a precautionary measure, to vaccinate all the inmates of the hospital, in order to check its further progress: the result so far has been satisfactory.

Measles and scarlatina are also prevalent, and from present appearances likely to continue for some time.

In the Obstetric Department, 278 women gave birth to 282 children. There were 4 twin cases, and 18 stillborn; 5 women died; 4 from diseases unconnected with parturition, and only one from puerperal fever. This latter fact is a source of satisfaction to me.

There were 330 children vaccinated during the year, a practice never omitted with all children born in the Institution; and in this manner a supply of healthy lymph is always kept up.

In the Insane Department, there were 204 cases treated: 57 were discharged to the city; 27 to Blackwell's Island; 21 transferred for different complaints to other divisions of the hospital; 5 eloped, and 7 died. Remaining at present, 87.

It is to be hoped that the building now being prepared for the reception of these patients, will tend materially to increase their comfort as well as promote their recovery.

In the Dispensary, or Refuge Department, all the wards have been visited daily by myself or assistant, so that any one ailing may have an opportunity of representing it, either by themselves, or nurse; by so doing, no contagious disease can remain long undiscovered. In this department there have been 2,924 cases prescribed for; 36 died, all infants under 1 year old. This is a decrease of deaths on former years; and is, I think, owing to the rule of not permitting the mothers to leave the Institution without taking their offspring along with them, as well as to the particular kindness and attention paid to them by the Superintendent.

To the Superintendent, James P. Fagan, Esq., I am deeply indebted for the service he has rendered, in aiding me to advance the comfort and ameliorate the condition of the sick.

Dr. Simrock having resigned his position, as my assistant, last June, I have been fortunate in securing the services of Dr. Guleke in his stead. I have implicit confidence in his abilities, and he has discharged his onerous duties to my entire satisfaction.

The bill for medicines is very small, and reflects credit on the apothecary, Dr. Dwyer, who co-operates with me in that respect, and is deserving of my commendation for his strict attention to this, as well as his general duties.

Very respectfully, your obedient servant,
GEORGE FORD, *Physician-in-Chief.*

Ward's Island, N. Y., Jan. 1, 1861.

To the Commissioners of Emigration:

Gentlemen:—I have the honor to inclose herewith, the annual report of the Surgical Department of the State Emigrant Hospitals, for the year ending the 31st December, 1860.

By these statistics it is shown, that the whole number of cases treated was 1,078; the number of cases cured and discharged, 817; and the number of deaths, 18, or about 1·66 per cent. on the whole number of cases treated.

During the past year, the department has remained free from erysipelas, hospital gangrene, or other epidemic disease.

A number of cases of acute and chronic diseases of the eye have been ad mitted, chiefly from the city, into the ophthalmic wards; purulent ophthal mia has, at times, manifested itself, but has speedily been arrested.

Many capital operations have been performed, such as amputations, resec tion of bones, exsection of joints, &c., generally with a successful result.

The Superintendent, Mr. Fagan, has given me his most thorough co-opera tion in all matters appertaining to the discipline and hygienics of the hospital

Dr. Guleke and Dr. Dwyer of the surgical staff, are entitled to high com mendation for their zealous and useful assistance. Most respectfully,

J. M. CARNOCHAN.

Table D(A),

Showing the avowed Destination of Emigrants landed at Castle Garden, from August 1, 1855 (*on which date the Emigrant Landing-Dépôt was opened*) *to December* 31, 1860.

DESTINATION.	1855. From Aug. 1.	1856.	1857.	1858.	1859.	1860.	TOTAL.
New York,	19,489	55,055	78,585	34,296	40,923	56,131	284,479
Pennsylvania,	4,469	11,749	16,660	6,708	7,370	9,512	56,468
Illinois,	3,444	11,064	15,750	6,690	3,940	4,077	44,965
Wisconsin,	4,667	13,327	12,704	4,953	2,441	2,589	40,681
Ohio,	3,250	7,085	10,054	6,176	4,668	5,195	36,428
Massachusetts,	2,037	6,494	6,904	3,212	5,119	6,371	30,137
Canada West,	3,346	8,526	9,673	4,218	2,202	1,872	29,837
New Jersey,	1,119	3,242	3,806	1,922	2,621	3,414	16,195
Unknown,	957	4,187	4,395	1,484	1,726	3,368	16,117
Michigan,	1,648	3,296	4,108	1,697	1,305	1,478	13,532
Connecticut,	829	2,292	2,974	1,227	1,929	2,579	11,840
Iowa,	795	2,380	3,775	1,724	664	776	10,114
Missouri,	434	1,064	2,366	1,690	1,598	1,614	8,766
Indiana,	881	1,388	2,474	1,271	1,122	1,106	8,242
Rhode Island,	551	1,354	1,389	510	1,001	1,291	6,096
Maryland,	485	1,164	1,535	907	902	1,014	6,007
Uncertain,	317	2,113	2,014	483	303	214	5,444
California,	447	778	877	1,084	1,108	1,141	5,435
Minnesota,	127	427	1,253	828	542	466	3,643
Utah,	250	1,579	14	3	740	905	3,491
Virginia,	292	567	702	548	575	452	3,136
Kentucky,	183	460	660	520	546	650	2,019
District of Columbia,	202	407	532	336	308	301	2,086
Vermont,	168	250	297	172	198	270	1,355
Louisiana,	60	171	206	240	255	321	1,253
South Carolina,	80	178	157	168	185	296	1,064
Maine,	143	148	186	210	122	142	951
Tennessee,	72	178	127	165	147	269	898
Georgia,	70	47	167	162	193	178	817
New Hampshire,	71	177	179	69	131	123	750
Delaware,	49	81	113	65	117	123	548
New Brunswick,	2	....	97	75	82	42	298
Texas,	5	76	55	43	52	63	294
Kansas,	1	11	25	88	77	92	294
North Carolina,	11	66	41	52	48	43	261
Mississippi,	6	14	62	21	50	15	168
Alabama,	7	30	21	24	39	45	166
Nova Scotia,	30	2	42	53	14	21	162
Nebraska,	....	2	27	42	31	46	148
South America,	25	30	18	14	36	18	141
Cuba,	....	....	25	32	46	29	132
Arkansas,	8	30	9	10	16	21	94
Florida,	13	12	5	11	32	17	90
Mexico,	....	12	1	5	7	9	34
Oregon,	1	....	7	6	6	13	33
West Indies,	2	11	....	6	5	9	33
New Mexico,	....	....	5	....	23	1	29
Central America,	....	....	....	3	9	8	20
Canada East,	....	....	....	....	10	5	15
Prince Edward's Island,	....	....	....	3	3	1	7
Vancouver's Island,	....	....	....	....	1	3	4
Washington Territory,	....	....	....	....	3	....	3
Australia,	....	1	....	....	....	1	2
Bermuda,	....	....	....	....	1	1	2
Sandwich Islands,	....	....	....	....	....	1	1
Total,	51,114	141,525	185,076	84,226	85,602	108,682	656,225

NOTE.—From August 1, 1855 (when Castle Garden was opened as the Emigrant Landing-Dépôt) to the close of 1856, a record was kept, so far as could be ascertained, of the cash means brought by the emigrants landing during that period; but owing to the impossibility of obtaining accurate information on the subject, the record was not continued. So far as kept, it showed an average amount of about $68 per head, as the *cash means* brought by the passengers who landed at Castle Garden.

Table D[B],

Showing the Ports and Countries whence Emigrant Passenger Vessels landing Passengers at the Castle Garden Emigrant Landing-Dépôt, have arrived, (together with the number of such Vessels), during the years 1855 (*in which year the Landing-Dépôt was opened*), 1856, 1857, 1858, 1859, and 1860.

Port whence sailed from.	Nation.	1855. From Aug. 1.	1856.	1857.	1858.	1859.	1860.	TOTAL.
Liverpool.....	Great Britain.	170	215	223	168	160	213	1,149
London.......	" "	57	49	52	47	44	47	296
Bristol	" "	4	4	5	1	3	1	18
Newport......	" "	....	3	....	....	....	....	3
Cardiff	" "	....	1	2	2	....	....	5
Sunderland...	" "	....	1	....	....	....	....	1
Southampton.	" "	....	1	....	....	....	....	1
Glasgow.......	" "	18	14	16	13	16	9	86
Tralee	" "	2	4	5	2	2	....	15
Belfast	" "	....	3	1	1	....	....	5
Galway.......	" "	1	....	1	8	13	11	34
Queenstown..	" "	....	....	1	1	....	....	2
Cork	" "	1	....	....	1	5	....	7
Hull..........	" "	2	....	....	....	....	....	2
Sidney,N.S.W.	" "	....	....	1	....	....	....	1
Havre........	France	55	78	87	58	54	54	386
Cette	"	....	....	1	....	....	....	1
Antwerp	Belgium.......	21	33	48	19	15	14	150
Flushing	"	1	....	....	....	....	....	1
Amsterdam.....	Holland	....	1	1	....	1	....	3
Rotterdam.....	"	18	16	13	11	3	9	70
Hamburg	Hamburg......	35	62	69	45	44	48	303
Bremen	Bremen	95	76	115	64	67	71	488
Emden	Hanover	1	1	1	....	....	....	3
Madeira.......	Portugal.......	....	....	1	....	1	....	2
Stockholm.....	Sweden.......	....	1	1	....	....	....	2
Gefle	"	2	2	2	....	....	....	6
Gothenburg...	"	....	4	1	1	2	2	10
Leghorn.......	Tuscany	3	7	5	3	1	1	20
Genoa........	Sardinia	1	4	5	5	5	1	21
Fayal, A. Is[lds]..	Portugal.......	....	....	....	1	1	1	3
Porto Cabello.	Venezuela....	....	....	....	....	....	1	1
Bergen........	Norway.......	1	....	....	....	....	....	1
	Total....	488	580	657	451	437	483	3,096

Table D(c),

Showing the number of Families relieved by Advances made on a pledge of baggage, without charge for Storage, or Interest on the amount advanced, and the amount of such Relief, together with the payments made on redemption during the years 1856, 1857, 1858, 1859, *and* 1860.

	Number of Advances.	Amount advanced.		Number of Redemptions.	Amount Repaid.
Advances during 1856	210	$2,097 25	1857, Jan. 1. Redeemed in 1856	158	$1,456 25
" " 1857	788	8,723 75	1858, " " in 1857	606	6,414 50
" " 1858	425	4,873 00	Do. " " of 1856 during 1857	31	350 50
" " 1859	239	2,345 00	1859, " " in 1858	346	3,759 00
" " 1860	173	1,756 00	Do. " " of 1856 during 1858	1	10 00
			Do. " " of 1857 " 1858	119	1,523 50
			1860, " " in 1859	211	2,031 50
			Do. " " of 1857 during 1859	8	150 00
			Do. " " of 1858 " 1859	50	694 00
			1861, " " in 1860	168	1,658 00
			" of 1858 during 1860	1	35 00
			" of 1859 " 1860	5	171 00
			Balance of 1856, '57, '58, '59, and '60	131	1,541 75
Total	1,835	$19,795 00	Total	1,835	$19,795 00
1861, Jan. 1. Unpaid balance of 1856	20	$280 50			
" " " " 1857	55	635 75			
" " " " 1858	28	385 00			
" " " " 1859	23	143 00			
" " " " 1860	5	97 50			
Total	131	$1,541 75			

Table D(D),

Showing the relative proportion of Sailing and Steam Vessels bringing Passengers landed at the Castle Garden Emigrant Landing-Dépôt from August 1, 1855, (*when the establishment was first opened,*) *to December* 31, 1860.

Months.	1855.				1856.				1857.				1858.				1859.				1860.			
	No. of Vessels.	Passengers.	Steamers.	Passengers.	Sailing Vessels.	Passengers.	Steamers.	Passengers.	Sailing Vessels.	Passengers.	Steamers.	Passengers.	Sailing Vessels.	Passengers.	Steamers.	Passengers.	Sailing Vessels.	Passengers.	Steamers.	Passengers.	Sailing Vessels.	Passengers.	Steamers.	Passengers.
January,	....	....	....	....	7	1,057	....	....	28	5,155	....	....	20	2,993	2	276	26	2,820	4	252	14	1,509	6	558
February,	....	....	....	....	20	2,246	....	....	26	3,390	2	185	18	1,110	3	261	8	290	6	732	7	597	8	953
March,	....	....	....	....	45	5,544	1	163	17	2,369	8	1,196	25	2,834	3	480	25	2,349	8	1,149	26	2,084	8	1,756
April,	....	....	....	....	34	7,033	1	361	67	19.661	6	2,089	15	2,880	5	1,577	17	2,453	6	1,634	22	3,896	7	3,134
May,	....	....	....	....	56	18,797	4	916	63	24,993	8	3,046	48	12,096	9	2,323	43	14,058	14	4,119	63	17,700	11	5,998
June,	....	....	....	....	60	18,926	2	402	64	20,302	11	3.944	35	8,266	6	1,524	38	9.850	9	2,511	26	8,780	8	3,514
July,	....	....	....	....	53	15,579	2	713	74	24,547	7	1,750	55	12.351	9	1,838	24	5,521	9	2,009	36	9,153	14	4,174
August,	39	8,145	....	....	71	15,802	2	523	54	12,091	8	2,375	33	5,343	12	2,260	32	4,439	7	2,179	35	6,399	10	2,419
September,	55	12,021	....	....	54	13,899	2	620	64	18,239	5	1,948	45	6,432	8	1,378	31	5,226	11	3,073	35	6,478	9	3,769
October,	65	14,033	....	....	60	15,777	2	663	52	15,390	7	2,187	32	6,832	10	1,810	21	4,090	8	2.249	51	8,591	8	3,168
November,	30	6,312	....	....	70	17,644	4	527	47	12,580	5	1,240	26	4,277	10	1,948	37	6,259	10	1,279	31	5,604	10	3,020
December,	61	10,603	....	....	22	4,155	2	223	32	6,233	2	276	15	2,423	7	705	30	4,029	13	3,032	27	3,644	10	1,787
Total,	251	51,114	*	*	552	136,459	22	5,111	588	164,650	69	20,236	367	67,837	84	16,389	332	61,384	105	24,218	373	74,435	109	34,247

* No record kept.

RECAPITULATION.

	No. of Vessels.	No. of Passengers.
Total.....1855, from August 1st...	251	51,114
" 1856	574	141,570
" 1857	657	185,186
" 1858	451	84,226
" 1859	437	85,602
" 1860	482	108,682
Total,............	2,852	656,380

Steamers under the Flag of	1856.	1857.	1858.	1859.	1860.
United States......................	..	3	14	13	6
Great Britain......................	12	48	47	58	72
Bremen..............................	..	1	6	15	10
Hamburg............................	7	10	17	19	21
Belgium.............................	2	7	..	..	..
France...............................	1	..	..	..	..
Total..........................	22	69	84	105	109

Table D(E),

Showing the number of pieces of Baggage belonging to and landed with Passengers at the Castle Garden Emigrant Landing-Dépôt, and stored until required by the owners, together with the quantity delivered, during the years 1857, 1858, 1859, *and* 1860.

MONTHS.	No. of Pieces Received.					MONTHS.	No. of Pieces Delivered.				
	1857.	1858.	1859.	1860.	Total.		1857.	1858.	1859.	1860.	Total.
January	......	2,556	2,498	1,699	6,753	January	......	2,831	2,428	1,780	7,039
February	......	1,206	1,006	1,245	3,457	February	......	1,272	1,082	1,259	3,613
March	......	3,163	3,148	3,307	9,618	March	......	3,178	2,948	3,160	9,286
April	......	4,350	3,468	5,438	13,256	April	......	4,185	3,849	5,125	13,159
May	......	12,566	15,210	18,146	45,922	May	......	12,381	15,009	16,910	44,300
June	......	8,163	9,983	10,055	28,201	June	......	8,119	10,006	10,884	29,009
July	......	12,224	6,454	11,217	29,895	July	......	12,325	6,537	9,716	28,578
August	13,518	7,308	6,545	8,028	35,399	August	13,725	7,040	6,566	8,770	36,101
September	21,581	7,511	7,185	9,096	45,373	September	19,386	8,160	6,997	9,430	43,973
October	18,736	7,994	6,503	10,351	43,584	October	15,407	8,092	6,682	9,752	39,933
November	10,730	5,497	7,235	6,788	30,250	November	12,551	5,333	7,325	7,619	32,828
December	4,920	2,605	4,438	4,414	16,377	December	7,067	2,864	4,277	4,410	18,618
Total	69,485	75,143	73,673	89,784	308,085	Total	68,136	75,780	73,706	88,815	306,437

ANNUAL REPORTS

OF THE

SUPERINTENDENT OF THE

EMIGRANT LANDING-DEPOT,

For the years 1856, '57, '58, '59, *and* '60, *and accompanying the preceding Tables.*

EMIGRANT LANDING-DÉPÔT,
Castle Garden, N. Y., Jan. 13, 1857.

TO THE COMMISSIONERS OF EMIGRATION:

Gentlemen:—In presenting the Table, marked A, which shows the destination of the emigrant passengers who landed at this dépôt, and the amount of cash means they possessed at the time of arrival, during the year 1856, I avail myself of the opportunity to congratulate the Commission on the large measure of success that has attended the establishment and working operation of a landing-place under the direct supervision of the Board.

Within the past year *one hundred and forty-one thousand six hundred and twenty-five* passengers have been landed here, from *five hundred and eighty* vessels, arrived from *twenty-two* different ports of Europe, without an accident occuring in any case, to mar the usual hilarity of disembarkation. Table B. shows the number of passengers and vessels from each port.

To nearly every passenger the dépôt seemed an acceptable place of reception. The major portion duly appreciated the efforts made for the safety and security of their persons and effects. The shelter they receive from the inclemency of the weather is palpable to all of them; while their protection from the fangs of the man-catchers does not seem to be so plain until after they have become victims.

Hence, a few of these strangers, under the evil advisement of agents sent to Europe expressly for the purpose, by their co-operators on this side of the ocean, have refused to receive the protection and counsel placed at their disposal in the dépôt, and have sallied forth, with their effects, immediately on landing, generally only to return again with complaints of imposition practised, or robberies committed, in most cases beyond remedy. The recurrence of such examples could be easily prevented by more decided measures of protection being adopted at the several points whence they embark. Could foreign governments be made to see the benefit an entire extinction of the booking system would render to the poor emigrant, doubtless all of them would speedily follow the example of the governments of Hamburg and Bremen in making it a penal offence to solicit or book an emigrant for inland travel in a foreign country. I would respectfully suggest a renewal of the efforts of the Board for the accomplishment of so desirable a result.

Notwithstanding the very large general average of cash held by passengers, a considerable number continue to arrive with not more than sufficient means to pay their way to their destination.

By the operation of the Landing-Dépôt this class are enabled to proceed at once to the end of their journey; not being delayed nor induced by interested parties to make unnecessary expenditure from their scanty means; whilst otherwise, as heretofore, they would, in most cases, become a charge on the fund, or, under special bonds, on the ships that brought them. Another class, who, although not in possession of sufficient means, in cash, to defray the necessary expense of further prosecuting their journey, have been aided with what cash was needed, on the pledge of baggage, under the condition that "no charge should be made for storage nor interest on the amount advanced." This mode of rendering aid has been practised to a limited extent at the principal office of the Board, for several years; but the facility the dépôt offers for discovering persons who can be so assisted, has enabled the management to systematize the operation, and make it effective. On the 22d of August last, it was commenced, since which time *two hundred and ten* families have been aided in the sum of $2,097 25; while the redemptions on the same, amount to *one hundred and fifty-eight* cases, and $1,456 25; leaving an indebtedness on 1st inst. of *fifty-two* advances, and in the amount of $647. The prompt manner in which redemptions have been made to this time, may be regarded as indicative of the redemption of the balance in charge, within a reasonable period.

The introduction of this feature as a legitimate portion of the operations of the Landing-Dépôt, will prove to be a benefit to the fund, as well as to the parties assisted. For, under the old system of landing passengers, nearly all of the persons so helped would have gone into boarding-houses to await remittances from friends, which failing, in whole or in part, their effects would have been sacrificed to meet the expenses of subsistence; and after all had passed from them, and they had been rendered penniless, and possibly debauched, would be turned into the streets, a charge on the fund or the ship. And, in many instances, a permanent incumbrance on rather than a benefit to the community.

The advantages resulting from a single emigrant landing-dépôt, is now universally conceded. Every philanthropist recognizes its efficacy in protecting the stranger, to a large extent, from being despoiled of his property, and his morals from degradation. Our own hospitals and other eleemosynary institutions, already attest to the diminished calls on their benefaction; and our public streets speak volumes on the reduced number who solicit aid from the hand of passing charity.

Castle Garden has been found by experiment to be the proper location for the Landing-Dépôt. No other spot in the harbor possesses the advantages for the operation that it has, in the fullest degree. To change the dépôt to any other place, would, at this time, be to destroy it. And, as the lease from the Corporation expires on the 1st May, 1859, would it not be advisable, at an early day, to adopt measures for a prolongation of the term, or to secure a yet more permanent tenure of the premises? At the same time, it would also be advisable to have the area of the premises enlarged to nearly double its present size. I find when passengers are arriving rapidly in large numbers, that the enclosure is not sufficiently extensive to permit a proper disposition of the baggage to ensure safety, and allow such a distribution of it as would facilitate the delivery to owners.

Several instances of sudden sickness from ordinary diseases, have occurred during the year, which made it necessary to call in medical aid from the neighborhood. I would respectfully recommend a suitable medicine chest to be placed in the dépôt, and that it be made a part of the duty of the medical inspector stationed here, to attend to such cases when they occur.

Very respectfully,

JOHN A. KENNEDY, *Superintendent.*

EMIGRANT LANDING-DÉPÔT,
Castle Garden, N. Y., Jan. 14, 1858.

TO THE COMMISSIONERS OF EMIGRATION:

Gentlemen:—The past year has afforded additional opportunity for yourselves and the community, to become satisfied that the Landing-Dépôt has accomplished all the good purposes for which it was established, the increased number of arrivals not having in any manner affected its efficiency or beneficence. The final destination of passengers, as avowed at the time of landing, is fully set forth in the accompanying Table A; but the financial information heretofore furnished in that Table, has been omitted, under the advisement of the Committee on the emigrant Landing-Dépôt.

The main object for inquiring of passengers the amount of cash means they possessed, was secured, when it was shown to the public that on the average they were in possession of a larger amount of such means than is held by the localized residents of any known community; and that although a part of the emigration is among that class of persons who seek our shores as a refuge, and for a subsistence by labor, with little or no cash means; yet a large portion bring with them of that kind of property a sufficient quantity to sustain themselves, and to aid in the enrichment of the country. It was also apprehended that a continuance of the report under that head might lead to mischievous results from their manifest inaccuracy. The Table of 1856 presents the average amount of cash means at $68 08 per head; subsequent, but reliable, information was obtained, that the concealment of large amounts had been constantly and successfully practised; and that, had full admission been made of the funds in possession, the average would have been at least double the amount reported.

One hundred and eighty-five thousand one hundred and eighty-six passengers have landed at the dépôt, within the year, brought by *six hundred and fifty-seven* vessels, from *twenty-four* different ports. For detail of which see Table B.

The plan of extending partial relief to persons who are deficient in the amount necessary to defray their expenses in prosecuting their inland journey, on the pledge of baggage, without subjecting them to charges for interest or storage, has been continued with excellent effect. Many have thus been aided in reaching their destination, who would otherwise have fallen by the way, while incitement to effort and self-dependence has been infused into others who would not, at least so early, have been made to feel and know the advantages resulting from their own exertions. There has been advanced during the year $8,723 75 to *seven hundred and eighty-eight* families; of which amount $6,414 50 has been repaid by *six hundred and six* of the families aided; leaving a balance of $2,309 25, due by *one hundred and eighty-two* parties. The balance due on account of advances made in 1856, has been more than half paid off; leaving but $290 50, due by *twenty-one* families. Table C sets forth the account.

I had the honor of presenting to your Board in July last, a statement intended to exhibit the increase in the number of emigrant passengers brought to this port by steam vessels as compared with sailing vessels; and to show how entirely this branch of business was done under the flags of foreign countries. In Table D, I respectfully present a continuance of the statement, to the end of the year.

The enlargement of the baggage-house, by the erection of the new building on the south side of the Castle, has greatly benefitted the working operations of the dépôt. It has enabled a system of receiving and delivering packages to be introduced, and has relieved us from the chaotic process theretofore necessarily prevailing; when the baggage was heaped up in a contracted space, and every person who had a claim, or pretended to have a claim, was necessarily permitted free access to overhaul it, disarrange checks, and thus, too frequently, had opportunity to purloin the property of other parties. Nothing of the kind has occurred since the new baggage-house has been in use; and losses of baggage on the premises are unknown, except where it occurs from the owners' carelessness in losing their checks, or heedlessly exchanging them. The only defect apparent in this department is the probability of more room being required should emigration increase on the number of the last year, or even should it remain as it then was. Every day seems to increase the proportionate quantity of personal effects brought over; and as the certainty of a greater safety for such things on landing becomes known to passengers before leaving their former homes, the quantity they bring will continue to increase.

The area of the baggage-house is 11,393 square feet. And this space is occupied by two office rooms, two apartments for pledged baggage, from lack of other accommodation, and thirty-eight stalls, with the necessary passage-ways. The stalls are as nearly of equal size as the ground-plan will permit; and are each capable of containing about eighty ordinary sized travelling boxes. Allowing eighty to be the capacity of each stall, there is storage for 3,040 packages at a time; being an abundant provision for the average rate of arrivals. But when unfavorable weather has prevented ships from making port in proper time, and unduly increased the number of vessels to arrive, a sudden change of the wind may bring in a large fleet of sail, as has frequently occurred; then the limited space must derange our system, and partially re-open the dépôt to the liability for such abuse as formerly existed. To illustrate, permit me to refer to such an occurrence in the latter part of June, when, for several days, no vessel could reach port, although many were due; on the 29th of that month they commenced arriving, and the rush continued until the 4th July; in these six consecutive days 13,734 passengers were landed, being an average of 2,289 per day. Since the baggage has been delivered solely on orders, we have found that the relative proportion of pieces of baggage to passengers arriving is nearly equal; in the last five months there being the proportion of $6\frac{813}{1000}$ pieces of baggage to $7\frac{255}{1000}$ of passengers. On this basis the number of pieces of baggages received in the week alluded to, was 12,897; too large a number to be properly stored and delivered in our present limits within the period of six days.

A very considerable extension to the present accommodation for baggage will be necessary at an early day, and is respectfully submitted for your consideration.

Table E contains a return of the pieces of baggage received, and stored, and delivered, from August 1st to December 31st, 1857.

At the time Castle Garden was opened as a landing-dépôt, no other establishment bearing any resemblance to it had ever had existence. All the details of its construction and management were necessarily experimental and uncertain. Many important requirements were omitted to be provided for; whilst other things were supposed to be indispensable which are found, on trial, to be of little or no value. Improvements have been introduced whenever they could be, to advantage, but daily observation satisfies me that much yet remains to be done to bring the dépôt up to the contemplated standard; my earnest efforts will continue to be directed to the accomplishment of it.

Respectfully submitted,

JOHN A. KENNEDY, *Superintendent.*

EMIGRANT LANDING-DÉPÔT,
Castle Garden, N. Y., Jan. 8, 1859.

TO THE COMMISSIONERS OF EMIGRATION:

Gentlemen:—The number of emigrants who arrived at this port during the past year having fallen so very much below the number of arrivals in many former years, the continued usefulness of the Emigrant Landing-Dépôt can now be best appreciated by comparing the number of those who have become a public charge, among those recently arrived, with the same class in any year previously to the establishment of the dépôt. The diminished proportion of those whom it was necessary to send from the dépôt to the principal office for aid, furnishes an indication that the average condition of the emigrants has become greatly improved. Although this may be attributed mainly to increased facilities furnished them by the Landing-Dépôt, for reaching their destination and friends, yet, in part, the improvement is due to the smaller number coming in each ship, affording better opportunity for the enforcement of the sanitary regulations which should be observed on board every well-regulated vessel—the average number of arrivals during this year being but *one hundred and eighty-seven* persons to each vessel, and these, as usual, were destined to nearly every State and Territory in the country, as well as to the neighboring provinces. Table A. exhibits the avowed destination of the passengers at the time of landing.

During the year, *four hundred and fifty-one* vessels have landed at the dépôt *eighty-four thousand two hundred and twenty-six* passengers, from nineteen different ports of Europe. The details are shown in Table B.

The system of rendering partial relief to parties who are deficient in the amount necessary to enable them to continue their journey inland, on a pledge of baggage, without charge for interest or storage, has proved itself both beneficial to the recipient and economical to the fund. During the past year there has been advanced to *four hundred and twenty-five* families, $4,873, of which *three hundred and forty-six* families have repaid $3,759, leaving a balance of $1,114 due by *seventy-nine* families. Of the balance due on January 1st, 1858, $1,533 50 has been repaid by *one hundred and twenty* parties, leaving a balance of $1,066 25 due by *eighty-three* families; which shows that of the whole amount advanced since August 22d, 1856, viz., $15,693 50, there remains unpaid $2,179 75 by *one hundred and sixty-two* families. Table C. shows the account in full.

The additional clerical force allowed by the Board gave opportunity to arrange the letter and message department more perfectly, and to render it more generally useful. Since the 30th of June last, there have been written 1,376 letters for passengers who had arrived, to which 562 answers have been received, containing $5,315 51; remittances amounting to $6,734 62 have also been received in anticipation of the arrival of the passengers, and numerous messages from emigrant societies and others in the city, of funds waiting for expected passengers on their arrival. It might be well for a more general notice to be given of the importance of having funds here awaiting the arrival of expected emigrants, as both time and expense would thereby be saved, and a greater certainty attained of the aid reaching the party intended to be benefited; as cases have occurred through the long delay in the receipt at this office of the answer from the friends of the emigrants obtaining employment where they could not be traced, and so remaining a longer time separated from their friends.

Table E shows the number of pieces of baggage received and delivered in each month during the year. Owing to the reduced number of passengers arrived, the baggage-house has proved to be sufficiently commodious for the purpose designed. The proportion of pieces of baggage to the passengers differs but little from that shown last year, it being then $6\frac{813}{1000}$ pieces to $7\frac{225}{1000}$ passengers, while during the year 1858 there were $7\frac{514}{1000}$ pieces to $8\frac{422}{1000}$ passengers.

To the report of last year a table was appended, in which the number of sailing vessels arrived, were separated from steamers, with the view of showing the gradual increase of steamers in the passenger business, and that this increase was mainly under foreign flags. The table is continued herewith, marked D, by which it will be seen that, while the steamers under foreign flags maintain their numerical superiority, a gratifying increase has taken place in the number of those sailing under the flag of the United States.

The buildings and wharf and the plank road in the Dépôt, are much in need of repair; and if not attended to at an early day, the expense therefor will be increased much beyond the difference gained by delay. The special attention of the Board is respectfully invited to this subject.

JOHN A. KENNEDY, *Superintendent.*

EMIGRANT LANDING DÉPÔT,
Castle Garden, N. Y., Jan. 12, 1860.

TO THE COMMISSIONERS OF EMIGRATION:

Gentlemen:—The operations at this Dépôt during the past year differ very little from those of the preceding year; a few less vessels brought a slightly increased number of emigrant passengers; thus increasing the average number of persons arrived in each vessel to *one hundred and ninety-six.* The number of passengers landed at the Dépôt during the year, was *eighty-five thousand six hundred and two*, being an increase on the year preceding of *one thousand three hundred and seventy-six.* Table A shows to what portions of the country these passengers purposed proceeding. *Four hundred and thirty-seven* vessels were employed in bringing this number of passengers from *eighteen* different ports in Europe, as shown in Table B.

The application of steamers to this branch of the passenger business has increased *twenty-five per cent.* during the year; but no portion of the increase is under the flag of the United States. The whole number of arrivals of this class of vessels under foreign flags is *ninety-two*, against *thirteen* under our own flag. There can be no doubt left that this mode of travel is rapidly gaining favor with emigrants. The relative proportions arrived on steamers and sailing vessels may be used to demonstrate the fact; for, while the average number of passengers by sailing vessels has been *one hundred and eighty-four* $\frac{296}{332}$, the average by steamers has been *two hundred and thirty* $\frac{68}{105}$, being an excess of about *forty-six* passengers per vessel. It is proper, however, to state, that persons who are returning from visiting Europe constitute a larger proportion on steamers than on sailing vessels. The whole number of such persons landed at the Dépôt was *eight thousand four hundred and sixteen*, of which number *four thousand four hundred and thirty-five* were from steamers; being about *eighteen* per cent. of all the passengers brought on them, while the remaining *three thousand nine hundred and eighty-one* are only about *six* per cent. of the passengers brought on sailing vessels. Table D gives a monthly exhibit of arrivals by steam and sailing vessels respectively, and the progress of each class since 1856.

The number of passengers to whom aid has been extended by temporary loan, on a pledge of their baggage, "without charge for interest or storage," has very much lessened during the year, fewer in number being in circumstances to need it, who were provided with property of sufficient value on which to make the advance. But during the year, *two hundred and thirty-nine* families have had $2,345 50 advanced to them; of which *two hundred and eleven families* have repaid $2,031 50, leaving a balance of $314 due by *twenty-eight* families. Of the balance due on January 1st, 1859, $744 have been repaid by *fifty-eight* families, leaving a balance of $1,336 25 due by *one hundred and four* families. The whole amount advanced in this way since August 22d, 1856, is $18,039 to *sixteen hundred and sixty-two* families. Table C shows the account.

There have been 1,564 letters written during the year for as many passengers, to their friends, soliciting aid to enable them to reach their destination; to the honor of this class of persons, very few answers have been received declining to render the desired assistance; several hundred have remained unanswered, probably from not having been received by the parties to whom sent, owing to the imperfect character of the address frequently furnished, or from removals from the last known place of abode. Seven hundred and eighty-nine of the answers received contained remittances to the gross amount of $6,283 76 for the purposes requested. There have also been received remittances amounting to $6,825 19 in anticipation of the arrival of passengers. This amount is much less than it was expected it would be, but no effort has been made to give general publicity of the facilities afforded by the management of the Dépôt, in aid of parties expecting friends to arrive. Means should be used to inform them that by having remittances on hand in the Dépôt, at the time their friends arrive, they would be enabled to pursue their journey without delay, and thus save expenses which accrue in waiting, as well as some suffering. Letters are constantly being received, making inquiries on this subject, which would be obviated by proper public notice being given.

The number of pieces of baggage received into, and delivered from the baggage-house, is shown in Table E.

The proportion of pieces of baggage to the passengers arrived, remains about the same as heretofore, it being $7\frac{367}{1000}$ pieces to $8\frac{560}{1000}$ passengers. In 1857, it stood $6\frac{313}{1000}$ to $7\frac{225}{1000}$, and in 1858, in the proportion of $7\frac{514}{1000}$ to $8\frac{422}{1000}$.

Whenever the funds of the Commission will afford the outlay, the Dépôt requires important repairs.

JOHN A. KENNEDY, *Superintendent.*

EMIGRANT LANDING DÉPÔT,
Castle Garden, N. Y., Jan. 15, 1861.

To G. C. VERPLANCK, Esq., President of Commissioners of Emigration:

Sir:—Herewith I beg leave to submit to the Board a report of the operations of the Emigrant Landing-Dépôt during the past year. As had been anticipated, the arrivals of passengers are much in advance of the two previous years. The total number landed, including those not subject to bonds or commutation, was 108,682 against 85,602 in 1859; and 84,226 in 1858. The avowed destination of the passengers will be found in Table A.

These passengers arrived from 14 different ports, in 582 vessels, as is shown by Table B.

Table C exhibits the relative proportion of steam and sailing vessels bringing these passengers, and a comparative statement of the same for the four preceding years. As an evidence of the favor with which the application of steam vessels to this branch of the passenger trade continues to be received, the number of steamers landing passengers at the Dépôt has increased from 22, bringing 5,111 passengers in 1856, to 109, bringing 34,247 in 1860; and which latter would undoubtedly have been larger, were it not for the partial suspension of one of the foreign lines, which stopped running towards the close of the year.

The relative proportion of passengers in steamers, as compared with sailing vessels, is even more marked than in 1859; for, while in that year the average number brought by steamers was $230\frac{63}{105}$ against $184\frac{296}{332}$, showing a difference in favor of the former of 49 passengers, the average number brought by steamers last year was $314\frac{21}{109}$ against $109\frac{208}{373}$ by sailing vessels, showing a difference in favor of the steamers, of 115 passengers per vessel.

Table D shows the number of pieces of baggage received into and delivered from the baggage-house. The proportion of pieces of baggage to passengers arrived, varies but slightly from previous years: it being $8\frac{976}{1000}$ pieces to $10\frac{363}{1000}$ passengers, against $7\frac{367}{1000}$ pieces to $8\frac{560}{1000}$ passengers in 1859; $7\frac{514}{1000}$ pieces to $8\frac{422}{1000}$ passengers in 1858; and $6\frac{313}{1000}$ pieces to $7\frac{225}{1000}$ passengers in 1857.

A quantity of baggage unclaimed and unredeemed, has accumulated in the store-rooms attached to the Landing-Dépôt appropriated therefor, and the greater part of which, from the length of time it has remained, and from other causes, is now nearly worthless and of no value to the owners, and is becoming quite an incumbrance to the establishment. I would respectfully suggest that it be recommended to the Legislature, to authorize the Commissioners to dispose by public auction, of all such baggage remaining uncalled for after a certain period of time has elapsed, the proceeds to be appropriated either to liquidate the advance made, or be held for the benefit of the owner, should he subsequently present himself.

Table E shows the number of families to whom advances have been made during the year, by temporary loan on a pledge of their baggage, without charge for interest or storage; as also redemptions from, and balances remaining of, previous years.

During the year 173 families have had advanced to them $1,756, of which $1,658 50 have been repaid by 168 families. The whole amount advanced under this plan, since August 22, 1856, is $19,795 to 1,835 families; thus enabling, without any additional expense arising from detention here, at least 7,340 persons (allowing four to each family) to take their departure for their intended destination without delay.

During the past year 1,867 letters have been written for recently arrived emigrants, to their friends in different parts of the country, soliciting aid to enable them to reach their destination. From many causes, such as a change of residence, or the decease of the parties addressed, or the imperfect character of the address frequently furnished by the emigrant, many of these letters fail. Of the replies received, 713 were accompanied with remittances to the gross amount of $7,654 45; there have also been received, in anticipation of the arrival of passengers, remittances amounting to $7,133 79: making a total amount of $14,788 24, and being an increase over last year of $1,679 29, in such receipts.

About one-half of the above amounts was received since the 27th of August last, on which date the new organization of the offices of the Commissioners, consequent on the resignation of the former able and energetic Superintendent, John A. Kennedy, Esq., went into effect, and which transferred that portion of the duties of the Landing-Dépôt to the Treasurer.

Respectfully,

BERNARD CASSERLY, *General Agent.*

FINANCIAL TABLES.

Table No. I.

COMMUTATION FUND AND MARINE HOSPITAL FUND ACCOUNTS FOR THE YEAR 1847.

Commutation Fund.

Receipts.

Amount of commutation money received from owners and consignees of vessels for alien passengers from May 5 to Dec. 31, 1847..................	$128,727 00	
From owners and consignees of vessels for violations of law, and errors in reports of passengers.......	500 00	
For board of masons at Ward's Island............	129 58	
For sale of crops, swill, &c., at do. do.............	116 75	
Total amount received..............		$129,473 33

Disbursements.

For erection of buildings, improvements, and repairs	$23,686 45	
For reimbursements to counties for the support of emigrants	2,270 68	
For reimbursements to Governor of Alms-house....	2,333 36	
For reimbursements to local Institutions..........	280 00	
For Commissioners' Office; salaries, and wages, &c..	9,612 19	
For disbursements on account of Emigrant Refuge and Hospitals, Ward's Island..................	27,134 76	
Total disbursements................		$65,317 44
Balance of fund in bank, Dec. 31, 1847...........		$64,155 89

Marine Hospital Fund.

Receipts.

Amount of hospital money received for passengers from May 5 to Dec. 31, 1847	$40,778 29	
Amount of drafts on State Treasurer	23,040 42	
Amount of dry goods transferred to Ward's Island establishment	1,100 90	
		$64,919 61

Disbursements.

For expenses of barge Vermont	$2,317 48	
Amount refunded vessels (having been twice paid)	5 25	
For disbursements on account of Marine Hospital establishment	80,507 14	
		$82,829 87
Amount of deficit due Bank of the State of N. York		$17,910 26

Table No. II.

Statement of Moneys received by the Commissioners of Emigration, on account of Minor Children becoming orphans, made in accordance with Section 5 of the Act of December 15, 1847.

Parents' Name.	Name of Vessel.	Where from.	Date of Death of Parents.	Names of Children.	Age.	Amount.	Disposition of Property.
John Hall	India	Liverpool	Feb. 19, 1848	Sarah	17	$190 00 and a watch.	$95 paid for clothing and nursing of infants. Balance on deposit in Seamen's Bank for Savings.
				Elizabeth	13		
				Jane	11		
				Mary			
				Hannah	2½		
Catharine Moore	Digby	Liverpool	March 23, 1848	Matthew	15	$140 07	In Seamen's Bank.
Andrew Hannon	Virginia	Liverpool	May 1, 1848	Anderoga	8	1 25	Do. do.
				Michael	7		
				Edward	4		
John Perry	Wm. Carson	Dublin	Aug. 16, 1848	Peter	12	4 83	Do. do.
				Mary	11		
Elizabeth Whaley	Memnon	Liverpool	Oct. 9, 1848	Lavinia	12	13 76	Do. do.
				James	10		

Note.—The Orphan account was transferred from the Seamen's Savings Bank to the Emigrant Industrial Savings Bank, July 8, 1852.

Table No. III.

COMMUTATION FUND AND MARINE HOSPITAL FUND ACCOUNTS FOR THE YEAR 1848.

Commutation Fund.

Receipts.

Balance of fund in the hands of the City Chamberlain, Jan. 1st, 1849	$64,155 89	
Amount of commutation money received from owners and consignees of vessels for alien passengers	189,554 00	
Amount received from captains, owners, and consignees, for violations of law and errors in reports of passengers	730 00	
Amount received for fines of boarding-house keepers for violation of law	250 00	
For board of masons at Ward's Island	132 68	
For sales of fat, barrels, &c.	200 87	
For forwarding money refunded by the German Society, and Irish Emigrant Society	682 16	
For forwarding money refunded by emigrants	61 00	
		$255,766 60

Disbursements.

For the purchase of real estate	$13,289 38	
For building and repairs	25,671 73	
For reimbursements to counties and towns	20,961 95	
For reimbursements to institutions, societies, &c.	1,487 93	
For support of Emigrant Refuge and Hospitals, Ward's Island, and office expenses	85,113 48	
For two transfers to Marine Fund, $10,000 each	20,000 00	
		$166,524 47
Balance of fund remaining in the hands of the City Chamberlain, January 1, 1849		$89,242 13

Marine Hospital Fund.

Receipts.

Amount of hospital money collected during the year		$112,092 38	
Of which amount was paid under protest.........		52,966 50	
Leaving available..................		$59,125 88	
Amount received from trustees of "Seamen's Fund and Retreat" for transportation of sailors chargeable to that institution......................		24 00	
Amount received for conveying sick.............		5 00	
" " sales of empty barrels, fat, &c.		236 79	
" " barge Vermont.............		100 00	
" " drafts on State Treasurer, April 15.........................	$55,835 22		
Do. do. June 28..............	4,164 78		
		60,000 00	
Amount transferred from Commutation Fund by authority of the Governor, Comptroller, and Attorney-General, in conformity with Section 11 of the Act of April 11, 1848:			
August 17.....................	$10,000 00		
Nov. 16......................	10,000 00		
		20,000 00	
			$139,491 67

Disbursements.

Deficit in the fund due the Bank of the State of New York on the 1st January, 1848.................	$17,861 75	
Total expenses during the year 1848.............	128,579 02	
		$146,440 77
Amount of deficit due the Mechanics' Bank, January 1, 1849.................		$6,949 10

Table No. IV.

COMMUTATION FUND AND MARINE HOSPITAL FUND ACCOUNTS FOR THE YEAR 1849.

Commutation Fund.

Receipts.

Balance of fund on deposit with the City Chamberlain in Mechanics' Bank, January 1st, 1849	$89,242 13
Amount of commutation money received from owners and consignees of vessels for alien passengers	310,687 50
Amount received from masters, owners, and consignees of vessels for violations of the law	853 00
Amount received for commutation of special bonds	782 96
" " fines of boarding-house keepers	100 00
" " sales of empty barrels, bones, fat, &c.	287 26
" " sales of live stock	64 41
" " damage by fire, from Insurance Company.	100 00
" " repairs to office from City Comptroller	123 48
" " transportation (being money refunded for advances made to emigrants forwarded to the interior)	237 81
Amount received for support of illegitimate children	144 00
" " board of steward at Ward's Island	110 50
" " board of masons at "	33 81
" " returned premium, Insurance Company	30 11
" " ferriage on board steamboat Stranger	61 55
" " expenses of bonded passengers	189 00
" " expenses of law suit from the Delaware and Hudson Canal Company	250 00
Amount received for one volume Natural History	1 00
	$403,298 52

Disbursements.

For the purchase of real estate at Ward's Island.....	$43,818 83	
For erection of buildings, improvements, &c., &c....	33,298 98	
For reimbursements to counties, institutions, &c....	44,644 78	
For the support of Emigrant Refuge and Hospitals, Ward's Island, and office expenses..............	151,684 03	
For transfers to the Marine Fund.................	30,000 00	
For expenses of Marine Hospital, subsequent to April 11th, 1849..................................	77,767 84	
		$381,214 46
Balance of fund in Mechanics' Bank, Jan. 1st, 1850..		$22,084 06

MARINE HOSPITAL FUND.

Receipts.

Amount of hospital money, to April 11th, 1849.......	$1,287 86	
Amount received for washing at the Marine Hospital..	41 08	
" " returned salaries...............	38 83	
" " postage.......................	9 91	
" " sale of shanty.................	250 00	
" " separate burials................	49 00	
" " board of patients not chargeable at the Marine Hospital..........	91 76	
" " sale of empty barrels, &c., &c....	29 31	
" " returned premium, Insurance Co.	12 02	
" " damage by fire, from Insurance Co.	10 00	
Amount transferred from the Commutation Fund by authority of the Governor, Comptroller, and Attorney-General..................................	30,000 00	
		$31,819 77
Balance of expenses of Marine Hospital (charged to Commutation Fund since April, 1849).............		$77,767 84

Disbursements.

Deficit in the Marine Fund on the 1st January 1849...........	$6,949 10
Total expenses of Marine Hospital, during the year............	95,961 06
" " Bedlows Island...........................	6,677 45
	$109,587 61

Table No. V.

Statement of Moneys received by the Commissioners of Emigration on account of Minor Children becoming orphans; made in accordance with Section 10, *Act of April* 11, 1849.

Parents' Name.	Name of Vessel.	Where from.	Date of Death of Parents.	Names of Children.	Age.	Amount.	Disposition of Property.
John Hall	India	Liverpool	19 Feb. 1848	Sarah	17	$190 00	$95 00 paid for clothing and
				Elizabeth	13	and a watch.	nursing infant. Balance on
				Jane	11	......	deposit in savings bank.
				Mary	...	......	
				Hannah	$3\frac{1}{2}$	......	
Catharine Moore	Digby	Liverpool	23 Mar. 1848	Matthew	15	140 07	In savings bank.
Andrew Hannon	Virginia	"	1 May, 1848	Anderoga	8	1 25	" "
				Michael	7	......	
				Edward	4	......	
John Perry	Wm. Carson	Dublin	16 Aug. 1848	Peter	12	4 83	" "
				Mary	11	......	
Elizabeth Whaley	Memnon	Liverpool	9 Oct. 1848	Lavinia	12	14 76	" "
				James	10	......	
Robert O'Reilly	New World	"	3 Mar. 1849	William	14	5 00	$2 50 paid to William; balance
				Eliza	...	......	in savings bank.
Jacob Burkle	......	......	7 June, 1849	Anton	8	316 17	
				Adam	10	......	$117 87 paid for clothing, board,
				Mary	5	......	&c. Balance in savings bank.
				Henry	2	......	
Auguste Pfau	E. Harbeck	Bremen	1 Aug. 1849	Carl	19	502 70	$66 05 paid for clothing.
				Edward	9	......	Balance in bank.
				Robert	8 mos.	......	
Matilda Pohlig	Belvidere	Antwerp	Oct. 1849	Albert	...	1,176 00	$10 75 paid for clothing, &c.
				Matilda	...	......	Balance in bank.
Ferdinand Seidler	Avalanche	Bremen	......	Ferdinand	9	120 90	$24 70 paid for clothing.
H. Jan Oonk	E. Denison	do.	......	......	...	25 25	$1 00 " cartage.

Table No. VI.

COMMUTATION FUND ACCOUNT FOR THE YEAR 1850.

Receipts.

Balance of fund on deposit with the City Chamberlain in Mechanics' Bank, January 1, 1850	$22,084 06
Amount of commutation money received from owners and consignees of vessels for alien passengers	316,267 00
Amount received for commutation of special bonds	81 35
" " from masters, owners, and consignees for violations of law	756 50
Amount received for mortgage of real estate	36,000 00
" " from trustees of "Seamen's Fund and Retreat"	1,459 29
" " advances made to orphans,	322 66
" " support of illegitimate children	661 12
" " advances made to emigrants for transportation into the interior	615 27
Amount for sundries	1,847 17
	$380,094 42

Disbursements.

For purchase of real estate on Ward's Island	$21,826 75	
For erection of buildings, improvements, and repairs.	24,629 65	
For reimbursement to counties	26,736 40	
For reimbursement to New York Alms-house, and other institutions	13,483 46	
For the support of Emigrant Refuge and Hospitals	173,800 04	
" " Marine Hospital	61,440 29	
For Commissioners' office; salaries and wages, &c.	12,875 61	
For contingencies	34,779 19	
		$369,561 39
Balance of fund in Mechanics' Bank, Jan. 1, 1851		$10,533 03

Table No. VII.

COMMUTATION FUND ACCOUNT FOR THE YEAR 1851.

Receipts.

Balance of fund on deposit with the City Chamberlain, in Mechanics' Bank, Jan. 1, 1851..........		$10,533 03
Amount of commutation money received from owners and consignees of vessels, for alien passengers.	$438,037 50	
For commutation of special bonds................	9,628 69	
From owners and consignees of vessels for violations of law.............................	621 00	
For mortgage of real estate......................	14,000 00	
From trustees of "Seamen's Fund and Retreat"...	1,710 27	
For advances made to emigrants, for transportation into the interior...........................	612 28	
For support of illegitimate children..............	350 00	
From the Comptroller of State of New York, for commutation money of passengers, in sundry vessels consigned to Joseph McMurray, unpaid in 1850....................................	3,321 00	
For sundries..................................	1,257 53	
		469,538 27
		$480,071 30

Disbursements.

For the purchase of real estate on Ward's Island...	$1,606 91	
For erection of buildings, improvements, and repairs	9,824 04	
For reimbursements to counties..................	67,781 17	
For reimbursements to "Governors of New York Alms-house".............................	13,042 94	
For reimbursements to local Institutions..........	8,784 40	
For office expenses (salaries, furniture, gas, &c.)....	14,727 49	
For expenses of Lodging-house and Labor Exchange, Nos. 25 and 27 Canal street...........	16,140 14	
For supply of Emigrant Refuge and Hospitals.......	193,568 76	
For contingencies (on account Commutation Fund).	64,436 77	
For support of Marine Hospital and Quarantine....	67,095 18	
For contingencies (on account Marine Hospital)....	6,646 20	
		$463,654 00
Balance in Mechanics' Bank, Jan. 1, 1852................		$16,417 30

Table No. VIII.

COMMUTATION FUND ACCOUNT FOR THE YEAR 1852.

Receipts.

Balance of fund on deposit with City Chamberlain, January 1, 1852		$16,417 30
Amount of commutation money received from owners and consignees of vessels, for alien passengers	$455,236 50	
Amount received for commutation of special bonds.	10,965 80	
Amount received from owners and consignees of vessels for violations of law	275 00	
Amount received for mortgage of real estate	80,000 00	
Amount received from trustees of "Seamen's Fund and Retreat"	689 56	
Amount refunded for advances made to emigrants for transportation into the interior	264 64	
Amount received from Irish Emigrant Society, for do. do	236 78	
Amount received for support of illegitimate children	388 00	
Amount from Insurance companies, for damage by fire	4,750 55	
Amount for sundries	3,105 46	
		555,912 29
		$572,329 59

Disbursements.

For erection of buildings, improvements, and repairs	$26,576 43	
For reimbursements to counties for support of emigrants	64,763 90	
For reimbursements to "Governors of Alms-house"	10,912 97	
For reimbursements to local Institutions	12,755 08	
For Commissioners' office, salaries, wages, &c.	15,428 52	
For salaries of agents in Buffalo, Rochester, and Albany	4,020 41	
For Lodging-house and Labor Exchange, Nos. 23, 25, and 27 Canal street	21,000 89	
For temporary refuge and Lodging-house in Third Avenue	6,857 50	
Carried forward	$162,315 70	$572,329 5

Brought forward........	$162,315 70	$572,329 59
For temporary refuge in the church, corner of Duane and Church streets..........................	6,249 44	
For support of Emigrant Refuge and Hospitals, Ward's Island..............................	210,268 77	
For contingencies on account of commutation fund.	64,373 19	
For support of Marine Hospital, and Quarantine....	107,187 55	
For contingencies on account of Marine Hospital...	19,122 09	
		569,516 74
Balance in Mechanics' Bank, Jan. 1, 1853................		$2,812 85

Table No. IX.

COMMUTATION FUND ACCOUNT FOR THE YEAR 1853.

Receipts.

Balance of fund on deposit with the City Chamberlain, January 1, 1853.........................		$2,812 85
Amount of commutation money received from owners and consignees of vessels for alien passengers..	$550,755 50	
For mortgage of real estate.............	20,000 00	
For compromises of special bonds................	11,661 67	
From owners and consignees of vessels for violations of law..	371 71	
From trustees of "Seamen's Fund and Retreat"....	616 23	
Amount refunded for advances made to emigrants for transportation into the interior............	280 99	
From Irish Emigrant Society, for do. do..........	618 06	
For support of illegitimate children..............	1,083 00	
For ship-fever cases admitted to Marine Hospital...	687 00	
For rent of premises, No. 23 Canal street.........	563 33	
For sale of barrels, bottles, bones, fat, rags, iron, &c., at Ward's Island and Marine Hospital......	3,779 99	
For sundries..............................	1,234 44	
		591,651 92
Carried forward........		$594,464 77

Brought forward........		$594,464 77

Disbursements.

For erection of buildings, improvements, and repairs....................................	$33,233 08	
For reimbursements to counties, for support of emigrants, during the years 1852 and 1853..........	122,135 16	
For reimbursements to "Governors of Alms-house"	20,000 00	
For reimbursements to local Institutions..........	9,737 01	
For Commissioners' office, salaries, and wages, &c..	18,220 36	
For salaries of agents (in Albany, Rochester, and Buffalo), and other employees..................	6,925 00	
For Intelligence Office and Labor Exchange, Nos. 25 and 27 Canal street..........................	5,372 60	
For disbursements by agent in Albany............	2,280 95	
For disbursements " Rochester..........	74 00	
For disbursements " Buffalo.............	4,024 57	
For disbursements on account of Emigrant Refuge and Hospitals, Ward's Island....................	214,077 30	
For unclassified expenses, commutation fund.......	79,007 31	
For disbursements on account of Marine Hospital..	56,713 75	
For unclassified expenses, Marine Hospital........	10,838 15	
For maintenance of passengers landed at Quarantine, from "cholera vessels,"..................	4,219 05	
		586,859 18
Balance in Mechanics' Bank, Jan. 1, 1854................		$7,605 59

Table No. X.

Commutation Fund Account for the Year 1854.

Receipts.

Balance of fund on deposit with the City Chamberlain, Jan. 1, 1854............................		$7,605 25
Amount of commutation money received from owners and consignees of vessels for alien passengers.	$633,210 00	
For mortgage of real estate......................	20,000 00	
For compromises of special bonds................	18,913 88	
From owners and consignees of vessels, for violations of law....................................	192 00	
Carried forward........	$672,315 88	$7,605 25

Brought forward.......	$672,315 88	$7,605 25
For support of illegitimate children...............	1,365 25	
Amount re-deposited, having been drawn from bank in August, 1853, to pay for real estate on Ward's Island, and charged as such in report of that year	6,000 00	
For rent of No. 23 Canal street..................	1,249 17	
From trustees of "Seamen's Fund and Retreat," for board and medical treatment of seamen.........	499 25	
For ship-fever cases, admitted into the Marine Hospital.......................................	86 00	
Amount refunded for advances to emigrants for their transportation into the interior............	1,171 54	
From Irish Emigrant Society for do. do.	50 50	
For sales of empty barrels, bones, fat, rags, iron, &c., at Ward's Island and Marine Hospital.......	3,951 19	
For sundries.................................	2,114 20	
		688,802 98
		$696,408 23

Disbursements.

For erection of buildings, improvements, and repairs		$17,105 16	
For purchase of real estate on Ward's Island......		10,868 75	
For reimbursements to counties for support of emigrants.......................................		78,532 85	
For reimbursements to local Institutions...........		9,117 50	
For " " Governors of New York Alms-house"................................		27,525 36	
For Commissioners' office (salaries, &c.)..........		21,316 21	
For Intelligence Office and Labor Exchange in Canal street......................................		5,113 61	
For disbursements by agent in Albany............		5,332 61	
" " " Buffalo		6,574 33	
" " " Rochester..........		880 00	
" " " Utica.............		2,335 75	
" " on account of emigrant Refuge and Hospital, Ward's Island....................		251,447 48	
For disbursements on account of Marine Hospital...		64,286 39	
Unclassified expenditures for Commutation Fund, comprising:			
Payment to Life Insurance Company, on account of principal of loan on bond and mortgage.....................	$40,000 00		
Interest on loan........................	10,537 62		
Carrried forward........	$50,537 62	$500,436 00	$696,408 23

Brought forward........	$50,537 62	$500,436 00	$696,408 23
Forwarding emigrants to interior.......	19,227 21		
Temporary board and lodging to emigrants	10,791 82		
Temporary relief to emigrants..........	7,670 53		
Steamboat hire......................	4,085 00		
Rent, insurance, and sundry unclassed expenses	32,990 60		
		125,302 78	
For unclassified expenses Marine Hospital.........		7,816 75	
Maintenance of well passengers landed at Quarantine from "cholera vessels"..................		1,660 24	
			635,215 77
Balance in Mechanics' Bank, Jan. 1, 1855................			$61,192 46

Table No. XI.

Commutation Fund Account for the Year 1855.

Receipts.

Balance of fund on deposit with the city Chamberlain in Mechanics' Bank, Jan. 1, 1855...........		$61,192 46
Amount of commutation money received from owners and consignees of vessels for alien passengers.	$279,954 00	
For mortgage of real estate......................	39,823 56	
For compromises of special bonds................	33,769 20	
From owners and consignees of vessels for violations of law.................................	122 66	
For support of illegitimate children...............	1,795 59	
Amount refunded for advances to emigrants for their transportation into the interior.................	2,806 17	
From Irish Emigrant Society, for do. do...........	292 37	
From merchants and underwriters for expenses of visit of New York Legislature.................	535 83	
For board of emigrants in city and institutions of Ward's Island, and Marine Hospital............	1,092 02	
For washing clothes of passengers at Marine Hospital..	116 85	
Carried forward........	$360,308 35	$61,192 46

Brought forward........	$360,308 35	$61,192 46
For separate graves of passengers at Marine Hospital	22 00	
From employers of wet nurses at Ward's Island....	222 63	
For sales of empty barrels, bones, fat, rags, iron, &c., &c., at Ward's Island and Marine Hospital...	3,787 94	
For sundries..................................	1,625 32	
		365,966 24
		$427,158 70

Disbursements.

Reimbursements to counties for support of emigrants......................................	$43,181 17	
Reimbursements to local Institutions.............	8,645 56	
Expenses of Commissioners' office; salaries, &c.....	26,182 31	
Expenses of Intelligence Office and Labor Exchange	4,297 80	
Expenses of Emigrant Landing Dépôt, Castle Garden	5,875 34	
Disbursements by agent in Albany...............	6,246 58	
" " Buffalo................	9,881 41	
" " Utica	4,021 71	
" " Rochester.............	1,180 69	
Disbursements on account of Emigrant Refuge and Hospitals, Ward's Island......................	190,231 81	
Disbursements on account of Marine Hospital......	43,196 25	
For erection of buildings, improvements, &c........	28,727 44	
Board and lodging of emigrants in the city of New York......................................	24,439 47	
Forwarding emigrants to interior................	28,343 71	
Temporary relief to emigrants in the city of New York......................................	16,175 39	
Interest on bond and mortgage and overdrafts.....	14,688 39	
Steamboat hire (contract).......................	3,437 50	
Unclassified Expenses on account of Ward's Island,&c.	23,480 31	
" " " Marine Hospital.	7,564 83	
Support of well passengers at Marine Hospital......	392 10	
		$490,189 77

Overdraft on Mechanics' Bank, Jan. 1, 1856.............$63,031 07

Table No. XII.

COMMUTATION FUND ACCOUNT FOR THE YEAR 1856.

Receipts.

Amount of commutation money received from owners and consignees of vessels for alien passengers.	$286,612 00	
Compromises of special bonds....................	9,050 97	
Transfer of amount paid, under protest, in 1849....	2,785 71	
From owners and consignees of vessels for violations of law....................................	565 31	
Penalties for deaths on board emigrant vessels (under law of United States) during the passage from Europe	2,800 00	
Amount refunded for advances to emigrants for transportation to interior.....................	1,582 78	
For support of illegitimate children..............	1,634 25	
For board of emigrants at Ward's Island, and in city	510 15	
For wet-nurses taken from Ward's Island..........	368 00	
For support of well passengers at Marine Hospital..	2,913 89	
For sale of empty barrels, casks, bones, rags, fat, &c., at Ward's Island..............................	1,814 05	
Do. do. at Marine Hospital........	359 77	
For sundries.................................	247 46	
		$311,244 34

Disbursements.

Reimbursements to counties for support of emigrants	$13,439 97	
Reimbursements to local Institutions..............	10,528 07	
Rent and expenses of Commissioners' office; salaries, wages, &c..............................	20,846 63	
Rent and expenses of Intelligence Office and Labor Exchange..................................	3,126 13	
Expenses of Emigrant Landing Dépôt, Castle Garden	5,065 10	
Disbursements and expenses at agency in Albany..	3,512 77	
" " " in Buffalo...	3,511 22	
" " " in Utica ...	2,484 69	
Carried forward........	$62,514 58	$311,244 34

Brought forward........	$62,514 58	$311,244 34
Consumption of stores and supplies by laborers while quarantined discharging infected ships.....	1,642 84	
Expenses of Emigrant Refuge and Hospitals.......	109,721 10	
Expenses of Marine Hospital....................	35,018 24	
Board and lodging of emigrants in city of New York.	3,357 38	
Temporary relief to emigrants in " "	166 25	
Forwarding emigrants to interior................	3,862 37	
Interest on bond and mortgage and overdrafts......	17,440 41	
Steamboat hire to Ward's Island and Marine Hospital	7,650 00	
Interments from Ward's Island and city	1,085 50	
Insurance on buildings at Ward's Island and Marine Hospital	1,862 14	
Unclassified expenses, Ward's Island, &c...........	12,308 81	
" " Marine Hospital............	786 40	
Total disbursements....................		$257,416 02
Add overdraft on Mechanic's Bank, Jan. 1, 1856........		63,031 07
		$320,447 09
Receipts.............................		311,244 34
Overdraft on bank, Jan. 1, 1857.....................		$9,202 75

Table No. XIII.

Commutation Fund Account for the Year 1857.

Receipts.

Amount of commutation money received from owners and consignees of vessels, for alien passengers.	$369,298 00
Compromises of special bonds...................	9,786 98
Penalties for deaths on board emigrant vessels (under law of United States), during passage from Europe.....................................	3,160 00
From emigrants, for their transportation to interior	636 24
From owners and consignees of vessels for violations of law................................	166 00
For support of illegitimate children..............	1,149 53
Ferriage on board steamer "King Philip,"........	406 33
Rent of part of building in Albany................	142 00
Carried forward........	$384,745 08

Brought forward........	$384,745 08	
For board of emigrants at Ward's Island..........	571 90	
From employers of wet-nurses, taken from Ward's Island	375 00	
For sale of empty barrels, bones, fat, rags, &c., at Ward's Island............................	1,492 22	
For support of well passengers at Marine Hospital..	4,660 18	
For board of patients at Marine Hospital..........	127 14	
For sundries, as per cash account................	298 91	
	$392,270 43	
Less overdraft, Jan. 1, 1857.........	9,202 75	
		$383,067 68

Disbursements.

Reimbursements to counties for support of emigrants	$85,563 85	
" to local Institutions.............	6,680 16	
Rent and expenses of Commissioners' office, salaries, wages, &c.	21,437 13	
Expenses of Emigrant Landing Dépôt at Castle Garden....................................	18,784 67	
Disbursements at agency in Albany..............	2,765 96	
" " Buffalo..............	2,352 27	
" " Rochester............	889 96	
" " Oneida County........	715 50	
Support of Emigrant Refuge and Hospitals, W. Isl'd	111,634 38	
" Marine Hospital......................	32,039 29	
Unclassified expenses on account of Ward's Island, &c., &c.,..................................	8,259 15	
" " " Marine Hospital	1,041 98	
Support of well passengers, Marine Hospital.......	2,355 62	
Interest on bond and mortgage and overdrafts.....	12,003 06	
Mutual Life Insurance Company, in part payment of bond of $150,000.......................... .	25,000 00	
Interments at Ward's Island and in city...........	724 50	
Insurance on buildings at Ward's Island and Marine Hospital....................................	1,867 14	
Board and lodging of emigrants in city............	1,798 11	
Forwarding emigrants to destination..............	3,040 29	
Support of illegitimate children......................	1,331 03	
Steamboat hire (contract) to Ward's Island and Marine Hospital................................	7,042 50	
Salaries of Chamberlain's clerk, clerk and nurse on steamboat, Metropolitan police, and superintendent at Seguine's Point..........................	2,254 74	
Repairs to Government Dock, Quarantine.........	1,330 50	
		$350,911 79
Balance in bank, December 31, 1857.............		$32,155 89

Table No. XIV.

COMMUTATION FUND ACCOUNT FOR THE YEAR 1858.

Receipts.

Amount of commutation money received from owners and consignees of vessels for alien passengers.	$157,412 00	
Compromise of special bonds....................	14,052 25	
Penalties for deaths on board emigrant vessels (under law of U. S.) during passage from Europe...	1,000 00	
From owners and consignees of vessels for violations of law..............................	140 00	
From emigrants for their transportation to interior.	1,534 66	
Support of illegitimate children..................	1,125 00	
Rent of part of premises occupied by agent in Albany	221 16	
Ferriage on board steamer "Island Home"........	279 38	
Interest on deposit in Shoe and Leather Bank.....	1,574 71	
Rent of Castle Garden.........................	2,500 00	
Board of children and others at Ward's Island.....	399 90	
From employers of wet-nurses taken from W. Island	340 00	
Sale of empty barrels, bones, fat, rags, &c., from Ward's Island..............................	1,603 47	
Support of well passengers at Marine Hospital.....	7,902 24	
Board and medical attendance of patients at Marine Hospital..................................	193 41	
Washing clothing of passengers at Marine Hospital.	530 65	
For separate graves, " "	47 84	
Sale of coal, old iron, rags, &c. " "	418 07	
Sale of hay at Seguine's Point..................	10 00	
Sundries, as per cash account..................	83 90	
	$191,368 64	
Add balance in bank, January 1st, 1858	32,155 89	
		$223,524 53

Disbursements.

Reimbursements to counties for support of emigrants	$16,893 16	
Reimbursements to local Institutions do. do.....	8,002 73	
Rent and other expenses of Commissioners' Office..	20,721 06	
Carried forward........	$45,616 95	$223,524 53

Brought forward........	$45,616 95	$223,524 53
Expenses of Emigrant Landing-Dépôt, Castle Garden	16,774 56	
Disbursements at Agency in Albany..............	2,386 98	
" " " Buffalo...............	2,725 53	
" " " Rochester	938 54	
" " " Oneida county........	724 17	
Support of Emigrant Refuge and Hospitals, W. Island	78,586 38	
" Marine Hospital and Quarantine........	32,613 49	
Board and lodging of emigrants in city............	1,153 42	
Care of well passengers in Marine Hospital.........	127 56	
Cartage and commissions on supplies sent to Ward's Island and Marine Hospital..................	903 69	
Drawing plans for new hospitals at Quarantine....	250 00	
Forwarding emigrants to destination.............	3,228 45	
Insurance on buildings at Ward's Island and Marine Hospital..................................	1,816 64	
To "Governors of Alms-house" for interments....	434 50	
Interest on bond of $150,000....................	10,157 19	
Steamboat hire to Ward's Island and Marine Hospital	8,455 00	
Support of illegitimate children..................	838 00	
Subsistence of Metropolitan Police at Quarantine...	609 26	
Temporary relief in city of New York............	237 50	
Salaries and wages of clerks in Mayor's office, and clerks and nurses on steamboat and wharf......	2,275 92	
Salary of Superintendent, Seguine's Point.........	328 00	
Repairs to wharf at Marine Hospital.............	145 25	
Sundry other expenses, as per account............	6,541 33	
		$217,868 25
Balance in bank, January 1st, 1859..		$5,656 28

Table No. XV.

Commutation Fund Account for the Year 1859.

Receipts.

Balance in bank, January 1st, 1859..............		$5,656 28
Amount of commutation money received from owners and consignees of vessels for alien passengers.	$159,112 00	
For compromise of special bonds.................	9,921 55	
Carried forward........	$169,033 55	$5,656 28

Brought forward........	$169,033 55	$5,656 28
Penalties for deaths on board emigrant vessels (under law of U. S.) during passage to this port.....	895 00	
For support of illegitimate children..............	779 56	
Steamboat fare on steamer "Island Home".......	180 55	
From emigrants, for their transportation to interior.	510 54	
Interest on balances in Shoe and Leather Bank....	1,173 73	
Licenses granted to emigrant runners.............	1,140 00	
For rent of Castle Garden......................	6,000 00	
For rent of premises in Albany..................	232 50	
From Germania Insurance Company for destruction of a barn by fire at Ward's Island..............	300 00	
For sale of old furniture from Office..............	19 00	
Returned premium from three Insurance Companies	11 25	
Returned salaries—Office, $32; Castle Garden, $1 25	33 25	
Board of children and others at Ward's Island.....	521 51	
From employers of wet-nurses taken from W. Island	507 00	
Sale of groceries, empty barrels, rags, bones, &c., &c., from Ward's Island......................	800 86	
Sale of old iron at Marine Hospital and Castle Garden	362 57	
Sale of sundries at Marine Hospital...............	43 82	
Board and medical treatment of patients on Floating Hospital..................................	13 15	
Sundries, as per cash account.....................	8 50	
		182,566 34
		$188,222 62

Disbursements.

Reimbursements to counties for support of emigrants	$23,555 75
Reimbursements to local Institutions.............	6,380 21
Rent, and other expenses of Commissioners' office..	16,486 18
Expenses of Emigrant Landing-Dépôt, Castle Garden	34,726 91
Disbursements by agent in Albany...............	2,160 00
" " Rochester.............	1,087 49
" " Buffalo	2,600 71
Support of Emigrant Refuge and Hospitals.......	57,019 78
" Marine Hospital and Quarantine.......	18,359 77
" Floating Hospital...................	4,647 71
Yearly interest on bond of $150,000, at 7 per cent.	10,500 00
Insurance on buildings at Ward's Island and Marine Hospital..................................	1,355 25
Forwarding emigrants to destination.............	1,012 74
Real estate purchased on Ward's Island...........	1,000 00
Carried forward........	$180,892 50

Brought forward	$180,892 50	
Steamboat hire to W. Island and Marine Hospital	6,922 25	
Salary of counsel to Commissioners of Emigration	1,500 00	
" City Chamberlain's Clerk	700 00	
Salaries of manifest and forwarding clerks, and physician of city prison	1,550 00	
Salaries and wages of clerk and nurses on board steamer Island Home	1,225 00	
Salary of agent in Oneida county	600 00	
Taxes on leased property at Ward's Island	468 65	
Temporary relief granted in city of New York	93 69	
Support of illegitimate children	956 00	
Stage fare of emigrants from Ward's Island	273 86	
Sundry other expenses	4,693 83	
		199,875 78
Overdraft, January 1st, 1860		$11,653 16

Table XVI.

COMMUTATION FUND ACCOUNT FOR THE YEAR 1860.

Receipts.

Amount of commutation money received from owners and consignees of vessels for alien passengers	$209,354 00	
From Mutual Life Insurance Company on bond and mortgage	57,500 00	
For compromise of special bonds	11,329 87	
For rent of Castle Garden	6,000 00	
For support of illegitimate children	1,442 92	
Penalties for deaths at sea on board emigrant vessels	820 00	
From emigrants for their transportation to interior	642 74	
Steamboat fares on board " Island Home "	182 25	
Rent of premises in Albany	180 00	
Licenses granted to emigrant runners	740 00	
From Quarantine Commissioners, for searches, &c., in procuring loan	106 45	
For board of children and others at Ward's Island	251 92	
From employers of wet-nurses taken from do	306 00	
Sale of empty barrels, rags, bones, &c., &c., from do.	536 53	
Sundries as per cash account	75 24	
		289,467 92
Deduct overdraft January 1, 1860		11,653 16
		$277,814 76

Brought forward........ $277,814 76

Expenditures.

Reimbursements to counties for support of emigrants	$51,113 59	
" " local Institutions for do..........	7,755 49	
Disbursements on account of Commissioners' office..	14,112 91	
Expenses of Emigrant Landing Dépôt, Castle Garden	23,060 57	
" at agency in Albany..................	2,340 45	
" " " Buffalo..................	2,391 68	
" " " Rochester..............	1,060 65	
Support of Emigrant Refuge and Hospitals........	58,913 41	
Disbursements on account of Marine Hospital......	3,025 62	
" " " Floating Hospital.....	49 82	
Interest on bond of $207,500......................	13,713 29	
Board and lodging of 3,242 emigrants in city......	945 17	
Blacksmithing and horse-shoeing in city...........	243 06	
Advertising in and subscription to newspapers.....	165 06	
Boats, oars, &c................................	226 01	
Cartage and commissions on supplies for Ward's Island......................................	509 90	
Forwarding emigrants to destination..............	1,522 29	
Horse feed in city.............................	602 16	
Insurance on buildings at Ward's Island..........	1,114 25	
Interments in City Cemetery......................	131 00	
Quarantine Commissioners, being amount received for mortgage of State property at Seguine's Point	7,500 00	
Printing annual reports..........................	253 60	
Support of illegitimate children..................	1,587 51	
Postage..	111 86	
Expenses of procuring loan on bond and mortgage..	277 63	
Steamboat hire to and from Ward's Island........	6,315 00	
Salary of counsel to Commissioners of Emigration..	1,250 00	
" City Chamberlain's clerk...............	855 56	
" physician in city prison................	416 60	
" clerk in mayor's office..................	600 00	
" forwarding clerk......................	450 00	
" nurses on steamboat...................	540 00	
" clerks on steamboat and wharf..........	685 92	
" agent of Commissioners of Emigration in Oneida county............................	600 00	
Sundry other expenses..........................	1,624 31	
		$206,064 37

Balance in bank December 31, 1860............. $71,750 39

General Table,

Showing the number of Aliens arrived and landed at the Port of New York, for whom Commutation and Hospital Moneys were paid, as also the total number of persons treated, cared for, forwarded, &c., classified under the different heads, together with the total amount of Receipts from all sources, and the whole amount of Expenditures, from the organization of the Commissioners of Emigration, May 5, 1847, *to December* 31, 1860.

YEAR.	Number of Aliens arrived, for whom Commutation and Hospital moneys were paid, or bonds demanded.	Number treated and cared for at Emigrant Refuge and Hospitals, Ward's Island.	Number treated at Marine Hospital.	Number supplied temporarily with board and lodging.	Number temporarily relieved with money, &c.	Number provided with employment.	Number of persons forwarded.	Number treated in other Institutions of this city, at expense of this Commission	Number relieved in the Counties of the State, and chargeable to this Commission	Grand Total of persons treated, cared for, relieved, forwarded, &c., by and at the expense of the Commissioners of Emigration.	Total Receipts of Commutation and Hospital Moneys, and from all sources.	Total Expenditures.
1847	129,062	1,629	6,474	....	503	....	798	1,190	....	10,594	$193,292 10	$148,147 31
1848	189,176	4,057	8,661	....	6,640	....	2,102	694	5,369	27,523	301,901 99	274,833 49
1849	220,791	8,320	6,159	....	16,854	....	2,999	1,360	5,566	41,258	318,608 29	378,817 34
1850	212,603	10 156	3,411	27,314	....	8,000	2,301	267	5,937	57,386	358,010 36	369,461 39
1851	289.601	14,939	6,343	23,941	....	18,204	7,391	1,658	12,550	85,026	469,538 27	463,654 00
1852	300,992	15,182	8,887	117,568	....	14,971	4,601	1,364	18.432	181,005	572,329 26	569,516 74
1853	284,945	14,365	4.796	24,317	20,197	14,334	3,262	1,152	9,351	91,774	591,651 92	586,859 19
1854	319,223	15,950	4,762	51,569	17,516	13,964	4,608	2,021	10,504	120,894	688.802 98	635,215 77
1855	136,233	12,901	2,402	59,520	34,405	15.151	4,996	807	12,175	142,357	365.966 24	490,189 77
1856	142,342	7,610	1,648	11,093	79	9,378	589	1,081	5,346	36,824	311,244 34	257,416 02
1857	183,773	8,539	1,856	5,108	303	10,933	529	864	4,253	32,385	392,270 43	350,911 79
1858	78,589	6,906	1,204	5,731	413	9,346	515	245	4,200	26,560	191.368 64	217,868 25
1859	79,322	4,361	274	3,860	722	7,150	176	485	2,407	19,435	182,566 34	199,875 78
1860	105,162	4,729	....	5,115	122	7,717	401	527	2,104	20 715	289,467 92	210,359 66
Total	2,671,819	129,644	56,877	333,136	97,754	129,148	35,268	13,715	98,194	893,736	$5,227,019 08	$5,153,126 50

Appendix No. 1.

Office of the Commissioners of Emigration
of the State of New York.

New York, November, 1848.

THE Legislature of the State of New York, admonished by the rapid increase of immigration at the port of New York, and considering the important interests connected therewith, has established a Board of Commissioners, acting under the authority of the State, and intrusted with the general care and supervision of the subject. The protection of the emigrant against the tricks and dishonesty of persons with whom he must necessarily come in contact immediately on his arrival, is one of the principal objects of the Commission; and in furtherance of this object, the undersigned have been appointed a committee to notice a great and frequent abuse, which is practised upon the emigrant even before he leaves the old world.

The number of passengers arrived at this port since the beginning of this year is nearly 160,000; and it may be assumed that at least 130,000 thereof have proceeded to the distant parts of the country at the West, and that the money paid here for their passage, amounts to more than half a million of dollars. As may be supposed, there are many people engaged in the business of forwarding these emigrants, and the individuals or companies thus engaged employ a host of clerks or servants, called "runners," who try to meet the new-comer on board the ship that brings him, or immediately after he puts his foot on shore, for the purpose of carrying him to the forwarding offices for which they respectively act. The tricks resorted to, in order to forestall a competitor and secure the emigrant, would be amusing, if they were not at the cost of the inexperienced and unsuspecting stranger; and it is but too true that an enormous sum of money is annually lost to the emigrants by the wiles and false statements of the emigrant runners, many of them originally from their own country, and speaking their native language.

Of late the field of operation of these "emigrant runners" is no longer confined to this city; it extends to Europe. Some have appeared there sent from here by forwarding offices, others have been engaged on the spot, and again others have commenced and are carrying on the business on their own account and responsibility; but all have the same object in view, namely, to make money out of the emigrant. They generally call themselves agents of some transportation or forwarding bureau, and endeavor to impress the emigrant who intends going farther than New York, with the belief that it is for his benefit, and in the highest degree desirable, to secure his passage hence to the place of his destination, before he leaves Europe.

It is well known that emigrants frequently arrive at the sea-ports in Europe, without having engaged their passage across the ocean, and not finding a vessel ready to take them on board, they are compelled to stop at a considerable expense, until an opportunity offers to proceed on their voyage; and it also happens that, even when they have secured a passage before going to the port of embarkation, they are delayed, and subject to perplexities and charges which they did not anticipate. This circumstance is taken advantage of by the so-called agents of New York transportation and forwarding houses, to induce the emigrant to take his passage from this port to his ulterior destination, before leaving Europe. He is told that, unless he does so, he runs great risk of being detained, or having to pay exorbitant prices.

These statements, and all similar ones, which may be used for the purpose, *are not true*, and whoever believes them, and acts upon such belief, is sure to be deceived.

There are but two routes hence to the west; the one is by way of Albany and Buffalo, the other by way of Philadelphia and Pittsburgh, and to these places there is no more than one conveyance daily, all the year through. There is never any difficulty in getting away from New-York, and so numerous are the establishments engaged in the business of forwarding passengers, that exorbitant or high prices of passage are entirely prevented by the competition among said establishments, and the traveller will never be exposed to them, if he will only be careful *not* to make an arrangement with the first comer, but will take some pains to find out which is the safest and cheapest office to apply to.

It is invariably the case, that those who in Europe take passage tickets for inland places in America, pay more, generally considerable more, than others, who wait until they are here. The agents in Europe who sell such tickets must have a compensation therefor, and this compensation, be it much or little, is added to the regular price of passage, and the emigrant has to pay it. Instances have come to the knowledge of the Commissioners, where the difference amounted to three dollars a person! But this is not all. The cases are by no means rare in which the tickets prove entirely worthless. They bear the name of offices which never existed, and then, of course, are nowhere respected; or, the offices whose name they bear, will be found shut up, and are not likely ever to re-open; or the emigrants are directed to parties refusing to acknowledge the agent who issued the tickets, and in all these cases the emigrant loses the money paid for them.

It is to be hoped that this publication will receive the attention it deserves. It would be gratifying to the Commissioners, and entirely for the interest of the emigrants, if the respective governments in Europe would prohibit the business alluded to; in any event, the Commissioners trust that emigrants will heed this warning, and henceforward will not pay, or arrange, for passage to the interior of America, until they are here.

On their arrival here they should not give ear to any representations, nor enter into any engagements, without obtaining first the advice and counsel of either the Commissioners of Emigration, or the Emigrant Society of the nation to which they belong, or its consul; and in inquiring for the office of the society, or consul, or the commissioners, they should be careful not to be carried to the wrong place. There are many individuals sufficiently unscrupulous intentionally to mislead the stranger. If the latter, for instance, inquire after the agency of the German society; the person applied to will say that he is the agent, or that he will take the stranger to the office of the German society, but instead of doing so, will take him to a place where he is almost sure to be defrauded. As a general rule, if the emigrant is urged to take passage, or has to pay for the advice he asks, he may take it for granted that he is not at the place where he wishes to be; and he should bear in mind to look for the names of the persons or office he is in search of, at the door of the houses into which he is shown. All the foreign consuls, and the emigrant societies, as well as the Commissioners of Emigration, have signs over the doors of their offices. The office of the German society is No. 95 Greenwich-street, of the Irish emigrant society at 22 Spruce-street, and of the Commissioners of Emigration in one of the public edifices of the city, in the park.

Finally we would remark, that if the emigrant be so situated as to render his immediate departure hence necessary, without having an opportunity to apply for advice to any of the places indicated, he should be careful not to take his passage for the whole distance he has to go, but should do so only to the first station of the route, say to Albany or Philadelphia. He should bear in mind that the passage hence to Albany is fifty cents, and to Philadelphia two dollars and twenty-five cents a person, and *no more.*

The Commissioners trust that this advice will be received and acted upon, with that confidence to which it is entitled, from being given by persons who have no interest but that of the welfare of the emigrant, whose duties make them perfectly familiar with the subject, and who act not as private citizens, but under the authority and supervision of the government of the State.

In behalf of the Commissioners of Emigration.

GULIAN C. VERPLANCK,
President of the Board.
LEOPOLD BIERWIRTH,
President of the German Society.
JOHN H. GRISCOM,
General Agent.
} *Committee.*

Appendix No. 2.

New York, Nov. 2d, 1848.

Hon. JAMES BUCHANAN, Secretary of State:

Sir:—I have the honor to address you on behalf of the Board of Commissioners of Emigration of the State of New York.

This Board (as you may perhaps be already informed) is a commission appointed by the authorities of this State, for the assistance and protection of foreign emigrants arriving in this State, by providing for the sick and destitute, and protecting all from imposition while here, and aiding them to their ultimate destination. We have lately learned from unquestionable authority (among others, from the United States Consul at Havre), that an organized system of imposition exists at the principal points of emigration from Europe, in the ports of Great Britain and Ireland, as well as those of the Continent, by which great and frequent frauds are committed in relation to the passages of emigrants to the interior of the United States. A circular has been accordingly prepared, under the authority of this Board, with the design of exposing these frauds: thus setting the emigrants on their guard against them. (A printed copy is herewith enclosed.) It has occurred to the Commissioners that this communication would be far more likely to promote its objects if it received the aid and sanction of the government of the United States.

This being a subject strictly relating to our intercourse with foreign nations, and in which other States must feel as much interest as that which first receives the emigrant; it appears to be legitimately within the constitutional sphere of the general government. It is, therefore, respectfully suggested, that copies of the enclosed circular should be transmitted to the several consuls of the United States, at all the points of great emigration to this country, with a note from the Department of State, recommending the subject to their especial attention, and requesting them to give publicity to the information and advice of the Commissioners.

Should this suggestion meet your approval, printed copies of the circular will be furnished and forwarded, as the Department may direct.

I am, with great respect, your obedient servant,

G. C. VERPLANCK, *Pres. of Com'rs of Emigration.*

DEPARTMENT OF STATE,
Washington, 6th Nov., 1848.

Hon. G. C. VERPLANCK, *New York:*

Sir:—I have received your letter of the 3d inst., addressed to me on behalf of the Board of Commissioners of Emigration, of the State of New York, referring to the existence " of an organized system of impositions at the principal points of emigration from Europe, in the ports of Great Britain and Ireland, as well as those of the continent, by which great and frequent frauds are committed, in relation to the passages of emigrants to the interior of the United States, together with a printed copy of a circular, prepared under the authority of the Board, with the design of exposing these frauds, thus setting the emigrants on their guard against them."

In the promotion of an object so honorable and benevolent, your Board may fully rely upon all the aid and support which this Department can properly afford.

In reply to your suggestion, that copies of this circular be transmitted to the several consuls of the United States, at all the points of great emigration to this country, and your offer to furnish them for that purpose, I have to state that I will, with great pleasure, cause them to be so addressed, with such instructions as may be best calculated to ensure the results you have in view.

I am, sir, respectfully, your obt. servant,
JAMES BUCHANAN.

Appendix No. 3.

New York, April 27, 1849.

HON. AMBROSE L. JORDAN, Attorney-general of the State of New York:

Sir:—The Commissioners of Emigration are in doubt as to their duties in relation to certain payments, formerly directed to be made from the moneys placed at their disposal, but which they may now be restricted from making by a general provision of the Act of the last session in relation to the Marine Hospital.

The Board has directed me to submit this subject to you for your advice, trusting that you will excuse the formality of an official application, in the first instance to the Governor or Comptroller by whom it would be referred to the Attorney-general.

By section 3, title IV., chapter XIV. of the Revised Statutes (2 R. S., 445), the expenses of the boat and boatmen for the use of the health officer, are directed to be charged to the funds of the Marine Hospital.

In section 12, title I. chapter XIV. (2 R. S., 424), it is enacted that the resident physician and health commissioner shall each receive an annual salary of one thousand dollars; and the health officer, as physician of the Marine Hospital, a like salary of four hundred and fifty dollars; and such *salaries shall be paid out from moneys* appropriated for the use of the *Marine Hospital.*

The act of April 11, 1849 (a copy of which is herewith enclosed), expressly enacts (§ 8) that "the moneys received under any of the provisions of this act as commutation money, or upon bonds given for or on account of any persons or passengers landing from vessels at the port of New York, shall not be applied or appropriated to any other purpose or use than to defray the expenses incurred for the care, support, or maintenance of such persons or passengers." It is to be observed that the moneys so designated in the section above quoted, are now the only "moneys appropriated to the use of the Marine Hospital."

In the same act (§ 14), the medical charge of the Marine Hospital is taken from the health officer, and it is presumed that his compensation ceases of course; but no provision is made anywhere in relation to the salary of the resident physician, or to that formerly allowed the health commissioner in addition to his fees of office. The salary of $2,000, provided in § 2 of the act, is in lieu of the fees.

Under these provisions, it would appear that the Commissioners are inhibited not only from paying the salary of the health officer, and the expenses of his boat—which they believe to be the intention of the Legislature to restrict them from doing—but also from applying their funds to the salaries of the resident physician and health commissioner, for whom, however, no other legal provision is made, while their salaries are left unrepealed.

Under these circumstances, the Commissioners respectfully ask your advice, whether or not they can apply any of the funds received by them to the purposes above mentioned, or any of them?

With respect, yours, &c.,

G. C. VERPLANCK.

Attorney-General's Office,
May 2, 1849.

Hon. G. C. Verplanck, President of the Commissioners of Emigration:

Sir:—In answer to yours of the 27th ult., I have the honor to state my opinion as follows: It was doubtless the intention of the Legislature to appropriate all moneys arising from the bonds executed on landing of emigrant passengers, or from commutation in lieu of such bonds, to the support of the Marine Hospital and quarantine establishment.

They intended to steer clear of the constitutional objection raised in the late case of Smith *vs.* Turner, and sustained upon the ground (partly at least), that the fund raised by taxation upon passengers had been employed for purposes foreign to Marine Hospital and quarantine regulation.

Not only was such the intention, but the provisions and language of the statute are full and clear. Let it first be observed, that no moneys are placed at the disposal of the Commissioners of Emigration, except such as arise from said bonds and commutations, and by the 8th section of the act the moneys so arising should not be applied or appropriated to any other purpose or use than to defray the expenses incurred for the care, support, and maintenance of such persons or passengers, who by the 6th section are to be received into said Marine Hospital. The health commissioner is now detached from all connection with the Marine Hospital, for which a physician is to be appointed by the Governor and Senate with power to appoint so many assistant physicians as the Commissioners of Emigration should determine to be necessary. The Commissioners of Emigration have the sole and exclusive control of the Marine Hospital and other lands and buildings, used for quarantine purposes, except in regard to the sanitary treatment of the inmates, their treatment being committed to the physician and his assistants.

The health officer shall not by virtue of his office have any other authority over the Marine Hospital, or medical charge as physician thereof, than is in this act provided, and all the powers given by the act are (§ 6) to send emigrants suffering under contagious or infectious diseases to the Marine Hospital, and to have free access at all times, to inspect all or any patients afflicted with any contagious or infectious disease, &c. The health officer being thus detached from the Marine Hospital and no longer physician thereof, his salary as such ceases. He cannot be entitled to a salary of $450 per annum, or any other sum as physician to the hospital when he is not such physician. The expense of his boat and boatmen can in no sense be considered as incurred for the care, support, or maintenance of persons or passengers received into the Marine Hospital.

The same remark is applicable, as it appears, to the salaries of the resident physician and the health commissioner. I am accordingly of the opinion, and do advise the Commissioners of Emigration, that they have no authority to pay said expenses or salaries or any part of them, out of the funds in their hands acquired under the operation of the said act of April 11th, 1849.

AMBROSE L. JORDAN.

Appendix No. 4.

The Committee appointed at the last meeting of the Commissioners of Emigration, to inquire and report in relation to certain abuses, alleged to have taken place, as to the bodies of persons who have died in the Hospitals and Refuge at Ward's Island,

RESPECTFULLY REPORT:

That on the morning after their appointment they went to Ward's Island, and spent the greater part of the day in examining into the several matters understood to be included in the inquiry given in charge to them; after conferring with the warden, and inquiring as to all matters which had fallen within his observation or knowledge, touching the treatment of the bodies of those who died in the establishment under his care, they proceeded to examine Drs. Hosack, Macneven and Cox, who were in attendance, the first as visiting surgeon, and the others as physicians, and afterwards separately Dr. Carnochan, one of the surgeons; they also examined separately the clerk of the hospital, the sexton who had charge of the dead-house, and an assistant, also two persons employed on Randall's Island, in the burying-ground, where persons dying on this island are interred.

These were questioned apart, and as closely as could be done where there was no power to secure any but voluntary testimony, or to compel attendance. There was however amongst those who appeared, but one instance of refusal to answer any question, and that (on the part of the clerk) referred only collaterally to the main subjects of inquiry.

The bodies of persons dying in the establishment at Ward's Island, are placed in plain but substantial separate coffins of stained wood, and then carried to the dead-house, a secure building near the bank of the inlet or narrow rocky channel separating Ward's Island from Randall's Island, where the public burying-ground of the city (known as Potter's Field) is situated. The building and its contents are under the charge of the sexton, and of the clerk of the hospital, nor can any body be removed thence without their knowledge, nor to any place except that of the intended interment, without a violation of the rules prescribed by this Board. The new by-laws and regulations passed by this Board, some weeks ago, have given additional security in this matter, by positively requiring the signature of the physician who attended the case, to the certificate issued by the clerk, a provision in conformity with the law of the State, which though always directed heretofore to be followed has for some time past been neglected, the clerk having given certificates with his own signature only, and the keeper of Potter's Field (so far as it appeared) receiving them without objection.

When the bodies have been received at Potter's Field, the control and responsibility of the Board cease entirely, and they are then under the charge of the proper authorities at Randall's Island.

The committee directed their inquiries, first, as to the taking of bodies for the purpose of dissection, that being one of the chief points of complaint.

Dissection, in its ordinary acceptation as well as in its strict professional sense, is understood to mean the cutting up and examining bodies for anatomical study, the bodies being commonly taken to some dissecting-room, and all the parts separately laid open.

Upon the fullest examination and inquiry, your committee cannot find that any such use has been made of the body of any person who has died at Ward's Island, and if any such case has occurred it must have been after the body had been duly delivered at Potter's Field, and by the neglect or connivance of the persons employed there, over whom this Board has no control.

There is no place at Ward's Island where any such dissection could be made without publicity, and the knowledge of the officers and employées and the evidence were to us conclusive, that no dissection of that nature had been made on the island, and that nobody had been taken or sent from there except to Randall's Island, or delivered to the care of friends.

As to the care of bodies after interment at Randall's Island, the committee had no sufficient means of inquiry, the keeper of Potter's Field who had been sent for not appearing; but they are satisfied to leave the care of their dead in the hands of the city authorities, where it is placed by law, in full confidence that it will not be abused. It appeared, however, on pursuing our inquiries that another species of medical or surgical examination of the dead was of frequent occurrence at Ward's Island, and of this the visiting surgeons and physicians neither made nor used any concealment. This is what is technically called *post mortem* examination, or examination after death of the seat of disease or the circumstances of the death, rendering such an inspection of special benefit to the living. It is sometimes ignorantly, and sometimes intentionally confounded with anatomical dissection, and the terms "dissection" and "dissected" were repeatedly used, in reply to questions by some of the witnesses, where, upon further examination, it was apparent that a post-mortem inspection was referred to. This differs widely from the dissection of the body, being simply confined to such incisions as may lay open to close inspection the part or organ specially injured or affected by the malady, and after such inspection the parts are restored to their place and as nearly as may be to their state before the incision, and the body is then consigned to the grave. Such examinations are made in most of the hospitals and infirmaries in this country and in Europe without any concealment; and your committee were informed by all the physicians and surgeons who were examined as well as since by other medical men of extensive practice not belonging to the medical board of Ward's Island, that they are very common in private practice when the case presents any peculiarity important to be studied for medical improvement or exciting any doubt as to the cause of death. The examination is of course never made in private families without the consent of the friends of the deceased, and it is very rarely that such consent is refused. It is performed with all care and respect to the dead, and takes place in the wealthiest families, and sometimes upon the bodies of the most distinguished members of the community, of which several recent instances are known to your committee.

It was stated by Dr. Carnochan, that the medical board had laid down the rule for themselves, of being governed in all their post-mortem examinations by the same rules as are established by usage or agreement in private practice in this or other cities. They are made only by authority of the superior physician, or surgeon who attended the case, and always under the inspection of the curator or medical officer specially charged with this duty.

According to a book made out by the sexton for his own use (for what purpose did not clearly appear), about thirty such inspections were made between the 1st October to the 14th November, inclusive, seventeen of which were made from the 24th Oct. to the 14th November, inclusive, during which later period 51 persons had died at Ward's Island. The bodies thus examined were all afterwards buried.

In the two cases of children, which had been stated in certain city papers to have been dissected, were both of them cases of such post-mortem examinations. One of them died of a disease of the throat, which was thought by the attending physician to be of much importance to examine, for the purpose of the medical knowledge of the disease and its treatment. The parts affected were opened, and the examinations made by Dr. Cox, and afterwards sewed up, the whole being done, as the committee was assured, precisely as it would have been done in the chambers of the wealthy in private practice, and without defacing the body. It was stated by Dr. Carnochan, that this post-mortem inspection was not only valuable as to general medical skill, but had resulted in immediate advantages in the treatment of similar cases in the practice of the hospital.

The other was a peculiar and very interesting case of abscess, extending across the stomach, and affecting the liver and stomach. This body was also opened by direction of Dr. Macneven, who had attended the case, and the examination made in the manner usual in private practice.

Some special circumstances in relation to the last case require a fuller statement, but as they do not relate to the post mortem itself nor at all affect the general conclusions to which your committee have arrived, the facts will be examined separately. Examinations of the kind which have taken place at Ward's Island, would not have been objected to in any hospital known to your committee either for the reception of the totally indigent or of the pay patients; and there are very few intelligent citizens of the most independent circumstances, who would (as all may infer from daily experience) hesitate to permit them to be made upon the remains of their dearest friends or children. As long as they are conducted under such regulations and inspection as may secure a decent care of mortal remains they ought not to shock the feelings of the most fastidious, whilst the practical results redound, not only to the general advance of medical and surgical knowledge and skill, but very often to the immediate benefit of the living requiring aid under similar diseases which may happen to prevail.

Whatever looseness in these examinations may have heretofore occurred, it is believed that its recurrence will be prevented by a rigid adherence to the new rules passed within the present month, and now in the press. It is therefore the decided opinion of the committee that no impediment should be placed in the way of continuing post-mortem examinations whenever they are thought likely to conduce to the public benefit.

There is yet another use made of the remains of the dead, distinct alike from regular anatomical dissection and from simple post-mortem examination. This is the preservation, by injection or otherwise, of some part or organ of the human body peculiarly afflicted by disease or injury, the rest of the body being committed to the grave. As such specimens are desirable only when they present some special or peculiar means of instruction to the student, it is obvious that the great majority of dead bodies afford nothing which would tempt the surgeon to any such use. Some cases, however, had occurred which induced the attending surgeon to retain particular organs for this purpose. In this your committee could not learn that there was any secrecy or concealment. On inquiry respecting the statement made in a newspaper publication, as to a large portion of a body remaining unburied, the following facts appeared: Dr. Carnochan had under treatment a complicated and interesting case of *hernia*. After the death of the party he was desirous to preserve the parts for the use of the hospital, as presenting a peculiarity instructive to the young surgeon for the future treatment of this distressing malady, to which persons employed in various sorts of hard labor are specially exposed. He had also, with the same object, preserved a foot exhibiting a complicated and badly-treated old fracture. These parts had been left in the dead-house, but had been since removed by some person without the knowledge of the physicians. When the committee went to the dead-house, the sexton said that he had found them, and produced them from under the roof.

Such preparations are made in very many public hospitals, and are often procured from private practice. The practice of making them and the amount of the collections are annually reported to the Legislature and published by some of our State institutions, and the collections themselves are open to all who desire to examine them. Of the great utility of such pathological specimens there can be no doubt, and the humblest citizen may, directly or indirectly, in his family or in his own person, experience their benefit. Still, if under the peculiar circumstances of the Ward's Island establishment, it is thought that the preservation of such morbid organs, a portion of persons dying there, though taking place in comparatively few instances amongst the whole number of deaths, is offensive to the feelings of those immediately interested in the welfare of the inmates of the establishment, it is for the Commissioners to decide whether, on this ground alone, the practice should be disallowed for the future.

Whether the change be made or not, your committee cannot find any ground to censure what has hitherto been done.

After presenting these general conclusions from the various examinations on points referred to them, it is proper to remark briefly upon the conduct of some of the younger medical assistants in respect to one of these cases. It is a matter quite personal to them, and does not touch either the mode of post-mortem examinations ordinarily pursued, or the character or conduct of any other physician or surgeon.

This occurred as to the body of a boy named Bennett, the examination of which has been above mentioned as in itself not only unobjectionable, but proper and beneficial. The boy had been under treatment by Dr. Macneven, for an abscess extending across the abdomen and affecting the liver and stomach.

After his death on Thursday, 7th Nov., Dr. Macneven requested the attending house physician, Dr. Ely, to have the body kept for a post-mortem examination.

The following day the body was sent, with a certificate of the clerk of the cause of death (without the physician's signature), to Randall's Island for burial. Dr. Macneven having expressed his disappointment in not being able to examine the corpse, Dr. Ely went in the afternoon to Randall's Island, and obtained from the sexton of Potter's Field the coffin containing the body in question.

The sexton, soon after changing his mind for some reason unexplained (he not being found when sent for by your committee), followed Dr. Ely across the channel to Ward's Island, and took back the coffin where it was returned. Dr. Ely, determined on obtaining the body, crosses over at midnight, accompanied by the sexton of Ward's Island, and, it is said, two other young physicians, had the coffin dug up, Bennett's body taken out, and after placing it in another coffin, took it back with his party to the dead-house at Ward's Island; where the next day, Dr. Macneven, without being apprised of the mode in which the body had been last obtained, proceeded to the post-mortem examination, which was performed in the usual way followed in private practice, and the body was then left for re-interment. The hospital clerk refused afterwards to give a new certificate for burial, and the body remained in its coffin in the dead-house until—Monday or Tuesday morning—it was discovered to have been secretly removed and, it is understood, re-interred.

Dr. Ely, who was the chief actor in these proceedings, left the Island suddenly, whilst the committee were pursuing their inquiries, without giving them an opportunity of questioning him.

The act itself may not amount to the violation of express law, as the body was not taken for the purpose of dissection, nor for pecuniary profit, and if requested for a proper and lawful object might, under the rightful authority, have been taken up and examined with perfect publicity. But the going to the public burying-ground secretly and at midnight, and there disinterring a body, are circumstances so nearly approaching to infraction of the law (if they do not actually amount to it, which it is not for your committee to decide), and are so capable, if overlooked, to lead on to some serious or habitual abuses, that it appears to us to be the duty of the Commissioners to take such measures in relation to the transaction as may exonerate this Board from giving any countenance to this act, and what is of still more importance may restrain other persons hereafter from similar or more serious abuses.

G. C. VERPLANCK.
ADOLF RODEWALD.

27th November, 1850.

REPORT OF MR. DILLON.

Gregory Dillon, one of the Committee appointed at the last meeting of the Board, to inquire into and report upon the management of the Hospitals at Ward's Island, in relation to the charges of dissections and exhumations alleged to be practised there, has the honor to report:

That, on Thursday last, the committee consisting of Messrs. Verplanck, Rodewald and myself, proceeded to Ward's Island, in the performance of the duty assigned to us; but before leaving the city, I proposed to the chairman, that some public officer, authorized to administer oaths, be requested to accompany us, in order that we might make a thorough examination, and be enabled to report to the Board the facts of the case, founded upon legal testimony. I regret to say that my views were not concurred in. Upon arriving at the wharf opposite to the island, we were accosted by a gentleman who represented himself to be a reporter from one of the daily papers of the city, and desired to have the permission of the committee to attend the investigation. Believing that the attention of the public cannot be too frequently called, or too closely directed, to the management of our public institutions—particularly to one so distant and so peculiarly circumstanced as that on Ward's Island—I was desirous that the reporter should be admitted, but was overruled by my associates of the committee. Immediately after our arrival on the island, we commenced the investigation, by examining, orally, three of the visiting physicians—Drs. Macneven, Cox, and Hosack—the hospital clerk, Mr. P. Coghlan; the sexton, John Faly; James Doyle, patient in the tenth shanty; and Matthew Gilmore, assistant sexton on Randall's Island.

It would encumber this report, and extend it to an unnecessary length were I to give in detail the examinations thus made. I have accordingly annexed them to this report, that the Board may refer to them for the purpose of deciding whether they justify the conclusions to which I have arrived. It is my opinion, as the result of these examinations, that the charges of improper conduct in the management at Ward's Island, to which the attention of the Board has been drawn, and which the committee was bound to investigate, have not in any degree been exaggerated, but are strictly true. The Board will recollect that I strenuously opposed the new plan for the re-organization of the medical department at the island, and that I frequently urged as a radical objection, that it would open the Emigrant Hospital as a school of experiment for mere medical students, who would operate upon the patients without the constant supervision of superior medical authority, which was absolutely necessary for the protection of the patients. All my anticipations, I regret to say, have been more than realized. Treated worse than the dead of the prisons, strange to say, no less than three-fourths in number of all the emigrants who have died since the new medical organization was established, have been subjected to post-mortem dissections.

If the dissections had been confined to those patients who were here without friends or relatives, it would then have involved simply a violation of the rights of the dead; but two cases were proved to us, in which children were dissected without the permission of their parents, and in wanton violation of their rights and feelings, although the parents had been to the island to make preparations for the decent burial of their offspring. In one of these cases, even after the child had been buried, one of the young physicians so far forgot the rights of the father and his own duty, that in the dead of night he, in company with two other house physicians, went to the grave-yard at Potter's Field, and with his own hands dug up the remains of the child and carried them to the dead-house for dissection, thus superadding to the other enormities of this transaction a violation of a law of the State. It also appeared before the committee, that in some cases, after dissection, the bodies were not buried entire, but parts were taken away by the physicians as it pleased them; and that portions of different bodies were thrown into the same coffin, and buried together. I must refer the Board, however, for a more particular statement, to the examination of the witnesses, annexed to this report, and which will be found to justify my opinion, that the late proceedings at Ward's Island are scandalous, and demand immediate action on the part of the Board. What action should be taken will be very apparent, when we consider the causes which have led to these proceedings; they are twofold:

First. The present organization of the medical department is radically defective. Ten visiting physicians and surgeons, at $600 a year each, residing in the city, alternately paying daily visits to the island, in which the mere going and returning consume three hours of the day, cannot possibly give proper attention to the sick, or afford to us that guarantee for the faithful discharge of their duty by the students, nurses, and others employed in the department, which we should require. A physician of known skill and established reputation, with such assistants as he may deem necessary, should be appointed, and should reside permanently on the island, and devote his whole time and energy to the emigrant sick. Such, I understand, is the practice at the Bloomingdale Asylum, and that it works admirably. If, in addition to one responsible head, it should be deemed advisable, as well for benefit of the sick as for the advancement of medical science, that eminent professors from the city should be allowed or invited to visit the hospital, I would interpose no objection. But then it must be distinctly understood that their attendance must be strictly confined to the mere purpose of prescription and of clinical lectures. They must be made to know that under no circumstances can they have any authority to dissect or exhume the friendless emigrant. If medical science cannot be advanced without violating the rights of the dead, the law of the land, or the sacred feelings of the living, I prefer that it should stand still.

Secondly. The late scandalous proceedings at Ward's Island may be traced to another cause, which penetrates through all our establishments, and works quietly but with the most baleful effect. I refer to the opinion entertained by many that the emigrants are paupers, and are, therefore, entitled only to pauper consideration. This is a radical error. It is a mistake of fact which leads to serious consequences, and (said Mr. Dillon, *viva voce*) I am sorry to say that the gentlemen associated with me on the committee are of the same opinion. They are not paupers in any just sense of the term; they were called paupers when they were a charge upon the city, and before this commission was established; but the returns show that they never have been paupers, and are not paupers now. Every emigrant that comes to our shores pays a dollar and fifty cents to this Commission. Those who have health spread over the country, to increase our wealth and prosperity; those who are sick are relieved by the fund to which all, both well and sick, have contributed, and the fund is sufficient, and in my opinion more than sufficient under proper management. The whole class, therefore, are, as it were, underwriters for each of their number, and by their own aggregate contributions alone relieve the misfortunes of one another.

It is true that we, the members of this Board, render our services gratuitously; but a fund, to which no citizen of this State contributes a farthing, and which is found sufficient to pay upwards of $5,000 per annum to a resident physician at the quarantine, and $3,000 to a general agent and his private secretary, cannot, with any propriety, be called a pauper fund—at least by those who contribute nothing to it. But so long as this opinion shall prevail—so long as your general agent, physicians and other employées shall consider the emigrants to be paupers, and their fund to be a pauper fund, so long shall we fail in securing to the sick and wretched emigrants that consideration which not merely humanity, but his rights, demand. Let us employ in our service only those who truly understand the nature and character of the fund which we are honored to disburse, and we shall then find that a general and proper sympathy for the emigrant will prevail, without which all our efforts in his behalf will be fruitless. It is my opinion, therefore, and I recommend that early measures be taken to reform the present organization of the medical department at Ward's Island, to remodel it upon the plan to which I have alluded, and to dismiss from service the general agent, and all others employed by this commission, who have failed to evince towards the emigrants that sympathy and consideration to which they are entitled. And, in the meantime, I recommend for immediate action, that the chairman notify those physicians who have been engaged in dissecting or exhuming bodies at Ward's Island, that this Board no longer require their services.

Respectfully submitted,

GREGORY DILLON.

November 20, 1850.

Grand Jury Room, 20*th Dec.*, 1850.

The grand inquest of the county having had under consideration certain charges in reference to mal-practices at Ward's Island, after investigating the same, and having heard all the evidence adduced in relation thereto, have adopted the following resolution:

Resolved, From all the testimony before the grand jury, they can come to no other conclusion, than that the Commissioners of Emigration, instead of being obnoxious to censure by them, deserve their highest commendation for the correct and humane manner in which they have managed the affairs of the Commission.

WM. S. CONELY, *Foreman*.

JOSHUA S. UNDERHILL, *Assistant Clerk*.

To the Court of General Sessions of the Peace in and for the city and county of New York.

The minority of the grand jury sent in the following communication:

The undersigned members of the grand inquest beg leave to present that they do not concur in the resolution adopted by the majority of their body in reference to the Commissioners of Emigration, and protest against the same, as they do not think the said Commissioners are entitled to the commendation contained in said resolution.

ANDREW CLARK,
BERNARD MAGUIRE.

New York, *Grand Jury Room*, 20*th Dec.*, 1850.

Appendix No. 5.

REPORT

On the subjects in dispute between the Commissioners of Emigration and the Alms-house Department of the City of New York.

To the Commissioners of Emigration:

The Special Committee on the laws, organization, and operations of the Commissioners of Emigration, to whom were referred a report of a Committee of the Governors of the New York Alms-house.

That while the Commissioners, in the judgment of this committee, have much cause to congratulate themselves and the public on the successful results, as well pecuniary as humane, of the great charity committed to their charge, they cannot but express their deep regret at the absence of that sympathy and harmony which a mutual benevolence and a common object ought to produce on the part of a sister Institution, to which has been confided the distribution of the alms of this city. This regret is increased by the fact that these differences have been made public at a time when an amicable submission of them to the arbitrament of distinguished citizens had been arranged, and before those gentlemen had an opportunity to decide or investigate the matters submitted.

Previously to 1847, the year in which this Commission was instituted the expenses of all the poor, both native and foreign born, who sought public relief here, were defrayed by the Commissioners of the Alms-house, and the tax-payers of this city assessed for their support. The same was the case in other cities and counties of the State. The amount thus paid was so large as to be the cause of frequent complaints. To these was added an apprehension, on the part of our citizens, of the spreading of the contagious diseases with which many newly-arrived emigrants were afflicted in the autumn of 1846, and spring of 1847. These grave subjects attracted the attention of the Legislature. To remove, or at least diminish them, was the object of the legislation, from which resulted this Commission.

It is true, that before 1847 there was a law requiring bonds to be given by ship-owners to indemnify the county from loss; but it was practically found that paupers were either supported in private establishments, by the agents of the ship-owners, in a manner often revolting to humanity, and producing disease and death, or the sums received, owing to the defects in the law, were so small as to be entirely inadequate, and scarcely worthy of notice. This provision, besides, was intended only for the relief of this county, and extended to no other.

The law of 1847 imposed substantially a tax of $1 50 for every emigrant arriving at this port in a vessel from a foreign country; and out of the funds thus raised the Commissioners of Emigration were directed to indemnify, as far as might be, the several cities, &c., of the State, for any expense which might be incurred for such persons, and that such appropriations should be in proportion to the expenses incurred by said cities, &c., severally. The powers and duties thus conferred were merely those appertaining to disbursing officers. The several cities, &c., were to be paid, as far as the receipts were sufficient for that purpose; but no one county, or town, or city, was to have any advantage over any other county, town, or city; but each was to receive a rateable portion with the others, according to the amount of expense it had incurred.

The Superintendents of the poor in other counties, the Governors of the Alms-house in this, and the Commissioners of Emigration, are each creatures of the law which specifies and defines their duties. It is not for them to decide what the law ought to be, but to perform their duties under the law as it is. A denunciation of the Commissioners for not doing what the law does not direct, but in substance prohibits, is as improper and as unreasonable as a refusal on the other side to perform what the statute requires.

As has been stated, the Commissioners—now called the Governors—of the Alms-house, were, previously to 1847, the general almoners of the city. No law since that time has changed their duties or diminished their responsibilities in that respect. They are as much liable now as ever to furnish accommodations for all the poor who reside and seek public relief here. In regard to emigrants, however, who have arrived at the port of New York since May, 1847, and who have not been in the country five years, the Commissioners of Emigration are directed to indemnify them "as far as may be," according to the expenses incurred.

It was never intended that the Governors should be the proprietors of a boarding-house for emigrants, out of which to make profit, but simply that they should be indemnified for their actual outlay, to the extent aforesaid. When the Commissioners of Emigration agreed to pay three dollars a week for the support of each emigrant lunatic (arriving as above stated) in the asylum on Blackwell's Island, it was on the supposition that the maintenance of each inmate would cost the Alms-house that amount. But when the Commissioners discovered, by the reports of the Governors, that this supposition was erroneous, and that the support of each emigrant cost considerably less, they put an end to the contract, as they were in duty to the other counties, towns, and cities of the State (regarding the rateable division of their fund) bound to do, and claimed that for the future they should not be obliged to pay more than the expenses actually incurred.

The Commissioners are invested by the same law with a discretion in regard to erecting buildings, and of themselves taking care of and supporting those who would otherwise become a charge on the several counties, towns, and cities of the State. Seeing the lack of accommodation, not arising from design or want of prudence on the part of the Governors, but from the vastly increasing and unexpected number of applicants for public aid, and believing that in this city they could take care of and support such emigrants, in certain cases, as comfortably as at the Alms-house, and at a less price than would be incurred by the city for them, the Commissioners determined to exercise this discretion to a certain extent, and therefore erected buildings for the reception and care of all emigrants who had arrived at this port, and who needed public assistance or medical treatment, except small-pox patients in the city, and lunatics. Of the latter there was not at first a sufficient number to justify the expense of erecting a special hospital, although that is now in contemplation, as soon as those to be supported and the means will justify the outlay. The Commissioners also thought it unadvisable and imprudent then to increase the number of hospitals for that highly contagious disease, small-pox, the Governors of the Alms-house having already such a hospital; although at present, and for some three years past, small-pox patients have been sent to a separate building at Quarantine, exclusively appropriated to their reception. All other cases the Commissioners are willing to, and do, receive into their institutions on Ward's Island; and when it is intimated that a numerous class "of syphilis patients, or those affected with a kindred disease, who are chargeable to this Commission," are treated or maintained by the Governors of the Alms-house, the intimation involves either a rhetorical fiction, or, if true, shows a neglect of duty in not sending them to Ward's Island, where, so far as this city is concerned, they by law belong.

The case of vagrants, as well as other cases involving imprisonment, is quite different. Vagrancy, by our law, is a misdemeanor. Men are imprisoned for it as for petit larceny or other misdemeanors, and committed for not more than six months, and "kept at hard labor." By the sentence of the Court they are deprived of the opportunity of earning their own livelihood, and are obliged to work for the benefit of the city. Why, then, should the Commissioners of Emigration be charged for their support, any more than for the maintenance of an emigrant sent to Blackwell's Island for theft, or to the State Prison for burglary, or arson, or any other felony, "there to be kept at hard labor"? The Commissioners are not penitentiary officers, but merely disbursing officers of a charitable fund collected to indemnify for paupers, not to pay for the support of criminals, who may, for aught that is known, earn enough to support themselves by the "hard labor" to which they have been sentenced.

That convicts from abroad, and inmates of foreign poor-houses, have been shipped to this country, and passed from shipboard into our Alms-houses, is no new matter. The Commissioners called the attention of the Legislature to these facts four years ago; but that body declined to act, doubtful, perhaps, of its powers under the Constitution. The Commissioners have also submitted the matter to the consideration of the General Government, whose powers upon the subject are undoubted. The Commissioners have endeavored to trace such cases, have imposed penalties upon the vessels bringing them, and aided to return them whence they came; and if they have not done more, it has not been from negligence or want of disposition, but purely from insufficiency of power. They cordially unite in the hope that this subject may become matter of treaty regulation; but whilst indulging in this hope, they also protest against this importation of criminals and paupers, to which they have interposed all the opposition with which the law has clothed them, being invoked as a cause of censure against them. Besides, any foreign pauper or foreign convict, whose support is chargeable to the fund under the control of this Commission, if in need of support, is sent to Ward's Island; but any other foreign pauper or foreign convict, arriving by way of Canada or otherwise, whose support is not chargeable upon this fund, must be supported in the same manner as a native pauper.

It seems to have been strangely overlooked by the Governors, that the Commissioners of Emigration are not responsible for all foreigners who have not been in this country five years. The law prohibits the expenditure of any of this fund except for those who have come in vessels from a foreign country, arriving at the port of New York, or for those who have not been in this country one year, and who have arrived at this port in a ship or vessel from any other of the United States, and have paid commutation, and by thus paying commutation have contributed to the only fund from which the Commissioners can defray their expenses. The unqualified statements, therefore, that "in the workhouses there are 173 inmates known to be less than five years residents," and "in the Penitentiary 112 foreigners resident less than five years," and "of the foreigners 582 had been resident less than five years," if made and published as evidence from which the public is to infer that the Governors are supporting those whom this Commission ought by law to maintain, are as unsatisfactory as unjust. Emigrants arrive at Quebec, Boston, Philadelphia, Baltimore, and New Orleans, not to mention other Atlantic ports, and without doubt many of these, within five years from the time of their arrival, find their way by inland routes to this city, and into its Alms-house and Penitentiary. None know better than the city almoners, that for such the Commissioners are in no way responsible. They know further, that the Commissioners are prohibited from using any of their fund for the support of such. Your Committee cannot believe that these statements, and the calculation based thereon, are made with intent to influence the judgment of our citizens in regard to this Commission, because, if thus intended, they would in fact amount to an attempt, by concealment of known enactments which are daily acted upon by the Governors, to mislead and deceive the public.

Your Committee regrets that the Governors in their statement, by neglect, or intentionally, should have omitted so material a fact in regard to the "nine hundred insane patients belonging to the Commissioners of Emigration," treated in the Asylum, as that the Commissioners have paid the Governors over $93,490 for such lunatics, and hold themselves ready and able to pay the balance, if any, when the gentlemen to whom it has been arranged to submit this and other matters, have made their decision in the premises.

The Commissioners do not cause this emigration, neither is it in their power, or within their province, to stop or attempt to stop it. It is the result of causes far removed from the control of any body of men—oppression, poverty, small wages, scarcity of land, and a thousand other causes abroad. Freedom, fair remuneration for services, abundance of fertile and unoccupied tracts, and innumerable other inducements in this country, produce this emigration. It is doubtless an evil to have either convicts or pauper emigrants introduced into the country; but your Committee submits that the advantages which the city derives from emigration to this port greatly overbalance that evil, and more than compensate for the fact gravely charged, that eight or ten stray emigrants have, according to the report of the Governors, found refuge in the Alms-house, instead of being sent to the institutions of the Commissioners.

Emigration employs, and profitably rewards, a large portion of our mercantile marine. The receipts from passage money exceed the amount received for freights on all the exports of the United States. On the arrival of the emigrants here, our laborers and cartmen are employed in the removal of their baggage, our boarding-house keepers in affording them food and accommodations, others in supplying them with such various necessaries as after a long sea voyage persons in their circumstances require; and when they take their departure from the city, our steamboats, and railroads, and canals, are profitably employed in their transportation. In addition to this, German emigrants alone have for the past three years, as is estimated by the best German authorities, brought into the country annually an average of about eleven millions of dollars. A larger amount of property in proportion to numbers is also estimated to have come from Holland and other countries. The amount of money thus expended for supplies and for labor, and introduced into the country, is incalculable; and when the profits to our citizens from these sources are duly considered, the expense of such eight or ten stray emigrants becomes an insignificant item.

The Commissioners are authorized to take care of emigrants alone. During the seven years of their existence, many emigrant females have been delivered of children in the hospitals of the Commissioners. These children are not emigrants, but native-born, and their care and maintenance belong to the Governors of the Alms-house; and the expense of taking care of them, your Committee is advised, is an equitable set-off, to some extent at least, to the claims of the Governors for lunatics and small-pox patients. This is denied by the latter, and the Commissioners are told to send such children to the alms-house. They are willing, and have offered, to do so provided the Governors will also take charge of the mothers, for whose expenses they will be indemnified. This is refused, on the ground that the mothers, being emigrants, are properly inmates of the Institutions on Ward's Island, and will not be received into the poor-house. And thus the Commissioners are obliged to be either guilty of the inhumanity of separating tender babes from their mothers, or must bear the expenses of thousands of infants chargeable of right to another fund and another body. The Commissioners have adopted the latter alternative, and will, for humanity's sake, continue so to do, although the Governors thereby may be relieved from a burden which they of right ought to bear.

Your Committee deems it proper, before concluding, to state that the laws under which the Commissioners act have been of great benefit, in a pecuniary point of view, to the tax-payers of the State, and especially to those of this city; and leaving out of view for the present the large amount yearly expended in returning paupers and others to Europe, in transportation of emigrants to their friends away from the city, and for indemnifying other counties in the State, your Committee proposes to show the amount annually laid out in this city by this Commission, for the support of those who otherwise would have been inmates of the Alms-house here, and a burden on our tax-paying citizens.

The Commission was organized in May, 1847. During the last eight months of that year there was expended, as above stated:

	$77,542
1848	149,564
1849	303,852
1850	246,498
1851	274,541
1852	292,595
1853	292,036
1854 (estimated)	365,000
In all	$2,000,658

Besides, from May, 1847, to first October of this year, the Commissioners have indemnified the other counties of the State to the amount of $420,040.*

Your Committee would call special attention to this fact,—that the fund under their charge is derived exclusively from emigrants arriving at this port direct from a foreign country, and that out of the sixty counties of this State the poor-officers of the county of New York alone seem to burden it with the support of those who never contributed a cent towards it.

In conclusion, your Committee invites the strictest examination into their operations, and the mode in which, under the law, the Commissioners have disbursed the moneys subject to their control. Your Committee is satisfied of a just intention in all such transactions.

All of the Commissioners of Emigration excepting the Mayor of Brooklyn, are, as all their predecessors have been, residents and tax-payers in this city, and have been and are, therefore, interested in the diminution of the taxes of the city. In all their dealings, however, with this sacred fund—a fund raised from the poor, the homeless, and the stranger—your Committee is satisfied that investigation will prove the Commissioners to have been as little influenced by their own private interests as by any sentiment of rivalry, or motives of jealousy or injustice towards those who are laboring in the same broad field of benevolence. In this work there is abundance of room for kindliness of feeling and harmony of action. These the Commissioners desire; but, if unfortunately denied, they then ask nothing more than that their motives should not be impeached or their actions misrepresented.

G. C. VERPLANCK,
AND. CARRIGAN,
E. CRABTREE.

New York, Dec. 15, 1854.

* For particulars see Table E.

Appendix No. 6.

REPORT

On the subjects in dispute between the Commissioners of Emigration and the Alms-house Department of the City of New York.

Mr. Verplanck, from the Committee to which was referred the recent Report of the Governors of the Alms-house, in regard to this Commission,

Respectfully reports:

That it is alike a matter of regret and astonishment, considering the opportunities and the duty of the Governors to become familiar with the facts and the law affecting the controversy between them and this Commission, that so many misstatements as are contained in their report should have been given to the public, and that the tone and language of such report should have been so overbearing and offensive.

It is well known that whatever may have been the matters in dispute between the Governors and the Commission, it has endeavored to observe due civility in action and words towards the Alms-house Department, and all its officers. It is therefore difficult to account for this unprovoked attack, unless the Governors suppose that the public may not distinguish between such angry and unjustifiable assaults and sound argument warmly argued. A good cause rejects all such extraneous and unworthy aids; and your Committee, in discussing the differences between the two boards, hope to avoid these peculiarities of the Governors, and will only notice them when they impugn the fair dealing of the Commission.

Before entering into an examination of the report, your Committee would suggest, for the consideration of the public and the Governors, this preliminary matter. The Governors, in all their discussions with this Commission, undertake, as they have done in this report, to announce the law, and define its meaning. This is done in a manner so off-hand and confident as almost to carry along with it the conviction that the Governors, like the king, can do no wrong and commit no error. Yet the action of the Governors fairly leads to the opinion that it is taken either in ignorance or contempt of the theory and the statutes upon which the Commission is organized. Nor is this Commission to blame for this want of knowledge, if such exist, on the part of the Governors. Almost a year ago, a public attempt was made to explain to them these statutes; and what was then said is now repeated:

"The law of 1847 substantially requires a payment of \$1 50 (since increased to \$2) for every emigrant arriving at this port in a vessel from a foreign country; and out of the funds thus raised the Commissioners of Emigration were directed to indemnify, as far as might be, the several cities

&c., of the State, for any expense which might be incurred for such persons, and that such appropriation should be in proportion to the expenses incurred by said cities, &c., severally. The powers and duties thus conferred were merely those of disbursing officers. The several cities, &c., were to be paid as far as the receipts were sufficient for that purpose; but no one county, town, or city, was to have any advantage over any other county, or town, or city, but each was to receive a ratable portion with the others, according to the amount of expenses it had incurred. The superintendents of the poor in other counties, the Governors of the Alms-house in this city, and the Commissioners of Emigration, are each creatures of the law, which specifies and defines their duties. It is not for them to decide what the law ought to be, but to perform their duties under the law as it is. A denunciation of the Commissioners for not doing what the law does not direct, but in substance prohibits, is as improper and unreasonable as a refusal on the other side to perform what the statute requires."

It is supposed that, holding such relation to the law, obedience to its directions would not be made a subject of condemnation or of sneers. Yet, whenever a refusal to comply with any of the unreasonable demands of the Governors is made, because a compliance would be without the authority or in violation of law, the Commission is accused of resorting to "quibbles."

Your Committee now propose to examine the complaints and some of the other statements contained in the Governors' report.

The causes urged against the Commission may be reduced to three points.

1. That bills for support of emigrants at the Penitentiary from 1849 to 1853, and on Blackwell's Island and at Bellevue Hospital, from "1849 to 1854, six years," amounting to $49,500, are unpaid.

Yet the Governors ought to know full well that there is neither substance nor legality in this claim. The persons for whom this charge is made were committed to the various institutions named, as vagrants; and last year this Commission presented the Governors with their views in regard to it as follows:

"The case of vagrants, as well as all other cases involving imprisonment, is quite different; vagrancy, by our laws, is a misdemeanor. Men are imprisoned for it, as for petit larceny, or other misdemeanors, and committed for not more than six months, and 'kept at hard labor.' By the sentence of the court, they are deprived of the opportunity of earning their livelihood, and are obliged to work for the benefit of the city. Why, then, should the Commissioners of Emigration be charged for their support, any more than for the maintenance of an emigrant sent to Blackwell's Island for theft, or to the State prison for burglary or arson, or any other felony 'there to be kept at hard labor'?"

The Commissioners are not penitentiary officers, but merely disbursing officers of a charitable fund collected to indemnify for paupers, not to pay for the support of criminals, who may, for aught that is known, earn enough to support themselves by the hard labor to which they have been sentenced.

With this view of the case, the Governors were not satisfied, and appealed to the Legislature last winter. That body, the creators of both the Governors and this Commission, by its action, declared that there was no validity in this claim, and utterly repudiated it. Yet, the Governors, with their habitual determination and pertinacity, without regarding this legislative action, again bring forth and parade their claim for public inspection, and when, in justification of its disallowance of this claim, this Commission invokes the argument above urged, the law and the repudiation of it by the Legislature, it is answered only by the contemptuous reply, "It is a legal quibble."

The Commissioners have had running accounts with an average of forty other counties in this State, for the last eight years, and of them all the Alms-house Department of this city is the only one that has ever made such a charge as this, or set up any such claim.

II. The next cause of complaint is this, that this Commission has not paid bills which "have been presented," amounting to $48,412, for support of inmates of lunatic asylums, workhouse, penitentiary, hospital, and for interments in the city cemetery.

If this Commission, considering the great numbers chargeable to its funds, being no less than the entire emigration of the last five years, were to pay all the "bills presented," especially as made up according to the peculiar ideas of the Alms-house Department, it could easily exhaust its annual fund at a very early period of the year. It is, however, customary to examine "bills presented," and to compare them with the ships' manifests on record in this office; and thus have been and are all such bills adjusted and liquidated by the auditor. That officer, after proper examination, has made to your Committee the following report of the bills presented and adjusted, according to the rules and practice between the Alms-house Department and this body:—

Balance due to New York Alms-house on January 1, 1853		$19,200 68
Amount of bills rendered and allowed for 1853		24,768 03
" " 1854		17,536 98
" " from Jan. 1, 1855, to July 1, 1855		5,900 42
Amount of bills rendered July and August, 1855, not yet examined		2,110 36
Total		$69,516 47
1853—July 6, cash	$5,000 00	
1853—Oct. 5, cash	10,000 00	
1853—Oct. 26, cash	5,000 00	
1854—May 31, cash	10,000 00	
1854—Nov. 8, cash	17,525 36	
1855—June 13, cash interments	1,109 50	
1855—Sept. 6, cash interments	140 00	— 48,774 86
Balance due		$20,741 61

Thus, instead of a proper claim of $43,412 32, the actual amount on this particular charge is only $20,741 61, somewhat less than one-half of the amount claimed thereon by the Governors, and a little more than one-fifth of the general indebtedness stated by them.

This Commission, in the judgment of your Committee, and of counsel, has a fair and equitable offset to this $20,741 61, and it is willing to submit it to the public decision.

This offset was last year stated, and is now repeated, as follows:—

"The Commissioners are authorized to take care of emigrants alone. During the seven years of their existence many emigrant mothers have been delivered of children in the hospitals of the Commissioners. These children are not emigrants, but native-born; and their care and maintenance belong to the Governors of the Alms-house; and the expenses of taking care of them, your Committee is advised, is an equitable set-off, to some extent, at least, to the claims of the Governors for lunatics and small-pox patients. This is denied by the latter, and the Commissioners are told to send such children to the Alms-house. They are willing, and have offered, to do so provided the Governors will also take charge of the mothers, for whose expenses they will be indemnified. This is refused on the ground, that the mothers, being emigrants, are properly inmates of the Institutions on Ward's Island, and will not be received into the poor-house. And thus the Commissioners are obliged to be either guilty of the inhumanity of separating tender babes from their mothers, or must bear the expenses of thousands of infants chargeable of right to another fund and another body."

The above has been the case for over eight years, and the amount expended for such children is computed to exceed $50,000. The Governors, however, refuse to allow it; and it is therefore to be the subject of arbitration or litigation. It is well worth while, however, to observe in the above statement, the ground upon which its disallowance is placed by the honorable the Governors, and to consider whether it may not be that the "quibble"—the mote in the eye of the Commission—is not seen by the Governors from behind a beam in their own optics.

Even, however, allowing that the Commissioners are in error in claiming an equitable allowance on this account, equal at least to the balance claimed by the Governors, still assuredly, when it is considered that this unadjusted balance of $20,700 is on a long account, upon which payments of seven times that amount have been actually made, and that over a hundred times that amount have been expended for the use of the city by this Commission, a little delay in settlement can hardly justify the broad charges of the Governors, and still less can it afford any ground for the assertion, that it will "compel this department to call for a sum of not less than $100,000 for the special purpose of providing for the impositions of the Commissioners of Emigration not otherwise provided for."

If a deficiency in the large grants to the Governors has occurred, requiring such an additional call from the department, it must arise from "impositions" from some other quarter than the Commissioners of Emigration.

In this connection, it may be well to advert to the remark of the Governors, that this Commission has paid large sums to the other counties, while it has passed New York by.

The Governors know very well, yet seem studiously to conceal the fact, that fifty cents out of every two dollars received by this Commission, are by express law appropriated and set aside as a separate fund, out of which expenses of emigration in all the counties, *except New York*, are to be paid. The Commissioners did not advise the enactment of this act, and are in no way responsible for it. This provision was first advised and recommended to the Legislature by a convention of county poor-officers. The Commissioners considering that the great mass of those who would otherwise fall immediately upon the city of New York, were taken care of in their own establishments, and that thus the city was always first relieved from this burden, saw no reason to oppose this appropriation of the additional fund, and assented to it. Since its passage in 1853, no money, except from this fund of fifty cents, has been paid to the counties, and that from time to time as the law requires. When, therefore, the Commission is reprimanded for paying the counties other than New York, the censure is simply for the performance of a duty, which the law specially enjoins.

In the next place, this Commission expends for the benefit of the county of New York an amount ten times greater than for any other county in the State, and four times as large as that paid to all the other counties together.

At an earlier period of the Commission, it was judged by the then Commissioners, Messrs. R. B. Minturn, Havemeyer, Bierwith, the late Messrs. Colden, Jacob Harvey, Dillon and others, advisable to establish hospitals and refuges in this county, instead of allowing the emigrants to be maintained in the city establishments. This was done after mature deliberation and calculation leading to the conviction that this fund could be thus administered with more economy than the then experience had shown the city's had been. A comparison of the expenses of the Commission in this city, and of the Almshouse Department during the same time, as exhibited in the reports, will show that these gentlemen were not in error in their decision.

In this county, therefore, this Commission purchased lands and erected refuges and hospitals; in no other county, except Richmond, where the Marine Hospital, for the protection of this city from the introduction of disease, is located, has this been done. In the other counties, all the emigrant poor requiring public aid, are maintained in the county poor-houses. Such would have been the case here had not the Commissioners institutions of their own. The amount expended in these is therefore in effect so much paid to the city of New York, for to that extent is this city relieved; yet the Governors report as though the Commissioners, who, with the exception of the Mayor of Brooklyn, are all residents and tax-payers in this city, paid nothing for the city, but were acting adversely to its claims and its interests.

The aggregate amount thus expended for the city, and to which extent it was relieved from taxation, is, since 1847, the year of the organization of this commission, over $2,250,000, and has been for the last five years at the rate of over $300,000 a year. It must be always borne in mind that the Commissioners of Emigration have no discretion as to the amount of their expenditures, nor any claim on the city or State treasury to make up deficiencies or enlarge their income, but they are the administrators of a limited and fluctuating fund raised from the emigration itself; that the Legislature never made it their duty, nor ever expected, that they should support or pay for all emigrant poor, under all circumstances, but merely prescribed that they should do so as far as the fund would allow, either by institutions of their own, or by repayments to the counties on which such persons became chargeable. The administration of the Commission, however imperfect, has thus far exceeded the expectation of the Legislature, having, during eight years, entirely supported the whole of such poor in this city, the whole quarantine and marine hospitals of this port, and refunded the counties in full to within the last few months, during which last period a dividend of 65 per cent. has been paid.

III. The third and last point of complaint by the Governors is the refusal of the Commissioners to receive the lunatics who have been tendered, according to their resolutions. On this the Governors expend a great deal of unnecessary indignation. If the spirit of fairness were as evident in the Governors' report as is their eagerness to embarrass and misrepresent the Commission, they would not have been guilty of some important omissions which your Committee will proceed to supply.

Last winter the Governors, in the same style as they now propose, "united themselves as a committee," and proceeded to Albany to correct the abuses in this Commission, and to amend the defects in the emigrant laws. A bill for that purpose was accordingly introduced into and passed the Assembly, without notice to this Commission. In that bill was a clause, authorizing the Governors to transfer lunatics to the charge of the Commissioners, just as they have recently attempted, and of the refusal to receive whom by the Commissioners they so much complain.

This clause was stricken out by the Senate, and the whole idea of such a thing repudiated. The Governors return to New York, and holding up the Commissioners to public view as adverse to the city—mal-administrators of the law—violators of "the legal pledge," under which they receive the commutation fund, exhibit the great respect entertained by themselves for law and legislative action, by attempting to do just exactly what the law forbids and the Legislature has but recently prohibited.

Then, again, the Commissioners have no authority or right to receive lunatics. The laws of the State are express on that point. Lunatics are to be examined by two Justices of the Peace, and committed to such secure place as may be provided by the overseers of the poor—in this city, by the Governors. It is made the duty of the Governors to provide such place, and if a public asylum, the approval of it by the supervisors is necessary. The Governors have not and cannot provide any of the institutions on Ward's Island as a fit place for lunatics, such as would meet the approbation of the supervisors, for there is no such edifice on that island. Yet, in full view of this law and these facts, the Governors undertake to transfer to an irresponsible place lunatics who have been committed to their charge by the judgment of a court, and for whose custody they are responsible to their friends and to the public. They complain, too, that the Commissioners, troubled perhaps by a "quibble," refused to aid them in their open and direct violation of the statutes.

The law makes such an act as the Governors contemplated and attempted a misdemeanor, punishable by fine and imprisonment; and but for the resistance of the Commissioners to this attempted unlawful act, the Governors might have found themselves inmates, instead of visitors, of their Penitentiary establishment on Blackwell's Island.

Your Committee, having thus disposed of the claims and charges in the report of the Governors, deem it a proper time to call attention to some past matters, and the action had thereon.

From time to time, during the last few years, differences of opinion have arisen between the Commission and the Governors in regard to the duties of each, and the meaning of various parts of the law under which they acted. Committees of conference were appointed and meetings held. A proposition was made by the Committee of this Board to submit the questions of law to the Corporation counsel, the legal adviser of the city and of the Governors; but this offer was declined by the other side.

Another proposition was then submitted and adopted, that certain points should be left to arbitration; and the Hon. J. I. Coddington, who had been one of the Governors, the Hon. William F. Havemeyer, formerly of this Commission, and Judge William Kent, were selected as arbitrators. Other points were on a case made to be submitted to the decision of the Supreme Court. After this had been done, new points were from time to time presented by the Governors, with the desire that they should be included in the above arrangement. Three several times, as these new points were thus presented, this Commission consented to the alteration; and in agreeing to the last gave their consent, on the assurance that there should be no more offered. This occurred last December.

As soon as the Legislature were assembled in January last, the Governors, unmindful of this arrangement, prepared and caused to be introduced into the Assembly a bill, retroactive in its effect, which was to settle, by legislation, the most material of the points which they had agreed should be decided as above mentioned. Your Committee have no comments to make upon this extraordinary movement, except to say that the Legislature refused to interpose or make any alteration in the emigrant laws, except to include for the future, but not for the past, (although this was proposed, desired, and advocated by the Governors,) among those chargeable to the emigrant fund, certain classes of emigrants who might be confined after conviction as vagrants or disorderly persons.

This law thus obtained, while matters involved in it had been made the subject of amicable adjustment, was soon followed by the commencement of an action against the Commissioners, which is now pending. Thus the Governors have taken even legal measures against this Commission; but, as usual, not satisfied with the laws, or the remedies which the laws afford, an offensive report is made, from which it is fairly to be inferred that no legal steps have been adopted against this Commission, although a suit had, before that report was made, actually been commenced.

Your Committee, nevertheless, would recommend, and do hereby offer, if this report be adopted and approved, to proceed with the agreement of submission to Messrs. Coddington, Havemeyer and Kent, as above stated, or agree to any other equally competent and known disinterested gentlemen, and thus, without litigation and without feeling, to dispose of the matters at issue between the Governors and this Commission.

Even had the claim of the Governors been far better founded than it has been shown to be, the Commissioners, after having for the last eight years diminished the burdens of the city, and paid annually large sums directly to the Governors, for the support of the insane, whom they had no means of keeping, had a right to expect a kind and liberal indulgence at this peculiar juncture. It is a matter of public notoriety, which must be familiar to all the Governors, that a great and unexpected diminution of emigration has occurred since January, 1855, and a consequent reduction of more than one-half of the usual income of the Commission; while the number of persons chargeable in former years, and the consequent expense, remained the same. A vigorous and efficient reduction of expense, in all departments, rendered practicable by the immense benefits arising from their lately-acquired Castle Garden establishment, will, it is expected, hereafter make the diminished income quite adequate to the diminished expenses. In the mean while, however, a period of temporary financial embarrassment in the affairs of the Commission could not but occur; and during the recess of the Legislature the Commissioners had a right to look for a confiding and generous forbearance, if not effective aid, from institutions laboring in the same cause. This they regret not to have found from the Governors.

Your Committee, in conclusion, utterly regrets these public discussions, and would have recommended silence in these matters, had not the report of the Governors been replete with misstatements, unfair imputations, unfounded claims, and angry charges. As, however, they have thought proper to submit these matters to the decision of the public, your Committee do not decline the cause or the tribunal.

This Commission has endeavored to administer the trust committed to it fairly and impartially, for the best interest of the emigrant and for justice to the entire State. When the large amount to be expended by it annually and the great numbers chargeable to the emigrant fund, are considered, it is not wonderful, and this Commission could not but expect, that differences and disputes should arise between those who claim and those who pay; but from no other source has this Commission, from the moment of its organization, met with half so much opposition, ill feeling, want of sympathy, and misrepresentation, as from the Alms-house Department of this city. This, in view of the pecuniary benefits which this city and many of its great interests have derived, and are deriving from emigration, was most unexpected. When, however, it is considered that this Commission has relieved our citizens of over $300,000 a year taxation—that disease has been kept from the city—that frauds upon strangers have been put an end to—that thousands of friendless men and women have been provided with employment—that the sick have been healed, the hungry fed, and the naked clothed, by hundreds—and that all these happy results have been in a great measure produced by this Commission and under its auspices, without any expense to the city—your Committee appeals with confidence to a discerning public for judgment on its efforts and its acts.

As to the immediate controversy in hand, and the charge of bad faith made against the officers of this Commission, your Committee humbly submit to public decision what they have and what they have not done in that behalf.

This Commission has always desired and acted for an amicable adjustment of points of dispute. It offered to submit them to the official counsel of the Governors—to gentlemen distinguished among our citizens for their intelligence, integrity, and experience—to the Supreme Court—it agreed to this last submission—consented to include points in such submission which were scarcely mooted when an agreement for it was arranged—and it now renews the offer for such an arbitration; and in all these things it endeavored to carry out its propositions in perfect good faith and honor.

The Commission has not declined the decision of the law officer of this city—the Governors' own legal adviser. It has not, when by agreement it was bound in honor to abide the award of unexceptionable gentlemen, rushed to Albany, to procure a legislative decision on matters which had been submitted. It has not, when frustrated in this, repudiated its agreement, and commenced a suit for the enforcement of its claims, and then informed the public, in substance, that no legal measure had been adopted; and it has not asked the Governors either to separate newborn children from their mothers, or else lose the expense of their support. These are some things which the Commission has done, and others which it has not done; and your Committee freely submit the whole matter to the public judgment.

GULIAN C. VERPLANCK, *Chairman.*

New York, Oct. 17*th*, 1855.

Appendix No. 7.

Grand Jury Room, September 9, 1856.

THE Grand Inquest of the county of New York, in the discharge of their duty, have been called upon to investigate certain complaints which have been preferred against certain employees of the railroad companies doing business with the emigrants landing at Castle Garden. In the discharge of this duty, they have felt called upon to visit the Landing-Dépôt itself, with a view to give a personal inspection to the mode of doing business within its inclosures. The landing and dispatching of a cargo of upwards of 400 passengers, taking place at the time of their visit, afforded a favorable opportunity to watch the whole proceeding. The passengers were brought from the ship on a barge, towed by a steamboat, persons and property sheltered from the rain by the upper deck of the barge. They landed in an orderly manner, having evidently been instructed by the officers from Castle Garden as to the nature of the Landing-Dépôt and its arrangements. They passed over the deck, answered the inquiries of the examining physician, whose duty is to note cases whose age or condition requires special bonds from the ship for their support in case of need, and to detect cases of sickness which may have escaped the notice of the Health officer at Quarantine. On entering the large rotunda of Castle Garden, they were registered by a clerk of the Commissioners of Emigration, who took down the names of the heads of families and single persons, whence they came, the State of their destination, their cash means, and the relatives (if any) they were going to join. The annual statistics of the current of emigration are made up from these notes. The passengers then passed on to the next desk, where clerks of the Transportation Companies ascertain the places of destination they wished to go, laid maps of the various routes of travel before them, explained the difference in time and price of travel by the various routes; and, after a selection was made by the passengers, provided them with an order on the cashier, setting forth the number of tickets required, the route selected, and the price of passage, and of over-freight per one hundred pounds by such route. The cashier, on receiving this order, issued the class of tickets it called for, and received the price therefor. The passengers were then shown by a different way from that by which they had entered the rotunda back to the dock, and there produced to the weigh-master the checks they held for baggage, which they had received on board of the vessel which brought them into port, previous to passing their trunks into the hands of the officers from Castle Garden. The property having the corresponding checks was then taken from the barge and weighed, each piece being labelled with a conspicious label, having a certain number and the place of destination printed thereon, the passenger receiving a baggage ticket with the corresponding number, and on which was inserted the number of pieces of baggage delivered, the route it had to be transported, the gross weight, and the amount of freight to be collected thereon, after deducting the amount to which each passenger is entitled. This freight was then paid to the collector, having his office at the scales, who copied the whole ticket into a book kept for reference, and then receipted for the money at the foot of the baggage ticket. The baggage was then taken on board of a steamboat employed to transport the passengers and their property, free of charge, from Castle Garden to the starting places of the various railroads and steamboat lines; and the passengers, having now fully prepared themselves at the usual hour of the day, had ample time to enjoy themselves in the dépôt, by taking their meals, cleansing themselves in the spacious bath-rooms, or promenading on the galleries or on the dock. The utmost order prevailed throughout; every requisite information was given passengers by officials conversing in different languages; letters from friends were transmitted to landing passengers, bringing them money or directions how to proceed, &c.

The Grand Inquest, having thus personally witnessed the whole mode of doing business at the Landing-Dépôt of Castle Garden, and having become satisfied that every care was taken of the emigrant that philanthropy could suggest, and devotion to a good cause, realized by perseverance and daily care, made further inquiries about the arrangements made for special cases which might not then have arisen or been witnessed by them. They learned that it is a frequent occurrence that passengers land expecting to find the means to pursue their route into the interior of the country without delay, but are disappointed. In such cases advances are made on the luggage of passengers, who being thus enabled to escape the necessity of waiting in expensive boarding-houses for communications from their friends, leave immediately for their destination, and after a short while send the amount advanced to them, without interest or charge for storage, and have their trunks sent after them. The amount of money saved to emigrant families by this beneficial arrangement, in keeping them out of boarding-houses, is immense; for it embraces not only the reasonable board for a few days. Before the establishment of Castle Garden, emigrants in such difficulties would go to a boarding-house and write to their friends for "money," not specifying amounts; the friends would send what they thought would pay for the passage, which was then swallowed up by the boarding-house bill, leaving the emigrant still without means to travel. The boarding-house keeper would probably extend a new credit on the security of the luggage (but not a cash advance thereon), and when thus all the means of the emigrant had been exhausted, he would be turned into the street a pauper, and a fit subject for the charities of the public institutions. This is proved by the statistics of Ward's Island Emigrant Refuge, which, at the time of the establishment of Castle Garden, had 3,000 inmates, whose number has, in one year, been reduced to about 1,000—the protection afforded by Castle Garden having cut off the supply of paupers.

Another admirable feature, to which the attention of the Grand Inquest was called, is the special arrangement of a large, airy and well-ventilated room for the accommodation of lying-in women, or such as have been confined so recently before the arrival of the ship as to require rest before travelling. They have all the necessary care of medical attendance and nursing, at the expense of the Commissioners of Emigration, and are not under any necessity of going to boarding-houses and expending money which will take them to their destination as soon as their strength is sufficiently established to bear the fatigues of a journey.

On inquiring into the causes of certain published attacks on the Emigrant Landing-Dépôt, the Grand Inquest have become satisfied that they emanate, in the first instance, from the very interested parties against whose depredations Castle Garden affords protection to the emigrant, and who are chiefly runners, in the employ of booking-agents, boarding-house keepers and others, who have lost custom by the establishment of a central dépôt, where the Railroad Companies have their own business done by their own clerks, and without the extensive intervention of passage brokers, &c.

This class has thrown great difficulties in the way of the proper development of affairs in Castle Garden, by constituting a noisy crowd around the gates, whose behavior is utterly lawless, and endangers the personal safety not only of the passengers who have to leave Castle Garden to transact business in the city, but also the employees of the Landing-Dépôt, and of individual Commissioners of Emigration, who are continually insulted in the public grounds surrounding the dépôt, and have been obliged to carry loaded fire-arms in self-defence against the violence which has frequently been offered to them.

This same class will swarm in boats around the ships in the bay, and bias the minds of passengers against the Landing-Dépôt, and when driven off by the police officers stationed by the Commissioners of Emigration on such ships, will abuse these officers in the most violent manner, and will lodge complaints against such officers in the Mayor's office, and such complaints will be listened to as though they emanated from respectable citizens.

The Grand Inquest witnessed a crowd of this class hovering around the gates of Castle Garden, and they learned with regret that in spite of repeated representations to the municipal authorities, the police utterly ignore the disturbances caused by this mob, who will pounce upon every person leaving the inclosures of Castle Garden, and, if they do not rob them of their money, valuables, tickets, baggage-checks, or the like, or commit gross assault and battery upon such as will not enter into conversation with them, will induce them, by force or argument, to go with them to places where they will be required to spend part or all of their money before they can find a chance to escape.

With a proper attention to their obvious duty on the part of the police there can be no doubt that this motley, noisy, and dangerous crowd could be entirely broken up, and prevented from re-assembling.

The Grand Inquest have learned with regret that this obvious duty of the police is absolutely neglected, to the great detriment of the emigrants, and to the great annoyance of the Commissioners of Emigration, who superintend the business of the Emigrant Landing-Dépôt.

The Grand Inquest having become satisfied that the latter in all its operations is a blessing, not only to the emigrants, but to the community at large, would feel remiss in the performance of a sacred duty if they failed to recommend this important philanthropic establishment to the fostering care of the municipal authorities; and they have dismissed the complaints preferred against certain employees of the Castle Garden, satisfied that they are not sustained by law, and have their origin in a design to disturb, rather than to further, the good work for which the establishment has been called into life by an act of Legislature of April, 1855.

HOWELL HOPPOCK, *Foreman of Grand Jury.*

Appendix No. 8.

New York, August 13, 1857.

To the Commissioners of Emigration:

Your Committee, in regard to the removal of Quarantine, respectfully report, that on Thursday afternoon, 6th instant, about three o'clock, a note was received from the Secretary of the Quarantine Commissioners, inviting your body to proceed to Seguine's Point, on the then next Saturday, to inspect the buildings erected there, preparatory to delivering them to you on Monday, August 10; that the Secretary of the Board, Mr. Casserly, was directed to notify the Quarantine Commissioners, that, owing to absence from the city of a majority of your body, it was impossible to obtain a quorum for the time fixed in their note, and requesting a postponement to some future day; that Mr. Casserly gave such notice personally, when Tuesday of this week was fixed by the Quarantine Commissioners for such visit. Mr. Casserly, thereupon, informed them that he doubted if a quorum of the Commissioners of Emigration would be present in the city on that day, but that if there were, he would so inform them; to which one of the Quarantine Commissioners replied, that he did not "care whether the Commissioners of Emigration went or not; for after having incurred an expense of $500, he didn't think that the Quarantine Commissioners should, for the accommodation of the Commissioners of Emigration, postpone their visit, to the disappointment of their other guests, of whom they had invited quite a number; and he for one was ready to notify the Commissioners to take the buildings at once, whether they saw them or not."

That your Committee, for the purpose of being enabled to report to your body, at the regular meeting to-day, the condition of the institutions at Seguine's Point and their sufficiency for the purposes intended by the law, invited the Commissioners of Health of this city—consisting of the President of the Board of Councilmen, President of the Board of Aldermen, the City Inspector, Resident Physician, Health Officer, and the Mayor—and some of the prominent shipping merchants and underwriters, to visit the Point on Monday last.

That on that day your Committee proceeded, with the parties invited, to Seguine's Point, and made a careful examination of the buildings and arrangements prepared by the Quarantine Commissioners.

By the act authorizing the establishment of a temporary quarantine, the Quarantine Commissioners are directed to provide accommodations for the reception of persons, &c.

Your Committee respectfully submit, that when the Legislature directed the Quarantine Commissioners to provide accommodations, it was their intent that the buildings should be erected, properly furnished, and ready in all respects for the accommodation and care of such patients as might be sent there according to law, and incidentally for those engaged about the hospital; and that the only duty devolved on your body consists in supplying physicians, nurses and orderlies, medicine and food, and such like matters, for the daily necessities and support of the diseased.

This view is strengthened by the fact that the Legislature, for the preparation of those temporary accommodations, put the large sum of $50,000 at the disposal of the Quarantine Commissioners, and that your body is prohibited by law from using any of its funds for any purpose other than the care and support of emigrants, whose contributions created and sustained it, and by the consideration that your body is authorized to collect $3 per week for each patient, not an emigrant, treated in any of the Quarantine establishments; that sum being about the actual cost for the care and treatment of a patient per week.

In all conferences with the Quarantine Commissioners, this view of the case was conceded to be correct; and on it your Committee have acted throughout.

Your Committee, on their visit, found that the Quarantine Commissioners had caused to be erected a dock, which, in so far as appeared, would answer all necessary purposes.

That two Hospital buildings of one story, and calculated for thirty-two beds each, had been erected; as also a wash-house and privy.

In the wash-house, no machinery whatever had been put up, although it is an ascertained fact that the clothes from yellow-fever patients cannot be washed by hand without certain danger to the employees.

These are all the buildings prepared by the Quarantine Commissioners.

Of furniture suitable for the purposes of the establishment, except in defensive operations, there is scarce any.

Your Committee found there, in one of the hospitals, nine bedsteads, and in the other a large number of muskets, and on the grounds two brass field pieces; and besides these enumerated articles, nothing else whatever in the way of furniture, or for the accommodation of physicians or employees, has been provided.

The law directs these temporary establishments to be used for the reception of persons arriving at the port of New York sick of yellow fever or other pestilential diseases. Now, there are times when cholera, ship-fever, and perhaps small-pox, are included under the head of pestilential diseases; and if the Commissioners of Emigration should put persons sick of these various diseases in the same hospitals, they would be justly condemned of murderous inhumanity.

There have been occasions (and no doubt such will occur again) when the Commissioners of Emigration have had in the institutions at Quarantine 1,400 patients; and yet here is provision for only 64.

Entertaining the above views, and aware of the exigencies of the service, your Committee have no hesitation in concluding, that no accommodations such as are required by the law, have been provided by the Quarantine Commissioners.

Nevertheless, since the visit, your Committee addressed a note to the Health Commissioners, Dr. Bissell, Physician of Marine Hospital, and Dr.

Thompson, Health Officer, requesting their opinion in regard to the sufficiency of the provision made at Seguine's Point. Answers have been received from all the above gentlemen, except the Health Officer.

These answers are annexed to this report, and your body, on referring to them, will find that these officers, to whom the care of the health of the city of New York has been specially committed by law, concur in the conclusions of your Committee.

Your Committee, concluding, respectfully submit:

1st. That the Hospitals provided at Seguine's Point are entirely inadequate in capacity.

2d. That these hospitals are unfurnished.

3d. That there are no accommodations for the physicians and employees required in the institutions.

4th. That there are no horses or carriages for the conveyance of the sick or dead, nor stables, coal-bins, or other conveniences indispensable to a hospital for Quarantine purposes. And your Committee, therefore, present the following resolution:

Resolved, That inasmuch as the Quarantine Commissioners have not provided the accommodations contemplated by the law authorizing the selection of a site for a temporary Quarantine and the provision of accommodations, the Commissioners of Emigration respectfully decline to take charge of the temporary hospital at Seguine's Point until the requirements of the law shall have been complied with.

ANDREW CARRIGAN, *Chairman*,
RUDOLPH GARRIGUE, } *Committee.*

Office of the Commissioners of Health,
New York, August 11, 1857.

To the Commissioners of Emigration:

Having received on Saturday last your very polite invitation to make an official inspection of the premises, buildings, and dock selected and erected by the Quarantine Commissioners at Seguine's Point as temporary accommodations for the sick under quarantine, and having on the 10th inst., in company with sundry other citizens of the port, made such inspection, we deem it our duty to comply with your request by stating our conclusions. We are of opinion that the accommodations which we observed at Seguine's Point are defective and incomplete even for temporary quarantine purposes.

Respectfully yours,

JONAS N. PHILLIPS,
WILLIAM ROCKWELL,
JEDEDIAH MILLER, } *Commissioners of Health.*

Marine Hospital, Quarantine,
Staten Island, N. Y. August 12, 1857.

ANDREW CARRIGAN, Esq., Chairman of Committee on Seguine's Point:

Dear Sir:—I have the honor to acknowledge the receipt of your favor of yesterday, requesting my opinion of the temporary accommodations for persons arriving in the port of New York with yellow fever "or other pestilential disease," which have recently been constructed at Seguine's Point by the Commissioners for the removal of the quarantine station.

In reply, I beg leave to state that I have examined the temporary accommodations at Seguine's Point, and while I believe for the most part they are suitable to the purpose for which they were intended, nevertheless, in several respects, in my opinion, they are deficient and incomplete for the reception, treatment, and general care of patients laboring under malignant disease.

Very respectfully yours,

D. H. BISSELL, *Physician Marine Hospital.*

Appendix No. 9.

Office of the Commissioners of Emigration,
New York, Jan. 23, 1857.

HON. WM. L. MARCY, Secretary of State, Washington City:

Sir:—At the last meeting of the Commissioners of Emigration of the State of New York, I was instructed to communicate to you their request that another effort should be made to induce the Governments of those countries of Europe whence emigration to this port chiefly flows, to prohibit altogether the booking passengers for inland passages or transportation in the United States, or selling abroad passage tickets or contracts for passage tickets to be used on this side of the Atlantic.

On this subject, permit me to refer you to a letter from a Committee of this Board to yourself of October 12th, 1855, to your reply thereto, and to the printed circulars issued in consequence thereof and circulated abroad through the facilities afforded by the Department of State.

The apprehensions expressed in the letter of the Committee, that the seat of depredation on the emigrant would be changed from this port to the port of embarkation, have been more than realized.

The chief operators in this system of fraud have not only opened offices in the several seaports where emigrants to this country usually embark, but have also established agencies in towns in the interior of those countries, and in the very villages whence families are likely to emigrate.

The effect of these agencies has been to renew, and even increase, the evils which have been checked by the establishment of an exclusive landing-place for emigrants at Castle Garden.

The more remote the place where the emigrant is induced to purchase a ticket for inland transportation in this country, the greater is the opportunity for imposition and fraud, and this is seldom suffered to pass unused.

The efforts made by our Government heretofore for protecting emigrants from such frauds abroad, have hitherto had little effect on the European Governments, with the exception only of Hamburg and Bremen. Not only is the privilege of booking passengers for distant inland points in the United States continued, but in some places it has been aided (it is hoped not intentionally) by means of Government licenses, giving an official character to the business, well calculated to mislead the ignorant. These are grossly overcharged for real tickets, or as often imposed on by fraudulent ones. After which, they are consigned to continued depredations by other confederates in this city and elsewhere in the United States.

These are facts of daily occurrence which our official position brings constantly to our notice, but seldom enables us to arrest or remedy.

There is a marked contrast in passengers coming by way of Hamburg and Bremen and those by other European ports. It rarely occurs that passengers from either Hamburg or Bremen are unable, on their arrival here, to pay their way to their destination in the interior, or to secure all proper comforts and conveniences on the way. Very many of those from other ports are first defrauded of their means by being induced to purchase tickets for railroad and water travel in this country, at high prices, which, when presented here, are found to be either quite worthless, or to carry the holders only to some point in the interior far short of their destination, where they are left destitute.

Other tickets are genuine, but are found to have been paid for at prices very far above the actual cost at the offices here.

It appears to us that the claims of humanity and justice, and the comity of nations, require and authorize our Government to invoke the aid of other Governments in protecting their own subjects during their pilgrimage from an over-crowded home to a region where vacant acres invite and reward the hand of industry.

To show the manner in which the business of the emigrant landing-place at Castle Garden, New York, under the exclusive control of this Commission, and established in pursuance of a special enactment of our Legislature, has been conducted, I inclose copies of a presentment* by a recent grand jury of this county. It will probably speak for us better than we can for ourselves on one of the most important points of our administration of the trust confided to us by the State of New York.

I am, with much respect, your obedient servant,

G. C. VERPLANCK, *President.*

Department of State, Washington,
Jan. 31, 1857.

HON. G. C. VERPLANCK, President Board of Commissioners of Emigration:

Sir:—I have received your communication of the 23d inst., with its inclosures, calling the attention of this department to the impositions practised

* For this see page 409.

upon emigrants to the United States, in the countries from which they depart, and suggesting that the aid of those governments should be invoked to protect their subjects from the arts of designing and unprincipled individuals.

The motives which led to the establishment of the Board of Commissioners by the State of New York are in the highest degree philanthropic and praiseworthy, and, accordingly, to further the objects which you have in view, I have addressed a circular letter, of which a copy is herewith inclosed, to the diplomatic and consular agents of the United States in those countries of Europe from which emigrants chiefly proceed, and instructed them to bring the subject of your communication to the notice of the governments to which they are respectively accredited, or of the authorities of the places where they reside, and to ask for the adoption of such measures on their part as may be required by the claims of humanity and the comity of nations.

I have likewise had the pleasure of conferring with Mr. Murray, the agent of the Board, and have furnished him with facilities for the accomplishment of the purposes of the Commissioners in his proposed visit to Europe.

I am, Sir, respectfully, your obedient servant,

W. L. MARCY.

CIRCULAR.

No. 17.

Department of State, Washington,
Jan. 31, 1857.

Sir :—The attention of this department having been recently called to the abuses to which emigrants are subjected in the countries from which they proceed, and on their arrival at certain seaports in the United States, it has been deemed advisable to bring the subject to your notice. I accordingly herewith transmit, in a printed form, a copy of a communication addressed to this department on the 23d instant, by the President of the Board of Commissioners of Emigration at New York, in which a mode of correcting the existing evils is suggested.

You are instructed to bring this subject, which is fully set forth in the annexed letter of Mr. Verplanck and its accompaniment, to the notice of the government to which you are accredited, or of the authorities of the place where you reside, and to ask for the adoption of such measures on their part as may be considered necessary for the protection of those intending to emigrate to this country. A step in this direction would no doubt be of service in correcting the evils complained of, and a regard for the interests of humanity demands that it should be taken.

I am, sir, your obedient servant,

W. L. MARCY.

Appendix No. 10.

New York, Nov. 8, 1858.

HON. GULIAN C. VERPLANCK, President of the Commissioners of Emigration:

Dear Sir:—In compliance with a request from a committee of your honorable Board, the undersigned visited the Quarantine grounds at Staten Island, on the 6th inst., for the purpose of inspecting the location and character of the new hospital buildings which are being constructed there.

The investigations which we have made respecting the questions proposed by your Board, enable us to unite in the following testimony, to wit:

"1st. As respects the location of the new hospital buildings.

"2d. As respects their liability to become infected places, or to communicate infectious diseases beyond the Marine Hospital inclosure."

First.—The hospitals are being erected on the northern and elevated section of the Quarantine grounds, where the natural ventilation or sweep of the winds is most constant and effectual.

The new structures are all placed at a much greater distance from the western wall inclosing the hospital grounds, and consequently at a much greater distance from the streets of the village of Tompkinsville, than most of the former hospital buildings were located. We found that the distance from the new building nearest the western wall, or limit of the hospital grounds, to the inhabited side of the nearest street in the village, is nearly three hundred feet; while several of the hospitals recently burned extended to within less than one hundred feet from the dwellings on that street. And all of the other new hospital buildings are located at a still greater distance from any dwellings beyond the hospital inclosure; and the relative as well as the general location of the several structures is well adapted for the preservation of a healthy atmosphere on the hospital grounds.

The buildings designed for cholera hospitals are judiciously located at the greatest practicable distance from the village population, and from the fever hospitals, the offices, and the physicians' former residences.

We regard the location of the several new hospital buildings as being the best that could be made upon the Quarantine grounds, and we believe them to be at such a distance from the streets of the village, and all residences outside the hospital grounds, that no disease or infection whatsoever can ever be communicated, from any class of patients that may be placed in those hospitals, to any residences or places beyond the Quarantine inclosure, by atmospheric agencies.

Second.—In respect to the liability of the New Hospitals to become infected places in consequence of being occupied by any class of patients, and as respects their liability to communicate any form of disease to persons or places beyond the Marine Hospital inclosure, we should regard those buildings as far less liable than the former Hospitals to become infected, as the provisions for ventilation are far superior to the arrangements for that purpose in the old Hospitals, while the position and construction of the new buildings are greatly superior.

But from careful inquiry, we are fully persuaded that even the old Hospitals at Quarantine, during their protracted history of overcrowding with all forms of disease subject to Quarantine restrictions, were never proved in a single instance to have communicated any form of infectious or contagious disease to any person beyond the walls of the Marine Hospital grounds. We believe, also, that a similar experience of the immunity of the immediate and populous neighborhood of Hospital establishments has always been enjoyed in the vicinity of the New York City Hospital and the great Bellevue Hospital; in the former of which, both Yellow Fever and Typhus have frequently been treated; in the latter, almost every form of disease that flesh is heir to. In short, the authentic results of medical observation in and about the great Hospital establishments throughout the civilized world, fully corroborate the opinion which we entertain respecting the innocuous character of such humane institutions to any population that may dwell in their vicinity, provided they are under proper medical management, and the Hospital wards and building themselves amply supplied with a pure atmosphere.

In conclusion, we would state that, without any reference to the opinions that we severally entertain respecting the much agitated and vexed questions relating to the Quarantine restrictions and regulations required for the protection of New York from important infectious diseases, or respecting the means by which Yellow Fever may be propagated, we unhesitatingly assert our belief that the new hospitals which are now being constructed on the Marine Hospital grounds will not, if under proper management, be liable to become infected places, especially as regards contamination from yellow fever or from typhus; and that much less will those buildings or the patients they may at any time contain, be liable to communicate infectious diseases to the inhabitants of the villages adjacent to the Hospital grounds.

In connection with the above, the undersigned beg leave to state that they have been severally engaged in the active practice of the medical profession, in the city of New York, for thirty-seven, twelve, and nine years respectively.

WILLIAM ROCKWELL, M. D.
HENRY G. COX, M. D.
ELISHA HARRIS, M. D.

New York, Nov. 8th, 1858.

I hereby set forth, that I have this day visited the Quarantine grounds on Staten Island, and inspected the buildings now in progress of erection thereon, and that I readily concur in the opinions and statements expressed in the preceding document.

I have been in the active practice of the medical profession forty-seven years and upwards.

JOHN W. FRANCIS, M. D.

Appendix No. 11.

Number of persons affected with contagious or infectious diseases admitted to the Marine Hospital during the following years:

Year		Number	Year	Number
1847	(From May 5th)	6,474	1853	4,478
1848	....	8,111	1854	4,438
1849	....	5,554	1855	2,107
1850	....	3,068	1856	1,556
1851	....	6,109	1857	1,777
1852	....	8,370		

Appendix No. 12.

Office of the Commissioners of Emigration,
Castle Garden, April 25, 1859.

Special meeting of the Board called at request of the "Commissioners for the Removal of Quarantine," of whom were present Messrs. Seymour and Green, (Mr. Patterson being absent on account of illness in his family,) was held at their rooms at Castle Garden on the 25th inst.

The President (G. C. Verplanck) and a quorum present.

The following resolution was, on motion, unanimously adopted:

"*Resolved,* That the Commissioners of Emigration will cheerfully co-operate with the 'Commissioners for the Removal of Quarantine,' and that this Board tender to said Commission the use of their office for the transaction of their business, and also will afford them every facility in their power for the accomplishment of the object of their appointment."

"*Resolved,* That in accordance with law, the Commissioners of Emigration be requested to remove the patients now at the hospitals on Staten Island, sick with diseases other than yellow fever, to their hospitals on Ward's Island."

Quarantine Commissioners' Office,
59 *Pine street, New York, May* 14, 1859.

To the Commissioners of Emigration:

Gentlemen:—I have the honor to send you herewith a copy of a resolution this day adopted by the Commissioners for the removal of the Quarantine Station. I am requested to ask for the subject the early consideration of your Board, and a reply at your earliest convenience.

Very respectfully yours,

S. C. HAWLEY, *Secretary.*

May 25, 1859.

Special meeting of the Board of Commissioners of Emigration, held at their rooms at Castle Garden on May 25th.

The President and a quorum of the Board present.

The following resolutions were, on motion, adopted:

"*Resolved*, That the Commissioners of Emigration acknowledge the receipt of a resolution passed by the Commissioners for the removal of Quarantine, on the 14th of May inst., and they hereby express their willingness to take charge of any of the patients now remaining at the Marine Hospital, at Castleton, or which may hereafter be sent to Ward's Island by the health officer or other proper authorities, with the exception of such as are afflicted with yellow fever, cholera, small-pox, and such other diseases as may endanger the inmates of the Institution or the inhabitants in the vicinity.

"*Resolved*, That this Board will pay the necessary expense of taking care of such small-pox cases as may be sent to Blackwell's Island, or any other place, and are properly chargeable to the Commissioners of Emigration and the fund under their control, with the understanding that the arrangement contemplated by the aforesaid resolution is one of a temporary character.

"*Resolved*, That a committee of three be appointed to carry out the above resolutions so far as may be necessary for any conference (or joint action) with the Quarantine Commissioners, and being in conformity with the law passed at the last session of the Legislature."

The President appointed as such committee Messrs. Curtis, Low, and Purdy, and to which, on motion of Mr. Purdy, the Mayors of New York and of Brooklyn were added.

Office of the Quarantine Commissioners,
59 *Pine street, N. Y., June* 15, 1859.

To THE COMMISSIONERS OF EMIGRATION, Castle Garden:

Gentlemen:—A copy of the resolutions of your Board adopted at the meeting held on the 25th of May, has been received, by which you agree to "take charge of any of the patients now remaining in the Marine Hospital at Castleton, or which may hereafter be sent to Ward's Island by the health officer, or other proper authorities, with the exception of such as are afflicted with yellow fever, cholera, small-pox, and such other diseases as may endanger the inmates of the institution or the inhabitants of the vicinity."

I am instructed by the "Commissioners for the Removal of the Quarantine," to inform you that the above proposition is acceptable to them, and is agreed to with the conditions contained in your resolution.

I am further instructed to inform you that there are now in the hospital at Castleton about forty patients. Of these, about 18 are sick of small-pox and 1 of scarlatina. The balance are ill of various diseases, none of which come within the excepted classes named in your resolutions.

These we will remove to your hospital at Ward's Island, as soon as we shall be advised that you are prepared to receive them. Those sick of small-pox we have provided for elsewhere.

Please inform us at your earliest convenience at what time we may send the patients to your hospital, and also send us any form of certificate you may wish to accompany them. An early reply is waited for.

I am very respectfully yours, for the Commissioners,
S. C. HAWLEY, *Secretary.*

Office of the Quarantine Commissioners,
59 *Pine street, N. Y., June* 15, 1859.

THE COMMISSIONERS OF EMIGRATION, Castle Garden, N. Y.:

Gentlemen:—In part performance of the duty enjoined upon us by law to provide temporary accommodations "for persons arriving at the port of New York, sick with yellow fever, or other pestilential diseases," we have prepared a "Floating Hospital" for the treatment of yellow fever, which will in a few days be ready to be placed at her anchorage below the Narrows.

It will be necessary immediately to place the Floating Hospital in charge of a ship-keeper and assistants for safe keeping. It would probably be desirable to furnish the hospital with beds, furniture, medicines, and other supplies composing a proper hospital outfit, before it is taken to the anchorage.

Arrangements also should be made beforehand for an appropriate force of physicians, nurses, and help to treat the sick that may be sent to the hospital.

As the payment of this class of expenses seems to belong to your Commission, it is proper that you should take charge of the matter and make such appointments and furnish such supplies as you shall deem needful.

It is specially desirable to know whether you would wish to put on board the Floating Hospital, furniture, supplies, medicines, and other hospital outfit before it is taken to the anchorage, and if so, where you would wish the hospital to be moored for that purpose.

Temporarily, and until you shall take up the matter, the Floating Hospital will be placed in the care of Capt. Willett Martin and his assistants for safe keeping.

Allow me to ask from you prompt consideration of the matters submitted, and a reply at your earliest convenience.

Very respectfully yours, for the Commissioners,
S. C. HAWLEY, *Secretary.*

New York, June 18, 1859.

TO THE COMMISSIONERS FOR THE REMOVAL OF QUARANTINE:

Gentlemen:—The Quarantine Commissioners' communication of the 15th June instant, acknowledging the receipt of a resolution adopted by the Commissioners of Emigration on the 25th May last, informing them that "their proposition was acceptable and agreed to, with the conditions contained in said resolution, and requesting them to inform the Quarantine Commissioners at their earliest convenience at what time the Quarantine Commissioners might send to their hospital the patients described by the Commissioners of Emigration in such communication, and requesting them to send the Quarantine Commissioners any form of certificate they may wish to accompany such patients," has been referred by the Commissioners of Emigration to the undersigned, for consideration and answer.

The undersigned now inform the Quarantine Commissioners that hospitals of the Commissioners of Emigration have been prepared and are in readiness for the reception of patients described in the above communication of the Quarantine Commissioners, as coming within the conditions of the aforesaid resolution of 25th May ult., and that whenever such patients may be removed from the hospital at Castleton, and transferred to Ward's Island, the Commissioners of Emigration will take charge and care of them.

In regard to the form of this certificate, the Commissioners of Emigration can only say, that such form as may seem proper to the Quarantine Commissioners, and be expressive of their power and the acts performed thereunder in this regard, shall be entirely satisfactory.

Very respectfully,

CYRUS CURTIS,
E. F. PURDY,
D. F. TIEMANN,
A. A. LOW,
S. S. POWELL, } *Committee.*

Office of the Commissioners of Emigration,
New York, June 22, 1859.

THE COMMISSIONERS FOR THE REMOVAL OF QUARANTINE:

Gentlemen:—Your communication of 15th inst., informing us that you have prepared a Yellow Fever Floating Hospital which would in a few days be ready to be placed at her anchorage below the Narrows, and suggesting to us the propriety of making certain arrangements in regard to ship-keepers, furniture, medicine and supplies, medical force and nurses, is received, and has been the subject of deliberate consideration.

In regard to the furniture, such as bedsteads, beds and bedding, chairs, tables, cooking apparatus, and such like articles, we had occasion to consider and express our views to your predecessors in office some two years ago. The law authorizes you, as it did them, to provide temporary accommodation, &c. * * * for persons arriving in the port of New York sick with yellow fever; and when the buildings at Seguine's Point, without furniture and other articles necessary to a complete arrangement, were tendered us, we declined to accept them, on the ground that accommodations had not been provided.

This decision in regard to a hospital on land we should feel constrained to apply to the Floating Hospital, and cannot doubt that on consideration you will not differ with us on this point.

The law under which we act expressly excepts from our control and jurisdiction the sanitary treatment of the inmates of the Marine or other hospital for quarantine purposes, and the appointment of nurses and help to treat and take care of the sick is by law conferred upon the physician of the Marine Hospital; and we are therefore without power to make any arrangement in regard to the medical force, nurses, and help to be employed on the Floating Hospital.

So far as a ship-keeper and crew are concerned, in our judgment they appear to be a part of the establishment to be provided by you.

We must therefore decline to assume the responsibility of appointing and paying such an officer and force.

We will wish to put on board the Floating Hospital medicines, fuel, and food, and some other articles required in the treatment or for the comfort of patients who may become inmates of it, and avail ourselves of your offer to move it to a convenient place for their reception. For that purpose the point we would indicate would be the wharf known as the Boat-house Wharf at the Quarantine Station at Staten Island.

On behalf of the Commissioners of Emigration,

I remain, gentlemen, yours, very respectfully,

G. C. VERPLANCK, *President.*

Office of the Quarantine Commissioners,
59 *Pine street, Aug.* 17, 1859.

To THE EMIGRANT COMMISSIONERS, Castle Garden, N. Y.:

Gentlemen:—The Act making an appropriation for the purposes of Quarantine, passed April 19th, 1859, requires this Commission, among other things, "to provide temporary accommodations" for persons arriving in the port of New York, "sick with yellow fever or other pestilential disease," to remove the sick from the hospital at Castleton, and designate places to which the sick should be thereafter sent.

This Commission, in obedience to the requirements of this law, prepared a Floating Hospital for the treatment of those arriving in port sick with yellow fever, &c., and formally *designated* it as the place to which such sick should be sent.

Considering that it was the duty of your Commission to undertake the charge and management of that hospital and pay its expenses, this Commission, by a communication dated the 15th of June last, requested you to make the necessary arrangements for doing so. This you declined to do, (except to place on board medicines and provisions, which were not then needed, as there were no sick to be fed or treated.) Among the reasons assigned for declining to accede to our request, was the allegation "that accommodations had not been provided."

Exactly what degree of perfection in finishing and furnishing the hospital would be demanded to meet your view of "providing accommodations," this Board had no means of knowing. They, therefore, have attempted to complete and furnish the hospital to such a degree of perfection as to render impossible any objection on that ground. This they believe they have now accomplished. The hospital was originally inclosed, arranged, divided, and fitted up in pursuance of plans furnished by the physician of the Marine Hospital.

On a careful examination, by a competent committee of experienced physicians, it became apparent that those plans were defective.

Alterations were required to be made, to remedy the errors of the first arrangement, which produced a considerable delay. They are now complete, according to the best medical authority. The hospital is finished and furnished, so as to abide the scrutiny and equal the demands of exacting criticism. During the time that the alterations and furnishing were being done, the yellow fever appeared in port. There was no other place to which the patients could legally be sent, and they were treated at the Floating Hospital. Dr. Elisha Harris, a physician of known repute and large experience in the treatment of yellow fever, was engaged to take charge of the sick, and such nurses and other help as the necessity of the service demanded, have been employed.

The safe keeping of the ship has been in charge of Capt. Willett Martin and his assistants.

The hospital and the force are now in an efficient condition for service.

There are now under treatment some five, six, or more, cases of yellow fever, and the number is likely to be increased by daily arrivals from infected places.

Safety to the public health, as well as decent regard to the welfare of the unfortunate sick, demand that the hospital be kept in its present effective condition.

This Commission have, in pursuance of the law of 1859, designated the Floating Hospital as the place to which the yellow fever, &c., &c., *shall be sent.* You are aware that the same law provides that the "Commissioners of Emigration shall send them (such sick persons) to such place as the said (Quarantine) Commissioners shall designate, and pay the expenses of their support."

The Floating Hospital having been finished and furnished, will have no expenses that will not properly belong to the "support of the sick" sent to it for treatment, covering the whole current expenditures of the hospital.

We presume you will agree with us in the opinion that the law of 1859 intends to throw upon the fund in your charge the whole of this expense from the beginning. The law does not say in terms that your Commission shall take the supervision and actual management of the matter; but inasmuch as you are to pay all the expenses, it is deemed to be but proper that you should have control and management of all the employées and of the purchase of supplies, and the right to stipulate as to all items of expenditure.

Possibly it would be a compliance with the intention, as it would seem to be with the words of the law, if you should pay all the bills incurred in carrying on the hospital from the beginning without taking the actual management of it. It is submitted, however, that it would be proper that the party who is bound to pay the expenses should supervise and control the making of them.

With these views submitted, the Quarantine Commissioners notify you that the Floating Hospital is finished and furnished and anchored according to law, and has been duly designated as the place to which certain classes of sick persons are to be sent; that there are now on board under treatment some four, five, or more persons sick with yellow fever; that Dr. Elisha Harris is the physician in charge, as the employée of this Commission for the purpose, with a small force (barely what is necessary) of nurses and help; and that Capt. Willett Martin is ship-keeper, with such assistants as the safety of the hospital requires.

The Quarantine Commissioners hereby request your Commission to take the charge, supervision, and management of this Floating Hospital, pay its expenses, and maintain it and the barge hereafter mentioned as a part of the temporary accommodation for persons arriving in the port of New York sick with yellow fever, or other pestilential diseases, until the Quarantine shall have been permanently located at some place to be hereafter provided.

The Quarantine Commissioners have also hired and fitted up the barge "Pilgrim" and anchored her opposite Castleton, to be used as a landing barge, where sick persons may be detained until the character of their diseases can be determined, and they can be distributed to the appropriate hospitals.

You are requested to undertake the same charge, management, and payment of expenses and maintenance in relation to this barge as to the Floating Hospital.

If you shall be of the opinion that your duty under the law will be fully and properly complied with by paying the current expenses of the hospital from the beginning, without taking upon yourselves its management, and are ready to do so, please advise us at once, and suggest some plan, by committee or otherwise, through which the business can be arranged on that basis.

The proper disposition and care of the sick; arriving in port at this season of the year are matters of the highest concern in relation to the public health, as well as to the welfare and comfort of the sick, and in order that the service may be well done, or perhaps done at all, it is necessary that the question, "Who shall pay the expense?" be decided without delay.

We therefore ask your early action and prompt decision upon the matters herein contained, with advice as to your conclusion.

Very respectfully yours,

By order of the Quarantine Commissioners,

SETH C. HAWLEY, *Secretary.*

Office of the Commissioners of Emigration,
New York, August 25, 1859.

To THE COMMISSIONERS FOR THE REMOVAL OF QUARANTINE:

Gentlemen:—Herewith you will please find copy of Report of Special Committee of this Board, to whom was referred your communication of the 17th instant, relative to the charge of the Floating Hospital, its supervision and management, made at the regular meeting of the Commissioners of Emigration, held yesterday, together with the resolutions in relation thereto, adopted also at the meeting yesterday:

"Your Committee, to whom was referred the communication from the Quarantine Commissioners of date 17th August, 1859, respectfully report:

"That the phraseology of the Act of 1859 making an appropriation to the Quarantine Commissioners, and containing certain provisions in regard to a temporary Quarantine establishment and arrangements for the care of the sick arriving at this port affected with pestilential disease, is uncertain and difficult of application, and is capable of different and even contradictory interpretations. Under the enactment, however, your Committee are of opinion that either body, the Quarantine Commissioners or this Board, in case this Floating Hospital were accepted, have the right and power, acting in good faith, and with the concurrence of the other Commission, to maintain and carry it on as a Quarantine institution. The Quarantine Commissioners have up to this time assumed the duty of conducting it, have officered it and manned it, employed a physician, nurses, and orderlies to treat and take care of the sick within it, and have organized and are carrying out a system which is the result of mature reflection on their part. To take the institution from their control would necessarily involve material changes in the system and organization, throw a sudden responsibility on the members of this Board, who are unfamiliar with the details of the arrangement, and at a period, too, when the Quarantine season has reached its height, and when even a transient error might result in serious public injury, and jeopard the health of the city and State. Under these circumstances your Committee would recommend that this Board should inform the Quarantine Commissioners that the public welfare in the judgment of this Commission, requires that they should retain the control and management of the Floating Hospital, and that this Commission will pay, as the law seems to intend, the current expenses of the care and treatment of the sick in the Institution.

"G. C. VERPLANCK, }
"J. E. DEVELIN, } *Committee.*

The report having been read, the following resolutions were, on motion, adopted:

Resolved, That the report of the Committee to whom was referred the communication of the Quarantine Commissioners be accepted; and that the Quarantine Commissioners be informed that, in the judgment of this Board, the public welfare requires that the Quarantine Commissioners should retain the control and management of the Floating Hospital; and that this Commission will pay the current expenses of the care and treatment of the sick, but not including the pay of the master and men employed in charge of the said ship, occupied as a Floating Hospital.

Resolved, That a copy of the report of the Committee and the aforesaid resolution be transmitted to the Quarantine Commissioners.

ERRATA.

Page ii., on 22d line, for "*fourth*" read "*fifth.*"

Page 37, first line, for "1846" read "1856."

The Legislature of the State of New York, observing the increase in emigration to the port of New York, and impressed by its great importance and the duty and interest of the State to extend to it every reasonable facility and encouragement, established, in 1847, an Emigrant Commission with very liberal powers. During and since that year numerous laws having reference to it have been enacted, which have gradually resulted in two systems. One of these, whilst it guarded against the introduction into this country of infirm and helpless persons, at the same time, by affording reliable information such as it might be supposed simple and inexperienced strangers would require, by providing a fund for the support of those among them whom misfortune or sickness might overtake after their arrival, and by assuring them that they would in such case be cared for and maintained during their disability, held out peculiar inducements to healthy emigrants to come to this port. The other was intended to protect emigrants from the frauds and impositions practiced upon them by unprincipled persons engaged in keeping emigrant boarding-houses, in selling tickets of conveyance, and contracting for the transportation of their baggage, to various points in this State and the other States of the Union, and the Canadas. The former system was committed for its practical application to the Commissioners of Emigration, and the latter principally to the civil magistrates in the various cities of the State.

The transfer to the Commissioners of Emigration, in 1847, of the Marine Hospital on Staten Island and its management, made them, in a modified degree, also Quarantine officers; and as various laws in regard to them and the public health have since been enacted (often upon a sudden exigency and without thorough examination and collation with existing statutes upon the same general subject), amending, modifying, and repealing previous acts—sometimes directly and at other times by implication—it has been thought proper, in publishing the laws affecting the Commissioners, to print all the statutes enacted in regard to them, so that whoever might have occasion or desire to examine them in this collection should be enabled to decide which of them had been changed or repealed, and which were existing and in force. These statutes at large will be found in the following appendix from first to forty-fourth page. The Counsel to the Commissioners, however, who supervised the publication of the appendix, has caused such portions of these statutes as in his judgment are now in force to be printed in large and such as have been repealed in small, type.

The remainder of the appendix is devoted to such of the laws for the protection of emigrants as are applicable to the present arrangement for landing emigrants at this port, and to a recent act of Congress for the protection of female passengers on shipboard. There are other existing protective statutes; but the establishment and maintenance of Castle Garden, by the Commissioners of Emigration, as an emigrant depot and the only landing-place in this city for emigrant passengers, having remedied in a great measure the evil practices which these statutes were enacted to suppress, it seems unnecessary to reprint them. These omitted statutes are as follows: Ch. 219 of Laws of 1848; Ch. 321 of Laws of 1849; Ch. 218 and Ch. 619 of Laws of 1853; and Ch. 103 of Laws of 1860.

There are other statutes relating to Quarantine which it is unnecessary to print, but proper to mention; Ch. 309 of Laws of 1849, Ch. 68 of Laws of 1857, and Ch. 465 of Laws of 1860.

The United States Passenger Act, which has been of great benefit to emigrants on shipboard, may be found at page 1492 of Dunlop's Digest of the General Laws of the United States, ed. of 1856.

New York, July 25, 1861.

APPENDIX.

CHAP. 195.

AN ACT *concerning passengers in vessels coming to the city of New York.*

Passed May 5, 1847, "three-fifths being present."

The People of the State of New York, represented in Senate and Assembly, do enact as follows :

Report to be made of all passengers.

§ 1. Within twenty-four hours after the arrival of any ship or vessel at the port of New York, from any of the United States, other than this State, or from any country out of the United States, the master or commander of such ship or vessel shall make a report in writing, on oath or affirmation, to the mayor of the city of New York, or in case of his absence or other inability to serve, to the person discharging the duties of his office, which report shall state the name, place of birth, last legal residence, age and occupation of every person or passenger arriving in such ship or vessel, on her last voyage to said port, not being a citizen of the United States, and who shall have within the last preceding twelve months arrived from any country out of the United States, at any place within the United States, and who shall not have paid the commutation money mentioned in the next section of this act, or have been bonded, or paid any commutation money, under the provisions of the act entitled "An act concerning passengers in vessels coming to the port of New York," passed February 11, 1824: The said report shall contain a like statement of all such persons or passengers as aforesaid, as shall have been landed, or been suffered to land from any such ship or vessel, at any place during such last voyage, or who shall have been put on board, or been suffered to go on board of any other ship, vessel or boat, with the intention of proceeding to or through the said city of New York: The said report shall further specify whether any of said passengers so reported are lunatic, idiot, deaf and dumb, blind or infirm; and if so, whether they are accompanied by relatives likely to be able to support them; and shall further specify particularly, the names, last place of residence, and ages of all passengers who may have died during said last voyage of such vessel: In case any such master or commander shall omit or neglect to report as aforesaid any such person or passenger, with the particulars aforesaid, or shall make any false report or statement in respect to any such person or passenger, in all or any of the particulars herein before specified, such master or commander shall forfeit the sum of seventy-five dollars for every such passenger, in regard to whom any such omission or neglect shall have occurred, or any such false report or statement shall be made, for which the owner or owners of every such ship or vessel shall also be liable, jointly and severally, and which may be sued for and recovered as hereinafter provided.

One dollar to be paid for each passenger.

§ 2. It shall be the duty of the said mayor, or other person discharging the duties of his office as aforesaid, by an endorsement to be made on the said report, to require the master or commander of such ship or vessel to pay to the Chamberlain of the city of New York the sum of one dollar, for every person or passenger reported by such master or commander as aforesaid, which sum shall be paid as aforesaid, within three days after the arrival of such ship or vessel at the said port of New York.

Condition of passengers to be examined into and reported.

§ 3. It shall be the duty of the Commissioners of Emigration, hereinafter named, to examine into the condition of passengers arriving at the port of New York in any such ship or vessel, and for that purpose all or any of the said commissioners, and such other person or persons as they shall appoint, shall be authorized to go on board, and through any such ship or vessel; and if on such examination, there shall be found among such passengers, any lunatic, idiot, deaf and dumb, blind or infirm persons, not members of emigrating families, and who, from attending circumstances, are likely to become permanently a public charge, they shall report the same to the said mayor particularly; and thereupon the said mayor, or the person discharging the duties of his office as aforesaid, shall, instead of the commutation money aforesaid, require, in the endorsement to be made as aforesaid, or in any subsequent endorsement or endorsements thereon, that the master or commander of such ship or vessel, with two sufficient sureties, shall execute a joint and several bond to the people of this State, in a penalty of three hundred dollars for every such passenger, conditioned to indemnify and save harmless each and every city, town and county within this State, from any cost or charge, which any such city, town or county shall incur, for the maintenance or support of the person or persons named in such bond, or any of them, within five years from the date of such bond. The sureties to the said bonds shall be required to justify before, and to the satisfaction of, the officer making such endorsement, and by their oath or affirmation shall satisfy such officer that they are, respectively, residents of the State of New York, and worth double the amount of the penalty of such bond, over and above all debts, liabilities, and all property exempt from execution.

Commissioners of Emigration.

§ 4. Gulian C. Verplanck, James Boorman, Jacob Harvey, Robert B. Minturn, William F. Havemeyer and David C. Colden, are hereby appointed Commissioners, for the purpose of carrying into effect the intent and provisions of this act, of whom the said Gulian C. Verplanck and James Boorman shall constitute the first class, and shall hold their office two years; the said Jacob Harvey and Robert B. Minturn shall constitute the second class, and hold their office four years; and the said William F. Havemeyer and David C. Colden shall constitute the third class, and hold their office for six years; and upon the expiration of their several terms of office their places shall be filled by appointments, to be made by the Governor, by and with advice and consent of the Senate, and the persons so appointed shall respectively hold their offices for the term of six years. The mayor of the city of New York, the mayor of the city of Brooklyn, the president of the German Society, and the president of the Irish Emigrant Society of New York, shall also severally, by virtue of their respective offices, be commissioners as aforesaid. The said Commissioners shall be known as the "Commissioners of Emigration," and by that title shall be capable of suing and being sued: The money so as aforesaid to be paid to the chamberlain of the city of New York, shall be paid out, on the warrant of the said commissioners, or a majority of them: It shall be the duty of the said commissioners to provide for the maintenance and support of such of the persons for whom commutation money shall have been paid as aforesaid, or on whose account bonds shall have been taken as aforesaid, as would otherwise become a charge upon any city, town or county, of this state; and the said commissioners shall appropriate the moneys aforesaid, for that purpose, in such manner as to indemnify, so far as may be, the several cities, towns and counties of the state, for any expense or charge which may be incurred for the maintenance and support of the persons aforesaid; such appropriation shall be in proportion to the expenses incurred by said cities, towns and counties, severally, for such maintenance and support. And the more fully to effect the object contemplated by this act, the said commissioners are authorized to apply in their discretion any part of the said money, to aid in removing any of said persons from any part of this State to another part of this or any other State, or from this State, or in assisting them to procure employment, and thus prevent them from becoming a public charge: The said commissioners are also authorized in their discretion to apply any part of the said moneys to the purchase or lease of any property, or the erection of any building, which they may deem necessary for the purposes aforesaid. But any expense so incurred by the commissioners in any city, town or county, shall be charged to the share of such moneys which any such city, town or county, shall be entitled to receive thereof, for expense incurred in the support or maintenance of the persons for whom commutation money shall have been paid as aforesaid, or on whose account bonds shall have been taken as aforesaid.

Their powers

Provision in case of persons becoming chargeable for whom bonds were given.

§ 5. In case any of the persons for whom commutation money has been paid as aforesaid, or for whom a bond has been given as aforesaid, shall, at any time within five years from the payment of such money or the execution of such bond, become chargeable upon any city, town or county within this State, it shall be the duty of the said Commissioners to provide for the payment of any expense incurred by any such city, town or county, for the maintenance and support of any such person, out of the commutation money to be paid as aforesaid, and the moneys collected on such bonds, so far as the same will enable them to do so. The said commisioners shall prescribe such rules and regulations as they shall deem proper, for the purpose of ascertaining the right, and the amount of the claim of any city, town or county, to indemnity under the provisions of this and the preceding section. The said Commissioners shall have power to provide for the support and maintenance of any persons for whom commutation money shall have been paid, or on whose account a bond shall have been given as hereinbefore provided, and who shall become chargeable upon any city, town or county, in such manner as they shall deem proper; and after such provision shall have been made by such commissioners, such city, town or county shall not be entitled to claim any further indemnity for the support and maintenance of such person.

Agents to be employed.

§ 6. The said Commissioners are authorized to employ such agents, clerks and servants as they shall deem necessary for the purposes aforesaid, and to pay a reasonable compensation for their services out of the moneys aforesaid.

Chamberlain to report annually.

§ 7. The Chamberlain of the city of New York shall, on the first Monday of January, in every year, and at such other times as he shall be thereunto required by the said Commissioners, report to them the amount of money received by him since his last previous report, for commutation money as aforesaid, and the amount of such moneys remaining in his hands.

Commissioners to report to legislature.

§ 8. The said Commissioners shall annually on or before the first day of February in each year, report to the legislature the amount of moneys received under the provisions of this act during the preceding year, and the manner in which the same has been appropriated particularly.

§ 9. In case of a vacancy in the said board of Commissioners, the same shall be filled by an appointment to be made by the Governor, by and with the advice and consent of the senate. The person so appointed shall hold his office for the remainder of the term of the person in whose place he shall be appointed. The said Commissioners shall in all cases be residents of the city of New York or city of Brooklyn. Vacancies how to be supplied.

§ 10. If any person for whom a bond shall have been given as aforesaid, shall within five years from the date of such bond become chargeable upon any city, town or county of this State, or upon the moneys under the control of the said Commissioners as aforesaid, the said Commissioners may bring an action on such bond in the name of the people of this State, and shall be entitled to recover on such bond from time to time, so much money, not in the whole exceeding the penalty of such bond exclusive of costs, as shall be sufficient to defray the expenses incurred by any such city, town or county, or the said Commissioners, for the maintenance and support of the person for whom such bond was given as aforesaid. Action may be brought on bond.

§ 11. If any master or commander as aforesaid shall neglect or refuse to pay over to the said chamberlain such sum of money as is herein before required for commutation money for each and every such person, *within three days* after the arrival of such vessel at the port of New York, or shall neglect or refuse to give any bond so required as aforesaid within the said three days, every such master or commander and the owner or owners of such ship or vessel, severally and respectively, shall be subject to a penalty of three hundred dollars for each and every person or passenger on whose account such commutation money or such bond may have been required, to be sued for in the manner hereinafter provided. Penalty in cases of neglect or refusal.

§ 12. The penalties and forfeitures prescribed by this act may be sued for and recovered with costs of suit by and in the name of said Commissioners of Emigration, in any Court having cognizance thereof, and when recovered, shall be applied to the purposes specified in this act. It shall be lawful for the said Commissioners before or after suit brought, to compound for any of the said penalties or forfeitures, upon such terms as they shall think proper. How recovered.

§ 13. Any ship or vessel whose master or commander, owner or owners, shall have incurred any penalty or forfeiture under the provisions of this act, shall be liable for such penalties or forfeitures, which shall be a lien upon such ship or vessel, and may be enforced and collected by warrant of attachment, in the same manner as is provided in title eight of chapter eight of the third part of the Revised Statutes, all the provisions of which title shall Ships or vessels liable to penalties.

apply to the forfeitures and penalties imposed by this act; and the said Commissioners of Emigration shall, for the purposes of such attachment, be deemed creditors of such ship or vessel, and of her master or commander, and owner or owners respectively.

Money collected for marine hospitals to be paid to Commissioners.

§ 14. The moneys now authorized by law to be collected by the Health Commissioner from the passengers in vessels arriving at the port of New York for the use of the Marine Hospital, except such as are paid under protest, shall be paid at such times as the said Commissioners shall direct, to the Chamberlain of the city of New York, and shall be drawn in the manner prescribed in the fourth section of this act, and the expenditures of the same for the purposes of the Marine Hospital, as now authorized by law, shall be made by the Commissioners constituted by this act, or by the Commissioners of Health under their supervision and direction. And any surplus which shall remain beyond such expenditures and the appropriations made by existing laws shall be applied by the said Commissioners to the general purposes of this act.

Appropriations by existing laws.

§ 15. Any appropriation made by existing laws from said moneys shall hereafter be paid out of the same by the Commissioners appointed by this act, and any moneys which have been or shall hereafter be paid under protest, shall, upon the settlement or judicial determination in favor of the State of the claims thereto, be paid to the Chamberlain of the city of New York to the credit of the Commissioners of Emigration, and shall be applied by them according to the provisions of this act.

Buildings may be erected, etc.

§ 16. The said commissioners are authorized to erect such buildings and make such improvements upon the land belonging to the State, known as the "Marine Hospital," as they shall deem necessary for the purposes of this act and of the said hospital, out of the moneys in the treasury of the State belonging to the "Mariners' Fund," which have not been paid under protest, or which have not been otherwise appropriated.

Provision in case of deficiencies.

§ 17. If the commutation money collected under the provisions of the second section of this act, and the surplus of the revenues of the "Mariners' Fund," applicable to the purposes of this act, as provided by the fourteenth section thereof, shall, at any time, be found insufficient to defray the expenses incurred by the said Commissioners, under the provisions of this act, and also to enable them to reimburse as hereinbefore provided, to the several cities, towns and counties of the State, such sums as shall have been expended by them for the maintenance and support of persons for whom commutation money shall have been paid, or bonds given as aforesaid, such deficiency shall be paid out of the surplus of the moneys in the treasury of the State, belonging to the "Mariners' Fund," which have not been paid under protest, remaining after the expenditures for buildings and improvements authorized by this act. Nothing in this section contained shall be applicable to the moneys paid to the credit of said "Mariners' Fund," by the Trustees of the "Seamen's Fund and Retreat," in the city of New York.

§ 18. The act passed February 11, 1824, entitled "An Act concerning passengers in vessels coming to the port of New York;" and the act passed April 12, 1842, entitled "An Act for the Relief of the County of Kings from the Support of Foreign Poor," are hereby repealed. Repeal.

§ 19. This act shall take effect immediately.

CHAP. 483.

AN ACT *to amend an act entitled "An Act concerning passengers in vessels coming to the city of New York," passed May* 5, 1847.

Passed December 15, 1847, "three-fifths being present."

The People of the State of New York, represented in Senate and Assembly, do enact as follows:

Marine hospitals, etc., transferred to Commissioners of Emigration.

§ 1. The hospital erected on the easterly shore of Staten Island, and the land adjoining thereto belonging to this State, heretofore known as "The Marine Hospital," together with all the buildings and improvements thereon, are hereby transferred from the Commissioners of Health to the Commissioners of Emigration, to be by them held in trust for the people of this State, and the sole and exclusive control of the same, except in regard to the sanitary treatment of the inmates thereof, is hereby given to the said Commissioners of Emigration, for the purposes and subject to the provisions specified in the previous enactments relative to the same; and from and after the passage of this act, the control of the said Commissioners of Health, and of each and every one of them over the same shall cease and determine, except as hereinbefore provided.

Except in regard to the sanitary treatment of inmates.

Statement of mariners' fund to be rendered to said Commissioners.

§ 2. The Comptroller of the State shall, within ten days after the passage of this act, render to the Commissioners of Emigration a full and particular statement of the condition of the Mariners' Fund, and the said Commissioners shall have full power and authority to sue for and collect all claims in favor of said fund, and the moneys so collected shall be deposited with the Chamberlain of the city of New York, and shall be drawn from him in the manner provided by the fourteenth section of the act hereby amended.

Powers of Commissioners of emigration.

§ 3. The Commissioners of Emigration, or any one or more of them, shall have and exercise the same powers and authority, in relation to poor children actually chargeable upon, or receiving support from said commissioners, as are now conferred by law upon the "Commissioner of the Alms-House Department," of the city of New York, respecting the "act concerning apprentices and servants."

To make the necessary regulations for the institution.

§ 4. The Commissioners of Emigration are authorized to make such regulations as they may deem necessary for the government of the institution, in which they may support such persons as become chargeable to them, and for the employment of the inmates thereof.

§ 5. In all cases in which the minor children of alien passengers shall become orphans, by their parents or last surviving parent dying on the passage to the port of New York, or in the Marine Hospital on Staten Island, the personal property which said parents or parent may have had with them shall be taken in charge by the Commissioners of Emigration to be by them appropriated for the sole benefit of said orphan children; and said Commissioners shall give in their annual report to the legislature, a minute statement of all cases in which property shall come into their possession by virtue of this section, and the disposition made of the same. And the Commissioners of Emigration are hereby authorized to prescribe rules requiring the Health Officer to make such reports to them respecting the persons and property at said hospital as they may consider necessary. **Provision respecting orphan children of alien passengers.**

§ 6. The second section of this act in relation to the collection of moneys by the Commissioners of Emigration shall not apply to the sum of sixteen thousand one hundred and sixty-six dollars and thirteen cents paid to the Commissioners of Health by the Trustees of the Seamen's Fund and Retreat, and now in the hands of the Commissioners of Health, but the said sum shall be paid into the treasury by the Commissioners of Health, and when so paid ten thousand dollars thereof shall be applied as provided by the second section of the act, chapter 373, of the Laws of 1847, and the residue thereof in such manner as may be hereafter provided by law. **Provision respecting $16-166 13 paid to Commissioners.**

§ 7. Nothing in this act contained shall be deemed to affect the present mode of appointment of the Health Officer, Resident Physician or Commissioner of Health in the city of New York; nor to prevent the Health Officer from selecting his own medical assistants. **Saving clause.**

§ 8. This act shall take effect immediately.

CHAP. 350.

AN ACT *to amend certain acts concerning passengers coming to the city of New York.*

Passed April 11, 1849, "three-fifths being present."

The People of the State of New York, represented in Senate and Assembly, do enact as follows:

§ 1. The first section of an act entitled "An act concerning passengers in vessels coming to the city of New York," passed May 5, 1847, is hereby amended so as to read:

Masters of ps or ves- s landing ssengers to port to yor of w York.

Within twenty-four hours after the landing of any passenger from any ship or vessel arriving at the port of New York, from any of the United States other than this State, or from any country out of the United States, the master or commander of the ship or vessel from which such passenger or passengers shall have been landed shall make a report in writing, on oath or affirmation, to the mayor of the city of New York, or in case of his absence or other inability to serve, to the person discharging the duties of his office, which report shall state the name, place of birth, last legal residence, age, and occupation of every person or passenger who shall have landed from such ship or vessel on her last voyage to said port, not being a citizen of the United States, and who shall have within the last preceding twelve months arrived from any country out of the United States, at any place within the United States, and who shall not have paid the commutation money, or been bonded according to the provisions of this act, or of the act hereby amended, or of the act of February 11, 1824, concerning passengers in vessels coming to the port of New York, nor paid commutation money under the provisions of this or any former act. The said report shall contain a like statement of all such persons or passengers, as aforesaid, as shall have landed or been suffered to land from any such ship or vessel at any place during such last voyage, or who shall have been put on board, or suffered to go on board of any ship, vessel or boat, with the intention of proceeding to and landing at the said city of New York, or elsewhere within the limits of this State. The said report shall further specify whether any of said passengers so reported are lunatic, idiot, deaf, dumb, blind or infirm; and if so, whether they are accompanied by relatives likely to be able to support them; and shall further specify particularly the names, last place of residence, and ages of all passengers who may have died during the said last voyage of such vessel; also the names and residence of the owner or owners of such vessel. In case any such master or commander shall omit or neglect to report, as aforesaid, any such person or passenger, with the particulars aforesaid, or shall make any false report or statement in respect to any such person or passenger, or in respect to the owner or owners of any such vessel, or in respect to all or any of the particulars hereinbefore specified, such master or commander shall forfeit the sum of seventy-five dollars for every such passenger, in regard to whom any such omission or neglect shall have occurred, or any such false report or statement shall be made, for which the owner or owners, consignee or consignees of every such ship or vessel shall also be liable jointly and severally, and which may be sued for and recovered as hereinafter provided.

§ 2. The second section of said act is hereby amended so as to read:

Owner or consignee of ship or vessel to give a several bond for each person or passenger named in report.

It shall be the duty of the said mayor, or other person discharging the duties of his office as aforesaid, by an endorsement to be made on the said report, to require the owner or consignee of the ship or vessel from which such persons were landed, to give a several bond to the people of the State in a penalty of three hundred dollars for each and every person or passenger included in such report, such bond being secured, as hereinafter provided and conditioned, to indemnify and save harmless the Commissioners of Emigration, and each and every city, town or county in this State, from any cost which said Commissioners or such city, town or county, shall incur for the relief or support of the person named in the bond within five years from the date of such bond, and also to indemnify and refund to the said Commissioners of Emigration any expense or charge they may necessarily incur for the support or medical care of the person named therein, if received into the Marine Hospital or any other institution under their charge. Each and every bond shall be secured by two or more sufficient sureties, being residents of the State of New York, each of whom shall prove, by oath or otherwise, that he is owner of a freehold in the State of the value of three hundred dollars, over and above all or any claim or lien thereon or against him, including therein any contingent claim which may accrue from or upon any former bond given under the provisions of this act; or such bond may, at the option of the party, be secured by mortgage of real estate, or by the pledge and transfer of public stock of the United States, or of the State of New York, or of the city of New York, or by deposit of the amount of the penalty in some bank or trust company; such security, real or personal, having been first approved by the said mayor. It shall be lawful for any owner or consignee at any time within three days after the landing of such persons or passengers from any ship or vessel in the port of New York, to commute for the bond or bonds so required, by paying to the Health Commissioner of the city of New York the sum of one dollar and fifty cents for each and every passenger reported by him as by law required; the receipt of such sum by such Health Commissioner shall be deemed a full and sufficient discharge from the requirements of giving bonds as above provided. The said Health Commissioner is hereby required to pay once daily the same money, with an account thereof, to the Chamberlain of the city of New York. The said Health Commissioner shall receive in lieu of fees and percentages a salary of two thousand dollars per annum, and shall give bonds, to be approved of by one of the judges of the Supreme Court, in the penalty of ten thousand dollars for the faithful performance of his duty.

Each bond to be secured by two or more sureties.

Owner or consignee may commute for the bonds.

Money, to whom paid by Health Commissioner.

§ 3. Section three of said act is amended so as to read as follows :

Commissioners of emigration to examine into the condition of passengers etc.

It shall be the duty of the Commissioners of Emigration hereinafter named to examine into the condition of passengers arriving at the port of New York in any ship or vessel, and for that purpose all or any of the said Commissioners, or such other person or persons as they shall appoint, shall be authorized to go on board and through any such ship or vessel, and if, on such examination, there shall be found among such passengers any lunatic, idiot, deaf, dumb, blind or infirm persons not members of emigrating families, or who, from attending circumstances, are likely to become permanently a public charge, or who have been paupers in any other country, or who from sickness or disease, existing at the time of departing from the foreign port, are or are likely soon to become a public charge, they shall report the same to the said mayor particularly; and thereupon and unless a bond as required in the second section of this act shall have been given, the said mayor, or the person discharging the duties of his office, shall require in the endorsement to be made as aforesaid, or in any subsequent endorsement or endorsements thereon, and in addition to the commutation money that the owner or consignee of such ship or vessel, with one or more sufficient sureties, shall execute a joint and several bond to the people of the State in a penalty of five hundred dollars for every such passenger conditioned to indemnify and save harmless the Commissioners of Emigration and each and every city, town or county within this State, from any further cost or charge which said Commissioners or any such city, town or county shall incur for the maintenance or support of the person or persons named in such bond or any of them within ten years from the date of such bond. The sureties to the said bonds shall be required to justify before, and to the satisfaction of, the officer making such endorsement, and by their oath or affirmation shall satisfy such officer that they are respectively residents of the State of New York and worth double the amount of the penalty of such bond over and above all debts, liabilities and all property exempt from execution. The subsequent endorsement authorized in this section may be made at any time within ten days after such examination, or of the landing of any such person or passenger.

The sureties required to justify.

Provision in case a person becomes chargeable to a city or town.

§ 4. If any person for whom a bond shall have been given as aforesaid shall within the time specified in such bond become chargeable upon any city, town or county of this State, or upon the moneys under the control of the said Commissioners as aforesaid, the said Commissioners may bring an action on such bond in the name of the people of this State, and shall be entitled to recover on such bond from time to time so much money, not in the whole exceeding the penalty of such bond, exclusive of costs, as shall be sufficient to defray the expenses incurred by any such city, town or county, or the said Commissioners for the maintenance and support of the person for whom such bond was given as aforesaid, and shall be authorized to collect and apply such money from any of the real or other security mortgaged, pledged or deposited therefor in conformity to this act.

§ 5. If any owner or consignee as aforesaid shall refuse or neglect to give any such bond or bonds and security therefor as hereinbefore required for each person or passenger landing from his ship or vessel, within three days after the landing of such persons or passengers, in respect to bonds required by the second section of this act, or shall not within that time have paid the moneys authorized by said second section to be received in cases where such bonds are herein authorized to be commuted for, every such owner or consignee of such ship or vessel severally and respectively, shall be subject to a penalty of five hundred dollars for each and every person or passenger on whose account such bond may have been required, or for whom such commutation money might have been paid under this act; such penalty to be sued for as provided for in the twelfth section of the said act hereby amended.

Penalty for neglect or refusal to give bond and security.

§ 6. The first section of the act entitled "An act to amend an act entitled 'An act concerning passengers in vessels coming to the city of New York,'" passed December 15, 1847, is hereby amended so as to read as follows:

Marine Hospital &c., vested in Commissioners of Emigration.

The institution belonging to this State now known as the Marine Hospital, and all the lands and buildings thereon, and all lands and buildings which may hereafter be purchased or erected and designated for such Marine Hospital, or lands and buildings used for quarantine purposes, are hereby vested in the Commissioners of Emigration, to be by them held in trust for the people of this State; and the sole and exclusive control of the same, except in regard to the sanitary treatment of the inmates thereof, is hereby given to the said Commissioners of Emigration, for the purpose of receiving therein all persons for whom bonds may be required, or for whom any bond or bonds may have been given, required, or commuted for under the provisions of this act, or the acts hereby amended, suffering under or afflicted with any contagious or infectious disease, or other disease preventing their immediate removal to any more distant hospital, and who shall be sent to such hospital by the direction of the Health Officer, or under his authority.

§ 7. The third section of the act entitled "An act to amend an act entitled 'An act concerning passengers in vessels coming to the city of New York,'" passed December 15, 1847, is hereby amended by adding thereto at the end thereof the words following:

Provision respecting bastards.

The Commissioners of Emigration shall also have, in relation to any illegitimate children so chargeable, or any child likely to be born a bastard, whose mother is so chargeable or receiving support, the same powers and authority to proceed to secure indemnity for the support of the mother and child, as are now or have heretofore been by law vested in the Commissioners of the Alms-House.

They may appoint a superintendent, officers,&c., for said hospital.

§ 8. The Commissioners of Emigration are authorized to employ and appoint a superintendent and such officers other than physicians, nurses and orderlies, and such servants as they shall deem necessary for the management and care of the Marine and other hospital used for quarantine purposes, and to pay all needful expenses therefor out of the moneys under their control. But the moneys received under any of the provisions of this act as commutation money, or upon bonds given for or on account of any persons or passengers landing from vessels at the port of New York, or elsewhere, shall not be applied or appropriated to any other purpose or use than to defray the expenses incurred for the care, support or maintenance of such persons or passengers, and nothing in this act contained shall be deemed to affect the authority of the Board of Health, nor the mode of appointment of the Health Officer, Resident Physician, or Commissioner of Health of the city of New York, or to prevent the Health Officer from selecting his own medical assistants for any duties required by law to be discharged by him, or under his authority. The said Health Officer shall at all times have access to inspect all or any patients affected with any contagious or infectious diseases, and to decide upon their detention at quarantine, or the further detention of the vessels from which such patients may have been received.

Amendment.

§ 9. The fourth section of said last mentioned act is amended by striking out the words "of the" before the word "institution," and inserting in lieu thereof the word "any."

§ 10. The fifth section of said last mentioned act is amended so as to read:

Provision relative to property of minors & alien passengers.

In all cases in which minor children of alien passengers shall become orphans by their parents or last surviving parent dying on the passage to the port of New York, or in the Marine Hospital, or any other establishment under the charge of the Commissioners, the personal property which such parents or parent may have had with them shall be taken in charge by the Commissioners of Emigration, to be by them appropriated for the sole benefit of said orphan children; and said Commissioners shall give in their annual report to the Legislature a minute statement of all cases in which property shall come into their possession by virtue of this section, and the disposition made of the same.

§ 11. The Board of Health of the city of New York may appoint any physician in their employ, or in that of the Commissioners of Emigration, to act as the agent of the Board of Health in all matters concerning the protection of the city against the introduction of contagious or infectious diseases.

Board of Health may appoint an agent.

§ 12. It shall be the duty of the superintendent of the Marine or other hospital, used for quarantine purposes, to furnish to the Board of Health, as often as may be required, a full and correct report of all persons in the said hospital affected with any contagious or infectious disease, and of all such patients as may die or be discharged as cured; such report shall be countersigned by the agent of the Board of Health, and no persons who may be, or who have been received as patients affected with contagious or infectious diseases, or under treatment as such, shall be discharged or removed from the Marine or other hospital used for quarantine purposes without a permit in writing from the Health Officer.

Superintendent to report to Board of Health.

§ 13. The Commissioners of Emigration shall receive into the Marine or other hospital for quarantine purposes, all alien passengers for whom bonds shall have been given or commutation paid, under the several acts of this State relating to alien passengers arriving at the port of New York, who shall be affected with any contagious or infectious disease, and sent to such hospital by the authority of the Health Officer. They shall defray the expenses of such patients out of the moneys by them received on account of bonds or commutation. They shall also receive and provide for all other patients or passengers who shall have landed from any vessel at the port of New York, affected with any contagious or infectious disorder, who shall be directed to be so received by the Health Officer or the Board of Health; they shall be entitled to receive for each person so admitted (other than aliens as above mentioned) at the rate of three dollars per week for their support and medical care, which shall be at the expense of the owner or consignee of any vessel in which such person shall have arrived, and from which they shall have landed, and no vessel shall be per-

What alien passengers are to be received into hospital.

mitted to leave quarantine until such expense shall have been paid, or secured to be paid to the satisfaction of the Commissioners of Emigration or the officer duly authorized by them for such purpose.

Restriction.

§ 14. The Health Officer shall not by right of office have any other authority over the Marine Hospital, or medical charge as physician thereof, than as in this act provided.

Repeal of a part of act of 1846.

§ 15. So much of the act concerning quarantine or regulations in the nature of quarantine at the port of New York, passed May 18th, 1846, as requires that any person shall be admitted into the Marine Hospital who shall have paid hospital money during any temporary sickness within one year after such payment, is hereby repealed.

Repeal of part of the Revised Statutes, &c.

§ 19. So much of the Revised Statutes in relation to the Marine Hospital and its funds, and the several acts and amendments thereto, passed April 18, 1843, and May 7, 1843, as authorizes or requires the Health Commissioner to demand or receive hospital money from or on account of any master, mate, sailor or passenger arriving in the port of New York, is hereby repealed.

Physicians of Marine Hospital and assistants how appointed.

§ 17. There shall be nominated by the Governor, and appointed by him with the consent of the Senate, a "Physician of Marine Hospital,"

And such number of assistants not less than four, to be respectively designated as "Assistant Physician of Marine Hospital," as the Commissioners of Emigration shall from time to time determine to be necessary for the proper care and medical treatment of the persons under their care at the Marine or other hospital for quarantine purposes. The number of "assistant physicians of Marine Hospital," shall not be at any time increased, unless the Commissioners of Emigration shall make and file with the Secretary of State a certificate, that in their judgment an increased number should be appointed to meet the actual permanent demand for medical services at such hospital, a copy of which certificate shall be furnished to the Governor of the State, and when any vacancy shall exist in the office of "Physician of Marine Hospital," or "Assistant Physician of Marine Hospital," and the Senate shall not be in session, such vacancy shall be filled by appointment, made by the Governor, until the next meeting of the Senate, and the confirmation thereof, or appointment of a successor.

Powers of the physician.

§ 18. The physician of Marine Hospital shall have the superintendence and control of, and shall make such regulations for the sanitary treatment of the patients in such Marine or other hospital for quarantine purposes as may be found necessary, and prescribe therein the duties of the assistant physicians thereof, and shall take upon himself and assign to such assistants respectively the charge of such portions of such hospital as shall seem to him best adapted to secure the objects and purposes of such institution, and the care and proper medical treatment of the inmates thereof; and the said Commissioners may employ from time to time such additional medical assistants as the temporary wants of such hospital and the inmates thereof shall require.

Assistants to appoint nurses and orderlies.

§ 19. Each assistant physician of such Marine or other hospital for quarantine purposes, shall from time to time, as shall be necessary, select and appoint such and so many nurses and orderlies in the department of such hospital which shall have been assigned to or be under his supervision and care, as shall be required for the proper care of the inmates of their respective departments; but the number of such nurses and orderlies shall be determined and controlled by the "Physician of Marine Hospital," and the compensation of such nurses and orderlies and of each of them, shall be fixed and determined by the Commissioners of Emigration.

Salaries of Physician & assistants.

§ 20. The "Physician of Marine Hospital" shall have and receive an annual salary of five thousand dollars, to be paid quarterly;

And each of the assistant physicians shall have and receive a salary of one thousand two hundred dollars per annum, to be paid quarterly or monthly, as the Commissioners of Emigration may determine; and in that ratio for any period of service of such physician or assistant,

And all salaries and other compensation of such physician and assistant physicians, and of all nurses, orderlies and servants, or others necessarily employed in and about the business, care and proper management of such Marine or other hospital for quarantine purposes, shall be paid by the Commissioners of Emigration, from and out of moneys collected upon the bonds hereinbefore required to be given by the owners or consignees of vessels arriving with and landing passengers at the port of New York, or from the commutation moneys paid upon or in lieu of such bonds, in accordance with the provisions of this act, and all the expenses of such marine or other hospital for quarantine purposes, shall, far as practicable, be defrayed by said Commissioners out of and from the moneys and securities in this act specified; but nothing in this act contained shall be so construed as to authorize the payment of any salary or compensation for services rendered by said Commissioners of Emigration or any of them.

Penalties & forfeitures how sued for and recovered.

§ 21. The penalties and forfeitures prescribed in and by this act may be sued for and recovered with costs of suit, by and in the name of the said Commissioners of Emigration in any court having cognizance thereof, and when recovered shall be applied to the support of such Marine or other hospital for quarantine purposes as specified in this act. It shall be lawful for the said Commissioners, before or after suit brought, to compound or commute for any of the said penalties or forfeitures upon such terms as they shall think proper, also to commute and compound with the owner or consignee of any ship or vessel for any such bond or bonds as are required in section three of this act, to be given by such owner or consignee for such person or persons, passenger or passengers as have been paupers in any other country, or whom from sickness or disease, existing at the time of departure from the foreign port, are or are likely soon to become a public charge, or who shall be sent to the Marine or other hospital for quarantine purposes in accordance with the provisions of this act, in consequence of sickness or disease existing at the time of departure from the foreign port, the commutation for said last mentioned bond or bonds to be fixed by said Commissioners at such sum as they shall deem just and equitable, and sufficient to defray the necessary expenses consequent upon the care, support and maintenance of the persons for whom such commutation shall be paid, during the existence and continuance of their then sick or diseased state.

§ 22. This act shall take effect immediately.

CHAP. 28.

AN ACT *to enable the Commissioners of Emigration to borrow money on mortgage in certain cases.*

Passed March 2, 1850, "three-fifths being present."

The People of the State of New York, represented in Senate and Assembly, do enact as follows:

§ 1. The Commissioners of Emigration are authorized to borrow from time to time such sums of money as may be needed for the support of the Marine Hospital, or for the reimbursement of the several cities or counties of this State, their expenses incurred for the support of emigrant paupers, or for any other expenditures as may be authorized by law to be made by the said Commissioners; and to mortgage for the securing the payment of the moneys so borrowed, any of the real estate held or purchased by the said Commissioners for the people of this State, or which may hereafter be purchased by the Commissioners.

May borrow money

And mortgage real estate.

§ 2. Before executing any such mortgage, the Commissioners of Emigration shall present to the governor, comptroller and attorney-general, a statement showing the reason of such loan and the intended application thereof, and a description of the real estate intended to be mortgaged; and no such mortgage shall be lawful, unless a certificate of approval thereof shall be first given, signed by the governor, comptroller, and attorney-general. Such certificate may be acknowledged, or framed, or worded in the manner by law provided in respect to conveyances of real estate. Every such mortgage shall be executed by a majority of the Commissioners.

Proviso.

§ 3. The moneys so borrowed shall in no case be a claim against the State, but shall be repaid out of the surplus funds received by the Commissioners, or from the proceeds of the lands mortgaged.

Moneys, how repaid.

§ 4. This act shall take effect immediately.

CHAP. 339.

AN ACT *to amend the act entitled "An act concerning passengers in vessels coming to the city of New York," passed May* 5, 1847*; also to amend the act entitled "An act to amend certain acts concerning passengers coming to the city of New York," passed April* 11, 1849.

Passed April 10, 1850.

The People of the State of New York, represented in Senate and Assembly, do enact as follows:

§ 1. The thirteenth section of the act entitled "An act concerning passengers in vessels coming to the city of New York," passed May 5, 1847, is hereby amended so as to read as follows:

ılty or iture enforc-

"Any ship or vessel, whose master or commander, owner or owners, shall have incurred any penalty or forfeiture under this act, or under the act of 11th April, 1849, amending the same, entitled 'An act to amend certain acts concerning passengers coming to the city of New York,' shall be liable for such penalties or forfeitures which may be a lien upon such ship or vessel, and may be enforced and collected by warrant of attachment in the same manner as is provided in title eight of chapter eight of the third part of the Revised Statutes, all the provisions of which title shall apply to the forfeitures and penalties imposed by this act; and the said Commissioners of Emigration shall, for the purposes of such attachment, be deemed creditors of such ship or vessel, and of her master or commander and owner or owners respectively."

§ 2. The fifth section of the act entitled "An act to amend certain acts concerning passengers coming to the city of New York," passed April 11, 1849, is hereby amended so as to read as follows:

"If any owner or consignee, as aforesaid, shall refuse or

neglect to give any such bond or bonds as hereinbefore required, according to the second section of this act, for each person or passenger landing from his ship or vessel, within *three days* after the landing of such persons or passengers, or shall not within that time have paid the moneys authorized by said second section to be received in cases where such bonds are herein authorized to be commuted for, or shall refuse or neglect to give the bonds required by the third section of this act to be given in certain cases, on the requirement of the mayor of the city of New York, or other person discharging the duties of his office, made according to the provisions of said section, within *six days* after such requirement being so made, every such owner or consignee of such ship or vessel, severally and respectively, shall be subject to a penalty of five hundred dollars for each and every person or passenger on whose account such bond may have been required, or for whom such commutation money might have been paid under this act; such penalty to be sued for as provided for in the twelfth section of the said act hereby amended, in every case where any fine, penalty, or forfeiture shall be incurred by the owner or owners, consignee or consignees, master, or commander of any vessel arriving at the port of New York, under any of the provisions of the acts concerning passengers coming to the city of New York, passed 5th May, 1847, and of this act, by reason of their neglect or refusal to give the bonds, or any of them, required by law, the consignee of such passengers, in relation to whom such neglect or refusal shall have occurred, shall be liable in the same penalties, and may be sued and recovered against in the same manner as is by law provided in relation to the owner or owners, consignee or consignees of the vessel.

Penalty for refusing to give bond.

§ 3. The fifth section of the aforesaid act, passed 5th May, 1847, and amended by the tenth section of the aforesaid act, passed April 11th, 1849, is hereby further amended so as to read as follows:

"In all cases in which minor children of alien passengers shall become orphans by their parents, or last surviving parent dying on the passage to the port of New York, or in the Marine Hospital, or in any other establishment under the charge of the Commissioners, the personal property which such parents or parent may have had with them shall be taken in charge by the Commissioners of Emigration, to be by them appropriated for the sole

Property of minors, how disposed of.

benefit of said orphan children ; and said Commissioners shall give, in their annual report to the Legislature, a minute statement of all cases in which property shall come into their possession by virtue of this section, and the disposition made of the same, unless it shall appear that there are other children or persons entitled by will or otherwise, to such property, or a distributive share thereof. Whenever it shall so appear, the portion only to which the said minor orphans would be legally entitled shall be applied to their use, and the remainder shall be received, held and distributed to the parties severally entitled thereto, in the same manner, and with the same authority as by law provided in respect to public administrators."

CHAP. 523.

AN ACT *to amend chapter four hundred and eighty-three, of the laws of eighteen hundred and forty-seven, chapter three hundred and fifty, of the laws of eighteen hundred and forty-nine, chapter two hundred and seventy-five, of the laws of eighteen hundred and fifty, and chapter three hundred and thirty-nine, of the laws of eighteen hundred and fifty, acts concerning passengers coming to the city of New York, and the public health.*

Passed July 11, 1851.

The People of the State of New York, represented i Senate and Assembly, do enact as follows:

Property alien e[illegible] grants.

§ 1. The third section of chapter three hundred and thirty-nine, of the laws of eighteen hundred and fifty, is hereby amended so as to be read as follows: Whenever any alien emigrant, whose personal property shall not exceed the value of twenty-five dollars, shall die on the passage to the port of New York, or in the Marine Hospital, or in any other establishment under the charge of the Commissioners, and in all cases in which minor children of alien passengers shall become orphans by their parents or last surviving parent dying, as aforesaid, the personal property which such alien emigrant, or such parent or parents may have had with them shall be taken in charge by the Commissioners of Emigration, to be by them appropriated for the sole benefit of the next of kin of such alien emigrant or of said orphan children; and said Commissioners shall give, in their annual report to the Legislature, a minute description of all cases in which property shall come into their possession by virtue of this section, and the disposition made of the same, unless it shall appear that there are other persons entitled by will or otherwise to such property or distributive share thereof. Whenever it shall so appear, the portion only to which the next of kin or said minor orphans would be legally entitled shall be transferred to them or applied to their use, and the remainder shall be received, held, and distributed to the parties severally entitled thereto, in the same manner and with the same authority as by law provided in respect to the public administrator of the city of New York, except that the said Commissioners are hereby authorized to distribute the same after a notice for creditors to appear and put in their claims within one week from the publication of the said notice. The said notice shall be published once in one of the daily papers of the city of New York.

Poor children.

§ 2. The third section of chapter four hundred and eighty-three, of the laws of eighteen hundred and forty-seven, is hereby amended so as to read as follows: The Commissioners of Emigration, or any one or more of them, shall have and exercise the same powers and authority in relation to poor children, actually chargeable upon or receiving support from said Commissioners, as are now by law conferred upon the Governors of the Alms-House, by section seven, of chapter three hundred and twenty-four, of laws of eighteen hundred and fifty.

Master of vessel to report age, &c., of passengers.

§ 3. The first section of an act entitled "An act concerning passengers in vessels coming to the city of New York," passed May fifth, eighteen hundred and forty-seven, as the same was amended by the first section of an act entitled "An act to amend certain acts concerning passengers coming to the city of New York, passed April eleventh, one thousand eight hundred and forty-nine," is hereby further amended so as to read as follows: Within twenty-four hours after the landing of any passenger from any ship or vessel arriving at the port of New York, from any of the United States other than this state, or from any country out of the United States, the master or commander of the ship or vessel from which such passenger or passengers shall have been landed shall make a report in writing, on oath or affirmation, to the mayor of the city of New York, or in case of his absence, or other inability to serve, to the person discharging the duties of his office, which report shall state the name, place of birth, last legal residence, age and occupation of every person or passenger who shall have landed from such ship or vessel on her last voyage to said port, not being a citizen of the United States, and who shall have, within the last twelve months, arrived from any country out of the United States, at any place within the United States, and who shall not have paid the commutation money, or been bonded according to the provisions of this act, or of the act hereby amended, or of the act of February eleventh, eighteen hundred and twenty-four, concerning passengers in vessels coming to the port of New York, nor paid commutation money under the provisions of this or any former act. The same report shall contain a like statement of all such persons or passengers aforesaid, as shall have been landed, or been suffered to land from any such ship or vessel at any place during such last voyage, or who shall have been put on board, or suffered to go on board of any other ship, vessel, or boat, with the intention of proceeding to and landing at the said city of New York, or elsewhere, within the limits of this state. The said report shall further specify whether any of the said passengers so reported are lunatic, idiot, deaf, dumb, blind, infirm, maimed, or above the age of sixty years, also designating all such passengers as shall be under the age of thirteen, or widows having families, or women without husbands having families, with the names and ages of their families, and shall further specify particularly the names, last place of residences, and ages of all passengers who may have died during the said last voyage of such vessel, also the names and residences of the owner or owners of such vessel. In case any such master or commander shall omit or neglect to report as aforesaid, any such person or passenger, with the particulars aforesaid, or shall make any false report, or statement in respect to any such person or passenger, or in respect to the owner or owners of any such vessel, or in respect to any of the particulars herein before specified, such master or commander shall forfeit the sum of seventy-five dollars for every such passenger, in regard to whom any such omission or neglect shall have occurred, or any such false report or statement shall be made, for which the owner or owners, consignee or consignees of every such ship or vessel shall also be liable, jointly and severally, and which may be sued for and recovered, as hereinafter provided.

Condition of passengers to be examined into.

§ 4. Section third of the said act, concerning passengers coming to the city of New York, passed May fifth, eighteen hundred and forty-seven, as the same was amended by section three of the act to amend certain acts concerning passengers coming to the port of New York, passed April eleventh, eighteen hundred and forty-nine, is hereby further amended so as to read as follows: It shall be the duty of the Commissioners of Emigration, hereafter named, to examine into the condition of passengers arriving at the port of New York in any ship or vessel, and for that purpose all or any of the said Commissioners, or such other person or persons as they shall appoint, shall be authorized to go on board and through any such ship or vessel; and if on such examination there shall be found among such passengers any lunatic, idiot, deaf, dumb, blind, maimed, or infirm persons, or persons above the age of sixty years, or widow with a child or children, or any woman without a husband, and with a child or children, or any person unable to take care of himself or herself without becoming a public charge, or who, from any attending circumstances, are likely to become a public charge, or who, from sickness or disease, existing at the time of departure from the foreign port, are, or are likely soon to become a public charge, they shall report the same to the said mayor particularly, and thereupon, and unless a bond, as required in the second section of this act, shall have been given, the said mayor, or the person discharging the duties of his office, shall require in the endorsement to be made as aforesaid, or in any subsequent endorsement or endorsements thereon, and in addition to the commutation money, that the owner or consignee of such ship or vessel, with one or more sufficient sureties, shall execute a joint and several bond to the people of the state in a penalty of five hundred dollars, for every such passenger, conditioned to indemnify and save harmless the Commissioners of Emigration, and each and every city, town or county within the state from any further cost or charge, which said Commissioners, or any such city, town or county shall incur for the maintenance or support of the person or persons named in such bond, or any of them, within five years from the date of such bond. The sureties to the said bonds shall be required to justify before and to the satisfaction of the officer making such endorsement, and by their oath or affirmation shall satisfy such officer that they are respectively residents of the State of New York, and worth double the amount of the penalty of such bond, over and above all debts, liabilities, and all property exempt from execution. The subsequent endorsement authorized in this section may be made at any time within thirty days after such examination, or of the landing of any such person or passenger.

§ 5. The eighth section of chapter three hundred and fifty, of the laws of eighteen hundred and forty-nine, is hereby amended so as to read as follows: The Commissioners of Emigration are authorized

Commissioners to appoint serv'nts a

To employ and appoint and dismiss at pleasure a superintendent, physicians and such other officers, nurses and orderlies and such servants as they shall deem necessary for the management and care of the Marine and other hospitals used for quarantine purposes, and

To pay all needful expenses therefor out of the moneys under their control; but the moneys received under any of the provisions of this act as commutation money, or upon bonds given for or on account of any persons or passengers landing from vessels at the port of New York, or elsewhere, shall not be applied or appropriated to any other purpose or use than to defray the expenses incurred for the care, support, or maintenance of such persons or passengers, nor shall such passengers be entitled to any aid from the Commissioners of Emigration after they shall have left the State of New York, and been absent therefrom for more than one year. Nothing in this act contained shall be deemed to affect the authority of the Board of Health, nor the mode of appointment of the Health Officer, Resident Physician, or Commissioner of Health of the city of New York, or to prevent the Health Officer from selecting his own medical assistants, other than those of the Marine Hospital, for any duties required by law to be discharged by him, or under his authority.

§ 6. Section seventeen of chapter three hundred and fifty, of laws of eighteen hundred and forty-nine, is hereby amended so as to read as follows: The Commissioners of Emigration are authorized to require the Health Officer to perform the duties of physician to the Marine Hospital; in which case he

Health Officer.

shall reside within the quarantine enclosure, and perform the duties of physician of Marine Hospital, and all other duties appertaining to that office, and discharge the patients from the hospital without compensation therefor, other than is now by law allowed him as Health Officer, and he shall not be entitled to demand or receive from the Commissioners of Emigration any pay or compensation whatever for services performed by him except where a written contract to that effect shall have been entered into by them. He shall also perform the duties of superintendent without compensation, if so required by the Commissioners of Emigration,

And at and after the expiration of the term of the present Health Officer, he shall pay the wages of the boatmen whom they shall respectively employ, and the Commissioners of Emigration shall in no respect be liable therefor.

Bond required of consignee of vessel.

§ 7. Section second of chapter three hundred and fifty of the laws of eighteen hundred and forty-nine, is hereby amended so as to read as follows: It shall be the duty of the said mayor or other person discharging the duties of his office aforesaid, by an endorsement to be made on the said report, to require the owner or consignee of the ship or vessel from which such persons were landed, to give a several bond to the people of the State, in a penalty of three hundred dollars for each and every person or passenger included in such report, such bond being secured as hereinafter provided, and conditioned to indemnify and save harmless the Commissioners of Emigration and each and every city, town, or county in this State from any cost which said Commissioners or such city, town or county shall incur for the relief or support of the person named in the bond, within five years from the date of such bond, and also to indemnify and refund to the said Commissioners of Emigration any expense or charge they may necessarily incur for the support or medical care of the persons named therein, if received into the Marine Hospital or any other institution under their charge. Each and every bond shall be secured by two or more sufficient securities, being residents of the State of New York, each of whom shall prove by oath or otherwise that he is owner of a freehold in the State of the value of three hundred dollars over and above all or any claim or lien thereon, or against him, including therein any contingent claim which may accrue from or upon any former bond given under the provisions of this act; or such bond may, at the option of the party, be secured by mortgage of real estate, or by the pledge and transfer of public stock of the United States or of the State of New York, or of the city of New York, or by deposit of the amount of penalty in some bank or trust company; such security, real or personal, having been first approved by the said mayor. It shall be lawful for any owner or consignee at any time within twenty-four hours after the landing of such persons or passengers from any ship or vessel in the port of New York, except as in the section hereinafter provided, to commute for the bond or bonds so required, by paying to the Health Commissioners of the city of New York the sum of

One dollar and fifty cents

For each and every passenger reported by him as by law required; the receipt of such sum by said Health Commissioners shall be deemed a full and sufficient discharge from the requirements of giving bonds as above provided. The said Health Commissioner is hereby required to pay over daily the said money with an account thereof to the Chamberlain of the city of New York. But no owner or consignee shall be authorized to commute for the bond so required for any passenger arriving in the port of New York, between the first day of December and the fifteenth day of April, who may be sent to the Marine Hospital from shipboard by the Health Officer, or by the authority of the Board of Health of the city of New York on account of illness from ship fever. The Commissioners of Emigration shall have authority to commute specially for any bond in such cases at such rates and in such manner as shall appear to them equitable and proper. It shall be the duty of the Health Officer to report without delay to the Commissioners of Emigration the names of all passengers sent by his order during the above mentioned period from ship board to the Marine Hospital on account of illness from ship fever. For the duties performed by the Health Commissioner and named in this section, he shall be paid by the Commissioners of Emigration at the rate of seventeen hundred and fifty dollars per annum, and he shall be paid the remainder of his salary by the Mayor, Aldermen and Commonalty of the city of New York. And at and after the expiration of the term of the present Health Commissioner, it shall be lawful for the Commissioners of Emigration to select for the performance of the duties named in this section and now performed by the Commissioner of Health, either the Mayor of the city of New York, or the Chamberlain of said city, or the Health Commissioner, and the compensation for the performance of said duties shall be so much as such officer so selected and the Commissioners of Emigration may agree upon, and thereafter the salary of the Health Commissioner shall be fixed by the Mayor, Aldermen and Commonalty of the city of New York, and paid from the treasury of said city.

Sale or exchange of land.

§ 8. The Commissioners of Emigration are hereby authorized and empowered by and with the consent and approval of the Governor, Comptroller and Attorney-general, to sell or exchange, and give conveyances for any lands or any portion thereof, which have been or may hereafter be purchased by them as such Commissioners.

§ 9. All acts and parts of acts inconsistent with this act are hereby repealed.

§ 10. The provisions of this act, so far as it relates to the abolition of the office and duties of the Physician to the Marine Hospital, shall not take effect until the first day of January next.

§ 11. This act shall take effect immediately.

CHAP. 224.

AN ACT *to amend the several acts relating to the powers and duties of the Commissioners of Emigration, and for the regulation of the Marine Hospital.*

Passed April 13, 1853, three-fifths being present.

The People of the State of New York, represented in Senate and Assembly, do enact as follows:

§ 1. The time allowed by the second section of chapter three hundred and thirty-nine of the laws of eighteen hundred and fifty to any owner or owners, consignee or consignees, of any ship or vessel bringing emigrants or passengers to the city of New York, for giving the bond or bonds first mentioned in said section, or paying the money, also therein mentioned, shall henceforth be twenty-four hours, instead of three days, from the landing of said passengers; and the time allowed by the said section to the said owner or owners, consignee or consignees, of any such ship or vessel, for giving other bond or bonds mentioned in said section, shall be twenty-four hours, instead of six days, from the making of the requirement for such last mentioned bond or bonds. **Bonds.**

§ 2. The said Commissioners of Emigration are and each of them is hereby vested with the same powers in regard to the administering oaths of office to employees, and to the binding out of children, with consent of parents or next of kin, actually chargeable upon them, and also in regard to persons in the institution, or any of them under the charge of said Commissioners, for the prevention or punishment of an infraction or violation of the rules or orders and regulation of such Commissioners or their officers in regard to such institutions, as are possessed by the Governors of tho Alms-House in the city of New York, or any of them, for the same purposes. **Powers of Commissioners.**

Annual Report. § 3. The Commissioners of Emigration shall annually, on or before the first day of February in each year, report to the Legislature the amount of moneys received, under the provisions of this act, during the preceding year, and the manner in which the same have been appropriated; stating particularly in detail the sum of each appropriation, and the purposes for which the same have been made.

Physicians. § 4. The office of Physician of Marine Hospital, as constituted by section seventeen of chapter three hundred and fifty of the laws of eighteen hundred and forty-nine, is hereby restored, together with the duties and compensation of the same, as specified in sections eighteen and twenty of said chapter three hundred and fifty of the laws of eighteen hundred and forty-nine.

Powers of Physician to appoint assistants. § 5. The Physician of Marine Hospital shall have power to select and appoint, subject to the approval of the Commissioners of Emigration, such and so many assistant physicians, graduates in medicine, as may be found necessary for the proper medical treatment of the inmates of the Marine Hospital, and to suspend or remove any of the same; but the number and rate of pay of said assistant physicians shall be regulated and determined by the Commissioners of Emigration. The Physician of Marine Hospital shall have power to select, appoint and dismiss at pleasure, Nurses and orderlies. such and so many nurses and orderlies for the departments of such Marine Hospital as he may deem requisite for the proper care of the inmates thereof; and the Commissioners of Emigration shall regulate and determine the rate of pay of the nurses and orderlies employed at the Marine Hospital.

Patients at Hospital. § 6. All discharges of patients from the Marine Hospital shall be in writing, and by the Physician of the Marine Hospital, who shall be responsible for the same, and who is hereby expressly prohibited from discharging any patient sent to the Marine Hospital, and affected with any contagious or infectious disease, until such patient shall be cured of such disease; and the said Physician of Marine Hospital shall receive into the Marine Hospital all cases of contagious, infectious, and pestilential disease which may be sent thither by the Health Officer, or under the authority of the Board of Health of the city of New York, except itch and syphilis, which shall not be construed as diseases entitling those suffering from them to be admitted as patients into the Marine Hospital.

§ 7. All officers and employees of the Marine Hospital, except chaplains, shall be required to reside within the quarantine inclosure, and the Commissioners of Emigration are hereby directed to provide suitable accommodations for the same. Officers and residence.

§ 8. The power granted to the Health Officer by an act entitled "An Act relative to the Public Health in the city of New York," passed April tenth, eighteen hundred and fifty, in so far as relates to the arrest and detention of persons eloping from the Marine Hospital, or persons invading the quarantine grounds, is hereby granted to the physician of Marine Hospital for the purpose of enabling him to maintain the Marine Hospital as a quarantine establishment, and the said physician of Marine Hospital is authorized and required to prescribe rules for regulating intercourse with the Hospital and its inmates, and he is expressly prohibited from admitting visitors at all, when in his judgment there may be danger of their communicating disease without the precincts of the quarantine grounds. Powers and duties of marine hospital physician.

§ 9. The physician of Marine Hospital shall present to the Legislature annually, on or before the first of March, a report of the general condition of the hospital under his charge, with the statistics of the institution in detail, and such other information and suggestions in regard to the same as he may deem advisable, and testify the same by his affidavit: he shall also furnish to the Board of Health of the city of New York and to the Commissioners of Emigration, whenever required by them so to do, an official return of the numbers and diseases of the patients in the Marine Hospital. Annual report.

§ 10. The Health Officer shall have no authority or control over the Marine Hospital, nor any charge or care of the sick inmates or employees of the institutions: he shall, at all times, however, have free access to the several wards, with the privilege of examining the condition of the sick inmates or employees of the institution: he shall, at all Health officer.

times, however, have free access to the several wards, with the privilege of examining the condition of the sick sent to the hospital under his authority, for the purpose of enabling him to judge as to the necessity for detaining the vessels from which said sick may have been landed; but nothing in this act shall be construed so as to interfere with the rights, duties, and powers of the Health Officer in regard to existing provisions of law, in so far as his control and authority over vessels and quarantine regulations upon the water may be concerned.

Removal of emigrants from hospital.

§ 11. The Commissioners of Emigration shall remove from the Marine Hospital and take charge of all emigrants whose quarantine has expired and who shall have sufficiently recovered from the diseases with which they were admitted, on the notification in writing of the physician of Marine Hospital that such removal will not, with ordinary care, endanger the safety of the individual or the health of the community.

Physician to act as superintendent

§ 12. The physician of Marine Hospital shall discharge the duties of Superintendent of Marine Hospital, under the Commissioners of Emigration, and without further pecuniary compensation than that allowed him as physician.

Commutation.

§ 13. The amount for which the master, owner, or owners, consignee or consignees, of any such ship or vessel may commute for any bond or bonds, authorized or required by or pursuant to the seventh section of chapter five hundred and twenty-three of the Laws of eighteen hundred and fifty-one, shall, from and after the passage of this act, be two dollars for each and every such passenger, instead of one dollar and fifty cents as now provided by law; and fifty cents of the amount commuted for any passenger or passengers shall be set aside as a separate fund for the benefit of each and every county in this State, except the county of New York. The Commissioners of Emigration shall deposit the moneys of said fund, so set apart, in any bank that the said Commissioners may select, and the same, or as much of it as may be necessary, shall be distributed to the several counties, except the county of New York, once in every three months, and the balance that may be left after such three months' payment shall be paid over to the Commissioners of Emigration for general purposes.

§ 14. All acts and parts of acts inconsistent with or repugnant to the provisions of this act are hereby repealed. Repeal.

§ 15. This act shall take effect immediately.

CHAP. 426.

AN ACT *to amend "An act concerning passengers in vessels coming to the city of New York," pased May fifth, eighteen hundred and forty-seven.*

Passed April 13, 1855.

The People of the State of New York, represented in Senate and Assembly, do enact as follows:

§ 1. The persons hereafter becoming chargeable upon any city, town or county, within this State, for the payment of any expense of whose maintenance and support incurred by any such city, town or county, it is made the duty of the Commissioners of Emigration to provide by the "Act concerning passengers in vessels coming to the city of New York," passed May 5th, eighteen hundred and forty-seven, or any act amendatory thereof, shall be deemed and taken to include all persons otherwise within the description and provisions of such act or acts, who are or shall become the inmates of any alms house, lunatic asylum, work-house, hospital, nursery, house of refuge, asylum for juvenile delinquents, house of correction, penitentiary, jail, bridewell, or prison, under commitment, sentence, or conviction, by an officer or officers, court or magistrate, under any law of this State as vagrants or disorderly persons.

§ 2. This act shall take effect immediately.

[*Extracts from Chapter* 147 *of the Laws of* 1846.]

OF THE MARINE HOSPITAL.

§ 35. The powers and duties of the "Physician of Marine Hospital" shall be as follows:

1. To select and appoint, subject to the approval of the Commissioners of Emigration, such and so many assistant physicians, nurses, orderlies, and other employees of the Marine Hospital as may be found necessary for the care and management of the said hospital, and the proper treatment of the inmates thereof, and to suspend or remove the same; but the rate of pay of said assistant physicians, nurses, orderlies, and other employees, shall be regulated and determined by the Commissioners of Emigration.

Powers and duties of physician of Marine hospital.

2. To have the general charge and control of the Marine Hospital, and to make and enforce such rules and regulations for the government of the same, and the treatment of the sick inmates thereof, as shall seem to him necessary and expedient to maintain the said Marine Hospital as a quarantine establishment.

3. To report to the health officer in writing, from time to time, and as often as may be, the persons sufficiently recovered from sickness to be discharged from said hospitals, or any of them.

4. To receive into the Marine Hospitals all persons of contagious, infectious, or pestilential disease, which may be sent thither by the Health Officer, or under his authority, or under the authority of the Board of Health of the city of New York, except itch and syphilis, which shall not be construed as diseases entitling those suffering from them to be admitted as patients into the Marine Hospital.

5. And to allow or permit the health officer at all times to have free access to the several wards of the Marine Hospitals, for the purpose of examining the sick inmates thereof, in order to enable the said officer to judge as to the necessity for detaining the vessels from which said sick may have been landed.

§ 36. Section five of chapter three hundred and fifty of the laws of eighteen hundred and forty-nine is hereby amended so as to read as follows: Any owner or consignee as aforesaid, who shall neglect or refuse to give any such bond or bonds and security therefor, as hereinbefore required for each person or passenger landing from his ship or vessel, within twenty-four hours after the landing of such persons or passengers, in respect to bonds required by the second section of this act, or shall not within that time have paid the moneys authorized by said second section to be received in cases where such bonds are herein authorized to be commuted for, every such owner or consignee of such ship or vessel, severally and respectively, shall be subject to a penalty of five hundred dollars for each and every person or passenger on whose account such bond may have been required, or for whom such commutation money might have been paid under this act; such penalty to be sued for as provided for in the twelfth section of the said act hereby amended.

Refusal by owner or consignee to give bond.

§ 38. This act shall take effect immediately.

CHAP. 515.

AN ACT *in relation to the Chaplains of the Marine Hospital.*

Passed April 15, 1857, three-fifths being present.

The People of the State of New York, represented in Senate and Assembly, do enact as follows:

SECTION 1. The annual compensation of the chaplains of the marine hospital, now located on Staten Island, shall hereafter be six hundred dollars each, in lieu of all other compensation to said chaplains now provided by law.

§ 2. This act shall take effect immediately.

CHAP. 672.

AN ACT *in regard to expenses of Emigrants, and to appropriate certain moneys to the use of the Commissioners of Emigration.*

Passed April 16th, 1857, three-fifths being present.

The People of the State of New York, represented in Senate and Assembly, do enact as follows :

SECTION 1. The payment by the Commissioners of Emigration of the amounts payable or coming to any of the cities, towns, or counties of this State, for any moneys paid out or expenses incurred previously to the first day of May next, by any of them, for the support or maintenance of any emigrant passengers who may have arrived at the port of New York, and who, or on whose account a bond may have been given, or commutation under and pursuant to chapter one hundred and ninety-five of the laws of eighteen hundred and forty-seven, or of any laws amendatory thereof, or in addition thereto, may be made by said commissioners at any time within three years from the said first day of May, and not before, unless the said commissioners shall be in funds applicable thereto. In the payment of said claims the said commissioners shall allow and pay to the said cities, towns, and counties, interest upon the amounts severally due them: provided always, that nothing herein contained shall postpone the payment to such cities, towns, and counties respectively, of the moneys which may have been appropriated for the reimbursement of said cities, towns, and counties respectively, by an act entitled "An Act for the removal of the quarantine station," passed March sixth, eighteen hundred and fifty-seven, whenever such moneys may be realized ; and provided, also, that the said sum of fifty cents mentioned in the thirteenth section of chapter two hundred and twenty four of the laws of eighteen hundred and fifty-three, shall be paid and distributed as provided in said act.

Support of emigrants.

Loan to Commissioners of emigration.

§ 2. There shall be loaned to the Commissioners of Emigration, out of any money in the treasury not otherwise appropriated, the sum of thirty thousand dollars, or so much thereof as may be necessary to repay and make up any overdraft made by the said commissioners for the support of the institution at Ward's Island, and Marine Hospital, on the presentation of satisfactory vouchers thereof to the comptroller; provided that the said Commissioners of Emigration shall enter into a contract in writing with the comptroller, to repay the State out of their commutation fund the sum so to be loaned within one year from the time when such loan shall be made; whereupon the treasurer shall pay the sum aforesaid to the Commissioners of Emigration on the warrant of the comptroller, and the comptroller is hereby directed to draw his warrant therefor.

§ 3. The sum of thirty thousand dollars is hereby appropriated for the purposes of this act.

§ 4. This act shall take effect immediately.

The commissioners of emigration shall annually make and return to the Legislature with their annual report, an affidavit, in and by which they shall respectively swear or affirm, each for himself, to the correctness of such report, and that he hath not, directly or indirectly, been interested in the business of boarding emigrants, in the transportation of any emigrant passengers through any portion of the interior of this country, or had made or received, directly or indirectly, any gain, profit, or advantage, by or through the purchase of supplies, the granting of any contract or contracts herein, or licenses, privilege or privileges, or the employment of any officer, servant or agent, mechanic, laborer or other person in the business, under the control of said commissioners. (§ 10 of Chap. 219 of Laws of 1848.)

Comm'rs to make an annual report with an affidavit.

It shall be the duty of the health officer to reside within the quarantine inclosure, and he shall have power:

Residence of Health Officer.

To cause any vessel under quarantine, when he shall judge it necessary for the purification of the vessel or her cargo, passengers, or crew, or either of them, to discharge or land the same at the quarantine ground or some other place out of the city.

Cargo and passengers to be landed.

To prohibit and prevent all persons, arriving in vessels subject to quarantine, from leaving quarantine, or removing their goods or baggage therefrom, until fifteen days after the last case of pestilential, contagious, or infectious disease shall have occurred on board, and ten days after her arrival at quarantine, unless sooner discharged by him, with the consent of the mayor or the commissioners of health.

Prohibition as to leaving Quarantine.

To permit the cargo of any vessel under quarantine, or any portion thereof, when he shall judge the same free from infection and contagion, to be conveyed to the city of New York or elsewhere; such permission, however, to be inoperative without the written approval of the mayor or commissioners of health.

Permit to proceed to N. Y.;

To cause all persons under quarantine to be vaccinated, when he deems it necessary, for the preservation of the public health.

Vaccination

To administer oaths.

To administer oaths and take affidavits in all examinations prescribed by this act, and in relation to any alleged violation of quarantine law or regulation; such oaths to have the like validity and effect as oaths administered by a commissioner of deeds. (Ch. 147 of Laws of 1856, § 12.)

Persons eloping from Marine Hospital may be arrested.

The health officer, or the physician of the Marine Hospital, may direct, in writing, any constable or other citizen, to pursue and apprehend any person not discharged, who shall elope from quarantine, or who shall violate any quarantine law or regulation, or who shall obstruct the health officer, or the physician of the Marine Hospital, in the performance of their duty, and to deliver him to said officer or officers, to be detained at quarantine until discharged by said officer or officers; but such confinement shall in no case exceed ten days. It shall be the duty of the constable, or other citizen so directed, to obey such directions; and every such person so eloping or violating the quarantine laws and regulations, or obstructing the health officer, shall be considered guilty of a misdemeanor, punishable with or by fine and imprisonment. (*Same ch.*, § 13.)

Care of the sick—Health Officer to discharge.

Every sick person sent to the Marine Hospital, by the health officer, shall be there kept and attended to with all necessary and proper care, and no such person shall leave the hospital until the health officer shall grant a discharge in writing. (*Same ch.*, § 14.)

Indigent emigrants.

The commissioners of emigration shall remove from the Marine Hospital and take charge of all indigent emigrants, whose quarantine has expired, and who shall have sufficiently recovered from the diseases with which they were admitted, on the notification in writing of the health officer, that such removal will not, with ordinary care, endanger the safety of the individual, or the health of the community. (*Same ch.*, § 15.)

Passengers under Quarantine how provided for.

All passengers being on board of vessels, under quarantine, shall be provided for by the master of the vessel in which they shall have arrived; and if the master shall omit or refuse to provide for them, or they shall have been sent on shore by the health officer, they shall be maintained by the commissioners of emigration at the expense of such vessel, her owners, consignees, and each and every one of them; and the health officer shall not permit such vessel to leave quarantine until such expense shall have been repaid or secured; and the said commissioners shall have an action against such vessel, her owners and consignees, and each and every one of them, for such expenses, which shall be a lien on such vessel, and may be enforced as other liens on vessels are enforced by said commissioners. (*Same ch.*, § 20.)

Persons charged with offense may be confined on shore.

The health officer, upon the application of the master of any vessel under quarantine, may confine, in any suitabale place on shore, any person on board of such vessel charged with having committed an offense punishable by the laws of this State or of the United States, and who cannot be secured on board of such vessel; and such confinement may continue during the quarantine of such person; or until he shall be proceeded against in due course of law; and the expense thereof shall be charged and collected as in the last preceding section. (*Same ch.*, § 21.)

Punishment for obstructing the health officer

Punishment for holding communication with vessels, &c. without permit.

Offender may be detained at Quarantine.

Every person who shall oppose or obstruct the said health officer in performing the duties required of him by law, and every person who shall go on board of, or have any communication, intercourse, or dealing with, any vessel under quarantine, or with any of her crew or passengers, without the permission of the health officer, or who shall, without such permission, invade the quarantine grounds or anchorage, shall be guilty of a misdemeanor, and shall be punished by a fine of not less than one hundred, nor more than five hundred dollars, or by imprisonment, not less than three nor more than six months in the penitentiary; and such offender shall be detained at quarantine so long as the health officer shall direct, not exceeding twenty days. In case such person shall be taken sick of any infectious, contagious, or pestilential disease, during such twenty days, he shall be detained for such further time, at the Marine Hospital, as the health officer shall direct. (*ch.* 147 of Laws of 1856, §§ 31, 32, as amended by § 4 of *ch.* 412, *of* Laws of 1857.)

When cargo may be removed or destroyed.

§ 6. The board of health, or the mayor and the commissioners of health, when they shall judge it necessary, may cause any cargo, or part of cargo, or any matter or anything within the city, that may be putrid or otherwise dangerous to the public health, to be destroyed or removed; such removal, when ordered, shall be to the quarantine ground, or such other place as the board of health shall direct; such removal or destruction shall be made at the expense of the owner or owners of the property so removed or destroyed, and the same may be recovered from such owner or owners, in an action at law, by the mayor, aldermen, and commonalty of said city. (§ 6 *of Title* 3 *of ch.* 275 *of Laws of* 1850.)

Non-resident sick to be sent to Hospital.

§ 7. The board of health may send to the Marine Hospital, or such other place as the board of health may direct, all aliens and other persons in the city, not residents thereof, who shall be sick of any infectious, pestilential, or contagious disease. The expense of the support of such aliens or other persons shall be defrayed by the corporation of the city of New York, unless such aliens or other persons shall be entitled to be supported by the commissioners of emigration. (§ 7 *of same title.*)

Trustees of Seamen's Fund and Retreat to contract for support of sick.

It shall be the duty of the said trustees (*of the Seamen's Fund and Retreat*) to contract with the health commissioners for the support of sick and disabled seamen who were subject to quarantine, and shall pay to the said commissioners the reasonable expenses, so contracted for, of all such sick and disabled seamen during the time they shall be subject to quarantine and remain at the Marine Hospital under their direction. (Laws of 1854, *ch.* 172, § 7.)

Burial ground on Staten Island

The Commissioners of Emigration shall, as soon as practicable after the passage of this act, procure a suitable place on Staten Island or elsewhere, remote from the premises of the Marine Hospital, for the burial of patients who may die in said hospital. (§ 5 of ch. 309 of Laws of 1849.)

Quarantine commissioners.

The sum of fifty thousand dollars, or so much thereof as may be necessary, is hereby appropriated out of any moneys in the treasury belonging to the general fund, not otherwise appropriated to the board of commissioners named in an act entitled "An act for the removal of quarantine station," passed march sixth, eighteen hundred and fifty-seven, if in their judgment the public health shall require it, to provide temporary accommodations at any locality which they may procure for persons arriving in the port of New York sick with yellow fever or other pestilential disease, until the present quarantine shall be removed; and it shall be the duty of the commissioners for the removal of the quarantine station to make some suitable arrangement for removing and taking proper care of such persons as may be sick at the hospitals at Castleton, and when such arrangement shall have been made, and notice thereof, in writing, shall have been given to the commissioners of emigration, they shall cease to send sick persons to said hospitals, but shall send them to such place as the said commissioners shall designate, and pay the expense of their support. (Laws of 1859, p. 1167.)*

---

* This arrangement was made and the notice given in the month of May, 1859. Soon after, the patients were removed and the hospitals at Castleton closed.

LAWS

FOR THE

PROTECTION OF EMIGRANTS.

CHAP. 474.

AN ACT *for the protection of immigrants, second class, steerage, and deck passengers.*

Passed April 13, 1855, three-fifths being present.

The People of the State of New-York, represented in Senate and Assembly, do enact as follows:

§ 1. It shall be the duty of all companies, associations, and persons, hereafter undertaking to transport or convey, or engaged in transporting or conveying, by railroad, steamboat, canal-boat or propeller, any immigrant, second class, steerage, or deck passenger, from the city, bay, or harbor of New York, to any point or place, distant more than ten miles therefrom, or from the cities of Albany, Troy, and Buffalo, the town or harbor of Dunkirk, or the suspension bridge, to any other place or places, to deliver to the mayors of the city of New York, Albany, Troy, and Buffalo, on or before the first day of April in each and every year, a written or printed statement of the price, or rates of fare, to be charged by such company, association, or person, for the conveyance of such immigrant, second class, steerage and deck passengers, respectively, and the price per hundred pounds for the carriage of the luggage, and the weight of luggage to be carried free of such passengers from and to each and every place, from and to which any such company, association, or person, shall undertake to transport and convey such passengers; and such prices or rates shall not exceed the prices and rates charged by the company, association, or person, after the time of delivering such statement to the said mayors; and such statement shall also contain a particular description of the mode and route by which such passengers are to be transported and conveyed, specifying whether it is to be by railroad, steamboat, canal-boat, or propeller, and what part of the route is by each, and also the class of passage, whether by immigrant trains, second class, steerage, or deck passage. In case such companies, association, or person, shall desire thereafter to make any change or alteration in the rates or prices of such transportation and conveyance, they shall deliver to the said mayors respectively a similar statement of the prices and rates as altered and changed by them; but the rates and prices so changed and altered, shall not be charged or received until five days after the delivery of the statement thereof to the said mayors respectively.

§ 2. Every ticket, receipt, or certificate which shall be made or issued by any company, association, or person, for the conveyance of any immigrant, second class, steerage, or deck passengers, or as evidence of their having paid for a passage, or being entitled to be conveyed from either or any of the points or places in the first section of this act mentioned to any other place or places, shall contain or have endorsed thereon a printed statement of the names of the particular railroad or railroads, and of the line or lines of steamboats, canal-boats, and propellers, or of the particular boats or propellers, as the case may be, which are to be used in the transportation and conveyance of such passengers, and also the price or rate of fare charged or received for the transportation and conveyance of any such passenger or passengers with his or their luggage.

§ 3. It shall not be lawful for any person or persons to demand or receive, or bargain for the receipt of any greater or higher price or rate of fare for the transportation and conveyance of any such immigrant, second class, steerage, or deck passengers with their luggage, or either, from either or any of the points or places in the first section of this act mentioned, to any other point or place, than the prices or rates contained in the statements which shall be delivered to the mayors of the cities of New-York, Albany, Troy, and Buffalo, and said commissioners, respectively, as in the said first section provided for, or the price or rates which shall be established and fixed for the transportation and conveyance of such passengers and their luggage, or either, by the proprietors or agents of the line or lines, or means of conveyance, by which such passenger or passengers and their luggage are to be transported or conveyed.

In all cases each immigrant over four years of age conveyed by railroad shall be furnished with a seat with permanent back to the same, and when conveyed by steamboat, propeller, or canal-boat, shall be allowed at least two and one-half feet square in the clear on deck. Such deck shall be covered and made water-tight over head, and shall be properly protected at the outsides, either by curtains or partitions, and shall be properly ventilated.

§ 4. Any company, association, person or persons, violating or neglecting to comply with any of the provisions of the first or second sections of this act, shall be liable to a penalty of two hundred and fifty dollars for each and every offence, to be sued for and recovered in the name of the people of this state; and every person violating any of the provisions of the third section of this act, shall be deemed guilty of a misdemeanor, and on conviction thereof, the person offending may be punished by a fine of two hundred and fifty dollars, or by imprisonment not exceeding one year, or by both fine and imprisonment, in the discretion of the court; one half of which fines, when recovered, shall be paid to the informer, and the other half into the county treasury where the action shall be tried or the conviction had.

§ 5. It shall be the duty of every magistrate who shall issue a warrant for the apprehension of any person or persons for violating the provisions of the third section of this act, within twenty-four hours after such person or persons shall have been taken and brought before him, to take the testimony of any witness who may be offered to prove the offence charged, in the presence of the accused, who may, in person or by counsel, cross-examine such witness. The testimony so taken shall be signed by the witness, and be certified by the magistrate, and in case such magistrate shall commit the accused to answer the charge, he shall immediately thereafter file the testimony so taken, with the district attorney of the county in which the offence was committed, to be used on the trial of or any further proceedings against the accused; and the testimony so taken shall be deemed valid and competent for that purpose, and be read and used with the like effect as if such witness were orally examined on such trial or proceedings. After the testimony of any witness shall be so taken, he shall not be detained, nor be imprisoned, or compelled to give any recognizance for his future appearance as a witness on any trial or proceeding thereafter to be had in the premises.

§ 6. The commissioners of emigration shall, from time to time, designate some one place in the city of New-York as they shall deem proper for the landing of emigrant passengers, and it shall be lawful for such passengers to be landed at such place so designated by the commissioners of emigration.

§ 7. The commissioners of emigration shall have authority to purchase, lease, construct and occupy such wharves, piers, and other accommodations in the city of New-York, as may be necessary for the accommodation of emigrant passengers for the purposes mentioned in the last preceding section.

§ 8. Whenever the health officers shall give notice in writing to the owner or owners, consignee or consignees, master, commander, or persons having charge of any vessel having emigrant passengers on board such vessel, to land such passengers at any pier or place in the city of New York designated specially by the commissioners of emigration for the landing of emigrant passengers, it shall not be lawful to land such passengers at any other pier or place, and the owners and master of any vessel from which passengers shall be landed in violation of the provisions of this section, shall be subject to a penalty of five hundred dollars for each and every violation thereof, to be sued for and recovered, with costs of suit, in the name of the commissioners of emigration, in any court having cognizance thereof, the said penalty when recovered to be applied and used by the said commissioners for the purposes for which said commissioners are constituted.*

§ 9. All acts or parts of acts inconsistent with the provisions of this act, are hereby repealed.

§ 10. This act shall take effect immediately.

The commissioners of emigration may, when in their opinion it shall seem necessary, appoint a proper person or

---

* *Amended Ch.* 579 *of Laws of* 1857, § 6.

persons, to board vessels from foreign ports at the quarantine ground or elsewhere in the port of New York, having on board emigrant passengers, for the purpose of advising such emigrants, and putting them on their guard against fraud and imposition; and the health officer is hereby required to prevent any person or persons from going on board such vessels, which may be subject to examination by him, until after the said person or persons appointed by the commissioners of emigration, shall have had sufficient opportunity to perform their duty. (§ 6 of Chap. 219 of Laws 1848.)

Persons may be apppointed to board vessels and advise emigrants.

No person holding office under the government of the United States, or of this State, or of any of its cities, or who shall be in the employment of the commissioners of emigration, shall solicit custom for any transportation line, or shall be interested in any way, directly or indirectly, in the forwarding of emigrants, under a penalty of not less than one hundred dollars, and not exceeding three hundred dollars, to be sued for in the name of the people of this State, and which money when collected, shall be paid into the County Treasury, for the use of the poor of said county. (§ 8 of same Ch.)

Restriction as to soliciting custom for transportation lines.

No keeper of any emigrant boarding-house shall have any lien upon the baggage or effects of any emigrant for boarding, lodging, storage, or any other account whatever, for any greater sum than shall be due from such emigrant for boarding and lodging according to the rates or prices so posted as above provided*; and upon complaint being made upon oath before the mayor or any police magistrate of the city in which such boarding-house is located, that the luggage or effects of any emigrant are detained by the keeper of any emigrant boarding-house, under pretence of any lien upon such luggage or effects, or on any claim or demand against the owner or owners thereof, for any other or greater sum than in accordance with such rates, it shall be the duty of the officer before whom such complaint is made, immediately to issue his warrant, di-

Restriction as to lien on effects of emigrant boarders.

* *See* § 3, *of Ch.* 219 *of Laws of* 1848.

rected to any constable or policeman of said city, commanding him or them to bring before him the party against whom such complaint has been made, and upon conviction thereof, the officer before whom such conviction shall be had, shall cause said goods to be forthwith restored to the owner thereof, and the party so convicted shall be punished by a fine not less than fifty dollars, and not exceeding one hundred dollars, and shall be committed to the city prison until the said fine shall be paid, and until such luggage or effects shall be delivered to such emigrants. Any person so convicted shall have the right of appealing from the decision of such mayor or magistrate to the same tribunals and in the same manner as is provided by law for appeals from the decisions of justices in civil cases, and all the provisions of law relating to appeals from justices, shall apply, so far as applicable, to appeals from such mayor or other magistrate. But such appeal shall not authorize the detention of such luggage or effects after the payment of the sum which such mayor or magistrate shall adjudge to be justly due from such emigrant. (§ 1 of Chap. 321 of Laws of 1849, amending § 4 of Chap. 219 of Laws of 1848.)

Right of appeal.

CHAP. 470.

AN ACT *to prevent Frauds in the sale of tickets to Passengers upon Railroads, Steamboats, and Steamships.*

Passed April 15th, 1857.

The People of the State of New York, represented in Senate and Assembly, do enact as follows:

SEC. 1. No person other than the agents or employees of railroad, steamboat, or steamship companies of this State, duly appointed by them for that purpose, by a proper authority in writing, shall offer for sale or sell within this State, any ticket or tickets, or any printed or written instrument issued by, or purporting to have been issued by any railroad, steamboat, or steamship company in this State or elsewhere, for the transportation of any passenger or passengers, upon any such railroad, steamboat, or steamship, or any instrument wholly or partly printed or written, delivered for the purpose or upon the pretence of the procurement to such passenger or passengers, of any such ticket or tickets, or in any other manner, charge, take, or receive any money as a consideration or price for such passage, or for the procurement of such passage ticket or tickets; and no ticket or tickets, or other evidence as aforesaid, shall be sold or offered for sale by the said agents or employees, except at the offices designated for that purpose by the said companies respectively, and at prices not exceeding their regular established rates. Sale of tickets.

§ 2. Whenever any person or persons shall be complained of and arrested for violating any of the provisions of the first section of this act, it shall be the duty of the magistrate before whom such complaint is made, to take and reduce to writing, in the presence of the person or persons complained of, the evidence of any witness which may be offered, either on behalf of the prosecution or the party accused, and the depositions so taken shall be respectively Violation of act.

subscribed by the witnesses making the same, and certified by the magistrate, and when so taken and certified, the said depositions shall be filed in the office of the clerk of the county in which the same shall be taken. Upon the trial of any person or persons charged with any offence under the provisions of this act, the testimony taken as aforesaid may be read by either party, with the like effect as if the said witness or witnesses were sworn in open Court upon said trial; provided it shall appear therein that the witness or witnesses were at the time of taking the same residents of another State, territory or province, or are immigrating from a foreign country, or are residents of this State, and on their way to some other State, territory, or province.

Penalty. § 3. Any person violating the provisions of this act, shall, upon conviction, be deemed guilty of a misdemeanor, and be punished by a fine of not less than one hundred dollars, or by imprisonment of not less than three months, or by both such fine and imprisonment.

§ 4. This act shall take effect immediately.

CHAP. 579.

AN ACT *for the protection of emigrants, and to amend chapter two hundred and nineteen of the laws of eighteen hundred and forty-eight, and chapter four hundred and seventy-four, of the laws of eighteen hundred and fifty-five.*

Passed April 16, 1857, three-fifths being present.

The People of the State of New York, represented in Senate and Assembly, do enact as follows :

SECTION 1. The commissioners of emigration are hereby authorized and required to grant and issue licenses, and the same from time to time, in their discretion, to suspend, revoke or annul, to the owner or captain of any steamboat, steamtug, propeller, or barge, used or engaged, or to be used or engaged, for the purpose, in whole or in part, of the removing, taking off, or conveying or transporting to any dock or pier in the city of New York, emigrant passengers, or their baggage, arriving at and being in any part of the port of New York, within this state, from the ship or vessel in which such emigrant passengers or their luggage shall have arrived at such part of said port, provided always that such licenses shall not be suspended, revoked, or annulled, except for cause after opportunity for the party complained of to be heard. Licenses.

§ 2. It shall not be lawful for any steamboat, steamtug, propeller, barge, or other boat or vessel, or the owner or captain, or person having charge of the same, to go or be taken along side of any ship or vessel having such passengers on board, being within this state, with the intent, or for the purpose of removing, taking off, conveying or transporting, or to remove, take off, convey or transport any of such passengers or the baggage of any such passen- Removing of passengers, &c.

gers, from such ship or vessel, being in this State, to any dock in the city of New York or Brooklyn, unless the license mentioned in the first section of this act shall have been granted, and issued to the then owner or then captain of such steamboat, steamtug, propeller, barge, or other boat or vessel, and be then existing and not suspended, revoked or annulled.

Penalties. § 3. The owner and owners jointly and severally, and the captain or person having charge of any steamboat, steamtug, propeller, barge, or other boat or vessel, violating the provisions of the second section of this act, or any of them, shall be liable to a penalty of five hundred dollars, for each and every violation thereof, and in case any of such passengers, or the baggage of any of them, shall be taken off or removed from such ship or vessel, so being within this State, in or by any steamboat, steamtug, propeller, barge, boat, or other vessel, without the license aforesaid, with the intent or for the purpose mentioned in said second section of this act, or in violation of any of its provisions, except in case of shipwreck or imminent danger thereof, the owner or owners, jointly and severally, and the captain or person having charge thereof, shall, in addition to the above penalty, be also liable to a further penalty of fifty dollars for each and every passenger, and for the baggage of each and every passenger so taken off, or conveyed from such ship or vessel; which penalties shall be deemed and be forthwith a lien on such steamboat, steamtug, propeller, barge, boat, or other vessel, and may be, immediately upon such violation, sued for, enforced and recovered by and in the name of the commissioners of emigration, either by an action in any court having jurisdiction thereof, or by an attachment under and pursuant to article first of title eighth of chapter eight, of first part of the Revised Statutes, for which purpose the said commissioners shall forthwith be deemed to be, and be creditors of such steamboat, steamtug, propeller, barge, boat, or vessel, and have a direct lien thereon.

§ 4. Section five of chapter two hundred and nineteen

of the laws of eighteen hundred and forty-eight, is hereby amended so as to read as follows:

No person shall, in any city of this state, solicit emigrant passengers or their luggage for emigrant boarding houses, passenger offices, forwarding transportation lines, or for steamers, ships, or vessels bound or about to proceed to any port not within this state, or for any person, or for any company selling, or offering for sale, passage tickets, or contracting or offering to contract for passage in any such steamer, ship, or vessel without a license for that purpose, which shall expire at the end of one year from its date: such license may be issued and revoked in the discretion of the mayor of the city where such license may have been granted, except in the city of New York, in which such license may be issued or revoked only by and in the discretion of the commissioners of emigration, for cause as hereinbefore provided. Such person receiving such license shall pay the sum of twenty dollars, and give a bond, with two sufficient sureties, in the penalty of five hundred dollars, conditioned for the good behavior and the observance by him of the provisions of this act, to the mayor of the city issuing the same, or to the commissioners of emigration, as the case may be. The money thus received or collected on said bonds shall be for the benefit of said city, or of the emigrant fund. Every person so licensed shall wear, in a conspicuous place about his person, a badge or plate, of such character and in such time* and manner as said mayor or, in the city of New York, as such commissioners shall prescribe, with the words "Licensed Emigrant runner," inscribed thereon, with his name and the number of his license. No person who is not of approved good moral character shall be licensed as such runner. Every person who shall solicit alien emigrant passengers, or others, for the benefit of boarding houses, passenger offices, or forwarding or transportion lines, or for any steamer, ship, or vessel bound or about to proceed to any port not within the state of New York, or for any person or company selling or offering for sale passage Emigrant runners.

* So in the original; should be "form."

tickets, or contracting or offering to contract for passage in any such steamship or vessel, upon any street, lane, alley, or upon any dock, pier, or public highway, or in any other place within the corporate bounds of any city in this State, or upon any waters adjacent thereto, over which any of said cities may have jurisdiction, without such license, shall be deemed guilty of a misdemeanor, and shall be punished by imprisonment in the county prison or jail not less than three months, nor exceeding one year.

Bonds. The bonds mentioned in the foregoing sections, may be sued by and in the name of the mayor of the city in which such license may have been issued, and in the city of New York, by and in the name of the commissioners of emigration, in any court having cognizance thereof, and in case of a breach, the said mayor, or the said commissioners, shall recover the full penalty of said bond.

Personal baggage. § 5. All personal baggage of emigrant passengers arriving at the port of and destined for the city of New York, shall be landed at the place or pier designated as the landing place in said city for emigrant passengers, and the captain, owner, and consignees of every ship or vessel arriving at said port with emigrant passengers destined for said city, shall be jointly and severally subject and liable to a penalty of fifty dollars for each and every emigrant passenger, or his personal baggage, landed at any place or pier other than the place or pier aforesaid: which penalty shall be a lien upon such ship or vessel, and may be enforced and recovered by and in the name of the commissioners of emigration, either by an action or by and in the name of the commissioners of emigration, either by an action or by warrant of attachment, under and pursuant to article first of title eighth of chapter eighth of the first part of the Revised Statutes.

§ 6. Section eight of chapter four hundred and seventy-four of the laws of eighteen hundred and fifty-five, is hereby amended so as to read as follows:

Duty of health officer. The health officer shall give notice, in writing, to the owner or owners, consignee or consignees, master, commander, or person having charge of every vessel, having emigrant passengers on board of such vessel, destined for the city of New York, to land such passengers and their personal baggage, at such pier or place in the said city of New York, as has been or may at any time be designated specially by the commissioners of emigration, for the landing of emigrant passengers and their personal baggage; and it shall not be lawful to land such passengers or their personal baggage, at any other pier or place; and the owner or master of any vessel, from which passengers or their personal baggage, shall be landed in violation of the provisions of this section, shall be subject to a penalty of fifty dollars for each and every person, or his baggage, so landed in violation thereof; which penalty shall be forthwith a lien on such ship or vessel, and may be immediately, upon such violation, sued for, enforced and recovered, with costs of suit, in the name of and by the commissioners of emigration, either by an action in any court having cognizance thereof, or by attachment under and pursuant to article first of title eighth, chapter eighth, of the first part of the Revised Statutes, for which purpose the said commissioners of emigration shall forthwith be creditors of such ship or vessel, and have a direct lien on such ship or vessel, for said penalty; the said penalty, when recovered, to be applied and used by the said commissioners for the purposes for which said commissioners are constituted.

§ 7. Nothing in this act contained shall be so construed as to alter, impair, or modify the existing laws and regulations regarding quarantine, or concerning the powers given to, and duties imposed upon, the health officer of the port of New York, for the protection of the public health.

§ 8. This act shall take effect immediately.

CHAP. 8

Of Laws of 36th Congress, Session 1, Passed March 24th, 1860.

AN ACT *to amend an Act entitled "An Act to regulate the carriage of passengers in steamships and other vessels," approved March 3d,* 1855, *for the better protection of female passengers, and other purposes.*

Be it enacted by the Senate and House of Representatives of the United States of America, in Congress assembled: That every master or other officer, seaman or other person, employed on board of any ship or vessel of the United States, who shall, during the voyage of such ship or vessel, under promise of marriage, or by threats, or by the exercise of his authority, or by solicitation, or the making of gifts or presents, seduce, and have illicit connexion with any female passenger, shall be guilty of a misdemeanor, and upon conviction shall be punished by imprisonment for a term not exceeding twelve months, or by a fine not exceeding one thousand dollars, *Provided*, that the subsequent intermarriage of the parties seducing and seduced, may be pleaded in bar of a conviction.

§ 2. And be it further enacted: That neither the officers, seamen, or other persons employed on board of any ship or vessel bringing emigrant passengers to the United States, or any of them, shall visit or frequent any part of such ship or vessel, assigned to emigrant passengers, except by the direction or permission of the master or commander of such ship or vessel first made or given for such purpose; and every officer, seaman, or other person employed on board of such ship or vessel who shall violate the provisions of this section shall be deemed guilty of a misdemeanor, and on conviction thereof shall forfeit to the said ship or vessel his wages for the voyage of the said ship or vessel during which the said offence has been committed. Any master or commander who shall direct or permit any officer, or seaman, or other person employed on board of such ship or vessel, to visit or frequent any part of said ship or vessel assigned to emigrant passengers, except for the purpose of doing or performing some necessary act or duty as an officer, seaman, or person employed on board of said ship or vessel, shall be deemed guilty of a misdemeanor, and shall, on conviction thereof, be punished by a fine of fifty dollars for each occasion on which he shall so direct or permit the provisions of this section to be violated by any officer, seaman, or other person employed on board of such ship or vessel.

§ 3. And be it further enacted: That it shall be the duty of the master or commander of every ship or vessel bringing emigrant passengers to the United States, to post a written or printed notice in the English, French, and German languages, containing the provisions of the second section of this act in a conspicuous place on the forecastle, and in the several parts of the said ship or vessel assigned to emigrant passengers, and to keep the same so posted during the voyage, and upon neglect so to do, he shall be deemed guilty of a misdemeanor, and on conviction thereof shall be punished by a fine not exceeding five hundred dollars.

§ 4. And be it further enacted: That in case of the conviction of any person under the provisions of the first section of this act, and the imposition of a fine, the Court sentencing the person so convicted may, in its discretion, by an order to be entered on its minutes, direct the amount of the fine, when collected, to be paid for the use or benefit of the female seduced, or her child or children, if any.

§ 5. And be it further enacted: That no conviction shall be had under the provisions of this act on the testimony of the female seduced, uncorroborated by other evidence, nor unless the indictment shall be found within one year after the arrival of the ship or vessel at the port for which she was destined when the offence was committed.

Approved March 24th, 1860.

www.ingramcontent.com/pod-product-compliance
Lightning Source LLC
LaVergne TN
LVHW021319110826
845150LV00003B/621

* 9 7 8 1 4 2 5 5 5 6 9 0 7 *